Yankee Singing Schools
and the
Golden Age of Choral Music in New England,
1760–1800

The frontispiece to William Billings's *New England Psalm Singer* (Boston, 1770) contains the only picture extant of a group of colonials engaged in part-singing, which was their favorite musical pastime. Long thought to be a representation of a singing school, this engraving is in reality a picture of one of the many informal singing groups, which, like the madrigal singers of Elizabethan England before them, gathered at each other's homes to sing music written by native-born composers. Both the groups pictured in this engraving and the music which they sang were an outgrowth of the Yankee singing schools which flourished during the golden age of choral music in New England. Engraving by Paul Revere (1735–1818). Courtesy, American Antiquarian Society.

A CANON OF 6 IN ONE WITH A GROUND

Wake ev'ry Breath and ev'ry String,
To Bless the great Redeemer King;
His Name thro' ev'ry Clime ador'd:
Let Joy & Gratitude and Love,
Thro' all the Notes of Music rove;
And Jesus sound on ev'ry Chord.

Double strike impression. For a later state of this plate see p. VIII.

Yankee Singing Schools

and the

Golden Age of Choral Music in New England,

1760–1800

ALAN CLARK BUECHNER

Published by Boston University for
The Dublin Seminar for New England Folklife

ISBN: 0-87270-132-8

Foreword

WE WELCOME this book with profound joy and relief. At last, future generations will have Alan C. Buechner's superb study of the beginnings of music education in our country in their hands: to read, to study, and to build on. Buechner's career was devoted to musical scholarship and to teacher education in music. His doctoral dissertation, which is comprised in this book, was completed at Harvard University in 1960. Because of institutional restrictions, it was made available only at Harvard. Scholars wishing to make use of Buechner's carefully researched and felicitously written work had to come to Cambridge to do so. And come they did, carrying away much information and new interpretations available nowhere else. Footnotes in myriad studies of the beginnings of music in America bear testimony to the debt owed to Alan Buechner's groundwork.

At Old Sturbridge Village, a reconstruction of an old New England village whose mission is to place American culture in accurate physical settings, Buechner's work was of compelling interest. Working with copies of music from original tune books and singing in the restored 1790s meeting house, the Old Sturbridge Singers, with his assistance, made a recording of the music that Buechner had studied. Released by Folkways Records in 1964, the seminal recording is still in print as "New England Harmony: A Collection of Early American Choral Music" (Smithsonian Folkways F32377).

It was this recording that brought Buechner's work to the attention of the late Gilbert Chase, author of the now classic text *America's Music* (1955). When he prepared the revised second edition in 1966, he used the dissertation as the basis for extensive revision of the chapter on "Native Pioneers." Chase was ahead of his time in his thinking that music should not be studied in iso-

lation from the society that produced it. He found a kindred spirit in Buechner, who had read wills, newspapers, diaries, court records, and old letters in his determined quest for the personal as well as the historical basis for changes in music performance and education in early America. In 1973, Buechner's work was among the forty books listed in *Landmarks of American Music History* by the Institute for Studies in American Music. Although it was an unpublished doctoral dissertation and was difficult to obtain, within thirteen years it was recognized as a work that had a major impact upon its field, both inside and outside of academia.

Alan Buechner's commitment to the study of his own nation's music when such was neither fashionable nor even acceptable in some circles led him and a group of his friends to band together to form a mutual support club. In honor of Oscar George Theodore Sonneck, an earlier pioneer in American music studies, they founded the Sonneck Society in 1975, a society committed to the dissemination of "accurate information about American music and music in America." The Society has prospered and grown into an international presence. Now a constituent member of the American Council of Learned Societies and with a revised name, the Society for American Music still honors Sonneck and in Sonneck's name honored Buechner in 1998 with its highest award for members: "Distinguished Service Citation."

In the words of Allen McConnell, Alan Clark Buechner (1926–1998) "was a remarkable man. He was distinguished by scrupulousness, intelligence, kindness, and courage. His scrupulousness marked all that he did, whether it was in speech, choosing the precise word, or in his impeccable scholarship, or in deciding the best course of action in a delicate human situation. He was a man of his word. He never 'blew his own horn.' . . . His discourse was marked by common sense, humor, and occasional irony . . . .

"His high intelligence facilitated a career as a scholar of music. His dissertation on American colonial music, written decades ago, has been one of the most consulted and cited. It is a reminder of his scrupulousness that he published so little when his gifts were so great, for he defied the harsh dictum of post–World War II American higher education: 'Publish or perish.' Translated this means: never mind the students; get the book out. He did mind the students. His students came first. And he took on the graduate program of music education at Queens College when it had sixty-five students to shepherd, a sure sign to me he could not think of his publications. He was still helping students in the last year of his life, five years into retirement."

Ave atque vale. Alan, we thank you.

Kate Van Winkle Keller
Executive Director, emerita
Society for American Music

ACKNOWLEDGMENTS

Born in El Paso, Texas, Alan C. Buechner graduated in 1947 from Rensselaer Polytechnic Institute and the Pennsylvania State College. After spending his early years as a school teacher and musical director in several secondary schools in Pennsylvania, he enrolled in the Harvard Graduate School of Education in 1951. There he received a Master of Arts in Teaching in 1952 and served as a Teaching Fellow and Instructor in Education while earning a Doctorate in Education degree in 1960. He subsequently taught at the University of Texas and at the University of Hartford. In 1967 he joined the Aaron Copland School of Music, Queens College, City University of New York, as a Professor of Music and Coordinator of Music Education. During that time his articles and reviews were published in the *Journal of the American Musicological Association*; in *Symposium*, the journal of the College Music Society; in *American Music*, the journal of the Sonneck Society for American Music; and in *Music Educators Journal*.

Professor Buechner arranged for the publication of his thesis with the Dublin Seminar shortly after he gave a talk at "New England Music: The Public Sphere, 1600–1900" held in Deerfield, Massachusetts, in June 1996. The subject of his paper was the musical and professional career of an early New England minister whose life was cut short by consumption at the age of twenty-eight. "Thomas Walter and the Society for Promoting Regular Singing in the Worship of God: Boston, 1720–1723" was one of twenty-one papers given at this meeting. We are grateful to Alan Buechner for sharing his insights into Reverend Walter's life, a man whose career in some ways was similar to his own. We are also grateful to him for making available a complete copy of his thesis manuscript and for his generous assistance organizing the material up to the time of his death in 1998.

We especially thank Kate Van Winkle Keller, who was critical in making the many arrangements necessary to get this project underway, and for her continuing assistance as the work progressed. Raoul F. Camus, Professor Emeritus of Music at Queensborough Community College, provided access to an initial version of the manuscript and several boxes of papers and photocopies related to Alan Buechner's research. The American Antiquarian Society, Worcester, Massachusetts, and the Eda Kuhn Loeb Music Library of the Harvard College Library, Cambridge, Massachusetts, generously provided help locating a number of early musical imprints. The Monroe C. Gutman Library at the Harvard University Graduate School of Education kindly provided a circulating copy of Dr. Buechner's thesis. Finally, we are grateful to the patience and generosity of Boston University, especially Harry Breger, Jan Hauben, Denise Doherty, Nick LaDuca, Maureen R. Moran, Patrick L. Kennedy, Peter Nebesar, and Lillian Laffan at the Office of Publications Production; Norman F. Wells at the Office of Scholarly Publications; Michael Longo of Boston University's Bulk Mail Service; and Hannelore A. Glaser, Peter W. Wood, and Patricia E. Barry of Boston University's Provost's Office, whose help was vital to the publication of this volume.

This publication was made possible by financial assistance from the H. Earle Johnson Fund of the Society for American Music.

—Peter Benes and Jane Montague Benes, Editors, The Dublin Seminar for New England Folklife.

Table of Contents

A later state of the print in the frontispiece illustration (shown in lower panel) was discovered as a photostat negative in Alan Buechner's papers. The mouths of the six singers have been removed or otherwise altered; the name "Byles" has been erased, and "Byles" added in script below it. These changes may have been the work of printers Benjamin Edes and John Gill in a later edition of William Billings's work perhaps done during the 1780s. The two men, along with many others, held a grudge against the Reverend Mather Byles, who remained a Loyalist throughout the Revolution and was put under house arrest. It also points to the continuing controversial aspect of organized singing in New England. Byles, minister of the Hollis Street Church in Boston, was not only known as a writer of religious music, but also as a poet and a leading proponent of musical education. *The editors.*

I

The Decline of Congregational Music in New England

THE HISTORY of an educational institution would be incomplete without some consideration of the circumstances which led to its establishment. In the case of the New England singing school, the low estate of congregational music during the first quarter of the eighteenth century was the principal reason for its founding.

That a genuine need to revive and reform congregational music existed prior to the advent of the singing school is a fact easily established by reference to contemporary documents. In 1720 Thomas Symmes, who was one of the most perceptive and articulate observers of the musical scene, bewailed:

> The Total Neglect of *Singing Psalms, by many Serious Christians, for want of Skill in Singing Psalm-Tunes.*There are many who never employ their Tongues in Singing God's Praises, *because they have not skill.* It is with great difficulty that this part of Worship is performed, and with great indecency in some Congregations for want of Skill: It is to be feared Singing must be wholly omitted in some Places for want of Skill, if this Art is not revived.[1]

A year later another observer, Cotton Mather, complained that even in those congregations in which the singing of psalms was not neglected the quality of the singing left something to be desired.

> It has been found accordingly in some of our Congregations, that in length of Time, their *singing* has degenerated into an *Odd Noise,* that has had more of what we want a Name for, than any *Regular Singing* in it; whereby the Celestial Exercise is dishonoured; and indeed the Third Commandment is trespassed on.[2]

He too saw the problem in terms of skill, since it was only by the acquisition of skill that the mode of singing in these wayward congregations could be reformed.

> The Skill of *Regular Singing* is among the *Gifts* of GOD unto the Children of Men, and by no means unthankfully to the Neglected or Despised. For the Congregations, wherein 'tis wanting, to recover a *Regular Singing,* would be really a *Reformation,* and a Recovery out of an *Apostacy,* and

what we may judge that Heaven would be pleased withal. We ought certainly to Serve our GOD with our *Best,* and *Regular Singing* must needs be *Better* than the confused Noise of a Wilderness. GOD *is not for confusion in the Church of the Saints;* but requires, *Let all things be done decently.*[3]

Regular singing, the standard by means of which he judged the singing of the congregations, meant musically literate singing. For this reason he suggested:

> . . . in the pursuance of this Holy Intention, it would be very desirable, that People, (and especially our YOUNG PEOPLE, who are most in the years of Discipline) would more generally *Learn to Sing* and become able to Sing by RULE, and keep to the NOTES of the TUNES, which our spiritual Songs are set unto; which would be to Sing, as Origen expresses it, εμμελως χαι δυμ–φουωϿ; Agreeably and Melodiously.[4]

It is a difficult task to account for the low estate of congregational music because the writers of the period were, with one notable exception, not particularly concerned about the historical antecedents of the musical problems confronting them. To attribute these problems to environmental difficulties or to the Puritans' alleged antipathy toward music would be to oversimplify that which in reality was a rather complex situation. There is reliable evidence that the Puritans kept a lively psalm-singing tradition going in spite of the physical hardships which they encountered in settling a new land. That they disliked music is a now thoroughly discredited concept.[5] Furthermore, their attitude toward music has relatively little bearing upon the matter at hand since the singing of psalms was one of the musical activities in which they are known to have participated wholeheartedly. This being the case, it can only be concluded that the low estate of congregational music was due to certain undefined musical factors in their singing tradition. Mather was explicit in stating that their singing had "degenerated" from an acceptable standard; thus it may be assumed that these factors had been operative for some time. To understand what these factors were and how they brought about a decline in congregational music it is necessary to trace the history of psalm-singing in New England from its first settlement.

The Puritan Ideal of Congregational Music

The first settlers of New England were children of the Reformation, be they Pilgrims or Puritans, in that they subscribed to the singing of a metrical version of the Psalms of David in the language of the people. From their first arrival on these shores, psalm-singing was an important part of their daily life. A striking example of this fact may be found in Edward Johnson's *History of New England* (London, 1654) in which he relates the circumstances under which the earliest settlers of Concord, Massachusetts, sang psalms in 1635.

> After they have thus found out a place of aboad, they burrow themselves in the Earth for their first shelter under some Hill-Side, casting the Earth aloft upon Timber they make a smoaky fire against the Earth at the highest side, and thus these poore servants of Christ provide shelter for themselves, their Wives and little ones, keeping off the short showers from their Lodgings, but the long raines penetrate through, to their great disturbance in the night season; yet in these poore *Wigwames* they sing Psalmes, pray and praise their God till they can provide them houses....[6]

He goes on to describe how many had to go barefoot and bare-legged in the winter, how their cattle sickened and died, how wolves made depredations on their flocks, how they had to supplement their diet with "Venison or Rockoons," and how they lived in continual fear of attack by hostile Indians in this "howling Desart." Yet all through these incredible hardships the people sang psalms and took heart.

A narrow strip of wilderness along the coast had hardly been tamed before the religious leaders of the new colony became concerned about the musical portion of the divine service. In two works, written in New England and published before 1650, they set forth and implemented their ideal of congregational music.

The first of these works originated in a very proper ministerial concern about the failings of the metrical translations of the Psalms then in use, i.e., those by Sternhold and Hopkins.[7] The feelings of these leaders in the matter were summarized many years later by Cotton Mather in his *Magnalia Christi Americana* (London, 1702).

> Tho' they blessed God for the Religious Endeavors of them who translated the *Psalms* into the *Meetre* usually annex'd at the end of the Bible, yet they beheld in the Translation so many *Detractions* from, *Additions* to, and *Variations* of, not only the Text, but the very *Sense* of the Psalmist, that it was an Offense unto them.[8]

Accordingly, the task of making a new translation was assigned to some "thirty pious and learned Ministers" that the people might have a more perfect version from which to sing. The result was, of course, the justly renowned Bay Psalm Book,[9] which was issued from the press of Stephen Daye in Cambridge.

The story of the Bay Psalm Book has been so well told elsewhere that it would be redundant to retell it here.[10,11,12] Suffice it to say that it more than fulfilled the expectations of those who produced it. In New England, twenty-seven editions were published, the last of which appeared in 1762. In England, where it was reprinted as early as 1647, twenty editions were published, the last of which was issued in 1754. Thus, aside from the two communities which clung to the Ainsworth Psalter (Amsterdam, 1612), this psalm book and its successor (a revision made by President Dunster in 1651, entitled *The New England Psalm Book*) became and remained the standard psalm book for several generations of New Englanders.

The second of these works, a treatise by the Reverend John Cotton of Boston entitled *Singing of Psalms a Gospel Ordinance* (London, 1647), originated in the need to amplify the Puritan position with regard to church music as it had been defined a few years earlier by the Assembly of Divines at Westminster.[13]

> It is the duty of Christians to praise God publickly by singing of psalms together, in the congregation and also privately in the family. In singing of psalms the voice is to be audibly and gravely ordered; but the chief care must be to sing with understanding, and with grace in the heart, making melody unto the Lord.[14]

This work, like the Bay Psalm Book before it, achieved recognition in the mother country and served to define and regulate musical practices in the meeting houses of New England for almost a century and a half.

Cotton divided his subject into four sections:

1. Touching the Duty itselfe.
2. Touching the Matter to be Sung.
3. Touching the Singers.
4. Touching on the Manner of Singing.

In the first section, cognizant that even in New England there were a few diehards[15] who questioned the wisdom of singing, he asserted:

> ...wee lay downe this Conclusion for a Doctrine of Truth; that singing of Psalms with a lively voyce, is an holy Duty of God's worship now in the dayes of the New Testament.[16]

At the same time he cautioned against the danger of letting the singing become an externalized act of worship.

> For God is a Spirit: and to worship him with the voyce without the spirit, were but lip-labour: which (being rested in) is but lost labour (Isa. 29.13), or at most profiteth but little, 1 Tim. 4.8. But this wee say, As wee are to make melody in our hearts, so in our voyces also.[17]

In this connection he was careful to explain that the use of musical instruments in support of this duty was unacceptable because it was a form of ceremonial worship.

> ...now in the growne age of the heirs of the New Testament, such externall pompous solemnities are ceased, and no externall worship reserved, but such as holdeth forth simplicitie, and gravitie; nor as any voyce now heard in the Church of Christ, but such as is significant and edifying by signification (1 Cor. 14.10, 11, 26) which the voyce of instruments is not.[18]

His thinking[19] was thus in accord with that of other Puritan divines in that they were chiefly concerned with the elimination of all distracting influences from public ritual.

In the second section, "Touching the Matter to be Sung," he revealed himself to be not only a good Calvinist,

> We hold and beleeve; that not only the *Psalmes of David*, but any other Spirituall Songs recorded in Scripture, may be lawfully sung in Christian Churches...[20]

but also a liberal whose views concerning the use of spiritual songs of "human composure" were considerably ahead of those espoused by his contemporaries.

In the third section, "Touching the Singers," he answered three important questions. In reply to the first, "Whether one for all the rest, the rest onely saying Amen: or the whole Congregation?" he affirmed the Protestant ideal of full participation by the people in religious services.

> The whole word of God dwelling richly in us, is to be improved to the Teaching and Admonishing of one another: but the *Psalmes* are to be improved, not onely to both these ends, (as all the rest of the Word beside) but to a threefold end also, even to the Singing of Praises to the Lord. Now in this third end, all the Congregation may joyne....[21]

In reply to the second question "Whether women as well as men, or man alone?" he found sufficient precedent in the Old Testament to justify "the lawful practice of women singing together with the men the Praises of the Lord."

> ...the Law, yea the Lawgiver *Moses* did permit Miriam and the women that went out after her to sing forth the praises of the Lord, as well as the men, and to answer the men in their Song of Thanksgiving; *Sing Yee to the Lord, for he hath triumphed gloriously: the horse and his rider hath he throwne Into the Sea.* Exod. 15. 20, 21.[22]

He concluded by asking, "Whether carnall men and Pagans as well as Church-members and Christians?" His reply anticipated the evangelistic use of religious song in America by a hundred years.

> ...the end of singing is not onely to instruct, and admonish, and comfort the upright, but also to instruct, and convince, and reproove the wicked, as hath been shown, Deut. 31.19.[23]

In the final section of his treatise, "Touching on the Manner of Singing," he discussed two practical problems which kept some communicants from participating in the musical portion of the service, namely illiteracy and the lack of psalm books. His solution to both of these problems was the same as that proposed by his colleagues in England.

> Then to this end it will be necessary helpe, that the words of the Psalmes be openly read before hand, line after line, or two lines together, so that they who want either books or skill to reade, may know what is to be sung and joyne with the rest in the dutie of singing.[24]

This practice which was known as lining-out, became nearly universal in the meeting houses of New England.

The Puritans' ideal of congregational music as amplified by Cotton was thus one of simple, heartfelt vocal expressions engaged in by all and performed without the support of instruments.

Formulated with scant reference to the musical problems inherent in group singing, it nonetheless served to guide the destiny of congregational music in New England for several generations.

Congregational Music in Seventeenth-Century New England

Data concerning the degree to which the Puritans succeeded in making their ideal of congregational music a reality during the seventeenth century are fragmentary at best. Accounts of congregational singing in Boston, Salem, and Plymouth must serve to suggest the answer.

That all was not well with church music in Boston even at the time when the Bay Psalm Book and Cotton's tract first appeared is suggested by one of the "Questions to the Elders of Boston" delivered by Thomas Lechford in 1640.

> #24. If Psalms, and Hymns, and spiritual songs are to be sung in the Church, and to sing melodiously, and with good harmony, is the gift of God, and uncomely singing a kind of sin in the holy Assemblies; why should not the chiefe leaders, and rulers of the Church, appoint some, in their stead, to take care of the singings of the Church? and may not some be fitter to lead in singing, than others? and lest they may fall out of their tunes to jarring, why may they not use the help of some musicall instruments? and lest they should want able men this way, why should they not take care, that some children be trained up in Musique?[25]

If all had been well, these suggestions would hardly have been necessary. Perhaps, congregations fell "out of their tunes to Jarring" far more often than theologians bound by dogma would have admitted.

Lechford's recommendations for the improvement of congregational music in Boston disclose many of the factors that later-day historians have considered of prime importance in explaining the decline in church music in New England. The lack of skilled musical leaders, the lack of instrumental accompaniment to sustain the singing, as well as the lack of some form of music education were problems blithely ignored by his contemporaries. Because the solutions which he proposed involved the restoration of the very things which the Puritans had discarded, and because he was personally unpopular, it is unlikely that his views received serious consideration.

Eyewitness accounts of congregational singing in other New England towns during this period are lacking. Evidence preserved in church records reveals that by the latter part of the seventeenth century, descendants of the early settlers were forced to abandon the more elaborate tunes sung by their forbears and substitute something easier. Such was the case at least in Salem and Plymouth, where the simple tunes associated with the Bay Psalm Book came to have precedence over the beautiful, yet complex tunes of the Ainsworth Psalter.[26]

The congregation at Salem was the first to experience difficulty in maintaining the musical portion of the service.

> At a Church Meeting 4th of 5th month 1667[.] The pastor having formerly propounded and given reason for the use of the Bay Psalm Book in regard to the difficulty of the tunes, and that we could not sing them so well as formerly, and that there was a singularity in our using Ainsworth's tunes; but especially because we had not the liberty of singing all the Scripture Psalms according to Col. 3.16. He did now again propound the same; and after several brethren had spoken there was at last a unanimous consent with respect to the last mentioned, that the Bay Psalm Book should be used together with Ainsworth's to supply the defect of it.[27]

Nothing is known concerning the musical level of this parish at its founding. It may be presumed that the congregation once was able to sing most of the Ainsworth psalms acceptably in spite of their diverse metrical patterns and their intricate tunes. Yet within a generation an expedient had to be found to compensate for an obvious decline in skill.

Much more is known about the sequence of musical events which took place in the congregation at Plymouth. There is little doubt that in the early days of the Plantation the musical portion of the service was sustained at a high level. Edward Winslow in his book, *Hypocrisie Unmasked*, tells of the departure of the Pilgrims from Leyden, a leave-taking made memorable by the music which they sang on that occasion.

> They that stayed at *Leyden* feasted us that were to goe at our Pastors house being large, where wee refreshed ourselves, after our teares with singing of Psalmes, making joyfull melody in our hearts as well as with the voice, there being many of the Congregation very expert in Musick; and indeed

it was the sweetest melody that ever mine eares heard.[28]

The story of their efforts to maintain this level in the New World affords further insight into the decline in musical literacy and skill which took place during the seventeenth century.

Considering the manifold hardships which they endured, it is remarkable that some sixty years were to elapse before any outward sign of difficulty appeared. The first may be found in the deliberations of 1681 when the unexplained disability[29] of one of the communicants forced the congregation to adopt the practice of lining-out.

A few years later agitation arose concerning the difficulties encountered when singing the noble tunes in their psalter.

> May 17, 1686. The Elders stayed in the Church after public worship was ended, & propounded to them a motion to sing Psalm 130 in another Translation, because in Mr. Ainsworth's Translation which wee sang, the tune was soe difficult few could follow it, the chh consented thereunto, & on May 24: sang, Ps. 130 in the Translation used by the churches in the Bay.[30]

The "Translation used by the churches in the Bay" was that of the Bay Psalm Book. The tunes associated with it were demonstrably shorter and easier than those included in the Ainsworth Psalter from which they customarily sang (see Figure 1).

The problem became acute in 1692 when it was realized that persons capable of setting the tunes of their psalter (reading the music and leading the congregation in it) could no longer be found. A resolution[31] that the equivalent version from the Bay Psalm Book be substituted whenever one of the Ainsworth psalms and its tune were found to be too difficult was soon proposed and adopted by the congregation. This resolution was followed by another one four years later which made the Bay Psalm Book supreme at last.

> June 7, 1696... the new translation of the Psalms was fixt upon & only sung, it being Judged most for aedification, because the former Translation had many difficult tunes that now wee could not sing.[32]

In just three generations the worthy tradition of Pilgrim singing had sunk to the mundane level existing elsewhere in the colony.

Congregational Music in Eighteenth-Century New England

The decline in congregational music implied by seventeenth-century sources is confirmed by eighteenth-century sources which demonstrate that precentors and congregations failed all too often in making the Puritan ideal a reality.

Since responsibility for the successful realization of this ideal rested largely upon the precentors, or deacons, who led the singing, it is proper to inquire as to their qualifications for this difficult task. Informed opinion did not rate them very highly. In the seventeenth century Lechford suggested that the chief rulers of the church appoint "some in their stead to take care of the singings of the Church," since some were "fitter to lead in singing than others."[33] That this suggestion probably went unheeded is seen in a "Letter" written to the editor of the *New England Courant* by an anonymous writer early in the eighteenth century.

> To old Master JANUS
> Sir:
> ...what makes this part of Divine Worship the more unedifying, is, that the Readers are generally such, whose only Qualification for parcelling out the Psalm to us, is, that they sustain the Office of a Deacon.[34]

The office of deacon was an important one in the hierarchy of religious leadership. It was only part of human nature that those who held this post were reluctant to delegate responsibility for one of their most important public duties to someone else.

The consequences of appointing deacons, less for their musical ability than for their standing in the community, were developed at length by the same writer.

The first of these consequences was that the rhetorical aspect of psalmody was often handled in a manner detrimental to the meaning of the sacred texts.

> ...and if we now and then meet with a Line which is a compleat Sentence of itself, the Words are often murder'd or metamorphos'd by the *Tone* of the Reader.[35]

This meant, of course, that those who had neglected to carry psalm books with them often sang without understanding the sense of the

Figure 1. An exact comparison between the tune used by Henry Ainsworth for his version of Psalm 130 in *The Book of Psalmes* (Amsterdam, 1612) and the tune used by the authors of the Bay Psalm Book (*The Psalms, Hymns and Spiritual Songs of the Old & New Testament* [9th ed.; Boston 1698]) is not possible because the authors cast their version in common meter. As such it could have been sung to any one of several tunes in that meter. A comparison is still possible, however, if the "Directionals" contained in the Bay Psalm Book are used as the basis for selecting a tune. Since Psalm 130 would have been classified as a "Psalm of Prayer," It could have been sung either to "York" or "Windsor" tune. "York" has been selected for purposes of comparison.

Ainsworth Psalm 130 (9 lines, all 6's) [Three lines of music]

York (4 lines, 8 6 8 6) [Two lines of music]

In the example both tunes have been transcribed into modern notation for ease of comparison. The length, the complex phrase-structure, the free melodic line, and the modal character of the Ainsworth tune explain in part the difficulties experienced by the Plymouth congregation in 1685. On the other hand, the brevity, the simple phrase structure, the straightforward melodic line, and the major tonality of "York" explain its adoption, or more correctly the adoption of common meter tunes by them.

Analysis of the Ainsworth version of Psalm 130 reveals that the author himself was at fault in suggesting that it be sung to the tune in question. This tune is designed to accommodate those poetic texts the lines of which are six syllables long throughout. The Ainsworth text is clearly defective in that many of its lines are highly irregular. The first line, which is twelve syllables long, is subdivided into two phrases of four and eight syllables, respectively. The second line which is eleven syllables long, is subdivided into two phrases of four and seven syllables, respectively. The tenth through thirteenth lines are so irregular as to defy meaningful application to the tune. Only the third through ninth lines are consistently six syllables (or twelve syllables evenly subdivided into two phrases of six syllables each) in length and are, therefore, easily applied to the tune.

Metrical Settings of Psalm 130

I. AINSWORTH PSALTER.

> Out of the deeps, I cal Jehovah unto thee.
> Lord hear my voice: let thine ears attentive bee, /
> unto voice of my suits-that-doo-for-grace-request.
> Iniquities, o Jah, observ if thou shouldest: /
> o Lord, who shal subsist?
> But wt thee pardo is: that thou mayst feared bee.
> I for Jehova look, my soul looks-earnestlie: /
> I also for his Word, have hopefully-forborn.
> My soul wayts for the Lord: more-than Watchmen for morn.
> Let Israel wayt for Jehova hopefully: for with Jehovah /
> there is bountiful-mercie. / and with him plentiful
> redemption there is.
> And he will Israel redeem: out of al his perverse iniquities.

II. BAY PSALM BOOK.

> LORD, from the depth I cryde to thee. /
> My voice Lord, doe thou heare:
> Unto my supplication voice / let be attent thine eare.
> Lord, who should stand if thou o Lord, /
> should mark iniquitee.
> But with thee there forgivenes is: /
> that feared thou maist bee.
> I for the Lord wayt, my soule wayts: /& I hope in his word.
> Then morning watchers watch for morn, /
> more my soule for the Lord.
> In God hope Isr'ell, for mercy / is with the Lord: with him
> there's much redemption. From all's sin /
> bee Isr'ell will redeem.

psalm, a serious matter for those who subscribed to the Puritan ideal of singing.

The second consequence was that the musical aspect of psalmody was often handled in a manner which resulted in tonal chaos.

> I have but one thing more to observe, and that is, that the same Person who sets the Tune, and guides the Congregation in Singing commonly reads the Psalm, which is a Task so few are capable of performing well that in Singing two or three Staves, the Congregation falls from a cheerful Pitch to downright *Grumbling,* and then some to relieve themselves mount an Eighth above the rest. Others perhaps a Fourth or Fifth, by which Means the Singing appears to be rather a confused Noise, made up of *Reading, Squeaking* and *Grumbling,* than a decent and orderly Part of God's Worship: Nor can I see but that the Arguments made use of against the People's *Praying after a Minister,* will ly as fairly against their *Singing after a Deacon.*

I am, SIR,
Your Humble Servant,
Jeoffrey Chanticleer[36]

Careful examination of this portion of the letter reveals that lining-out,[37] as it was then practiced, actually consisted of three steps: reading, setting, and singing. The first verse of the psalm was read or intoned by the deacon in a singsong manner. Then he proceeded to set that verse to music by singing each line of the text to the correct musical phrase of the tune, a line at a time. This meant that he would sing the words of the first line of the verse to the first phrase of the tune and the congregation would sing this line in imitation of him immediately thereafter. He next would sing the words of the second line of the verse to the second phrase of the tune and the congregation would sing this line in imitation of him. This process went on line by line until the verse was completed. Then the process would begin over again as the second verse was taken up and read. The continual interchange between deacon and congregation accounts in no small measure for the chronic flatting noted by "Chanticleer." That many people were reduced in the course of a long psalm to singing at various intervals above the depressed pitch of the group is entirely understandable, since this would have been the only way that they could continue in the duty of singing after the tune had fallen below their singing range.

Deeper insight into the significance of "Chanticleer's" remarks may be gained by referring to commentaries upon the state of English psalmody written by two professional musicians during the previous century.

The first of these commentaries was written by Thomas Mace, who was "one of the Clerks of Trinity College, in the University of Cambridge" and an accomplished teacher and player of the lute. Mace so deplored the "whining, toting, yelling or screeking" of the country congregations of his day that he devoted the first section of his magnum opus, *Musick's Monument*, to an analysis of the musical factors underlying this problem.[38] He believed that it was "absolutely impossible to have the Psalms rightly and well performed according to the common way," i.e., lined-out and sung unaccompanied, because Nature herself had failed to endow men with the ability to sing perfectly in tune for long periods of time. He argued

that the antiphonal interchange between clerk and congregation, which went on line after line until the conclusion of the psalm, would bring about a gradual lowering of the pitch because so few could be depended upon to match accurately the pitches given to them by the clerk.

Mace's solution to this problem was identical to that which has become practically universal in the churches of our time.

> ...if you will *Sing Psalms* in Churches well, and in Tune, *you must needs have an Organ* to Sing unto; by which means the whole Congregation will be drawn (or as it were compell'd) into *Harmonical Unity*; even so, that 'tis impossible for any person, who has but a *common or indifferent Ear*, (as most people have) to Sing *out of Tune*.[39]

As far as the country parishes of his time were concerned, his solution was not entirely realistic. Many were too poor to purchase an organ much less support an organist, while others like those in New England would have rejected the idea outright because of religious scruples.

The second of these commentaries was written by the music publisher, John Playford. In the preface to his *Psalms and Hymns*, he makes it clear that even in the city of London congregational music was in a languishing condition because there were but few parish clerks to be found who had "either Ear or Understanding" to set the tunes musically, it having been the custom to choose men "more for their Poverty than Skill and Ability."[40] A few years later, in the preface to still another work, *The Whole Book of Psalms*, he placed ultimate responsibility upon the shoulders of the clergy. At the same time he applauded those parish clerks who had begun to take their work seriously by setting up an organ and practicing the singing of Psalms.[41]

Unlike their colleagues in London, the deacons in New England had to succeed entirely by means of their own efforts. A guild of parish clerks such as Playford described would have been impractical in a provincial society. Furthermore, there were no organs in seventeenth-century New England meeting houses much less skilled persons to play upon them. Had they been available, it is doubtful that the pious deacons would have availed themselves of this opportunity for training. Samuel Sewall, who served for many years as a deacon in Boston's South Meeting House, expressed the prevailing sentiment when he wrote to a friend about a visit he had made to Oxford, England, in 1689:

> The next Sabbath day after the Coronation I heard a Sermon at St. Mary's. I am a lover of Musick to a fault; yet I was uneasy there: and the justling out of the Institution of Singing Psalms, by the boisterous Organ, is that which can never be justified before the great Master of Religious Ceremonies.[42]

Valuable in itself, Sewall's account demonstrates how thoroughly Cotton's admonition concerning the use of instrumental music in public worship had been assimilated by the faithful.

So strictly was this admonition adhered to that not even an innocuous pitch pipe was permitted within the meeting house. Deacons were expected to produce the correct pitch for each psalm tune with nothing more to guide them than their musical intuition. The difficulties inherent in such a system are clearly seen in the introductory remarks to the musical directions included in the ninth edition of the Bay Psalm Book.

> Some few directions for ordering the voice in Setting these following Tunes of the Psalms.
>
> First, observe how many *Notes* compass the Tune is. Next, the place of your first Note; and how many Notes above & below that: so as you may begin the *Tune* of your first *Note*, as the rest may be sung in the compass of your and the people's voices, without *Squeaking* above, or *Grumbling* below. For the better understanding of which, take notice of the following directions.[43]

Although these directions, which had been taken from Playford's *Introduction to the Skill of Musick*, were simply and logically worked out, they contained a serious defect as far as the lay singer was concerned. Even if he understood them, his voice type would have seriously influenced the pitch ultimately selected. For example, that which was a "cheerful high pitch" for a tenor voice would not have been the same for a bass voice. Obviously, considerable knowledge of the scope of one's own voice in relation to that of the group was necessary for even a modicum of success.

Because the responsibility entrusted to the deacon was very great, it is not surprising to find that musical failures were as common as successes in the period under discussion. Samuel Sewall kept a careful record of his career as a deacon in his diary. Insight into the practical problems which he faced in setting tunes without instrumental aid may be gained from a typical entry.

> Dec. 28, 1705. Sixth Day. Mr. Pemberton prays excellently, and Mr. Willard preaches from Ps. 66.20 very excellently. Spake to me to set the Tune; I intended Windsor, and fell into High Dutch; and then, essaying to set another Tunes went into a Key much too high. So I prayed Mr. White to set it; which he did well, Litchf. Tune. The Lord humble me and instruct me, that I should be the occasion of any interruption in the Worship of God.[44]

This entry and another[45] like it should not be dismissed as the confessions of a musically incompetent person. Sewall was an enthusiastic and successful singer on social occasions.[46] Yet even he could not approach the arduous task of setting the psalm in the meeting house with reasonable assurance that the musical portion of the service would proceed with decorum.

If the short-term result of the New Englanders' rejection of instrumental aids to singing was recurrent difficulty in setting and sustaining the psalm tunes at the proper pitch, the long-term result was confusion as to the identity of particular tunes.

When Samuel Sewall bewailed his congregation's inability to maintain the melodic integrity of an assigned tune throughout the singing of an entire psalm,

> Feb. 6, 1714/15. This day I set Windsor tune, and the people at the second going over into Oxford, do what I could.[47]

he recorded a phenomenon which must have been fairly widespread at that time. A few years later the ministers of Milton, Dorchester, and Taunton discussed the problem in detail in an essay entitled, *Cases of Conscience* (Boston, 1723).

> We cannot but think that some of our Congregations have too much indulged themselves in ignorance and Carelessness; while they have forgot, or never learned to distinguish one Tune from another by its Name; as to know which is Oxford Tune and which is Windsor Tunes and so the rest; and therefore it is high Time to learn to know them by their Names; and that it is conducing thereunto to have the Tune Named before hand as well as the Psalm to be sung in it; so that People may know that there is a difference between one Tune & another and may come by degrees to observe & keep that difference, and may leave off

Figure 2. The two tunes, "Windsor" and "Oxford," mentioned by Deacon Samuel Sewall in his Diary are given in the original diamond-shaped notation. They have been taken from the ninth edition of the Bay Psalm Book. Corrections for obvious errors in printing have been made after reference to other psalm books. The bar lines represent phrase endings rather than measures.

Windsor Tune

Oxford Tune

being so disorderly, as to sing part of two or three Tunes, in singing four or eight Lines.[48] Identical charges were lodged by another minister, Josiah Dwight, in a sermon delivered at Framingham in 1725.[49]

Whether the ministers were entirely fair in blaming the congregations for this confusion about the identity of the standard tunes is open to question. Examination of "Windsor Tune" and "Oxford Tune" (*Figure 2*) reveals that although they are deficient in rhythmic life by modern standards, they are different enough melodically to be easily distinguished one from another. Denied the support of instruments, the congregations could be no stronger than the men who led them. These men were also victims of the dogmatic rejection of instrumental aids to singing. Lacking a standard by which the melodic integrity of the tunes could be preserved and employing a method of performance which frequently resulted in tonal chaos, leaders and followers must have become more and more confused as to the character of the tunes which they tried to sing.

The difficulties noted by "Chanticleer," Sewall, Thacher, and others were in part responsible for two additional problems which plagued the congregations during the first quarter of the eighteenth century.

The first of these was the reduction in the number of tunes which they were able to sing.

The abandonment of difficult musical materials first noted toward the end of the seventeenth century seems to have become quite general by the first quarter of the eighteenth. Even the thirteen common tunes contained in the later editions of the Bay Psalm Book were subject to the winnowing process. In 1721 Thomas Walter in the introduction to his singing book, *The Grounds and Rules of Musick Explained*, pointed out that many congregations were confined to eight or ten tunes and that some were limited to little more than half that number.[50] Examination of another source lends support to his assertion.[51] That some congregations were in fact reduced to as few as four or five tunes is entirely credible in view of the lack of opportunity for musical training, the omission of music from many psalm books, and the rejection of instrumental aids to singing. When these factors are considered in the context of their manner of singing, i.e., "after a Deacon," it is apparent that they had gravitated as a matter of practical necessity toward a repertory of the simplest tunes.

The second of these problems was the failure of many persons to participate in singing divine praise. This failure became one of the chief justifications cited by the reformers in urging the adoption of the singing school. Thomas Symmes observed that there were many who never employed their tongues in singing God's praises and that great difficulty attended this part of the divine service.[52] It is hard to estimate in any quantitative way how widespread was this failure to participate. As pastor to an isolated rural congregation in eastern Massachusetts, Symmes was able to speak only from a limited vantage point. That it was something more than a condition unique to that region is seen in the remarks addressed to the General Association of the Clergy in Connecticut by another reformer, Nathaniel Chauncey.

> . . . a multitude of Persons live in a neglect of this duty. Many neglect it in Publick, they open not their Mouths to Praise God.[53]

Both Symmes and Chauncey attributed this failure purely and simply to a lack of skill. While this was undoubtedly true in many cases, the tonal confusion resulting from the common way of singing, described in the following section, was enough to discourage all but the most confident singers.

The Common Way of Singing[54]

The reports of widespread non-participation must not be taken to represent the total picture of congregational singing in New England during the first quarter of the eighteenth century. Many persons still sang with reverence and gusto, albeit in a manner uniquely their own. This manner of singing came to be known as the "customary way," the "usual way," or the "common way" of singing and as such was one of the evils which the reformers hoped to correct by having everyone sing according to the "Rules of Musick."

What was the common way of singing? To answer this question properly, a long forgotten performance practice which was never preserved in musical notation must be reconstructed from contemporary documents. Probably the most complete description of the actual sound that issued forth from the meeting house on a Sabbath morning is found in the essay *Cases of Conscience Concerning the Singing of Psalms.*

> Forasmuch as in our late Customary Way of Singing we have degenerated from the Right and Established Rules of Musical Singing; and many Congregations have Sung near one third too long, and some syllables have been Quavering, as in the singing of Mass; end in their singing have borrowed and taken some half a line, some a whole line, out of one tune and put it into another; and the singing of the same pretended Tunes in one

Congregation, hath not been alike to the singing of them in another, and several Singers in the same Congregation have differed one from another in the turns and flourishes of the Tune which they have sung, and have been too discordant; and sometimes He that hath set the Tune has been forced to sing two or three lines, before the generality of the Congregation could know what Tune was set, so as to fall in with it; Nor are the Musical Counter parts set to the Tunes, as we sing the said Tunes, in the late Customary way, to make the Melody, most harmonious.[55]

This description is, of course, suggestive of the confusion noted earlier. Contained within it, however, are certain key phrases, an analysis of which reveals characteristics of the common way of singing.

First of all, what was meant by the statement that in some congregations the "syllables have been Quavering, as in the singing of Mass"? Was this "quavering" the overall impression created by the equally indefinite "turns and flourishes" mentioned in a later phrase, or was it an effect separate in itself? Two other writers of the period also employ the term "quavering." Thomas Walter associated it with the corrupt forms of the psalm tunes sung by many congregations,

> ...the Tunes...when they first came out of the hands of the Composers of them, were sung according to the Rules of the *Scale of Musick*, but are now miserably tortured, and twisted, and quavered, in some Churches into a horrid medley of confused and disorderly noises.[56]

while Nathaniel Chauncey employed it to designate notes of specific time duration.

> Nothing makes more against the common way; for they will readily grant that they use many quavers and Semi-quavers.[57]

Both writers apparently were following the correct usage of their day. Grassineau makes it clear in his *Musical Dictionary* (London, 1740) that the word "quaver" has two meanings: (1) a note of specific time duration, i.e., an eighth note; (2) a type of ornament. With regard to the second definition, he seems to equate the English "quaver" with the Italian "trillo."

> The chief graces in singing are the Trillo and the Quaver. It is to be performed by making easy small Inflections of the voice on two sounds distant a tone or a semi-tone.[58]

In still another definition he states that the act of producing this ornament is called "quavering."

Quavering, the act of trilling or shaking, or running a division with the voice.[59]

Unfortunately, Grassineau did not define either "turns" or "flourishes" in his *Dictionary*. A quotation from a tract by Thomas Symmes provides a clue to the meaning of these terms.

> There is a Reason to be given why each *Note* in a *Tune* is placed where it is, *why* and *where every Turn* of the voice should be made, how *long* each *Note* should be Sung &c. Now *Singing by Note* is giving every *Note* its proper *Pitch* and *Turning* the voice in its proper Place, and giving every *Note* its true *Length* and *Sound*, &c. Whereas the *Usual Way* varies much from this: In it some Notes are sung too *high*, others too *low*, and most too long, and many *Turnings of*, or Flourishes with the Voice, (as they call them) are made where they should not be, and some are wanting where they should have been.[60]

It would appear that "turns and flourishes" were terms employed by laymen, not to designate a musical ornament, but rather to describe the process of directing the voice from note to note. Thus, if the voice was directed rapidly to several notes, many "turnings" would result. These "turnings," which Symmes makes synonymous with "flourishes," were probably like a modern turn in their ornamental effect, though freer in design and execution.

The significance of the above terms becomes clear when it is recalled that the writers of these descriptions were literate men who were thoroughly familiar with the original Puritan psalm tunes in their notation of semibreves and minims. Secure in the knowledge that these tunes were designed to be sung syllabically (one note for each syllable of the text), they hoped to discourage the practice of embellishing each syllable with additional notes of shorter duration. Because this practice resulted in a florid style which was vaguely reminiscent of the melismas of Gregorian chant, it is not surprising that they described the syllables as "quavering as in the singing of Mass."

Another significant aspect of the common way of singing was its lack of rhythmic organization. The failure of singers to synchronize their efforts and the agonizingly slow tempo which they used in singing the psalms were described by Thomas Walter in the preface to his singing book, *The Grounds and Rules of Musick Explained*.

> THERE is one more advantage which will accrue from the instructions of this little Book; and that

is this, That by the just and equal *Timeing* of the Notes, our Singing will be reduced to an exact length, so as not to fatigue the singer with a tedious Protraction of the Notes beyond the compares of a Man's Breath, and the Power of his Spirit: A Fault Very frequent in the Country, where I myself have twice in one note paused to take breath. The keeping of Time in Singing will have this Natural effect upon us that the whole Assembly shall begin and end every single Note, and every Line together, to an instant, which is a wonderful Beauty in singing, when a greet Number of Voices are together sounding forth the Divine Praises.[61]

Evidently, every singer sang as best pleased himself without the slightest regard for his neighbor. The consequences of this practice were vividly set forth by the same writer in another passage.

> ...I have observed in many Places, one Man is upon this note, while another is a note before him, which produces something so hideous and disorderly as is beyond Expression bad. And the evens unaffected and smooth sounding the Notes, and the omission of those unnatural Quaverings and Turnings, will serve to prevent all that Discord and lengthy Tediousness which is so often a Fault in our singing of Psalms. For much time is taken up in shaking out these Turns and Quavers; and besides, no two Men in the Congregation quaver alike, or together; which sounds in the ears of a good judge, like Five Hundred different Tunes roared out at the same times whose perpetual interferings with one another, perplexed Jars, and unmeasured Periods, would make a man wonder at the false Pleasure which they conceive in that which good Judges of Musick and Sounds, cannot bear to hear.[62]

Proof that their singing was slow and unsynchronized need not rest upon the veracity of a single source. Walter's contemporaries were as explicit as he, if not so colorful in their remarks upon the subject. For example, the anonymous author of the *Pacificatory Letter* (Boston, 1725) in discussing the necessity for reform, eventually arrives at the crux of the matter, namely, the lack of synchronization.

> We should not grudge to be at some Cost or Paine to apply some Study, thought and Care, that we may at least join in Singing, without causing Confusion and Disorder.... if in the same Congregation as the same time, when a Psalm is nam'd by the Minister, should some sing it in *one Tune*, and some in *another*; or some greatly raise, and others as evidently lower their Voice on the *same*

Syllable twice as long as others, what Discord, Jarring and Confusion would this make?[63]

Another example may be found in the essay *Cases of Conscience,* mentioned earlier. The reverend authors, concerned that some congregations sang "near one third too long," elaborated the point and in so doing provided a clue as to the meaning of Walter's phrase, "roared out."

> Question XI. What Convenience and Benefit would ensue upon it, if Men's voices were somewhat Lower'd in Singing (when otherwise very Loud voices are ready to drown all other voices in a Congregation); and what advantages would Ensue if all the Singers in a Congregation would keep time?[64]

Only the beginning of the long, tangential "Answer" need be given.

> Answer. Were our Tedious Length of Singing (which is contrary to the Standard or Primitive Rule, and more like the Mass, than our reformed English Musick) reformed and reduced unto the Length pointed out in the Musical Notes at the End of our Psalm Books; and were they who sing so Loud as that they can hear no Bodies Voice but their own, reclaimed from that Absurdity.[65]

The musical effect created by those who refused to observe the amenities of singing can well be imagined.

The Folk Psalmody Hypothesis[66]

That embellishments were incorporated into the structure of the syllable psalm tunes is but a part of the total melodic picture. This effect, which Walter designated by the term "quavered," does not account for the "tortured and twisted" character of the tunes. The latter phrase suggests something more, namely, that the tunes then in use followed melodic pathways which were far more winding than those indicated by the original notation. A clue to the meaning of this phrase is to be found in a quotation, a section of which appeared earlier in the discussion.

> But suppose by Solemn you mean Grave and Serious. Nothing makes more against the Common Way, for they will readily Grant that they use many Quavers and Semi-quavers &c. And on this very account it is they are pleased with it and so very loath to part with it. Now all these Musical Characters belong wholly to Airy and Vain Songs; neither do we own or allow any of them in the Song of the LORD. Judge then which is most Solemn.[67]

A similar statement by Symmes confirms the true nature of these "tortured and twisted" psalm tunes.

> And further I affirm, the *most* of the *Psalm Tunes,* as sung in the *Usual Way,* are much more like *Song-Tunes* than as Sung by *Rule;* because you've more *Supernumerary Notes & Turnings of the Voice* in your way, than in ours. An ingenious Gentleman, who has prick'd Canterbury, as some of you Sing it, finds (as I remember) no less than 150 Notes, in that Tune, in your way, whereas in our's there are but 30. Did we propose so many *Crochets,* and *Quavers,* and *Semi-quavers* and *Demi-semi-quavers,* in every Tune, I should not wonder if you were discouraged from endeavoring to learn to Sing.[68]

Symmes was arguing for a return to the austere semi-breves and minims of the original tunes, and in so doing revealed that lines once composed of whole notes and half-notes had, in time, become colored by a profusion of quarters, eighths, sixteenths, and even thirty-second notes. This melodic elaboration made them appear similar in character to the "Airy and Vain" tunes of traditional folk songs and ballads, which were, of course, unsuitable for use in church.

Walter described this remarkable change in the structure of the tunes perfectly when he wrote:

> But our Tunes have passed through strange *Metamorphoses* (beyond those of Ovid) since their first introduction into the World.[69]

He correctly perceived that the decline in the literate tradition of psalm singing had opened the door to this transformation.

> For to compare small things with great, our *Psalmody* has suffered the like inconveniences which our Faith had labored under, in case it had been committed and trusted to the uncertain and doubtful Conveyance of *Oral Tradition.* Our Tunes are, for want of a Standard to appeal to in all our Singing, left to the mercy of every unskilful Throats to chop and alter, twist and change, according to their infinitely divers, and no less odd Humours and Fancies.[70]

In a similar vein Thomas Symmes demonstrated precisely how this transformation took place.

> The Declining from, and getting beside the Rule was *gradual* and *insensible.* Singing-Schools and Singing-Books being laid aside, there was no Way to learn; but only by hearing of Tunes Sung, or by taking the *Run of the Tune* (as it is phrased). The Rules of singing not being taught or learnt, every one sang as best pleased himself, and every *Leading-Singer,*

would take the Liberty of raising any Note of the Tune, or lowering of it, as best pleased his Ear; and add such Turns and Flourishes as were grateful to him; and this was done so gradually, as that but few if any took Notice of it. One Clerk or Chorister would alter the Tunes a little in his Day, the next a little in his, and so one after another, that in *Fifty* or *Sixty* Years it Caus'd a *Considerable Alteration.*[71]

That many congregations lacked a standard to appeal to in their singing for a period of fifty or sixty years prior to the time of Walter's and Symmes's observations may be deduced from the bibliographical history of the Bay Psalm Book. Issued originally in 1640 without music, it was reprinted again and again without music. This failure to provide the congregational singer with practical help was belatedly rectified in 1698 with the publication of the ninth edition which included simple, two-part arrangements of the standard tunes and instructions for singing them. Prior to its appearance, the musical aspect of psalmody had been sustained by surviving copies of Sternhold and Hopkins's *Whole-Booke of Psalms* and such copies of Ravenscroft's *Psalter*, Playford's *Introduction to the Skill of Musick*, and Playford's *Whole Book of Psalms* as had found their way into the hands of relatively few individuals. The majority, of course, sang from the Bay Psalm Book and thus were forced to rely upon oral tradition in sustaining their singing.

The process described by Walter and Symmes was essentially the same as that which accounts for the innumerable variants of particular folk songs. These songs also experience the "Conveyance of Oral Tradition" so that in time no definitive version can be said to exist. When several versions of the same song are collected and compared, they exhibit regional differences, as well as the subtle fancies of the singers from whom they were obtained. When they are compared with other folk songs, a curious intermingling of melodies and texts is occasionally found. If the two processes described are the same, it might reasonably be expected that psalm-tune variants would be mentioned in their reform literature. Such is the case.

Both Chauncey and Symmes were very explicit about the existence of these psalm-tune variants even though they did not employ that phrase. The former noted that:

> The difference among Towns in Singing is Great, scarce any two Towns that Sing perfectly alike, and some differ very much.[72]

while the latter deplored the inconvenience to visitors and newcomers caused by the lack of standardization of the familiar tunes.

> If Congregations would unanimously *Reform* their Singing, and conform to the Notes in our *Psalm Books*, then all Congregations would Sing alike; whereas now they *vary* greatly, and their different *Modes* of Singing are hurtful on this Account. Many who have some Ability to sing in the Usual Way, are blunder'd when they go to a Congregation they have not been us'd to Sing withal; and if they move their Habitations they have their Tunes to learn again, as much as if they knew nothing about them, or at least to learn in a different manner.[73]

The differences between the tunes sung by various congregations were even more dramatically stated by Walter who pointed out that the differences between variants of the same tune were as great as between two totally unrelated tunes!

> I appeal to the Experience of those who have happened to be present in many of our Congregations, who will grant me that there are no two Churches that sing alike. Yea, I have myself heard (for instance) *Oxford* Tune sung in *three* Churches (which I purposely forbear to mention) with as much difference as there can possibly be between *York and Oxford*, or any two other different Tunes.[74]

That the same tune could have varied as widely as this within a single region seems almost incredible today. However, when the comparative isolation of New England towns and villages and their modest opportunities for cultural exchange are considered, the picture painted by Walter and the others becomes more plausible.

Convincing proof that a kind of folk psalmody had replaced the literate tradition in New England by the beginning of the eighteenth century is to be found in the psalm-singing tradition of another country. During the seventeenth and eighteenth centuries, congregational singing in Scotland followed a course of development that was strikingly similar to the one which it followed in New England. Enumeration of the more important points of coincidence serves to validate the use of cross-cultural data.

In Scotland, a series of national psalters[75] had provided the people with metrical translations of the psalms that were in closer conformity to the originals than those previously available. This series culminated in the Rous *Psalter* of 1650,[76] which, like its counterpart in New England, was issued without tunes. Scotchmen came under the edicts[77] of the Westminster Assembly, as did their brethren in the New World. Lining-out[78] was initially adopted under protest, but was later clung to as a vital principle. Similarly, the complex tunes[79] of the earlier psalters withered away and were replaced by simpler tunes. In time the number of tunes which they sang became standardized at an even dozen[80] in the *Psalter* of 1666, a development which brings to mind the eventual supremacy of the thirteen tunes which were included in the 1698 edition of the *Bay* Psalm Book.

By the end of the seventeenth century and continuing through the first half of the eighteenth century, Scottish psalmody became increasingly non-literate[81] in nature. As such, it was soon to become the object of a reform movement. This movement,[82] which originated a generation later than the one in New England, had as its leader Thomas Channon, former English soldier and singing master. Beginning in 1753 with the members of the rural parish of Monymusk in the Presbytery of Garioch, Channon soon developed a choir which sang according to the "reformed way," or "by rule," as the colonials would have called it. In 1755 he demonstrated the new way of singing in Aberdeen[83] where it became the subject of much controversy. Reason soon prevailed, and within a year or two most of Scotland had embraced the reformed way of singing.

The Scottish choir movement, which was very similar to the New England singing school movement, soon attracted other singing-masters who began to produce instruction books specifically designed for the task at hand. One of these men was Robert Bremner, who styled himself a pupil of the Italian composer Geminani. His book, *The Rudiments of Music*, which was published in Edinburgh in 1756, is especially noteworthy in that it contains a good description of the non-literate tradition. In the preface, the author related a story about an old precentor, which brings to mind remarks by the New England reformers concerning the embellishment of standard psalm tunes.

Endeavoring once to convince an old man who was precentor in a country church how absurd he rendered the music by allotting so many different sounds to one syllable, when there was only one intended, he replied with a good deal of briskness that he believed that the people of the present generation knew nothing of the matter: for his master was allowed to understand that there ought to be eight quavers in the first note of Elgin tune.[84]

In another passage he outlined the consequences of this practice and in so doing revealed that Scottish congregations sang in a manner which was similar to that which was employed by congregations in New England.

Had these nonsensical graces been the same everywhere, it would have been the less matter, but every congregation, nay, every individual, had different graces to the same note, which were dragged by many to such immoderate length that one corner of the church, or the people in one seat, had sung out the line before another had done: and from the whole there arose such a mass of confusion and discord as quite defaced this noblest part of worship.[85]

This manner of singing was not entirely eradicated by Channon's movement. In the Highlands of Scotland it survived for at least another century, where it contributed to the development of a distinctive non-literate tradition of religious singing. This tradition was studied during the last quarter of the nineteenth century by John Spencer Curwen, a latter-day English choir master and authority on church music. In his *Studies in Worship Music* (London, 1888) he noted:

There are five tunes—French, Martyrs, Stilt (or York), Dundee, and Elgin—which are the traditional melodies used for the Psalms. These have been handed down from generation to generation, amplified by endless grace notes, and altered according to the fancy of every presenter. When used they are sung so slowly as to be beyond recognition.[86]

It need hardly be pointed out that the limitation of the repertory to less than a dozen tunes, the elaboration of these tunes by embellishment, and their transmission by oral means were basic features of the New England singing tradition. It is not surprising, therefore, to find that psalm-tune variants were also a characteristic feature of Highland singing. Some of these Scottish psalm-tune variants had been recorded in modern

Figure 3. The Scottish psalm tune "French," which may be traced back to the Psalter of 1666, has been copied from the bibliography of psalm tunes appended to H. C. MacDougall's *Early New England Psalmody*. The variant, which was collected in the Highlands around the middle of the nineteenth century by Dr. Joseph Mainzer, has been copied from John Spencer Curwen's *Studies in Worship Music*, 1st ser., pp. 145–46. It is impossible to estimate how long "French" underwent the "Conveyance of Oral Tradition" in the congregation from which it was obtained. Since the tune is, as Curwen remarks, beyond recognition, and since the congregation apparently was never touched by Channon's reform movement, it is reasonable to assume that it is the product of at least a century of alteration at the hands of precentors and congregations. The notes of the original tune have been placed at appropriate points in the variant according to Curwen's observations.

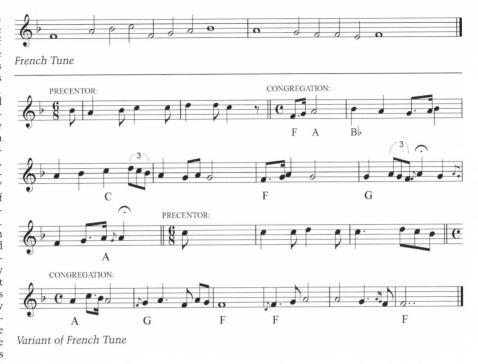

French Tune

Variant of French Tune

notation by Dr. Joseph Mainzer some forty years earlier when he resided at Strathpeffer in Ross-shire. In the notes to his *Gaelic Psalm-tunes* (Edinburgh, 1846), he reported that each parish and each precentor had differences in detail and that these variations were never written down but were handed down by tradition.

Curwen drew upon Mainzer's work to illustrate his own study of Highland singing. The illustration which he used, a variant on the tune called "French," has been included in the present discussion as *Figure 3*. Both the response chanting of the lines by the precentor and by the congregation are given. When the variant is compared with the original tune, it is clear that a process of elaboration similar to that which was described by Walter and Symmes has taken place. It will be recalled that Symmes had observed that one hundred fifty notes had crept into the thirty-note original version of "Canterbury." In the same manner forty-nine notes have crept into the fourteen-note original version of "French." Since no contemporary transcriptions of the New England psalm-tune variants have survived, this Scottish example may be taken as a possible facsimile of one of them. Only the manner of "deaconing" the

line appears to be at variance with the method employed in New England.[87]

Having noted the striking similarities between congregational singing as it was practiced in the meeting houses of New England at the beginning of the eighteenth century and as it was practiced in the kirks of the Scottish Highlands at the middle of the nineteenth century, it remains to reconcile certain differences between the two traditions. Significant aspects of the singing in New England such as the lack of synchronization, the interim changing of lines, the confusion as to the identity of tunes, the inability of some congregations to maintain the same tune throughout an entire psalm, and the failure of some individuals to participate are not mentioned in Curwen's account of Highland singing. That one tradition but not the other should be afflicted with obvious weaknesses is explained by the relative ages of the two traditions. If it be granted that both traditions began about the same time, i.e., the second half of the seventeenth century, it is apparent that the New England tradition was little more than two generations old at the time of Symmes's description and that the Scottish tradition was about six generations old at the time of Plainter's description. The development of coherent musical patterns among the folk may be considered an evolutionary process; thus, it is logical that the "younger" tradition would be afflicted with certain weaknesses not found in the "older" one because it would still be in the process of transformation from a semi-literate tradition to a non-literate one.

CONCLUDING REMARKS: Congregational singing in New England had declined during the first hundred years after its founding to the point where educated men could only describe it as an "Odd Noise." That this unflattering term was an appropriate one is seen in a summary of the diverse and often incompatible factors operative in their singing tradition. Entrusted to the none-too-skillful ministrations of the deacons, and performed without the support of instruments by musically illiterate congregations, the singing had in time become tedious and discordant. Slow and unsynchronized, freely and haphazardly ornamented, roared out by some, squeaked or grumbled by others, the psalmody must have been a torture to the musically sophisticated reformers who described it.

These men could hardly have been expected to perceive that the crude psalmody of their day might eventually have evolved into a coherent style of religious singing. Furthermore, they were confronted with a number of practical problems such as the inability of some congregations to maintain the melodic integrity of a given tune throughout the singing of an entire psalm, which demanded an immediate solution. As the official guardians of the Puritan ideal of congregational music, they could not have countenanced the introduction of instrumental music into the meeting houses. They chose, therefore, the only alternative open to them, namely the inauguration of an institution devoted to teaching the rudiments of music. Thomas Symmes spoke for all of the reformers when he proposed:

> Would it not greatly tend to promote singing of psalms if singing schools were promoted? Would not this be a conforming to *scripture* pattern? Have we not as much need of this as God's people of old? Have we any reason to expect to be inspired with the gift of singing, any more than that of *reading?* Or to attain to it without suitable mean, any more than they of old, when *miracles, inspirations &*c. were common? Where would be the difficulty, or what the disadvantages, if people who want skill in singing, would procure a *skillful person* to *instruct* them, and meet two or three evenings in the week, from five or six o'clock to eight, and spend the time learning to sing?[88]

In so doing, he disclosed the essential features of an institution which was to become the educational cornerstone of musical life in New England during the next century and a half. Succeeding chapters of this book will attempt to follow the fascinating pattern of its development as a popular institution for music education.

II

The Establishment of Regular Singing

THE RECONSTRUCTION of the major events associated with the establishment of regular singing in New England is an exceedingly complex task since no single narrative which tells the story in a comprehensive way has survived to the present day. Fragmentary material related to these events may be found in many of the diaries, letters, newspapers, tracts, and tune books of the period. These fragments, though of limited significance in themselves, may be combined to form a coherent picture of the approximate dates and places where singing schools were first established, the extraordinary efforts made to promote regular singing, the equally extraordinary controversy which arose over regular singing, and the eventual acceptance of regular singing and thus the singing school throughout New England.

The First Singing Schools

An apocryphal account concerning a man who reputedly attended the first singing school in Boston serves as the starting point for this reconstruction.

Sacred Musick

We are in possession of an anecdote which seems to fix the era when singing by notes was first introduced into the churches of Boston. Mr. Timothy Burbank, who died in Plymouth Oct. 13, 1793, aged 90 (precisely to the hour) was born in Malden, and during his apprenticeship at the tailor's trade in Boston, attended Dr. Colman's Meeting. He was always uniform in relating that he attended the first singing school* and religious society which introduced singing by notes at Boston. This era, therefore, must have been between the years 1717 and 1724.

*Mr. B. was a chorister many years at Plymouth, also an officer in the militia. He kept a bill of mortality in Plymouth for many years, which is in the possession of his descendants.[1]

Curiously enough, the records[2] of the church in which Dr. Colman served as pastor, i.e., the Brattle Square Church, do show that one Timothy Burbank was accepted into the church on March 6, 1726. Unfortunately, the records are very incomplete. No mention whatsoever is made of a singing school during the period of 1717–1724, or earlier, even though the congregation and pastor were among the most progressive in the province with regard to musical practice. Many years before the period under consideration they voted to abandon the cumbersome process of lining-out in favor of singing without interruption.

Dec. 20, 1699. Voted unanimously that ye psalms in our public Worship be sung without reading line by line.[3]

This vote, which came less than a year after the publication of the ninth edition of the Bay Psalm Book (the first to contain music), would seem to indicate that the level of musical literacy which prevailed in this church was considerably in advance of that which prevailed elsewhere at this time.

The search for the first singing school in Boston along the lines suggested by the Burbank story comes to a fruitless conclusion at this point. The sources available simply will not permit it to be carried further. While it is regrettable that such is the case, this gap in our knowledge is not so serious as it would first appear to be. The concept of an all-important first singing school established in a kind of musical wilderness is in all probability an oversimplification. Boston was by no means such a wilderness during Burbank's apprenticeship. That at least a few ministers were musically literate is attested to by their tracts upon church music. Also there is good reason to believe that a number of musical amateurs were active in Boston several years before the movement to reform congregational singing began. Three advertisements which appeared in local newspapers reveal the probable source and extent of their knowledge about music.

As early as 1713 George Brownell, a man who is now remembered chiefly as the master of a grammar school attended by Benjamin Franklin, offered instruction in the playing of several musical instruments.

AT THE HOUSE of Mr. George Brownell in Wings-Lane, Boston, is taught Writing, Cyphering, Dancing, Treble Violin, Flute, Spinnet, &.

Also English and French Quilting, Imbroidery, Florishing, Plain Work, Marking in several sorts of Stiches and several other works, where scholars may board.[4]

A year later one James Ivers specifically listed the singing of psalm tunes among the polite accomplishments which the young ladies of the town might acquire at his boarding school.

At the House of *Mr. James Ivers,* formerly called the Bowling Green House in Cambridge Street, Boston is now set up a Boarding School, where will be carefully taught Flourishing, Embroidery, and all sorts of Needle-Work, also Filigrew, Painting upon Glass, Writing, Arithmetick, and Singing of Psalm Tunes.[5]

Finally, a remarkable advertisement published in 1716 suggests that a sufficient number of musical amateurs lived in Boston at that date to warrant the importation of an extensive line of musical goods by an enterprising dancing master.

This to give Notice that there is lately sent over from London a choice Collection of Musickal Instruments, consisting of Flageolets, Flutes, Haut-Boys, Bass-Viols, Violins, Bows, Strings, Reads for Haut-Boys, Books of Instructions for all these Instruments, Books of Ruled Paper. To be Sold at the Dancing School of Mr. Enstone in Sudbury-Street near the Orange Tree Boston. *Note,* Any Person may have all Instruments of Musick mended, or Virgenalls and Spinnets Strung and Tuned at a reasonable rate, and likewise may be taught to Play on any of these Instruments above mention'd, dancing taught by a true and easier method than has been heretofore.[6]

Any one of these men, or any one of their more successful pupils, could have been of material assistance in initiating instruction in the rudiments of music. Evidence that they were formally associated with the reform movement has not survived. The lack of such evidence does not rule out the possibility that they may have been involved in the first informal efforts to provide instruction in music for members of particular congregations. The existence of even a few musically literate tutors and amateurs permits the formulation of a hypothesis that reform probably began, not as a highly organized effort in which a unique first singing school was all-important, but rather as a thing dependent upon initiative of particular ministers, who would have drawn upon such musical resources as were available to them in their congregations. This hypothesis would be in accord with latter-day practice in that responsibility for the musical aspect of the service was delegated to a chorister, or leading singer, who selected the tunes, supplied the proper key note for each tune, led the singing, and kept the youthful singers in order.

The essential soundness of this hypothesis as well as the approximate date of the initial efforts to effect reform may be deduced from two entries in Cotton Mather's diary. The first entry merely reflects the mounting concern felt by the more responsible members of the clergy for the low estate of congregational music.

Sept. 24, 1716. The Psalmody in our Assembly must be better provided for.[7]

The second suggests that changes had already begun to occur in the overall situation.

Oct. 13, 1718. The Psalmody is but poorly carried on in my Flock, and in a Variety and Regularity inferior to some others: I would see about it.[8]

Clearly, if the singing of his congregation was now inferior to that of other congregations in the number of tunes employed and in the manner in which they were sung, some improvements must have been initiated in neighboring churches during the period between the two entries.

Confirmation that efforts to reform congregational singing had been initiated by 1718 may be found in the introduction to the tract, *The Reasonableness of Regular Singing,* which appeared in 1720. Among the reasons listed by the author for its publication are the following:

3. THE *Difficulties & Oppositions which some Congregations have met withal, in their attempting & accomplishing a Reformation in their Singing.*

4. THE Success which has followed suitable Endeavours to remove those Cavils, which some (while they labor under their Prejudices to Singing by Rule) *have tho't were unanswerable Reasons in their Favour.*[9]

These statements imply that attempts to reform congregational singing had been in progress long enough to have aroused opposition in some quarters; thus the purpose of this tract was to provide encouragement for a movement that was underway.

The First Singing Books

Although not specifically mentioned by Symmes, one of the chief difficulties attending the earliest efforts to reform congregational singing was the lack of adequate instructional materials.[10] This lack was remedied soon after the establishment of the first singing schools by two of the reformers, who with characteristic Yankee ingenuity created new instruction books specifically for the task at hand. The magnitude of this task and its two-fold nature was revealed in an advertisement announcing the publication of these books.

> A Small Book containing 20 Psalm Tunes, with Directions how to Sing them, contrived in the most easy Method ever yet invented, for the ease of Learners, whereby even Children, or People of the meanest Capacities, may come to Sing them by Rule and may serve as an Introduction to a more compleat Treatise of Singing, which will speedily be Published. To be sold by Samuel Gerrish, Bookseller, near the Brick Church in Cornhill.[11]

The careful differentiation between a set of directions suitable for persons of modest talent and a formal dissertation on music, which by implication was suitable for the musically gifted, suggests that they were cognizant of the vast range of musical ability in the congregations of their day and were anxious to provide instruction appropriate for each in the singing schools.

The "Small Book" was in fact a slim pamphlet[12] by the Reverend John Tufts of Newbury, Massachusetts, entitled, *An Introduction to the Singing of Psalm-Tunes.* The "plain and easy method" mentioned in its title page (see *Figure 4*) was a system of letter notation wherein the pitch of the notes was represented by the *fasola solmization* syllables and the duration of the notes by dots and slurs. In addition to being the first American music textbook, this work was the first of a number of attempts made during the history of the singing school to facilitate the reading of music by means of special notational devices. Issued initially with a set of unharmonized tunes, it seems to have been intended for congregational singing. Later, as more persons became adept at singing by rule, it was issued with a collection of thirty-four tunes arranged in two-part harmony (treble and bass), and finally with a collection[13] of thirty-seven tunes arranged in three-part harmony (cantus, medius, bass). In this form it was equally suitable for choral singing and as such provided the fledgling choral singer with a much needed steppingstone to the more complex "Treatise of Singing."[14]

Figure 4. The title page to *An Introduction to the Singing of Psalm-Tunes* by the Reverend Mr. Tufts, the fifth edition (Boston: Printed for Samuel Gerrish, 1726). Courtesy, American Antiquarian Society.

The identity and purpose of the latter book was disclosed in an advertisement which appeared a few months after Tufts's *Introduction* was published.

> Just Published and to be Sold by Samuel Gerrish, The Grounds and Rules of Musick Explained: Or, an Introduction to the Art of Singing by Note, Fitted to the Meanest Capacities. By the Rd. Mr. T. Walter, M.A. Recommended by the Ministers of

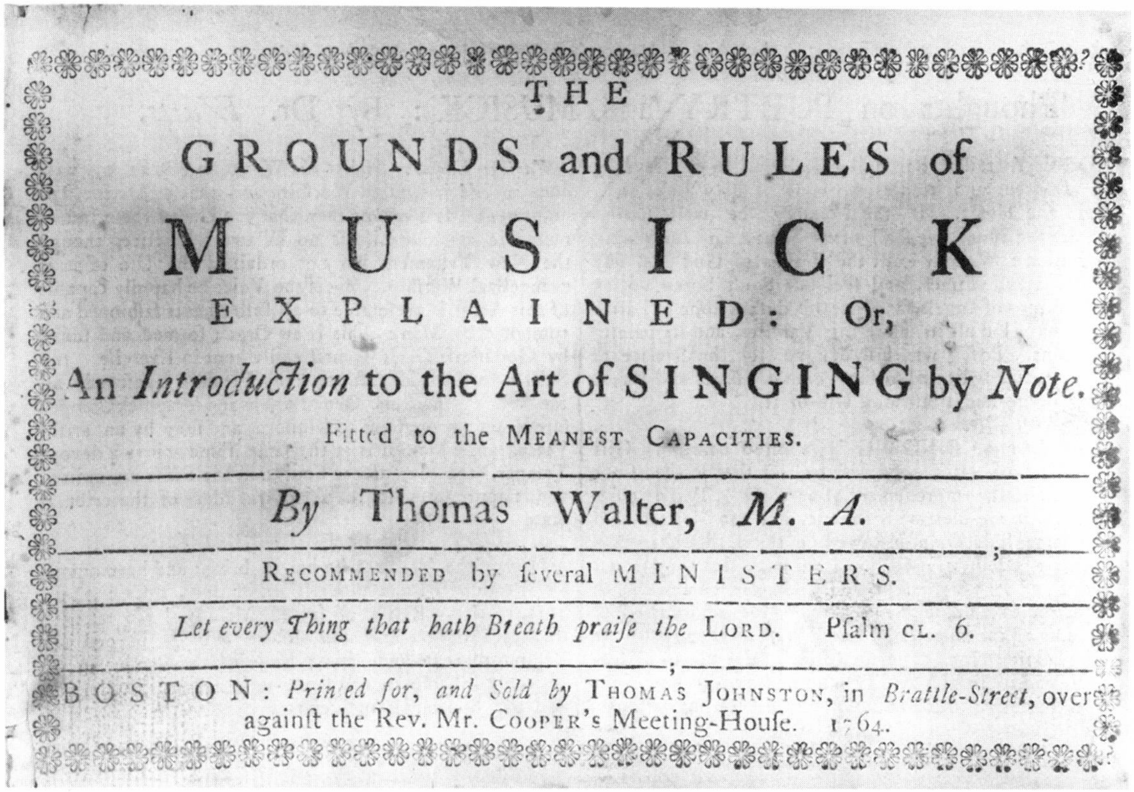

THE
GROUNDS and RULES of
MUSICK
EXPLAINED: Or,

An *Introduction* to the Art of SINGING by *Note*.

Fitted to the MEANEST CAPACITIES.

By Thomas Walter, *M. A.*

RECOMMENDED by several MINISTERS.

Let every Thing that hath Breath praise the LORD. Pfalm CL. 6.

BOSTON: *Printed for, and Sold by* THOMAS JOHNSTON, *in Brattle-Street*, over against the Rev. Mr. COOPER's Meeting-Houfe. 1764.

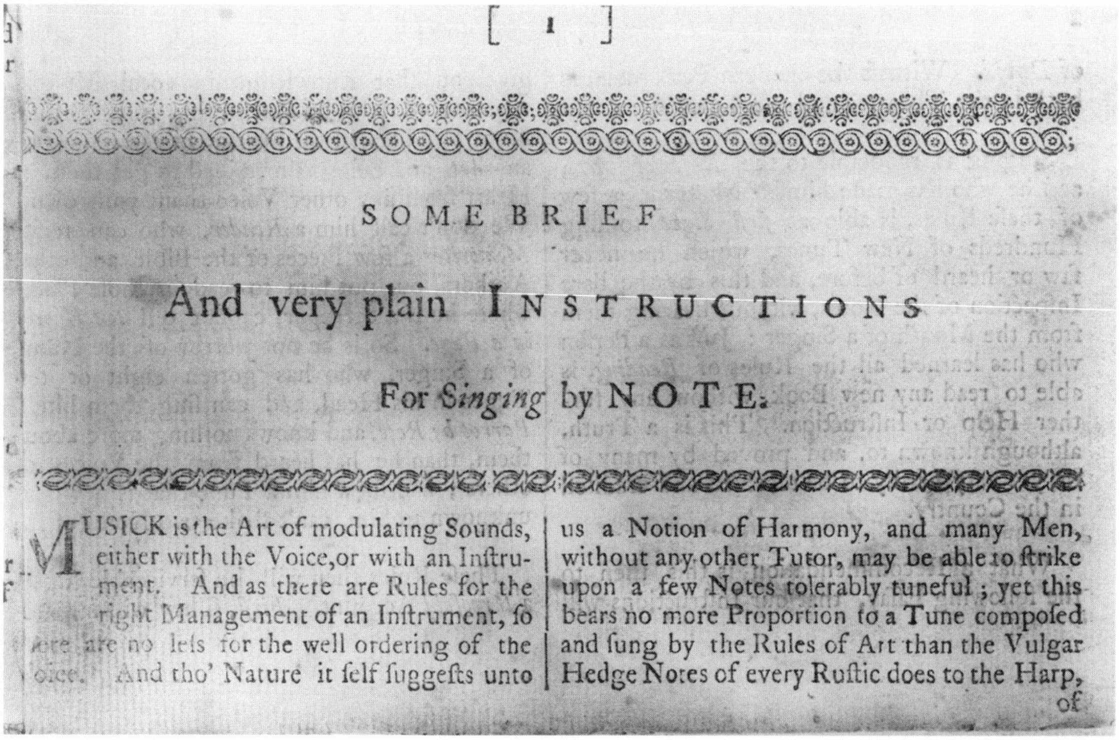

[1]

SOME BRIEF

And very plain INSTRUCTIONS

For *Singing* by NOTE.

MUSICK is the Art of modulating Sounds, either with the Voice, or with an Inftrument. And as there are Rules for the right Management of an Inftrument, fo are there no lefs for the well ordering of the Voice. And tho' Nature it felf fuggefts unto us a Notion of Harmony, and many Men, without any other Tutor, may be able to ftrike upon a few Notes tolerably tuneful; yet this bears no more Proportion to a Tune compofed and fung by the Rules of Art than the Vulgar Hedge Notes of every Ruftic does to the Harp, of

Figure 5. The title page and first page of the introductory essay to *The Grounds and Rules of Musick Explained* by Thomas Walter, M.A. (1721; Boston: Thomas Johnston, 1764). Courtesy, American Antiquarian Society.

Boston, and Others. With a Collection of Psalm Tunes, in 3 parts Printed from Copper Plate, engraved with great Curiosity & Exactness....[15]

Examination of Walter's *Grounds and Rules* shows that in spite of the announcement to the effect that it had been "fitted to the meanest capacities," its author had made no concessions to the singing public (see *Figure 5*). The rudiments of music were presented with great thoroughness and no attempt was made to simplify the difficulties involved in applying the *fasola* solmization syllables to the music. The uncompromising presentation of the rudiments, plus the inclusion of a collection of twenty-four tunes arranged in three-part harmony and printed in standard notation, suggests that it was intended for use by musically literate amateurs in choral singing.

The contribution to the movement to reform congregational singing made by Tufts's and Walter's books should not be underestimated. Tufts's *Introduction* went through eleven editions[16] between 1721 and 1744, while Walter's *Grounds and Rules* went through six editions[17] between 1721 and 1764. Thus, for nearly half a century they served as the foundation for the program of instruction offered by the singing schools. For this reason, if for no other, some study of the methodology employed by the authors of these works is in order.

In approaching the subject of singing by note Tufts and Walter used the time-honored English method of the *gamut*, or scale of music. Associated with the gamut was a set of four solmization syllables: *fa, sol, la, mi*, which were applied to the diatonic scale in the following manner.

scale degree	1	2	3	4	5	6	7	8
pitch letter	c	d	e	f	g	a	b	c
18th-century syllable	fa	sol	la	fa	sol	la	mi	fa
19th-century syllable	do	re	mi	fa	sol	la	ti	do

Unlike the nineteenth-century systems of solmization in which every scale degree is represented by a different syllable, the eighteenth-century system made the first three syllables, i.e., *fa, sol, la*, do double duty in the hexachord *c d e f g a*, the *mi* being used exclusively for the seventh scale degree, or leading tone (see *Figure 6*).

This system, which was commonly known as *fasola*, was applicable to scales in all keys through transposition of the *mi*. The *mi* was placed on any given line or space, the new tonic was determined, and the scale was sung as before, i.e., *fa, sol, la, fa, sol, la, mi, fa*, from the new tonic which was called *fa*. Reading a piece of music printed in an unfamiliar key involved locating the *mi* in terms of the key signature. Rather than confuse their readers with a general theory of scales, Tufts and Walter limited the number of keys in their books to seven major keys and their respective relative minors (Key signatures: no sharps or flats; one sharp, two sharps, three sharps; one flat, two flats, three flats) and gave specific directions for locating the *mi* in each of them. Walter's directions were especially compact (see *Figure 7*).

Take this short Scheme

The natural place for the *Mi* is in B, but if

B			E	
B and E	}	be flat, *Mi* is in	{ E / A	and if
F			F	
F and C	}	be sharp, *Mi* is in	{ F / C / G	
F, C and G				

And when you have found *Mi* in any of these variations, the notes above are *Fa, Sol, La, Fa*, &c. and below, *La, Sol, Fa, La*, &c. as before.[18]

Once the leading tone had been located on the staff, the reader was expected to assign the remaining syllables to the music by inspection. A convenient table, or gamut, in which the application of the syllables to the notes in several keys was summarized was included for reference purposes (see *Figure 8*).

It was in respect to this point that Walter and Tufts were in some disagreement. Walter saw no particular problem either in locating the *mi* or in using the gamut. Tufts, however, believed that both tasks were far too difficult for the average beginner and endeavored to assist him by supplying the correct syllable at all times in the music itself. He accomplished this by discarding the notes altogether and placing the letters *F, S, L, M* which stood for the syllables *fa, sol, la, mi*, respectively, on the staff (see *Figure 8*). In so doing he eliminated two of the most perplexing problems inherent in the English method of solmization.

The substitution of solmization letters for notes was not without its disadvantages since the letters by their very nature lacked mensural characteristics. This problem was solved by means of without any further Preamble, proceed to give the Reader some brief and plain Inftructions for finging by Note and Rule.

The Inftructions *for finging.*

I. There are in Nature but *feven diftinct Sounds,* every *eighth* Note being the fame. Thus when a Tune is fung by another upon a Key too low for the Compafs of my Voice, if I will fing with the Perfon, it muft be all the Way, *eight Notes above* him. I naturally found an *Eighth* higher. So a Woman naturally ftrikes eight Notes above the grum and low founding Voice of a Man, and it makes no more Difference than the finging of two Perfons upon a *Unifon,* or a Pitch. So on the contrary, when we would fing with a Voice too high and fhrill for us, we ftrike very naturally into an *Octave,* or Eighth below. And

here let it be obfervd, that the *Height* of a Note and the *Strength* of finging it, are two different Things. Two Notes of equal Height may be founded with different Degrees of Strength, fo as that one fhall be heard much further than the other.

II. Thefe eight Notes, for the fake of the Learner, are called by the Names, *Fa, Sol, La, Mi.* As thus,

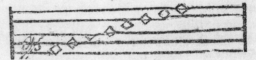

Fa Sol La Mi *Fa Sol La Fa*

Where it muft be obferved, that from *Mi* to *Fa,* as alfo from *La* to *Fa* is but a *Semitone* or *Half note* ; and from *Fa* to *Sol* ; from *Sol* to *La* ; and from *La* to *Mi,* is a *Tone,* or *whole Note.*

Figure 6. A page which describes the *fasola* solmization syllables and a page which contains the gamut reproduced from Thomas Walter's *Grounds and Rules of Musick Explained* (1721; reprint 1764). Courtesy, American Antiquarian Society.

---

an ingenious system of dots and slurs which was worked out in terms of the rhythmic values found in most psalm tunes. This system, which was explained to the reader entirely in terms of counting out the beats, did away with the need for the usual terminology of breves, semi-breves, minims, and so forth. Reference to the following table of equivalent note values and to the tunes, "Canterbury" and "St. Mary's" (see *Figures 8* and *10*), will serve to clarify the relationship between Tufts's system of rhythmic notation and the conventional one used by Walter.

Inspection of Tufts's settings of the above tunes reveals yet another simplification that was in keeping with his intention to employ a method that was adapted to the "meanest Capacities." Bar lines are missing except at the ends of the phrases. This convention, which was in accord with the practice of lining-out and singing the psalms a phrase at a time, enabled him to avoid the knotty subject of meter.

Walter felt that the singer should understand not only the conventional terminology for the notes, but also their "absolute" and "comparative" values.

XV. The Notes in *Musick* do come under a further Consideration, and that is their *Length,* or *Shortness* in Timing of them. They are known by the Names of a *Breve, Semibreve, Minim, Crotchet, Quaver,* and *Semiquaver.* These last are seldom used in Psalm Tunes but are frequent in Songs, Madrigals, and Light Airs. The other Better Becoming the Grave and Solemn Worship of the Temple. As for their *Absolute* Length and mea-

Beats	Tufts's letters	Walter's notes	English terms	Modern American terms
4	F:	⊟	breve	double whole note
2	F.	◇	semi-breve	whole note
1	F	♩	minim	half note
2 notes in one beat	FF	♩♩	crotchet	quarter note

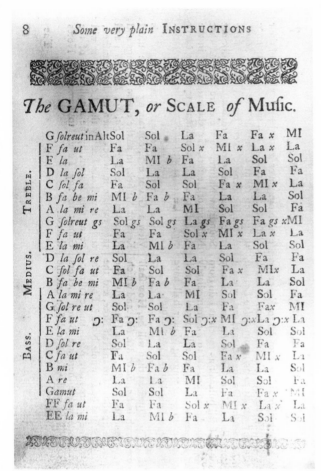

Figure 6.

sure of Time in Sounding; a *Semibreve* is sounded in the Time that a Man may let fall his hand slowly, and raise it again; letting his Hand fall at the first sounding, and taking it up when it is half done, which lifting up of the Hand finishes it. As for the *Comparative* Length, one *Breve* contains two *Semibreves*, one *Semibreve* contains two *Minims*, one *Minim* two *Crotchets*, &c. So that if a *Semibreve* is sounded while a Man lets fall his Hand, and raises it again, by Consequence, a *Minim* is sounded while the hand is falling, and another *Minim* while it is rising. And two *Crotchets* while it is falling and two while it is rising, &c.[19]

To make the "comparative" length of the notes clear he included a pyramid-shaped diagram of note values similar to those found in the instrumental music instruction books of the present day (see *Figure 9*).

Knowledge about the rhythmic aspect of the notes was the basis for understanding the principal meters used in the psalm tunes.

XV. From this different length of Notes, arises what we call the *Time* of a Tune. Which is two-fold, either *Common Time*, or *Triple Time*. *Common Time* is when all go by two, as one *Breve* is two *Semibreves*, and one *Semibreve* is two *Minims*, and so the rest. But in *Triple Time* all go by two except the *Semibreve*, which contains three *Minims*. Thus one *Breve* is two *Semibreves*, one *Semibreve* is three *Minims*, one *Minim* two *Crotchets*, &c. So that in *Triple Time* the *Minim* is one *Third* swifter, and must be sounded accordingly. And in *Triple Time* you will find *Semibreves* and *Minims* mingled together, and for the most part every other note is a *Minim*. The Proportion of *Common Time* to *Triple Time*, is as Three to Two, (3/2).[20]

This explanation was made necessary by the fact that the music in his book was barred in the customary manner, the single bar being used to indicate measures and the double bar to indicate phrase endings.

Walter was also concerned that the singer know something about the aesthetics of the music which he was learning to sing. This involved the presentation of two additional concepts in terms that laymen could understand.

The first of these concepts was that of sharp and flat keys. This concept had little to do with the key signatures per se but with the mode of the music.

To know whether your Tune be upon a flat Key, or a sharp Key, this is the general rule. If the Two Notes above the last Note of your Tune be *whole Notes*, it is upon a *sharp Key*, but if the Two Notes above be one a *whole Note*, and the other an half Note, then it is a *flat Key*.[21]

In the terminology of the day he was referring to the intervals of the major third (two whole tones) and the minor third (one and a half tones), respectively.

From this Difference of the greater and lesser Third it follows, that Tunes upon a Sharp Key are more chearful and sprightly, and therefore more suitable to Psalms of Praise and Thanksgiving. And the Flat Keys, being more grave, and mournful, and therefore best set and sung to Penitential Psalms, and melancholy Airs.[22]

there be no Flats, but Sharps, look up to F, and if that be the sharped Note, there is Mi; unless when you look down to C, and find it sharped, and then is the Mi in **C**. Or, lastly, look down to G, and if that be sharp'd too, the Mi is there. *Take this short Scheme.*

The natural Place for M*i* is in B, but if

B ------ } be flat, Mi is in { E
B & E }   { A

And if

F ------ }   { F
F and C } be sharp, Mi is in { C
F, C & G }   { G

And when you have found your M*i*, in any of all these Variations, the Notes above are *Fa, Sol, La, Fa, Sol. &c.* and below, *La, Sol, Fa, La, Sol*, &c. as before.

XI. The following Examples will shew us the several Removes of Mi; and here the Rea-der is desired to compare every Example with the Gamut, and he will find it answering, Note for Note ; only he must observe the distinct Columns of the Gamut. You will find the Letters, the Notes, the Place of the Mi to cor-respond exactly. So, compare the first Column of the Gamut with the first Example, where Mi is in B ; the second Example with the se-cond Column, where B is flat, and Mi is in E, and so of the rest. The Tune will answer the Gamut in all Points, as much as the Figures and Inches upon two Carpenter's Squares are alike, and answer one another.

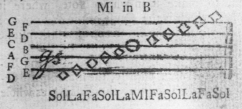

Mi in B

SolLaFaSolLaMIFaSolLaFaSol

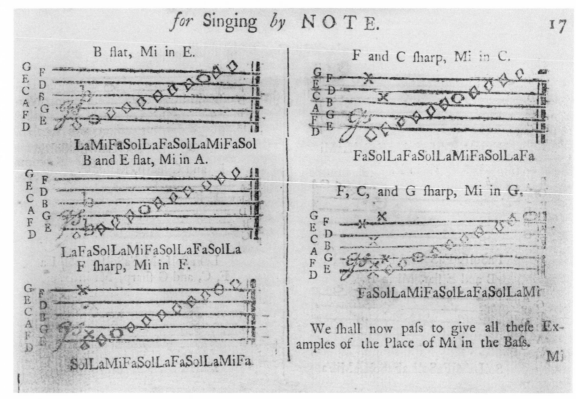

B flat, Mi in E.

LaMiFaSolLaFaSolLaMiFaSol

B and E flat, Mi in A.

LaFaSolLaMiFaSolLaFaSolLa

F sharp, Mi in F.

SolLaMiFaSolLaFaSolLaMiFa

F and C sharp, Mi in C.

FaSolLaFaSolLaMiFaSolLaFa

F, C, and G sharp, Mi in G.

FaSolLaMiFaSolLaFaSolLaMi

We shall now pass to give all these Ex-amples of the Place of Mi in the Bass.

Mi

Figure 7. A page which describes a "short scheme" for transposing the leading tone, or *mi*, and a page which illus-trates the positions of the *mi* in the keys of C, F, and B Flat major reproduced from Thomas Walter's *Grounds and Rules of Musick Explained* (1721; reprint 1764). Courtesy, American Antiquarian Society.

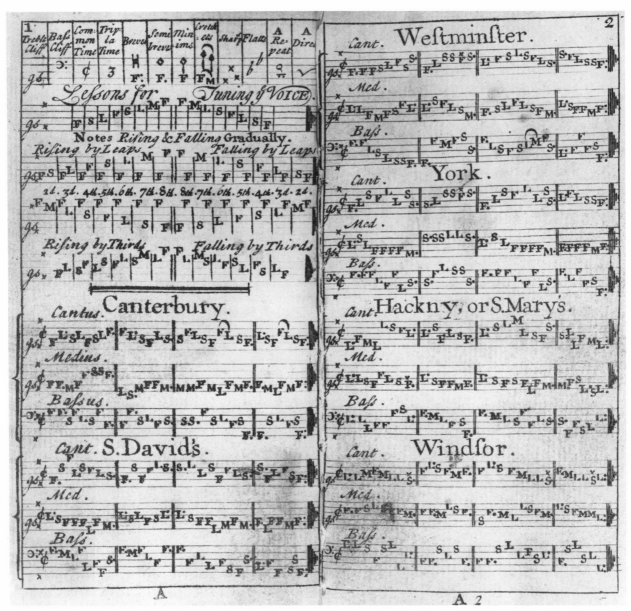

Figure 8. A page of instructions and a page of tunes in letter notation reproduced from the tenth edition of John Tufts's *Introduction to the Singing of Psalm-Tunes*. See also *Figure 10* in which the tunes "Canterbury" and "St. Mary's" are given in standard notation. Courtesy, American Antiquarian Society.

The singer was expected to recognize the difference between the major and minor mode and to combine texts and tunes in an acceptable manner.

The second of these concepts was that of concord and discord. With some condescension he remarked:

> XVIII. The last thing we have to treat of is the Doctrine of *Concord* and *Discords*. It would be but an unintelligible Amusement to the vulgar Reader (for whom this little Book is chiefly designed) to give the Physical and Mathematical Solution of the Grounds, Cause, and Effect of Harmony, as also the Reasons of Descant, which I might easily do. I only say that among the *Seven* Notes (for there are no more in Nature as we have already said, every *Eighth* being the same, only in a higher Key) a *Third*, lesser and greater, a *Sixth*, lesser and greater, a *Fifth*, lesser and greater are *Concords*. That is, if I sound a *Third*, or a *Fifth*, or *Sixth* above a Man, my Voice sounds harmoni-

The Scheme of *triple Time.*

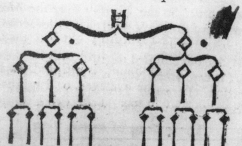

You may observe, that in the Scheme of triple Time above drawn, there is a Prick upon the right Side of the Note, which is by Musicians called a *Prick of Perfection,* which makes the Note before half as long again. Thus that Semibreve with a Prick is as long as a Semibreve and a Minim. Now if that Semibreve with a Prick after it, which makes it half as long again, be just as long as the three Minims under it,

then if that Prick were taken away, it would be as long as but two of those Minims. Therefore in your triple Time Tunes (where there is no Prick after the Semibreve) the Semibreve is to be sung just as long again as a Minim. Now one Minim and an half of a Minim in triple Time, is as long as one Minim in common Time ; therefore the Semibreve in triple Time being unpricked, amounting to the Length of two Minims in the same Time, it must be as long as a Minim and a third of a Minim of common Time; that is a Semibreve in triple time is a third shorter than a Semibreve in common Time.

XVII. There are several Adjuncts of Musick, such as a *Repeat* (whose Mark see at the Beginning of the Book) which signifies, that that Part of the Tune which went before it, is to be sung over again. There is also a *Direct* (whose Mark also see at the Beginning of the Book) which serves

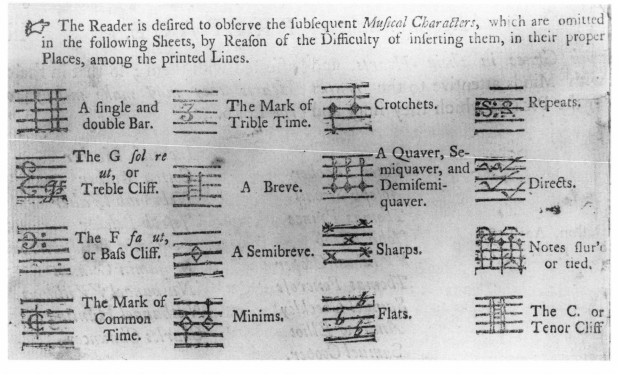

Figure 9. A page which describes the principal meters of psalm tunes, i.e., "Common Time" and "Triple Time," and a page which contains a table of "Musical Characters" reproduced from Thomas Walter's *Grounds and Rules of Music Explained* (1721; reprint 1764). Courtesy, American Antiquarian Society.

ously with his. A *Second*, and *Seventh*, are discords; a *Fourth* is by some accounted a *Chord*, by others a *Discord*; but I am inclined to think the former.[23]

This concept, which was immediately applicable to the practice exercises appended at the end of his essay, was an appropriate one for singers of an age that was just discovering the delights of harmony.

> Finally, observe, That *Discords* are sometimes made use of in *Musick*, to prepare the Ear by their Harshness, to relish better the Sweetness, and Melody of the following Concord. Thus oftentimes, there will be an imperfect Concord, then a Discord, which is still more grating; this serves to keep the Auditor in a longing Suspense, till all the Parts fall into a perfect Set of Chords, which finishes and compleats the Harmony, and strangely charms the Hearer.[24]

Once the content of Tufts's and Walter's books is understood it is possible to reconstruct the course of study as it was followed from day to day in the early singing schools. Initial sessions were undoubtedly spent in learning about the gamut, the rhythmic and metric aspect of the music, and the "musical characters" used in its notation (see *Figure 9*). Later sessions were devoted to applying what had been learned to a set of musical exercises and finally to the tunes themselves.

It was in the former activity that students came to grips with the heart of the matter, namely the vocalization of the solmization syllables. Tufts gently explained the necessity for this step in his introductory essay.

> A few Lessons are next plac'd to assist in *Raising & Falling* of Notes, either Gradual or by Leaps; the *Ground-work* of all good Singing, & is not to be attained ordinarily without the help of some skilful Person, or an Instrument. But being attained, and observing the few foregoing Rules, you will be able to leap with your voice from one Note to another, as they occur in their various Distances, and with a little Practice, to sing all the Tunes in this Book in any of their parts, with Ease and Pleasure.[25]

His "Lessons" (see *Figure 8*) were by comparison with Walter's "Rules for Tuning the Voice" (see *Figure 10*) very modest. Examination of Walter's "Rules" confirms that they are *solfeggio* exercises designed to acquaint the beginner with the most common intervals found in vocal music and to train him to sing them at sight. The scale is first established and then all of the intervals are stepped-off in a scale-wise fashion. Next, they are made to leap consecutively up and down from a point of reference, the tonic. Finally they are placed in the context of the octave or the triad whichever is most appropriate.

Mastery of the exercises led inevitably to mastery of the psalm tunes, since the intervals of the exercises were in fact the building blocks out of which the tunes and their accompanying parts were constructed. Granted such mastery, it was a comparatively simple matter to replace the solmization syllables with the words of the psalms.

From the vantage point of history it is rather easy to render superficial judgments concerning the worth of these two books. The simplicity, the naiveté and the very real limitations of Tufts's "plain and easy method" are obvious. The turgidity and complexity of Walter's essay are equally so. Yet when the problem confronting them, namely that of raising the musical literacy of the masses, is considered in the light of the difficulties inherent in the traditional system of solmization, it is apparent that between the two of them they had met the musical needs of their time. Such at least was the opinion of three influential ministers of the day who obliquely acknowledged their contribution to the movement to reform congregational singing in a tract published in 1723.

> The time is now come, when & wherein God is affording us more & better helps for right singing of the Psalms, than many Years we have had, and has stirred up many Young Ones to be willing to take pains to learn to sing by Rule.[26]

The First Singing Societies

Earlier in the present chapter it was concluded on the basis of such evidence as has survived that the first efforts at promoting regular singing were dependent upon the initiative of particular ministers and the resources available to them in their congregations. Both ministers and congregations varied considerably in these respects; thus it is not unreasonable to assume that at the time when the first singing books were published, perhaps a majority of congregational singers had not yet been introduced to the new way of singing. Credence is lent to this assumption by the fact that concurrently with the appearance of the new books a number of societies dedicated to "promoting regular singing in the worship of God"

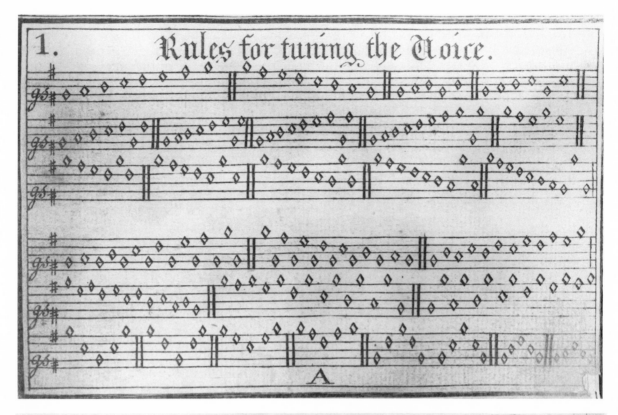

Figure 10. A set of "Rules for Tuning the Voice" and two tunes, "Canterbury" and "St. Mary's" reproduced from Thomas Walter's *Grounds and Rules of Musick Explained* (1721; reprint 1764). Courtesy, American Antiquarian Society.

were organized in Massachusetts. These societies not only played a significant role in bringing about the adoption of regular singing in this area, but also bequeathed to the singing school that which was to become one of its most characteristic features, the singing lecture.

Knowledge about the principals involved in the organization of these societies and the precise relationship between them is fragmentary at best. The first, and probably the most important, was the one established in Boston at about the time when Walter's *Grounds and Rules* was in the press. The first intimation of its existence is found in two entries from Sewall's diary relative to what must have been the dress rehearsal and first public appearance of that society.

> Mar. 15, 1721. Great Singing at night in the Court Chamber.[27]

> Mar. 16, 1721. At night Dr. Mather preaches in the School-house to the young Musicians, from Rev. 14.3 — no man could learn that song. House was full and the Singing extraordinarily Excellent, such as has hardly been heard before in Boston. Sung four times out of Tate and Brady.[28]

The principal speaker also recorded the event in his diary and in so doing revealed that the society was involved in providing instruction in the new way of singing.

> Mar 16, 1721. In the Evening I preached unto a large Auditory, where a Society of persons learning to Sing, began a quarterly solemnity. On Rev. XIV.3.[29]

That the society was actually involved in running a singing school is seen in the youthful age of the "persons learning to sing" and in the fact that they, like the thousands of young people who followed after them, were destined to engage in this activity for the usual three-month semester.

After the successful opening of its singing school the society in Boston is lost from view for a time. It reappears eight months later in a newspaper advertisement in which its full name, the nature of its activities, and the reasons for its absence from the musical scene are revealed.

> Whereas the Society for promoting Regular Singing in the Worship of God, did, upon the spreading of the Small Pox among us, think it proper to forbear their usual Meetings, while the Distemper continu'd; And the Town being now almost free of Infection, the Moderator and several others of the said Society, desire a Meeting of all the members thereof at the Town-House in Boston,

on Thursday Evening next, at 7 of Clock, to consider if it may not be proper to begin their Weekly Meetings, for Improvement in that delightful and heavenly Exercise.[30]

A frightful epidemic,[31] which had claimed the lives of over eight hundred persons between May and December of that year, was reason enough for the temporary cessation of its activities.

With the return to a more normal state of affairs, the society in Boston seems to have come into its own as an organization of considerable influence. In the spring of the next year, it held its second public concert, an event which attracted sufficient attention to warrant its being reviewed in the principal newspaper of the day.

> March 5, 1722. On Thursday last in the Afternoon, a Lecture was held at the New Brick Church, by the Society for promoting Regular Singing in the Worship of God. The Reverend Mr. Thomas Walter of Roxbury preach'd an excellent Sermon on that Occasion, from 2 Sam. 23.1.— *The Sweet Psalmist of Israel.* The Singing was perform'd in Three Parts (according to Rule) by about Ninety Persons skill'd in that Science, to the great Satisfaction of a numerous Assembly there present.[32]

Knowledge concerning the publication dates of the first singing books suggests that this concert was the first to demonstrate to the public at large the beauties of three-part music as performed by musically literate singers. The first edition of the singing book by their distinguished lecturer, Thomas Walter, had been available for some months. His only rival, John Tufts, had yet to bring out a three-part edition of his singing book; thus it is reasonable to assume that the music performed was taken from the *Grounds and Rules of Musick Explained.*

Walter's other contribution to the occasion, *The Sweet Psalmist of Israel,* was deemed remarkable enough by those[33] who heard it to warrant its immediate publication. Perusal of its contents discloses that it is not just another tedious sermon upon the fine points of religious dogma, but a serious essay in which eighteenth-century views on the aesthetics, the acoustics, and the psychology of music are reconciled with the Scriptures. Worthy of extended examination in any monograph dealing with the history of music in America, it reflects with the greatest credit upon its author and his audience.

In the preface to his *Sweet Psalmist*, Walter lauded the efforts of the Reverend Mr. Brown[34] of Reading who had delivered a singing lecture for the benefit of a society of that town. This event was also considered newsworthy enough to be reviewed in the *Courant*.

> March 26, 1722. On Thursday last a Lecture was held at Redding, by a Society of that Place for promoting Regular Singing in the Worship of God. The Rev. Mr. Brown preach'd from Psalm 100.2, *Come before his Presence with Singing*. The Singing was performed in Three Parts by about Fifty Persons, some of whom came from the Towns adjacent to assist in the Performance. 'Tis said a Singing Lecture will shortly be held at Newbury.[35]

The Newbury lecture went unchronicled by the *Courant*, but another pair of lectures, one of which demonstrates the existence of still another village singing society dedicated to promoting regular singing, received full coverage.[36]

The first of these events occurred in Dorchester. Like the one in Reading, its success was due in no small part to the active support and encouragement of singers from neighboring communities.

> May 14, 1722. On Tuesday last a Singing Lecture was held at Dorchester, by a Society of that Place for promoting Regular Singing in the Worship of God. The Rev. Mr. Danforth preach'd an excellent Sermon on that Occasion, from the 16th of the Acts, the 25th and 26th Verses. The Singing was perform'd in Three Parts, by about 100 Persons, many of whom went from Boston and Cambridge to assist the Society in that Part of Divine Worship.[37]

The happy custom of bringing together kindred musical spirits from several communities for the purpose of making a "joyful noise unto the Lord," which was so characteristic of the singing schools of a later era, thus had as its precedent the singing lectures promoted by the regular singers of Reading and Dorchester.

The second of these events took place in Boston a few weeks later. The Reverend John Barnard, a man who would one day publish his own versification[38] of the Psalms, was the principal speaker on that occasion.

> June 4, 1722. On Thursday last a Lecture was held at the New Brick Church, by the Society of this Place for the promoting or Regular Singing in the Worship of God. The Rev. Mr. *John Barnard* of Marblehead preach'd. an excellent Sermon on that Occasion from Psal. 57.7, 8. The Singing was

> perform'd in Three Parts as usual, by about 100 Persons skill'd in that Science.[39]

This lecture, which was the second to be given that year in Boston, brought the spring musical season to a close.

The fall musical season in Boston began with a singing lecture presided over by the Reverend Benjamin Colman of the Church in Brattle Square. His appearance before the Society went unrecorded in the columns of the *Courant*, even though he had long been an advocate of regular singing. The event itself would have remained unknown but for the fact that two of the members of the audience privately recorded their experience in manuscripts which have been preserved to the present day. One member, Joseph Green, was particularly impressed with the musical aspect of the lecture.

> ...on Friday last was ye delightfull exercise of singing performed att ye New Brick Church, Mr. Colman pr. from Rev. 5.9. and they sung a new song &c. ye Singing was managed only by ye masters of it, viz. men & women, seated in the front Gallery on purpose for it; they sang four times, all which were performed with a great dexterity and pleasancy.[40]

Another member, Jeremiah Bumstead, a humble mechanic who made it a habit to attend all of the singing lectures given in Boston, was most impressed by the textual aspect of the lecture.

> Sept. 21, 1722. A sing lecture att ye North Brick. Mr. Colman preached from those words, "They sung a new Song," revelations 5 & 9. Sung Tate and Brady 4 psalms, namely 108, first; 147, next; 89, next; 98, last; noted by titles in that psalm book.[41]

Taken together their impressions confirm the belief that the society in Boston was an able, forward-looking group that was worthy of being called the first choral society in the Colonies.[42]

The successes of the Society for Promoting Regular Singing in Boston were repeated again in 1723 when the society engaged Cotton Mather and John Tufts, respectively, to deliver sermons at two singing lectures. Both the ever-faithful Bumstead and the reviewer from the *Courant* attended the spring and fall lectures given that year. Both[43,44] recorded these events so laconically that nothing new is added to our knowledge of the society. The very brevity of their remarks suggests that part-singing was coming to be such a commonplace event in Boston that it was no longer particularly newsworthy.

The circumstances attending the demise of the Society for Regular Singing in Boston and its sister societies in Dorchester and Reading are as much a mystery as those attending their birth. No references are made to any of them after 1723 by the omnipresent Bumstead or the music-minded *Courant.* For this reason their disappearance from the musical scene must remain a matter of conjecture. The most likely explanation is that they had disbanded once they had achieved their objectives, i.e., the adoption of regular singing by the churches of their respective communities. Credence is lent to this explanation by Peter Thacher's statement[45] that regular singing had been adopted in the "Holy Churches of Boston, Roxbury, Dorchester, Cambridge, Taunton, Bridgewater, Charlestown, Ipswich, Newbury, Andover, and other Places" by 1723. Further credence is lent to this explanation by the curious coincidence between the dates when the societies ceased their activities and when Thomas Walter[46] retired from public life. Unfortunately, knowledge about his relationship[47] to these societies is too meager to permit the formulation of a definite hypothesis concerning this point.

Harvard College, the Wellspring for Regular Singing

From the chronicle presented thus far it is apparent that the first singing schools, the first singing books, and the first singing societies were chiefly the work of an enlightened group[48] of clergymen who possessed musical knowledge and skill far above those of their congregations. How they came to possess such a high degree of knowledge and skill in that which appears to have been a musical wilderness is a question not answered by the mere chronicling of events. The musical training offered in Boston by Brownell, Ivers, and Enstone was neither intensive enough to account for the remarkable accomplishments of men like Tufts and Walter, nor extensive enough to account for the general knowledge about music possessed by their fellow ministers. The only other place where they could have received training in music was their alma mater, Harvard College. This possibility seems at once to be a very doubtful proposition, since, as Morison has remarked, "Music and singing we have been taught not to expect in a puritan college."[49] His own researches into the history of the college in the seventeenth century, however, cast doubt upon the validity of this popularly held concept. He found reliable evidence[50] that secular music-making, such as ballad singing and fiddling, was a part of undergraduate life at that time. He also found a small amount of circumstantial evidence[51] that the serious study of music was part of the curriculum. Unfortunately, he did not carry his investigation any further than this point.

Certainly, the single manuscript page in the Harvard College Papers (1, no. 31) pertaining to the curriculum of 1723 would have discouraged additional research along this line, since music is not mentioned in it.

> A particular Account of the present Stated Exercises Enjoyed the Students.
>
> The first year the Freshmen recite the Classick Authors learn't at School viz Tully Virgil Isocrates Homer with greek Testam[en]t & greek Catechism & Dugards or Farnabys Rhetorick & the latter part of the year the Hebrew Grammar & Psalter Ramus's & Burgesdicius's Logicks.
>
> The Second year The Sophimores recite Bu[r]gesdicius's Logick and a Manuscript called the New Logick Extracted from Legrand and ars Herebords Meletemata continuing stil most part of the year recitations in the forementioned greek & Hebrew books and dispute on Logical Questions twice a week.
>
> The third year The Junior Sophisters recite Herebors Melletemata Mr Mortons Physicks Dr Mores Ethics a system of Geography & a System of Metaphysicks Wollebius's Divinity on Saturdays & dispute twice a week on Physical and Metaphysical & Ethical Questions.
>
> The fourth year the Senior Sophisters recite Alsted's Geography Gasendus's astronomy goe over the arts viz Gramma Logick & Natural Phylosophy Ames Medulla & dispute once a week on phylosophical & astronomical questions.[52]

This statement about the curriculum is clearly at odds with Symmes's assertion that music:

> ...was studied, known and approv'd of in our *College,* for many years after its first founding. This is evident from the Musical Theses which were formerly Printed, and from some Writings containing some *Tunes* with Directions for *Singing by Note,* as they are now Sung; and these are yet in being, though of more than *Sixty Years* standing; besides no Man that studied Music as it is treated of by *Alsted, Playford* and others, could be ignorant of it.[53]

That Harvard men not only studied music in college, but also indulged in part-singing is evident from an entry in Samuel Sewall's diary in which he noted the passing of an old friend and classmate.

> Satterday, January 11th, 1718. Enquiring at Mrs. Phillips, a Sherbourn man tells me Mr. Gookin dyed on Tuesday night, and is to be buried today. He was a good Scholar and a solid Divine. We were fellows together at College, and have sung many a Tune in Consort, hope shall sing Hallelujahs together in Heaven.[54]

The solution to this problem lies in the identification and analysis of the "Musical Theses" and of the works by Alsted and Playford. Most musical scholars have assumed that both the theses and the writings to which Symmes referred were lost in the fire that destroyed the college library in 1764. Not all of the theses were lost, however, because of their unusual nature. As Morison[55] has pointed out, they were not extended dissertations, but single sentence "propositions upon the several liberal Arts and other subjects studied in the undergraduate course, which any member of the graduating class, if challenged, was supposed to be able to defend, in Latin, by the recognized rules of syllogistic disputation." A commencement broadside devoted to the theses was published each year. Fortunately, many of these broadsides were not discarded once their usefulness was over but were preserved among the papers of those who used them.

The most complete collection[56] of these broadsides is in the possession of the Harvard Archives. Careful analysis of this collection with special reference to musical topics not only confirms Symmes's assertion concerning their existence, but also provides valuable insight into the type of musical training offered by the college.

The earliest surviving broadside which contains a musical thesis is that of 1711. Here a simple statement[57] about the nature of music is listed among the *Theses Mathematicae*.

> No. 10. Musica est sonus modulatus ad temporis et soni quantitatem.
>
> (trans.) Music is sound properly measured as to duration and pitch.

No copies of the broadsides for the years 1712, 1713, 1714, 1715, 1716, and 1718 have survived. Every broadside from 1717 through 1730 with the exception of that for 1720 contains one or more musical theses. With the year 1721 they were accorded a place of their own on the broadsides under the heading, "Theses Musicae." Inexplicably, none were included in the broadsides which were printed after 1730.

Careful analysis of the musical theses[58] yields much specific information about the course of study upon which they were based. Many, such as one[59] for the year 1730, are concerned with definitions of music.

> No. 25. Music est Ars sonos Voce et Instrumentis modulandi.
>
> (trans.) Music is the art of regulating sounds by means of voices and instruments.

Some, such as one for the year 1719, are concerned with the harmonic aspect of music.

> No. 18. Dias et Trias harmonia sunt fundamenta contrapuncti Musici.
>
> (trans.) The harmonious dyad (the interval of two notes) and triad (the common chord) are the foundations of part music.

Others, such as another one for the year 1719, are concerned with the melodic aspect of music.

> No. 20. Coeunt Melodiae motu graduali, non Saltatorio.
>
> (trans.) Melodies move gradually, not abruptly.

Still others, such as one for the year 1729, are concerned with the acoustics of music.

> No. 24. Corpora majora graviorem, minora acutiorem, producunt Sonum.
>
> (trans.) Large bodies produce a deeper tone, small bodies a higher one.

Additional insight into the type of musical training offered at the college during this period is afforded by examination of the books mentioned by Symmes. The most important of these was Alsted's *Encyclopedia*, a work[60] written in Latin which served as the standard reference book for several generations of Harvard students. The third volume of this work, entitled *Philosophia Theoretica* contains a chapter on musical theory as it might be construed by a classical scholar and mathematician. The topic headings[61] within this chapter are good indicators of the kind of musical knowledge students were expected to master.

> I. Of the Subject of Music.
> A definition of music as the "science of singing well, otherwise called harmonical and *Musathena.*"
> II. Of the Principles of Cognition in Music.
> A logical basis for the theory of music.

III. Of the Efficient End of Harmonical Song.
A theological basis for music.

IV. Of the Quantity of Musical Song.
Simple acoustics: intensity, pitch, duration. The scale of music. Intervals.

V. Of the Signs of a Musical Sound.
Rhythmic and tonal notation. The cleffs and the staff.

VI. Of the Musical Dyas.
Detailed study of the intervals and the mathematical ratios underlying them.

VII. Of the Musical Trias.
Detailed study of the triad, or common chord.

VIII. Of the Form of an Harmonical Song.
Mathematical analysis of melodic lines, part-music, and imitative writing in terms of pitch and duration.

IX. Of the Affections of an Harmonical Song.
The aesthetic doctrine of the affections as seen in the study of the ancient modes.

X. Of Special Music.
Types of music, i.e., sacred and secular. Means of production, i.e., voices and instruments.

That the students actually mastered the material in Alsted is seen in Walter's boast[62] that he could give the "Physical and Mathematical Solution of the Grounds, Cause, and Effect of Harmony" and in the fact that many of the musical theses are almost literal quotations[63] from that work.

Symmes's reference to the works of John Playford suggests that Harvard men were encouraged to put their theoretical knowledge to practical use in their daily lives. It is impossible to state with exact certainty which of his many publications, either secular or sacred, were known to them. Walter's allusion[64] to the type of note values found in "Songs, Madrigals, and Light Airs" suggests that he may have been familiar with one or more of Playford's collections of secular music. Be that as it may, the most likely examples of Playford's handiwork with which he and his fellow ministers were acquainted were the *Whole Book of Psalms* (London, 1677) and the *Introduction to the Skill of Musick* (London, 1654). Tufts's and Walter's indebtedness[65] to the former may be established by tracing the origins of the psalm tunes in their respective books. Their indebtedness[66] to the latter is less easily established because the sections of their books which deal with the rudiments are original restatements of common musical practice. The fact that this work, which went through twenty editions[67] in England between 1654 and 1730, was the principal tract[68] upon the rudiments of music available to New Englanders before the advent of their own works cannot be ignored. It is not unreasonable, therefore, to assume that the *Whole Book of Psalms* and the *Introduction to the Skill of Musick* were the works by means of which Harvard undergraduates rounded out their theoretical knowledge of music.

Having demonstrated the nature of musical study at the college, it remains to reconcile the fact of its existence with the fact of its omission from the "Account" about the curriculum of 1723. The best clue to the resolution of this paradox is the curious practice of classifying musical propositions under the heading of *Theses Mathematicae*. The rationale for this practice is to be found in the place accorded music in Alsted's systematization of knowledge. To him music was a "mathematical science subalternate to arithmetic."[69] It is difficult to believe that arithmetic, the humblest branch of mathematics, was a part of the college curriculum at that time. That it was, indeed, a part of the curriculum is confirmed by S. E. Morison's investigation[70] into the matter. Both arithmetic and geometry were a part of the senior sophisters' studies during the seventeenth century. While neither of these subjects is specifically mentioned in the "Account," it is reasonably certain that they continued to be a part of the curriculum during the first quarter of the eighteenth century because of the mathematical propositions[71] which were included each year in the commencement broadsides.

The classification of music among mathematical studies is not a completely satisfactory solution to the problem of determining its place in the curriculum, because such a classification fails to account for those musical theses which deal with acoustics. Here again the content of a textbook which was in use at the college between 1687 and 1728 provides insight into the way in which music was incorporated into the curriculum. This textbook was Charles Morton's *Compendium Physicae*, which is listed in the "Account" among the junior sophisters' studies as "Mr. Morton's Physicks." Included in this volume[72] is a chapter which deals essentially with the acoustics of music. The physiology of the ear, the nature of sound, the theory of concord and discord, the "Gamut or Scale of Musick," as well as the aesthetics of music are briefly discussed. Serious attention must have been given to Morton's discussion of these topics since some of the arguments which he employed were utilized in the musical theses.[73] Taken as a whole, this chapter afforded a good introduction to the more profound treatment of the subject in Alsted.

Confirmation of the fact that music was a regular part of the curriculum at the college not only explains why the ministry was ready and able to initiate musical reform in the congregations of their day, but also provides additional insight into the still much debated problem of the relationship between Puritanism and music. It was no flight of fancy that guided Mather's hand when he penned his advice to candidates for the ministry.

> For MUSIC, I know not what well to say. Do as you please, if you *Fancy* it, I don't *Forbid* it. Only do not for the sake of it Alienate your Time too much, from those that are more Important Matters. It may be so that you may serve your GOD the better for the Refreshment of One that can play well on an Instrument. However, to accomplish yourself at *Regular Singing*, is a thing that will be of *Daily Use* to you. For I would not have a day pass you without *Singing*, but so as at the same time to make a *Melody in your Heart* unto the Lord, besides the Part you may bear, In Hymnis suavisonantis Eccelesiae.[74]

Rather, it was the commonly held conviction that music served man best as the handmaiden of religion. As such it formed a very necessary part of the education of those destined to be the leaders of both the religious and the musical life of New England congregations.

The Great Controversy over Regular Singing

As has so often been noted by social historians, New England has always seemed to possess more than its share of the type of individual who is much given to thinking and acting according to the dictates of his own conscience. Historically speaking, one of the earliest examples of this characteristic was the great controversy over the adoption of regular singing. The nature of this controversy and the alignment of various segments of the community into opposing factions was revealed in a letter to Thomas Hollis by Cotton Mather.

A mighty Spirit came Lately upon abundance of our people to Reform their singing which was degenerated in our Assemblies to an Irregularity which made a Jar in the ears of the more curious and skilful singers. Our ministers generally Encouraged the people, to accomplish themselves for a Regular singing, and a more beautiful Psalmody. Such Numbers of good people, (and Especially young people) became Regular Singers, that they could carry it in the Congregations. But who would beleeve it? Tho' in the more polite City of *Boston*, this Design mett with a General acceptance, in the Countrey, where they have more of the Rustick, some Numbers of Elder and Angry people bore zealous Testimonies against these wicked Innovations, and this bringing in of Popery. Their zeal transported some of them so far (on the behalf of Mumpsimus) that they would not only use the most approbrious Terms, and call the Singing of these Christians, a worshipping of the Devil, but also they would run out of the Meetinghouse at the Beginning of the Exercise. The Paroxyms have risen to that Heighth, as to necessitate the Convening of several Ecclesiastical Councils, for the Composing of the Differences and Annimosities arisen on the occasion.[75]

This controversy, which raged sporadically throughout New England for some twenty years, arose chiefly from the refusal of many conservatives to accept the musical innovations advocated by religious leaders. The impasse created by their refusal was further aggravated by the intemperate lengths to which these leaders went in trying to bring about reform. So great was the ill feeling created by the actions and pronouncements of these men that townspeople became arrayed against country folk, and the younger generation became estranged from their elders.

Although this controversy was an unfortunate episode in the history of the New England singing school, it was, as far as the historian is concerned, not unproductive of some good. The polemical tracts upon religious music which were published during this period have remained the best single source of information about the decline of congregational music and the establishment of regular singing. The following list[76] of tracts is useful in confirming the identity of some of the principal figures involved in reform and in dating roughly the period of the controversy.

Symmes, *Reasonableness of Regular Singing*, 1720.
Mather, *Accomplished Singer*, 1721.

Symmes, *Discourse*, 1722.
Walter, *Sweet Psalmist of Israel*, 1722.
Symmes, *Utili Dulci*, 1723.
Thacher, *Cases of Conscience*, 1723.
Anon., *Pacificatory Letter*, 1724.
Anon., *Brief Discourse*, 1725.
Dwight, *Essay to Silence the Outcry*, 1725.
Woodbridge, *Duty of God's People*, 1727.
Chauncey, *Regular Singing Defended*, 1727.
Seccombe, *Essay*, 1741.

Of these tracts the most interesting is *Utili Dulci* by the redoubtable Thomas Symmes. Cast in the form of a "Joco-Serious Dialogue" between an ignorant but well-meaning country bumpkin and his minister, it summarizes and answers under ten headings the chief objections to the adoption of regular singing which were voiced by the more "Rustick" type.

1. It is a new way, an unknown tongue.
2. It is not so melodious as the usual way.
3. There are so many tunes we shall never have done learning them.
4. The practice creates disturbances and causes people to behave indecently and disorderly.
5. It is Quakerish and Popish and introductive of instrumental music.
6. The names given to the notes are bawdy, yea blasphemous.
7. It is a needless way, since our fathers got to heaven without it.
8. It is a contrivance to get money.
9. People spend too much time learning it. They tarry out nights disorderly.
10. They are a company of young upstarts that fall in with this way, and some of them are lewd and loose persons.

However picayune they may appear now, these objections were very real in their day. Furthermore, Symmes's answers to them are invaluable in that they provide a vivid picture of the real issues involved in the controversy.

For example, the first part of Symmes's answer to the complaint that regular singing was not so "melodious" as the common way of singing demonstrates the tremendous hold which tradition had upon the popular mind and the imprudent lengths to which the ministry went in trying to break that hold by means of ridicule.

N. My *Second Objection* is this, That this Singing by Note is not so Melodious & Pleasant, as the Usual Way. *Some have called it Yelling. Others have Said, they'd as leeve hear the Wolves howl.*

M....I'll honestly confess to you that before I was pretty well acquainted with the Rules of Singing, I rather fancy'd the *Usual*, than the Regular way: But my *Judgment* satisfy'd me the Regular must be the best. And I know; one reason why my Fancy for the present was most gratify'd with my singing the Usual Way, was, because I was used to *that*, and not Master of the *other*. And hence it is, that *Home is Home*, be it ever so Homely. And even so the miserable *Hottentots* (pardon the Comparison) who think to adorn themselves with the *Guts of Beasts*, with all the Garbage in them; prefer these Guts to a *Chain of Gold*, because its what they're used to, land it pleases their Fancies. But surely if they'd exercise Reason, the Ornaments us'd by other People, are more beautiful and becoming; or else all the Civilized & Polite part of the World are deceiv'd and those Dregs of Mankind are in the Right of it.[77]

The second part of Symmes's answer demonstrates the consternation experienced by intelligent men when they are forced to deal with persons who insist upon making value judgments without reference to the facts.

M. *Furthermore*, I've said to some of my Hearers, that if any of you A.R.S.'s would take the pains to *acquaint yourselves* with the Rules of Singing, so as to be able to Sing 6 or 7 Tunes tolerable by Art, *If they did not then say as I do*, that singing by Note is unspeakably preferable to singing the Usual Way; *I'd give up the Cause as to them.*

Besides, there are few of you A.R.S.'s that ever heard Singing in several parts of Musick: and some of you don't know the *Difference* between Treble & Bass. Hence I heard one, (that your Fraternity set much by) say, that the *Treble & Bass must be sung with the Same Voice!* And another that was pleas'd to say in my Hearing, That one Sabbath-day in a certain Meeting-House, there was *Four Parts* of Singing! for some sung *Rowly Way*; and some sung the *Usual Way*; and some sung the *New Way*; and some sung *Bass*. Whence I learn't that the Usual Way at one Town, and the Usual Way at another, were very *Different*: Fasest—. Now there is no man can judge aright of the Melody of Singing by Note; that has not heard Tunes sung in the several Parts or in Consort; and that not by Beginners only, but by Adeptists, or at least persons *well skill'd* in the Science of Music;

any more, than a man can judge or *Reading*, by Hearing one Read that *just begins* to put his *Syllables* together.[78]

The designation of those in opposition to regular singing as A.R.S.'s, or anti-regular singers, was a pun not lost upon Symmes's more sophisticated readers.

The use of such invective was particularly unfortunate in that it tended to unify those opposed to regular singing and to obscure the basic question, "Is an austere and strictly disciplined homophony the best solution to the musical difficulties engendered by a free and unfettered monophony?" The ministry could not, of course, argue the issue in these terms because the masses were musically illiterate. Instead, the issue was joined in terms of a host of minor misunderstandings about the nature and value of musical literacy.

Typical of these misunderstandings was the almost superstitious attitude which the country people had toward the solmizations of syllables.

N. My *Sixth Objection* was, that the Names given to the Notes are Bawdy, yea Blasphemous.

M. But then as to the Bawdiness of *La, Sol*; all I need say is, That as the *Fool thinketh*, so the *Bell Clinketh*. No Mortal that can spell would ever have had such a Tho't, and it's a shame to mention it. And I'm sure I'd never have done it, but to let the world see, what Treatment we have from you, who have a *Zeal without Knowledge*, as I must bear you Record.

But that we may hear no more of this Nasty Objection; I'll tell you, that the very Letters F.S.L. are in some Editions of *our Psalm Books*, and the whole Mystery of the Business is this, That these Names of the Notes were given (as *Alsted* and *Playford* tell us) by *Guido Aretinus*, several Hundred Years ago; they being the *First* Syllables of that Sophick,

Mi-ra Gestorum Sol-ve Polluti

Fa-muli Tuorum La-bii Reatium.

And these Names have been retained ever since. Because they answer the End as well as any other. And *some* Names there must be for the Advantage of the Learner. But if any will use, A,B,C, or *Bo-Ce-Di-Ga*-lo-ma-ni, as proposed by Alsted, instead thereof, it will serve the turn.... [79]

The underlying, but unstated, reason for this objection was that the uneducated had come to believe that the tunes used for the psalms were in themselves sacred; thus, the performance of these tunes by other means than the customary words was held to be a sacrilegious act.

The debate was not limited to the readers of tracts, but was carried to the readers of newspapers as well. In the columns of the *Courant*, several anonymous writers did battle on behalf of the traditional and liberal points of view. A city man, "John Harmony," begged several parishioners of his church to desist in their "irregular singing."[80] Another city man, "Harry Consort," made light of the furor[81] over regular singing which split the church at Braintree in twain.[82] A country man, "Ephraim Rotewell," who set great store by hearsay, argued that the adoption of regular singing would open the way for that most dreadful of fates, Popery.[83] And finally, a wit named "Jeoffrey Chanticleer" exposed the failings of existing performance practices for all to see.[84]

And so the debate over regular singing went on, the Harvard trained ministers on one side and the common people on the other, each thoroughly convinced as to the soundness of their respective positions and each stubbornly reluctant to yield a foot of ground. And so it might have continued, but for the fact that early in the controversy the ministers hit upon a solution to the problem which ensured the eventual victory of the new way over the common way of singing. Secure in the knowledge that the younger generation, which had proved itself to be very receptive to the new way of singing, would one day play a dominant role in the affairs of the church, the ministers made them the standard-bearers of reform.

With the publication of Walter's *Ground and Rules*, they went on record concerning their unanimity in this course of action.

...and we would encourage all, more particularly our *Young People*, to accomplish themselves with Skill to *Sing the Songs of the Lord*, according to the Good Rules of Psalmody: Hoping that the Consequence of it will be, that not only the Assemblies of *Zion* will *Decently* & in order to carry on this Exercise of PIETY, but also it will be the more introduced into private *Families* and become a part of our Family-Sacrifice.

Increase Mather	Peter Thacher
Cotton Mather	Joseph Sewall
Nehemiah Walter	Thomas Prince
Joseph Belcher	John Webb
Benj. Wadsworth	William Cooper

Benj. Colman   Thomas Foxcroft
Nathanael Williams   Samuel Checkly[85]

Having done so, they proceeded to defend the younger generation vigorously against all comers, especially their elders who often found them "too light, airy and vain" in learning to sing by rule. Many of the ministers, such as Peter Thacher, argued that the younger generation had been chosen in preference to the older generation because the younger learned the new way so much more readily.

> God bestows these choice Talents on Young Persons as well as on Elder Persons; and Persons in their Youth do learn the Art of Musick with greater ease and speed than such as are Aged; and therefore should be encoraged to learn it while they are Young; and having obtained this Gift of God, by God's blessings on their industry and instructions, they are to be Allowed and Encouraged to Exercise it peaceably in Publick Assemblies,...[86]

Others, such as Nathaniel Chauncey, were less tactful in explaining why the younger generation had been chosen.

> And as for Young Persons being so forward in the matter, a Good Account may be given.
>
> (1) They are generally more free from prejudice than Elderly people, and then besides,
>
> (2) Their present age disposes them to Mirth, and it should be a very Joyful and Acceptable thing unto Elderly People to see them forward to improve their Mirth according to Scripture directions. *Is any merry? Let him sing Psalms.*[87]

Still others, such as Thomas Symmes, who was noted for his pastoral work[88] with young people, justified the selection of the younger generation in terms of that generation's special need for more wholesome forms of musical recreation. In his original proposal for singing schools he asked:

> Would not this be an innocent and profitable recreation, and would it not have a tendency to divert young people, who are most proper to learn, from learning *idle, foolish,* yea, pernicious *songs* and *ballads,* and banish all such trash from their minds? Experience proves this.[89]

Symmes's query is especially significant since it raises a problem with which the ministry of New England had long been concerned, namely the people's taste for what Walter called the "licentious *Poesey* and *Music* of the Present Age."[90] As early as 1713 Mather had observed that:

> ...the Minds and Manners of many People about the Countrey are much corrupted, by foolish Songs and Ballads, which by the hawkers and Pedlers carry into all parts of the Countrey. By way of Antidote, I would procure poetical Composures full of Piety, and such as may have a tendency to advance Truth and Goodness, to be published, and scattered into all Corners of the Land. There may be an Extract of some, from the excellent Watt's hymns.[91]

His concern was shared by other Puritan divines[92] who believed that vocal music was amongst the most precious of God's gifts to men and ought, therefore, to be dedicated chiefly to His greater glory.

> A pleasant and strong Voice, with Ability to Modulate the same, is the Gift of GOD, and a Tallent that should be Improved to the Glory of his Name.[93]

They looked with horror upon its use for other, less noble purposes.

> What a pity and what a shame it is to abuse so sweet and heavenly an Art to the base Ends and Designs of Impiety, Vice and Debauchery! To commit such a Sacrilege, as to prostitute our Glory to the Devil, and serve the Interests of Hell thro' the Means of the heavenly Science! Verily, such Music shall finish in everlasting Weeping, Wailing and Gnashing of Teeth![94]

The truth of the matter was that the last quarter of the seventeenth and the first quarter of the eighteenth century was a period in which love songs, profane catches, and bawdy ballads formed the musical diet of all classes both in England and in America. In England solid Anglican divines such as Bedford,[95] Lavington,[96] and Senhouse[97] railed against the musical excesses of a Hogarthian age in terms that would have struck a sympathetic chord in their Puritan colleagues on the other side of the Atlantic.

> As the *Devil, like a roaring Lion,* walks continually about, seeing such Men whom he may devour; so he makes use of Musick for a Bait, whereby to deceive them in all Parts of the Nation, and among all Degrees, Ages, and Sexes. He knows too well, that all Mankind is addicted to Pleasures, that *Singing* is the natural Consequence of Mirth, and that when Men are merry, they are less apt to stand upon their Guard, and therefore he thinks it is in his Interest to mix his Poison among the *Songs* of all Sorts. The Ballads,

which are sung in most, and sold in all *Market-Towns* of this Nation, are a dreadful Instance of this Corruption; and the Tunes being fitted to a vulgar Capacity, are presently learn'd by those who are not able to pay for a better *Education.*[98]

Among their solutions to the problem of popular balladry was the further encouragement of the village singing societies which were beginning to be common in England at this time.

> It is to be wish'd that there were many more *Societies*, who did promote the *Singing of Psalms* together in *Consort.* The Effects of such an Exercise are very many, and very good; and it is a Pity, that an Affair of such Consequence in *Religion* should be either neglected or discouraged. The Knowledge thereof is very easily taught, and quickly learn'd, where there is a good *Master* and an apt *Scholar.* Here are no difficult Turnings and Windings the Voice. Here are no Varieties in Time, but everything so plain, that many Persons have learn'd to sing in Consort purely by Ear, without Assistance.[99]

Faced with the same problems, spiritual leaders of both faiths had thus arrived at the same solutions more or less independently of each other.

Needless to say, the youth of New England enthusiastically embraced the new way of singing. Hardly a single controversy tract fails to mention them favorably for the zealous way in which they applied themselves to the task of learning the "Rules of Musick." Whether the ministry succeeded entirely in winning them away from popular balladry is a moot question. Ballads continued to be published in respectable numbers throughout the remainder of the century. Be that as it may, the decision to make the younger generation the standard-bearers of reform set a precedent which largely determined the character of the later day singing school as an institution devoted to the education of youth through music.

The Eventual Triumph of Regular Singing

The task of documenting the establishment of regular singing in Boston is a simple one because it was the center of the reform movement. As such, it witnessed the formation of the first singing schools, the publication of the first singing books, and the founding of the first choral society in the colonies. It was inevitable, therefore, that the first fruits of the reform movement would be harvested in Boston and in the communities adjacent to it.

The task of documenting the establishment of regular singing throughout the rest of New England is a difficult one because the church records for this period are often unavailable and incomplete. Such information as has been gleaned from town and church histories suggests that in spite of its early adoption by those communities directly influenced by one or more of the reformers, regular singing had a long, arduous road to travel before it became anything like a universal practice in the meeting houses of New England.

On the basis of *Table 1*, it is apparent that two decades often elapsed before the smaller and more isolated towns adopted regular singing. One of the principal reasons why they lagged so far behind Boston is that a lack of skilled instructors in music existed at the time when reform was initiated. Timothy Woodbridge made this point very clear when he described the estate of congregational music in Connecticut.

> The following Discourse was delivered at a Lecture for the Encouragement of *Regular Singing,* a Comely & Commendable Practice; which for want of *Care* in preserving, and skilful *Instructors* to revive, has Languished in the Country till it is in a manner *Lost* and *Dead*; Yea has been so long Dead, as that with some it *Stinketh*; who judge it a great Crime to use means to *Recover* it again.[100]

In some instances this lack was remedied by the efforts of musically literate ministers,[101] but in most instances it was not remedied until one of the itinerant singing masters,[102] who were just beginning to become active, appeared on the scene.

Even when the services of the itinerant singing masters became more generally available, there was no guarantee that a particular congregation would adopt regular singing. Long accustomed to picking their own ministers, the congregations often refused to be guided by the dictates of higher ecclesiastical authority. In the case of regular singing, they treated it like any other matter affecting the operation of the church, i.e., they made it the subject of serious deliberation and formal parliamentary action.

As might be expected, their deliberations often reflected the conservatism of the times. Some congregations, such as the one in New Britain, Connecticut, rejected regular singing out of hand.

April 7, 1724. It was Proposed whether they should continue the present way of singing or would admit of regular singing.

May 9, 1724. Voted, to take a year's time to consider whether regular singing should be tried or not. Voted that if any person or persons shall presume to sing contrary to the lead of the Quoirister appointed by the church to the disturbance of the assembly, and the jarring of their melody, he or they shall be looked upon and dealt with as offenders.

March __ 1726/27. Voted, that we do declare our full satisfaction with the former way of singing psalms in this society, and do earnestly desire to continue therein.[103]

Others, such as the one at Hartford, adopted regular singing after a trial period.

June 20, 1733. *Voted* that this Society are willing and Content that Such of them as Encline to Learn to Sing by Rule should apply themselves in the best manner they can to gain knowledge thereof. *Voted* and agreed that after the Expiration of three months, Singing by Rule shall be admitted to be practiced in the congregation of this Society in their Publick Worship on the Lord's day & until their annual meeting in December next; & that then a Vote be taken whether the Society will further proceed in that way or otherwise.[104]

December __ 1733. *Voted* that Singing by Rule be admitted and practiced in the Congregation of this Society in their publick Worshipping of God; and this Society by their Vote manifest their desire that Mr. Joseph Gilbert, Junr., would take upon him the Care of setting the Psalm in the Congregation to the above Vote.[105]

Still others, such as the congregation at Hanover, Massachusetts, accepted regular singing in a forthright manner, which suggests that it never had been the subject of controversy.

May 7, 1742. The Church took a vote to see if the Society would sing the new way and it passed in the affirmative, nem con. Then being desired to bring in their votes for Turner, Mr. Ezekiel Turner was chosen by a considerable majority.[106]

The transition from the old way to the new way of singing was not always an easy one. Some congregations, such as the one at Wallingford, Connecticut, made it easier by alternating the new and the old until the people were familiar with the new. In 1731 they voted:

...that this Society Desire and agree to Sing in ye public assembly on ye Sabbath half ye time in ye new and half in ye old way for six Sabbaths; and after that wholly in ye new way.[107]

Others, such as the one at Glastonbury, found that the only way to ensure a smooth transition from the old to the new was to require the entire congregation to attend singing school.

Voted, that the Regular or new way of singing be deferred, and not be sung in the Congregation of this Society on the Sabbath days, until the meeting of this Society in December next, and that, in the mean time this Society, or as many inhabitants thereof as can conveniently attend it, do meet once a month at the place of public worship on the second Wednesday in each month, at two of the clock in the afternoon, to learn the said way of singing; and that there be also three private meetings set up for said singing once a week or fortnight, two in the Town Platt, and one at Naighuig, viz., at Mr. John Hollister's House at Naighuig on the first Monday in each month at four of the clock in the afternoon; —at the House of Jonathan Hale on the third Wednesday in Each month, at the same time of day, and at the house of Mr. Daniel Wright on the fourth Wednesday in Each month, at the same time of day.[108]

This method for accomplishing the transition was surely the most systematic on record. As such it stands in contrast to the more usual procedure of training up a group of young people who were expected to "carry" the new way in the congregation.

The votes of these and other congregations make it clear that the eventual triumph of regular singing in New England was also a triumph of sorts for the democratic process. Necessary changes in the mode of singing came about, not as the result of administrative fiat, but as the result of the participation of all in the life of the church. Free to think for themselves, even those congregations which had originally voted to reject regular singing eventually recognized its worth and moved its adoption. The deliberations of the Congregation at Mattapoisett, Massachusetts, are typical of those congregations which followed this pattern.

April 16, 1744. The Chh met to see whither something might be done to remove the great uneasiness that had arisen and had been long subsisting among us about the Rule of Singing in divine worship, or Singing by Rule, and after a considerable debate concerning a Vote or a Covenant (as some called it) which was consented unto by a certain Number of Persons in this place before there was a church gathered here, viz., that the new way of singing (for so they stiled regular singing) should forever be kept out of ye Prect. Hereupon the vote was called whether the Chh did look upon said act to be put a Vote. Voted in the affirmative; and hereupon the Vote was called whether this Chh do no Judge it most proper for ye future to sing by Rule in ye publick worship of God among us? Voted in ye affirmative.[109]

Given such freedom of conscience it was thus only a matter of time before the congregations were of one mind with regard to regular singing.

CONCLUDING REMARKS: With the establishment of regular singing, the singing school became an accepted feature of community life throughout New England. Designed initially to provide the congregations with instruction in the art of singing psalms by rule, it eventually expanded its activities to include instruction in more complex forms of music such as canons, fuging tunes, and anthems. This expansion of the course of study was but one manifestation of a burgeoning choral tradition which would one day place New England in the vanguard of musical culture in Federalist America.

III
The Singing School as an Educational Institution

THE ESTABLISHMENT of regular singing throughout New England was an arduous task which was made all the more difficult by the shortage of instructors and the slow process of self-government whereby individual religious societies could, and often did, take their time in adopting the new way of singing. Many of the smaller, more isolated communities apparently were still contemplating this move in the 1740s when they were swept up in the first great wave of revivalism in America known as the Great Awakening. Contemporary observers reported that there was a great deal of singing associated with this revival. Unfortunately, much of it was antithetical to the solemn, dignified, and carefully measured style of singing advocated by the reformers. For this reason the Great Awakening contributed relatively little to the further establishment of regular singing and thus the singing school in those areas which had remained untouched by the first efforts at reform.[1] In time the people's interest in revivalism waned and the singing school came to be recognized more and more widely as the proper means for improving congregational music.

The singing school would probably have continued along without any significant change in its essential nature after the Great Awakening was over but for the importation a decade later of two collections of English religious music, William Tans'ur's *Royal Melody Compleat* (London, 1755, 1760, 1764–66) and Aaron Williams's *Universal Psalmodist* (London, 1763, 1764, 1765, 1770). These collections were also reprinted eleven times in America between the years 1767 and 1774 by Daniel Bayley of Newburyport, Massachusetts, who issued them in a composite edition entitled *The American Harmony*.[2] The success of these collections was due not so much to Bayley's skill as an editor but to the fact that they provided New England psalm singers with their first introduction to some of the major forms of choral music such as canons, fuging tunes, anthems, and occasional pieces. So great was their impact that within a few years after their appearance a num-

ber of Yankee singing masters began composing choral music in the forms and styles included in their pages, and the regular singers who heretofore had been dispersed throughout their respective congregations began agitating for the right to form themselves into choirs. It would be no exaggeration to state that these collections were responsible in large measure for initiating the great flowering of choral music which took place in New England between 1760 and 1800.

Inevitably, the wide acceptance of these collections induced significant changes in the nature of the singing school. Masters and singers who had discovered the joys of singing extended choral compositions could hardly have been expected to remain content with an institution whose course of study was limited to the simple tonal and rhythmic patterns found in the psalm tunes of Tufts's and Walter's books. The performance of the new music demanded a much higher degree of musical literacy and vocal skill than the old music did. The singing school was, therefore, called upon to expand its course of study to include the complex tonal and rhythmic values and the performance skills demanded by the new music. By expanding its course of study, the school was thereby transformed from an institution oriented chiefly toward congregational singing to an institution oriented chiefly toward choral singing.

The emergence of a distinctive group of native-born singing master-composers, the widespread establishment of choirs, and the transformation of the singing school were closely interrelated phenomena. These facts suggest that they ought to be discussed together in the same chapter. It would, however, be difficult to do them equal justice by such a procedure, because the story of each is so rich in detail and of such significance to the history of the singing school as a whole. The discussion of these topics has, therefore, been divided into two chapters which follow each other logically. The first of this pair of chapters is devoted to an analysis of the singing master-composers and the singing schools which they taught, while the second is devoted to the choirs and singing societies which flourished mightily as the result of their labors.

The analysis of the singing school as an educational institution is a challenging one because it was different from most musical institutions in existence today. The scholar looks in vain for the kind of documents by means of which it might be studied. Catalogs, curriculum statements, courses of study, examinations, reports, graduation programs, diplomas, teachers' certificates, and so forth are completely lacking. Only the music books, the announcements in newspapers, and the personal papers of those who participated in the life of the school are available for study.

In spite of the lack of the usual paraphernalia, the New England singing school was a genuine institution because it fulfilled in its day most all of the responsibilities to the field of choral music which are now delegated to denominational choir schools, public school music programs, and college music departments. Furthermore, the paraphernalia listed above would have been useless to an institution which had evolved perfectly adequate, though relatively informal, means of accomplishing the same things. These equivalent means are readily apparent if the singing school is studied in the same manner as it was viewed by its contemporaries, namely, as a going concern involving the best efforts of ministers, members of congregations, singing masters, and singing scholars.

The relationships which existed between these persons suggested the plan of organization for the present chapter. The singing masters and their scholars are examined first, because they were the two principal elements in a singing school. Consideration of the traditional ways in which the ministers and their congregations brought these two elements together by "raising" a singing school follows. The materials and methods by means of which the real work of the school was accomplished are studied next, and the chapter closes with a discussion of the singing lectures and exhibitions which brought the school to its conclusion.

Singing Masters

The singing masters are worthy of serious study for two reasons. First, the singing school, unlike the heavily staffed, multi-departmental institutions of today, was a venture which succeeded or failed largely in terms of one man, the singing master. Second, when the history of the later-day singing school (1805–1825) is studied, it will be found that the singing masters of the previous period (1760–1805) became the subject of violent and scurrilous attacks which were promulgated by the apostles of a new taste which was sweeping the country at that time.

The importance of the first point is so obvious that it hardly needs elaboration here. The importance of the second is less obvious because this aspect of American musical history has received relatively little attention from scholars. Its significance is easily established by reference to two out of some twenty-five published documents[3] written by the proponents of the new taste. In 1809 Solomon Livermore in a lengthy diatribe delivered before the Musical Society at Pepperell, Massachusetts, declared:

> Liberty, the glory of our country, while it cherishes the growth of virtue and knowledge, gives latitude to vice and folly. Quacks are multiplied in all professions. The quack jurist disseminates contention and animosity. The quack physician, equipped from his indigenous magazine, sallies forth and bids defiance to the esculapian band. The quack politician mounts an exhausted cask, and intoxicates a gaping auditory by harangues more stale, than the dregs of his rostrum. The quack theologian ascends a splendid hayloft, and fulminates doctrines fit to be heard by none but proper tenants of the agrarian temple, built for flocks and herds. His incoherent declamation is succeeded by a fanatic choir, who with nasal solemnity profane sacred poetry in notes, wont to be vociferated by bacchanalians, or whined in dire historical ditties. Clans of quack musicians have for a long time infested the community. Unable to originate a musical idea, and without ingenuity, sufficient to arrange tones melodiously, from predatory spoils, tinctured by their own confusion, they have produced innumerable heterogeneous non-descripts, less grateful to the ear, than cantations of nocturnal reptiles.[4]

In 1811 Oliver Bray in an address delivered before the Hans Gram Musical Society at Fryeburg, Maine, attacked the singing masters and their works in a similar manner.

> Had they been content with mutilating every sound in the octave, and destroying the effect good music is calculated to produce, there is one crime of which they would have been innocent.

But they have not paused here. The prostituted airs of the debauchee have been stolen from the treasury of the bacchanalian, and converted to the worship of the Almighty. Like Milton's infernal messenger escaped from the regions of darkness, they have found their way into the Garden and defiled it, have entered the temple of Jehovah, and devotion has fled from their presence. With an impiety little short of blasphemy, these infamous productions have been employed in the exercise of praise to the God of heaven, taught to those who were preparing to be performers in the sanctuary, until all relish for the grave and impressive music of Handel and other eminent masters is lost, and nothing will excite pleasing emotions, but the merry airs of a march of dance, as metamorphosed by Billings and other modern Pretenders.[5]

Proper evaluation of these utterances[6] will rest upon accurate knowledge about the subjects under attack.

Who were these "quacks," these "Pretenders"? How did they enter the profession? How did they make their way in the world? Answers to these questions will not only add to our present knowledge of the singing school but also will provide a basis for understanding the pressures to which the later-day singing school was subjected.

The best introduction to the inquiry at hand is afforded by a remarkable set of recollections[7] written in 1841 by Moses Cheney,[8] one of the old-time singing masters. In 1788, as a boy of twelve, Cheney attended his first singing school in an unnamed village in the mountains of New Hampshire. Here he received his first introduction into the mysteries of musical notation and into the beauties of choral music.

> ...and it came to pass when I was about twelve years of age, that a singing school was got up about two miles from my father's house. In much fear and trembling I went with the rest of the boys in our town. I was told on the way to the first school that the master would try every voice alone to see if it was good. The thought of having my voice tried in that way, by a singing master too, brought a heavy damp on my spirits. I said nothing, but traveled on to the place to see what a singing school might be.
>
> When we came to the house, quite a number of young ladies and gentlemen had come, and were coming to the school. This was the first school which I attended of any kind, with very little exception. I did not pay much attention to the scholars, but I watched the master closely. We

were soon paraded all around the room, standing up to boards supported by old fashioned kitchen chairs. I being the youngest of the company managed to get the lowest seat, hoping thereby to be the last to have my voice tried. The master took his place inside the circle, took out of his pocket, a paper manuscript, with rules and tunes all written with pen and ink, read to us the rules, and then said we must attend to the rising and falling of the notes.

I shall take the liberty now to call ladies and gentlemen, and things, just as they were called in that school. And I begin with the rules as they were called, first:

RULES

Flats	Letters
The natural place for mi is in B.	G
But if B be flat mi is in E.	F
If B and E be flat mi is in A.	E Ten. & Treb.
If B, E, and A be flat mi is in D.	D
If B, E, A, and D be flat mi is in G.	C
	B
Sharps	G
But if F be sharp mi is in F.	F
If F and C be sharp mi is in C.	E
If F, C, and G be sharp mi is in G.	
If F, C, G, and D be sharp mi is in D.	

Rising and Falling Notes

These rules, as then called were all that was presented in that school. The books contained only one part each, bass books—tenor books—counter books, and treble books. Such as sung bass had a bass book; he that sung tenor had a tenor book; he who sung counter, had a counter book, and the gals, as then called, had treble books, I had no book.

With all these thing before the school, the good master began, "Come boys, you must rise and fall the notes first and then the gals must try." So he began with the oldest, who stood at the head, "Now follow me right up and down; sound." So he sounded; then the boy sounded, and followed the master up and down as it was called. Some more than one half could follow the master. Others would go up two or three notes, and then fall back lower than the first note. My feelings grew acute. To see some of the large boys, full twenty years old, make such dreadful work, what could I do! Great fits of laughing, both with boys and gals, would often occur. This scared me, and I was at my wit's end. Now my eyes were fixed on the

Master's mouth, if possible to learn the names of the notes before he came to me. I saw all that was needed was to make just the same sound that he made; and it come to my mind that I could mimic every beast, and bird, and thing, that I had ever heard make any noise, and it was no more to mimic my master than it was anything else. And then I had a firm belief I could do it. And I had only time to draw a long breath, and blow out the flutter of my heart, when the master came to me. "Well my lad, will you try?" "Yes sir." I looked him in the mouth, and as he spoke a note, so did I, both up and down. I did not wait for him to call the note first; I spoke with him. Now by watching him so closely, and observing how he spoke the notes, I had not only learned the names of the notes, but I had got also, by the form of his mouth what name would come so as to speak with him. The master turned away, saying, "this boy will make a singer." I felt well enough.

Then the gals had their turn to rise and fall the notes. "Come gals, now see if you can't beat the boys." So when he had gone through the gals' side of the school, he seemed to think the gals had done rather the best.

Now the rules were left for tunes. Old "Russia" was brought on first. The master sang it over several times, first with the bass, then with the tenor, then with the counter, and then with the treble. Such as had notes looked on, such as had none, listened to the rest. In this way, the school went on through the winter. A good number of tunes were learned in this school, and were sung well as we thought; but as to the science of music very little was gained.

At the close of the school, and after singing the last night, we made a settlement with the master. He agreed to keep, as then called, for one shilling and sixpence a night, and to take his pay in Indian corn at three shillings a bushel. A true dividend was made of the cost among the boys, (the gals found candles for their part) and it amounted to thirteen quarts and one pint of corn apiece. After the master had made some good wishes on us all, we were dismissed, and all went home in harmony and good union.

Now my benevolent father had given me a small plot of ground the summer before this school on which I had raised nearly two bushels of corn. Early the next morning I shelled out the corn. My mother handed me a clean pillow case with a smiling face and helped me measure up the corn, good measure. I took it on my shoulder, and away I carried it, four miles on foot to my master. I knocked at the door, went in, took off my hat in one hand, made a low bow, reached out the pillow case with the other, saying, "here is your corn, sir." The master took it with sparkles in his eyes, emptied it, and handed the cloth back to me. I made another low bow, came out, and went on my way rejoicing, singing along home. I should not mention how I took off my hat and made bows, if the practice among boys nowadays was not as much out of fashion as old fasola.

In the eyes of singers at this time, with the advance of the science of music for half a century past, this school must appear very insignificant indeed. But suffer me to try to express some of my feelings at that time. To me the whole movement of the school was of the brightest cast. Carrying with it, all through, from first to last, the most striking and affecting realities that I had ever been made to witness before, and I expected it was all that could be done in regard to the glorious work of singing for ages to come. A School! A Singing School!! O those words! Every other word vanished at the sound.

Think for a moment. A little boy of twelve years of age, growing up in the shade of the deep and condensed forests of the mountains of N.H., seldom out of sight of his mother, or the hearing of her voice, never saw a singing master or a musical note—seldom ever heard the voice of any human being except his own domestic circle, by the fireside of his Father's humble hearth.

Think again; now he is a member of a school; more, a Singing School! Singing tunes by note! Singing the "We Live Above!" Carrying any part all in the same high boy's voice. O, that winter's work! The foundation of many many happy days for more than fifty years past. The master too! Ah, that blessed form of a man. His bright blue sparkling eyes—his sweet angelic voice—his manifest care and love to his pupils—everything combined to make him one of a thousand.

Not long after this school was closed, I heard that there were plenty of printed singing books in Boston; and that our storekeeper would have some to sell before the next winter. It was my whole concern to be ready by the time they came up to buy one. I would persuade my father to give me a stint, to hoe by myself, to gain time to peal red-oak bark, burn it, and save the ashes for the purpose of buying a printed singing book. When the books came I was ready to pay in ashes. This I did, and then I owned a singing book.

I looked at the rules with astonishment. I do not remember the name of the book, or the author's name; but this I perfectly remember, it was a

Singing Book. In my new book, I had possessed myself of not far from a hundred new tunes. This was more than I ever expected to see. Now I could read but very poorly indeed, must spell all large words, and had it not been for singing, I should not have been able to read at all. Singing did more for me by far, in learning me to read than every other way of teaching. So on I went, studying my new book, and when I came to a hard name, or word, I would go to my mother, and in this way I made some progress.

In my book I found that notes had another name, Semibreve, Minim, Crotchet, Quaver, Semiquaver, and Demisemiquaver. I learned also that the semibreve was the longest note in singing and that it was as long as two minims, four crochets, eight quavers, sixteen semiquavers, or thirty-two demisemiquavers. This put one link more into the chain of my understanding.

My new book taught me likewise more modes of time than one. In my school without a book, I had only learned to beat up and down; but now I saw different ways, some two down beats and one up, another two down and two up. Some were slow, and some fast. This swelled my mind a little larger still. So I went on, committing from memory all that came in my way, until I had eaten that book up.

I attended some kind of singing school every winter but two until I was twenty-one years old. Forty-three years ago, or the winter after I was twenty-one, I followed Mr. Wm. Tenney, the best instructor that I had ever found. He taught every afternoon and evening in the week, Sunday excepted. When he left us, he gave me his singing book and wooden pitch-pipe, and told me to believe I was the best singer in the world, and then I should never be afraid to sing anywhere. He and myself could take any singing book that we met with and sing through at easily as we could read many other books. That was something then, and no small thing at this day. After this last school, from the time of my age twenty-one, I have taught singing until I became fifty, that is, more or less from time to time. . . .[9]

Cheney's account of how he became a singing master, for all of its full-blown rhetoric and its anecdotal quality, proves on closer examination to be surprisingly accurate. Singing schools customarily began with individual voice trials of the type which he described. Much of the instruction offered was based upon manuscript materials. The first tune which he learned, "Russia" *(Figure 11)*, was a great favorite throughout New England.

Payment of the master in Indian corn and the purchase of a printed singing book by means of barter was characteristic of many frontier communities at this time. The best singing masters were respected and loved by their scholars.

Equally accurate was Cheney's demonstration that potential singing masters got their training by attending singing schools at every opportunity until they were letter perfect in the rules and were able to read music as fluently as their masters. This informal method of training was perfectly in keeping with the apprenticeship system which was common in the early days of the republic. Singing masters did not employ apprentices in the usual sense of that word, but good teachers that they were, they were always willing to encourage the gifted few who aspired to their calling.[10]

Once an apprentice had received his master's blessing, he was ready to enter the world of music teaching as a full-fledged instructor. Often his first opportunity to teach came in his hometown where his musical ability was best known. Not infrequently, his election to the post of chorister, or leading singer, in the village choir gave him an easy entrée into the field because it was the chorister to whom the congregation looked for guidance in musical matters. Experienced singing masters were not always available on short notice; thus he was the logical candidate to teach the local singing school proposed by his friends and neighbors.

Local success inevitably caused the youthful singing master to consider expanding the scope of his activities to include adjacent communities. In such cases there was usually no problem in persuading people to subscribe to his proposed school because his good reputation had preceded him. However, as he traveled farther and farther afield, there came a time when he entered communities in which he was not known to anyone, a circumstance which raised, as it would in our own day, questions about his qualifications and his character. Modern methods of handling problems, i.e., the accrediting of schools, the granting of degrees, and the issuing of certificates, had, of course, yet to come into being. A single document, the traditional letter of recommendation, was employed in their place.

Of all the memorabilia pertaining to the personal lives of the singing masters, the letter of rec-

Figure 11. "Russia," a fuging tune composed by Daniel Read of New Haven, was reprinted many times in the tunebooks issued by other composer-compilers, who, often as not, published it without permission and misspelled the composer's name. The present reproduction has been taken from the second edition of Thomas Attwill's *New York and Vermont Collection of Sacred Harmony* (Albany, 1804). Courtesy, American Antiquarian Society.

RUSSIA
False are the men of high degree, / The baser sort are vanity;
Laid in a balance both appear, / Light as a puff of empty air.

---

ommendation seems to have had the least survival value. Only one such letter has come to light in the present investigation, namely, one which belonged to Daniel Read, the eminent singing master from New Haven, Connecticut.

New Haven Nov'r 27, 1786

To all to whom this shall be presented.

The following is for information to those who are Strangers to the bearer, Mr. Daniel Read. He is a respectable citizen of this city, a gentleman of respectable character & abilities, an uncommon proficient in the art of vocal music, and is the author of a singing book which has met with extensive approbation, entitled the *American Singing Book.* We sincerely wish him the attention of all respectable gentlemen among whom he may be conversant. As he is a man of integrity,

fidelity and benevolence we cannot apprehend that any who favour him with their attention or assistance will be disappointed in acquaintance.

We recommend Mr. Read most chearfully to the Gentleman, or Gentlemen to whom this shall be given, and should esteem any favours shewn as obliging us. We are &c.

Ezra Stiles, President of Yale Coll.

Samuel Wales, Professor of Divinity, Yale College

Samuel Austin, Pastor of Church in New Haven.[11]

Most singing masters could not boast of a recommendation of the quality of Read's. Their recommendations were undoubtedly of the usual sort, i.e., testimonials from the various ministers whom they had served during their travels through the country. These were useful in establishing contact with the more important citizens of the communities to which they traveled. Once contact had been made, it was not unusual for the singing master to secure their permission to use their names in the advertisements for the proposed school. That this procedure was customary even in those situations in which the singing master was fairly well known is seen in an advertisement which Sewall Short inserted in the *Nantucket Inquirer* for September 10, 1822.

SACRED MUSICK

The Subscriber proposes to open an evening School for instruction in the rudiments of Sacred Musick — to commence on or about the first of October next. Persons wishing instruction in the above science, will please apply previous to that period to the subscriber, who will give information as to terms, &c. Parents desirous of placing their children in this school, may depend on the utmost efforts of this subscriber towards perfecting them in this delightful, rational and now necessary accomplishment.

SEWALL SHORT

Nantucket, Sept. 9.

RECOMMENDATIONS

The Subscribers from a long and intimate acquaintance with the abilities and qualifications of Mr. *Sewall Short,* are happy to recommend him to the public as an experienced and able teacher of *Vocal Musick* — and hesitate not to express our belief that those who may enter his proposed School will derive satisfaction and profit from his instructions.

SAMUEL H. JENKS

SETH F. SWIFT

O. C. BARTLETT[12]

That parents had good reason to be concerned about the qualifications and character of those who taught music to their children is seen in two entries from the Bentley *Diary.*

Mar. 26, 1803....We have our singing School four evenings in a week. We cannot get able instructors for the sums we are able to give them.[13]

Oct. 18, 1807....I proposed to my Chorister a new School. Two of the best masters were introduced to me. Their request was for a loan of money & one of them was in a state of intoxication. They have published much & all say the best musick.[14]

Many singing masters did possess only a modicum of musical knowledge, and some of them did succumb to intemperance. The majority, however, as is proven by other entries in the Bentley *Diary,*

were worthy members of their profession. The practice of providing "certification" by means of letters of recommendation was thus a very useful one because it served the best interests of both the parents and the more responsible of the instructors.

The typical Yankee singing master has been described as an itinerant who made his living by traveling from town to town teaching the "Rules of Psalmody" to all and sundry. An itinerant he often was, but this description does not do justice to the scope of his activities nor to his ingenuity in making a livelihood in a society that was as yet unready to support full-time music teachers.

There were actually two aspects to his itinerancy. The proceeds from a singing school, meeting one evening per week, were, depending upon the size of the group, often hardly enough to keep body and soul together. Consequently, singing masters often arranged to teach several schools in surrounding communities on different evenings of the week. This was accomplished either by riding a circuit and lodging with a different family each night or by selecting a place of lodging that was equidistant from all points and using it as a base of operations. Insight into this aspect of the singing master's existence may be gained from perusal of the Reverend Ebenezer Parkman's *Diary* for 1777–1778 in which the comings and goings of an itinerant singing master named Lemuel Badcock are recorded in detail.[15]

The practice of circuit riding led in time to "union singing schools,"[16] in which all of the master's scholars from the several communities which he served met occasionally at a central location, usually a tavern, to enjoy the experience of singing choral music in a large group. The town historian of Sutton, New Hampshire, described the impact which such schools had upon her community during the era from 1790 to 1800. They were taught by a veteran of the Revolution, Captain Mathew Buell (1758–?), who was a native of Somers, Connecticut.

Capt. Mathew Buell, of Newport, taught singing schools in Sutton many years, about the close of the last century and afterwards. He used to teach three afternoons and three evenings in a week while the term continued, one day at Mathew Harvey's tavern, one day at Enoch Page's tavern, and one day at Caleb Kimball's tavern.

His schools became one of the greatest social institutions of the winter season, and were looked forward to with much interest at a period when young people in Sutton were so numerous that some school districts, which are now so much reduced as to be merged with others, then numbered one hundred scholars every winter.

The recess between the afternoon and evening schools afforded a fine opportunity for the young men to display their gallantry to the girls, by treating them to a supper of such good things as the tavern afforded. "On one occasion," says our informant, "Capt. Buell's Newport school, by special invitation came down to visit the Sutton school, had supper together, and a fine entertainment in every way."[17]

Union singing schools were thus the spiritual, if not the lineal, descendants of the singing lectures of the Tufts era in which regular singers from various communities united to demonstrate the advantages of the new way of singing.

Some communities had a singing school almost every winter. The majority, however, seem to have spaced their schools so that they occurred every two or three years. This practice was only to be expected, since once a new crop of singers had been elevated to the gallery choir there would be no further need for the services of a singing master until the normal process of attrition made the training of new singers a necessity. For this reason singing masters were forced to move periodically to fresh fields of endeavor once they had infused new life into the choral music of a given region. This then was the second aspect of their itinerancy, the periodic search for congregations in need of their skill.

An advertisement which appeared in the *Newport Mercury* for January 8, 1770, shows that some of the singing masters became prodigious travelers as a result of the imperatives of their calling.

The Public are hereby informed that a singing school will be opened at Mr. Bradford's Schoolhouse, next Thursday Evening, by a Person who has taught the various branches of psalmody in the Provinces of New York, Massachusetts Bay and Connecticut, when those Gentlemen and Ladies who have an inclination to improve in this excellent Art, may expect all that Care and Dilligence which is necessary to their being rightly *instructed* in the same. N.B. For further Particulars enquire of Mr. Bradford, School-Master.[18]

That this unnamed singing master was in no way unique is seen in a footnote to a singing lecture delivered by Aaron Kinne at Groton, Connecticut,

in 1798. In eulogizing the accomplishments of a group of scholars from his parish who had been instructed by a Mr. Redfield, he noted:

The author, returning from the western settlements in the state of New York, found Mr. *Redfield* at the house of his son, on the *Susquehannah*, preparing to return to his family in *Vermont*. As they were to take the same route, they agreed to travel together, and were five days in company. At this time the proposition was made for his teaching singing, in this town.

Mr. Redfield has exercised his talents in teaching the delightful art of melody, for many years, in the several states, and various parts of New England; in the course of which he has taught 71 Schools, containing 3786 scholars. The two schools in this town, consisted of 139 members.[19]

Redfield's achievement seems all the more remarkable when the inclement weather, the poor roads, the uncomfortable conveyances, and the miserable accommodations, which the travelers of that time had to endure, are taken into consideration.

Not all of the singing masters found the life of an itinerant a congenial one. Some elected to remain at home and found other means of making up for the meagre wages which they received for their teaching. John Stickney, the author of *The Gentleman and Ladies Companion* (Newburyport, 1774), cultivated the soil on his farm at South Hadley, Massachusetts, in the summertime and boarded lumbermen and fishermen in the wintertime.[20] Justin Morgan, a contributor to many singing books, bred horses, kept a tavern, and taught writing and common schools in and around his home town of Randolph, Vermont.[21] Solomon Howe, the author of *The Worshipper's Assistant* (Northampton, 1799), eked out a living on his farm at Greenwich, Massachusetts, and worked also as a preacher, a printer, and a teacher.[22] Supply Belcher, the author of *The Harmony of Maine* (Boston, 1794), lived the life of a country squire, kept a tavern, served as a member of the legislature, and taught school in his adopted town, Farmington, Maine.[23] Abraham Wood, co-author with Joseph Stone of *The Columbian Harmony* (Boston, 1793), worked as a fuller or dresser of cloth in Northborough, Massachusetts, and served as a captain in the militia.[24] Joel Read, the author of *The New England Selection* (1808), taught common schools, worked as a surveyor, and served as a selectman, an assessor, and a member of the legislature from the Town of Attleborough, Massachusetts.[25] Amos Bull, the author of *The Responsory* (Worcester, 1795), taught a school for "Reading, Writing, and Arithmetick" and ran a hardware store in Hartford, Connecticut.[26] Daniel Read, the author of *The American Singing Book* (New Haven, 1785), manufactured ivory combs, served as a director of the library, and took an active part in the public affairs of New Haven.[27] Timothy Swan, the author of *The New England Harmony* (Northampton, 1801), worked as a hatter in Suffield, Connecticut, and Northfield, Massachusetts.[28] Jacob Kimball, the author of *The Rural Harmony* (Boston, 1793), frequently taught common school while living at Topsfield, Massachusetts.[29] Jeremiah Ingalls, the author of *The Christian Harmony* (Exeter, 1805), kept a tavern and worked off and on as a farmer and as a cooper in Newbury, Vermont.[30] Oliver Holden, the author of *The Union Harmony* (Boston, 1796), began life as a humble carpenter and went on to become a real estate operator, the proprietor of a music store, and a member of the legislature from Charlestown, Massachusetts.[31] Abraham Maxim, the author of *The Northern Harmony* (Second edition, Exeter, 1808), taught reading schools in and around Turner, Maine.[32]

Of the various multiple occupations followed by the Yankee singing masters, that of teaching common schools and singing schools was the combination which was most often adopted. This fact is readily established by reference to the advertisements which appeared in the newspapers of their day. Typical of these was the advertisement which Abia Holbrook, master of the South Writing School in Boston, inserted in the *Boston Gazette* for June 26, 1744.

> ABIA HOLBROOK Writing Master & Edward Macom, propose to open a singing School to instruct Children in the Rules of Psalmody, at 20s. a quarter old Tenor; the first Quarter to be paid at Entrance, to begin Thursday next the 21st Instant at 6 o'Clock in the Afternoon; to continue on Thursdays and Saturdays at the Hour aforesaid during the Summer Season. The utmost Care will be taken of the Children, of either Sex; and the Place appointed, is the South Writing School in the Common.[33]

Also typical was the one which Noah Webster inserted in the *Connecticut Courant* for June 1, 1781.

> The subscriber, desirous of promoting Education, so essential to the interest of a free people, proposes immediately to open a school at Sharon, in which young Gentlemen and Ladies may be instructed in Reading, Writing, Mathematicks, the English language, and if desired, the Latin and Greek Languages—in Geography, Vocal Music, &c. at the moderate price of Six Dollars and two thirds per quarter per Scholar. The strictest attention will be paid to the studies, the manners and the morals of youth, by the public's very humble servant,
>
> NOAH WEBSTER, Jun.
>
> P.S. If any persons are desirous of acquainting themselves with the French Language, they may be under the instruction of an accomplished master in Sharon.[34]

Further study of the activities[35,36] of these men reveals that the teaching of the "three R's" was their principal occupation and that the teaching of the "Rules of Psalmody" was their secondary one, a circumstance which was dictated as much by the ephemeral nature of the singing school as by their personal feelings in the matter.

The most convincing proof of the hypothesis that the teaching of common schools and singing schools was the most typical vocational pattern followed by the Yankee singing masters is found, not in the world of reality, but in the world of fiction. When Washington Irving created Ichabod Crane, one of the most famous characters in American literature, he took the Yankee school master as his model.[37] Ichabod, as his creator would have the reader believe, found it very hard to make a living solely by teaching school. Like his counterparts in real life, he also taught the local singing school in an effort "to make ends meet."

> In addition to his other vocations, he was the singing master of the neighborhood, and picked up many bright shillings by instructing the young folks in psalmody. It was a matter of no little vanity to him, on Sundays, to take his station in front of the church gallery, with a band of chosen singers; where, in his own mind, he completely carried away the psalm from the parson. Certain it is, his voice resounded far above all the rest of the congregation; and there are peculiar quavers still to be heard in that church, and which may even be heard half a mile off, quite to

the opposite side of the mill-pond, on a still Sunday morning, which are said to be legitimately descended from the nose of Ichabod Crane. Thus, by divers little makeshifts, in that ingenious way which is commonly denominated "by hook and by crook," the worthy pedagogue got on tolerably enough, and was thought, by all who understood nothing of the labor of head work, to have a wonderfully easy life of it.[38]

And like one of his counterparts[39] he fell in love with the prettiest girl in his singing school, thus ensuring the development of an interesting plot. In short, Ichabod was the kind of hero who would be instantly recognized as an authentic country village type.

Equally authentic, but less characteristic, were those singing masters, such as Billings and Holyoke, who attempted to make a living entirely by musical activity. Although their musicianship was generally superior to that of their brethren in the country, they too found it very difficult to secure an adequate living in music. Two, and sometimes three, additional ways to supplement their income were available to them depending upon the scope of their training.

The first of these ways, and one which they shared with many part-time singing masters, was the compilation and publication of characteristic oblong singing books of their day. The typical compilation consisted of old favorites, which were often used without their authors' consent,[40] and new works by the master himself in the most popular forms, i.e., psalm and hymn tunes, fuging tunes or "flying pieces," and anthems for special occasions.

Warwick Palfray, a singing master who was active in Salem about 1800, was more candid than most when he explained to the public how and why he had ventured into the exacting field of musical composition.

To the Public

The Author of the following musical Compositions was led to the study of music more from inclination than education. But having been called to instruct in schools, and with some success, he was induced to add parts, and to correct such compositions as fell into his hands, in order to accommodate them to his own instructions. Being obliged to use measures not ordinarily found in psalmbooks, he ventured upon original composition; and, having given satisfaction, at the request of his friends he has ventured to offer the following compositions to the Public. He hopes they will prove as acceptable from the press; as they have been to his friends in the performance, and humbly submits them to public judgment.[41]

The author's candor was very much in order since his book was certainly one of the less distinguished of the many productions which had been published up to that time.

William Bentley, who had written the preface to Palfray's book, and who was the first bibliographer of what are now called "early American tunebooks," had noted a few years before the appearance of that work:

Apr. 29, 1793. Messrs. Atwell & Mansfield of Lynn, musicians, with me this evening. They recommended and performed the music of one Oliver Holden. From a great scarcity of such kind of Books, & almost the want of Composers in the Bay, we find the market glutted with their productions. The most successful Books in this way now are the "Collections," which have a little of each, excite a curiosity, & gratify it enough to keep the music in circulation.[42]

And a few years after its appearance he noted:

Nov. 2, 1806. Every master of a town School feels privileged to print his own books & they are worth accordingly. Next to School Books are Singing books with this circumstance that many new editions of Singing Books have a new name even from the same author. We are now told of the Bridgewater & Norfolk Collections. For Mr. Ebeling, at his request, I attempted to collect from Mr. Holyoke, who standing among the foremost, a list of such Singing Books as he knew. The list was at first a large one & the additions have been so great that I have given over all thoughts of completing it.[43]

Lacking the perspective of history, he was unable to see that in the proliferation of singing books he was actually witnessing the first great flowering of musical composition in America.

Prompted by the lack of materials for their schools, and spurred on by their own financial needs, the Yankee singing masters had become the largest and most significant group of composers in the country. Modern scholarship has been able to account for one hundred and eleven collections such as Bentley described, which were published up to 1800. Of these, thirty-six appeared in more than one edition, making a grand total of two hundred seventy-two editions.[44] With the exception of a few works, such as James Lyons's *Urania* (Philadelphia, 1761) and Andrew Adgate's *Rudiments of Musick* (Philadelphia, 1788), the vast majority of these collections were works by New England singing masters. As a body of musical literature, these works played a role in America's cultural development which "far transcended the narrow implications of the term 'Psalmody.'"[45]

The two remaining ways in which the full-time singing masters supplemented their incomes were by offering instruction in vocal and instrumental music and by promoting concerts for their own benefit. These activities, which were feasible only in the larger towns and cities, were modest in scope. They were, nonetheless, important because of the significant contribution which they made to the musical life of these communities.

The instruction in vocal and instrumental music inevitably reflected the interests and skills of particular singing masters. Thus, it was Andrew Law, a staunch advocate of soft singing, who established in Salem that which may well have been the first music school in New England devoted exclusively to the cultivation of the voice.

> Aug. 2, 1796. Mr. Law has new formed his Music School from the object of particular singing for religious societies, to the mere teaching of the art, which is a commendable exchange. Singing has never been taught in New England as a Liberal Art, in public schools, but by private tuition. Our Song Singers are generally self taught & sing best alone. By learning music upon a large scale, real advantages are to be hoped. Mr. Law has not the extent of the plan. But he teaches the Rules without regard to performance in the churches, tho' by Psalmody only.[46]

And it was Samuel Holyoke, a skillful clarinetist, who established in Salem that which may well have been the first society for instrumental music in New England.

> Nov. 21, 1797. This day we were assured the assistance of the Musical Society who have formed to promote instrumental music. Music has ever been low in this place. They who taught it knew little of composition & had no acquaintance with the best masters. The compositions were not excellent used in the churches, being chiefly mangled from the old Psalmody. Mr. Billings, with more genius than Taste, introduced new composition, but vocal music had its greatest progress in Connecticut. A few years since a Mr. Kimball, & Mr. Johnson, taught in Marblehead, &

last year a Mr. Law from Connecticut, a Mr. Holyoke of this country. Law was calculated for solemn, slow & soft music, but it could not well succeed to the noise to which had been accustomed. Holyoke was more indulgent to the common taste, tho' far above in his genius. Holyoke introduced much instrumental music & from his instructions has commenced the society now forming. Every effort of this kind has been short, but this is more general than any other, being not formed for any choir but for all the societies for private amusement.[47]

Of the two ventures,[48] Holyoke's instrumental music society apparently had the longest and most productive existence. The next reference to it reveals that it was composed largely of string players and that it had begun to play an important role in the musical life of Salem within a short time after its founding.

> Nov. 30, 1797. The Day of public Thanksgiving, clear, cold, & very windy. We had for the first time a band of instruments in our Choir. The members were from different parts of the Town & were kind enough to give us the first exhibition they have ever made in public & the first of the kind ever on a public religious solemnity in the Town. The scandalous indifference to vocal music has obliged us to have recourse to such expedients or our Church music must have been lost. In all our societies the Bass Viol has been used, having been introduced about two years since. A Violin & Clarionet followed in our worship. The number of these, with the Tenour Viol, formed our Band on this solemnity. The order of service was, An air—Hymn 73, the instruments going over the tune, before the vocal music joined—Introductory prayer—An air—Lesson—Hymn 4—Prayer—32 Psalm—Sermon—Collection for the Poor, An air, with a chorus—Prayer—42 Hymn—Blessing— Concluding air.[49]

The success of this string band, which was here employed as a gallery orchestra, seems to have encouraged the organization of several more amateur instrumental groups.

> Dec. 18, 1798. Some efforts are making in this Town to create a love of Musick. A musick society was formed by young mechanics who met occasionally. Another of a different class united key with wind instruments, to which the first were confined. A Selection of members formed another Society, who have provided an hall in Cambridge Street, of 30 by 20 feet properly arched. To this Mr. Dodge is to send his Organ which he has built in this Town, importing the

stops. Other Instruments are to be conveyed to this place. The hall is to be used on common occasions to teach Vocal Musick....[50]

A final reference to this curious amalgam[51] of instrumental music societies, which appeared in the *Salem Gazette* for April 2, 1805, suggests that they formed, in all likelihood, the nucleus of one of the first town bands in New England.

MUSIC SCHOOL

Those Persons who may have made some progress upon Musical Instruments and who may wish to make farther improvement, are informed that they can have an opportunity, by joining with the Instrumental Club, directed by S. HOLYOKE. A second quarter commences this evening at the Hall formerly occupied by Mr. Biglow.[52]

The soundness of this hypothesis is confirmed by examination of *The Instrumental Assistant*, a two-volume work which was compiled and published by the director of the Instrumental Club during this period. Perusal of its pages reveals not only the repertory but also the instrumentation of such organizations. The first volume[53] contains pieces such as "The President's March," Handel's Water Piece, "The Rakes of London," "Dog and Gun," and "Oh Dear, What Can the Matter Be?" Each piece is arranged in three parts (two treble parts and a bass part) in such a way as to be suitable for almost any combination of the instruments for which the volume was designed, namely, the violin, the flute, the clarionet, the oboe, and the bass viol or cello. The second volume[54] contains pieces such as the "March from the Battle of Prague," "A Turkish Quick Step," "The March from Scipio," "Wine Cannot Cure," and "The Blue Bells of Scotland." Two types of arrangements are employed. The simplest is scored for French Horn (*primo* and *secundo*), Clarinet (*primo* and *secundo*), and Bassoon. The more complex is scored for Oboe or Clarinet (*primo*), Oboe or Clarinet (*secundo*), Violino (*primo* and *secundo*), French Horn in D (*primo* and *secundo*) and Basso, which was intended for the Bass Viol and the Bassoon. In addition to these arrangements, each volume contains carefully written instructions for the various instruments, which reflect with much credit upon their author. It was, in short, a compendium of band music.

It is difficult to evaluate the contribution made by Holyoke to the field of early American instrumental music, because a comprehensive history of that field has yet to be written. This much is certain. Although his work as an author and compiler was outstanding, his work as a teacher of instrumental music was by no means unique. At least one other singing master, Ichabod Johnson of Woburn, Massachusetts, who had served in the Revolutionary Army as a fifer, taught wind and string instruments throughout New England with equal success and earned a fine reputation as a conductor of "bands of martial music."[55] Furthermore, many other singing masters, such as Supply Belcher,[56] who played the violin, and Abraham Maxim,[57] who played the bass viol, were adept at instrumental music. It would have been out of character for them to have restricted the exercise of their skill to the singing school. Much of their skill undoubtedly contributed to the development of the gallery orchestras which accompanied their choirs. These orchestras were in fact small ensembles composed of wind and string instruments which may very well have served, as they did in Salem, as the nuclei of the town bands of New England. Such seems to have been the case in New Ipswich, New Hampshire, where in 1805 Ichabod Johnson taught a singing school, which was the first to be granted a permanent station in the gallery as a choir, and transformed the instrumental players of the town into a first-class military band.[58]

The third way in which the full-time singing masters sought to augment their earnings was the promotion of concerts, the proceeds of which were specifically designated as being for their own benefit. A typical concert promoted by Samuel Holyoke with the assistance of the Salem Band was chronicled by that ever-faithful friend of music, William Bentley.

Oct. 10, 1806. Yesterday afternoon was the Musical Exhibition of Mr. Holyoke in the New South Meeting House. Its first motive was to relieve a man who had been indefatigable in assisting Church Music & had been disappointed in his many publications. He has laboured much but without a friendly genius, tho' with greater science than has commonly fallen to the possession of instructors in Music in our Country. Charity led to encourage the contribution from the public, but Genius did not preside at the exhibition. The Salem Band performed the principal parts. Many performers from friendship stepped in. Mr. Kimball, who has less skill in composition but better talents in execution than Holyoke, was urged to assist. Farmington was from *Andover*, Mann from Worcester did not assist. A few performers of Salem took this opportunity to display their powers on the Flute & from them all Holyoke obtained his end a musical exhibition which all present paid for & none dared to blame because they must blame their own friends. The house was not filled & tickets were at 1-4 D. I went & paid for 2 tickets.[59]

This was evidently the first of several such concerts[60] given more or less annually by Holyoke in Salem and Newburyport. The one given in Salem in 1809 is of particular interest because it illustrates a second type of benefit concert, namely, one given largely with vocal forces, and because it featured one of the earliest performances of Handel's "Halleluiah Chorus" outside the metropolis of Boston.

Feb. 9, 1809. This evening with H.H., I attended Mr. Holyoke's Concert in the Baptist Meeting, Marlborough Street. This Mr. H. has done more for Psalmody than any may of the present generation & has been poorly rewarded. He lately had a Concert in the Tabernacle which was poorly attended. His price this evening for the best seats 25 cents. The Company was far from being large, or well informed, chiefly young. Besides a few performances on the Instruments to keep time, the Bill announced the following compositions, Old Hundred, Champlain, Finale & Grand Alleluia Chorus of Handel. The treble was feeble without a commanding voice. The Echo of Champlain was ill-composed, the finale had not expression enough. In the Chorus some began to feel. As a Work of Genius it had not high Claims, but comparatively it was excellent & did honour to the exertions of the Master.[61]

It is of interest too because it confirms the fact that events which of necessity relied upon the efforts of amateurs were probably not too successful in competing with the more professionalized forms of entertainment such as the theatre.

It was unfortunate that a man who had done so much to make Salem one of the most musical cities in New England was reduced to the expedients described above. It may be argued that his case was a special one because at that time Salem was in the throes of a severe economic depression which had been brought on by the Embargo. But careful investigation reveals that even in normal times those singing masters who attempted to make a livelihood entirely by means of music found the going very difficult. Two of the very best masters, Billings and Kimball, died in great poverty and not a single one can be named who amassed anything more than a very modest estate as a result of his work in teaching.

The real wealth of the singing masters lay in the high esteem with which they were held by their scholars, in the satisfaction that comes from a job well done, and in such honors as the communities which they served could bestow upon them. For example, Justin Morgan, who was "greatly liked wherever he went," was remembered for "his urbane manners and upright character."[62] Similarly, Asahel Benham, who was "respected for his correct manners and kind heart," was also revered for "his good sense and intelligence."[63] Jeremiah Ingalls had the pleasure of knowing that travelers on long journeys often arranged to stop over at Newbury, Vermont, in order to hear his choir, which had gained a statewide reputation for excellence.[64] Supply Belcher acquired the appellation, "the Handel of Maine," a title which was entirely justified in terms of the freshness and originality of his choral compositions.[65] Andrew Law enjoyed the honor of receiving one of the earliest LL.D. degrees awarded by Allegheny College.[66] And William Billings, who was eulogized as one who "spake and sung and thought above the common abilities," achieved posthumously the greatest distinction of all, that of being called "the Father of our New England Music."[67] Taken individually or as a group, these humble yet remarkable men would have been worth knowing in any age.

Singing Scholars

Although long neglected by the authors of secondary works, the singing scholars are as worthy a subject for study as the singing masters. Considerable misunderstanding exists not only about the claims which were made by and for certain later-day singing masters concerning the scholars whom they taught but also about the role which the singing school played in the lives of these scholars. Actual knowledge about the age groups involved in the singing school, the social classes represented among the singing scholars, and the attitudes which they possessed provides the best basis for setting these misunderstandings aright.

One of the writers upon whom the authors of secondary works have relied extensively is Nathaniel D. Gould, a later-day singing master who wrote a very uneven book[68] on the history of church music. In its pages Gould claims to have been the first singing master in New England to teach "juvenile singing schools" which were specifically designed to introduce children to the rudiments of music. He notes that he commenced teaching such schools in Boston, Cambridge, and Charlestown in 1824 and that three or four years later Lowell Mason adopted this plan of instruction and made it the basis for his campaign to have music admitted to the public school curriculum in Boston.[69] While the extent to which Mason was indebted to Gould remains in doubt, there is no doubt whatsoever concerning Mason's success in introducing music into the public schools.[70] Indeed, his success in this campaign was so great that his most recent biographer,[71] A. L. Rich, has ventured to call him "The Father of Singing Among the Children." Both Gould's claim and Rich's claim on behalf of Mason that they were uniquely or jointly responsible for the initiation of mass instruction in music for children prove on closer examination to be demonstrably false in terms of easily documented facts about the singing scholars and the singing schools of the previous era.

In Chapter II of this book it was established that the reformers made the youth of New England the standard-bearers for regular singing because of the opposition of their elders. It was also suggested that this policy largely determined the character of the singing school as an institution devoted to the education of youth through music. To identify the singing scholars simply as "youth" is, however, inadequate for present purposes. Reformers such as Thacher,[72] Symmes,[73] and Tufts[74] were deeply concerned that children as well as youth should receive instruction in music. Advocacy is one thing; fulfillment is often another. Thus it becomes necessary to establish as precisely as possible the age groups represented among the singing scholars.

That the old-time Yankee singing masters were accustomed to making provision for children as well as youth is apparent from some of the advertisements which they placed in the newspapers of their day, from some of the instruction books which they published, and from some of the records of the singing schools which they taught.

John Waghorne was one of the earliest singing masters to set up singing schools especially for children. In the issue of the *Boston Gazette* for July 9–16, 1739, he notified the public:

WHEREAS JOHN WAGHORNE, now resident in Boston, has been often requested by some of the principal Gentlemen of this Town, to instruct their Children In Vocal Psalmody, with a Promise of Encouragement; and he having now a suitable House for that Purpose, therefore is to inform such Persons who will think proper to send their Children, that said Waghorn intends to instruct Youth in the Gamut and Measure of Notes &c. according to the Method of the famous Dr. Crafts late Organist and Composer to his Majesty's Chappel, and will attend on Monday, Wednesday, and Friday, from 4 to 6 o'Clock in the afternoon....[75]

His example[76] was followed by Abia Holbrook[77] in 1744 and by Jacob Bucknam[78] in 1768.

Other masters, such as Mr. Munson of Salem, made it quite clear in their advertisements that they were prepared to accommodate both children and "young Gentlemen and Ladies" by holding separate classes for them in the afternoons and evenings.

MR. MUNSON

Respectfully acquaints the Gentlemen and Ladies of the Town of Salem that he opens a Singing School this day, at the Assembly-Room, where Parents and other Subscribers are desired to send their Children at 5 o'Clock P.M., and Young Gentlemen & Ladies to attend at seven in the Evening. N.B. Subscriptions are taken in at Mr. Samuel Field's in School Street, and at the Printing Office.[79]

Munson's method of handling the two age groups seems to have been fairly common throughout New England at this time.[80,81]

Daniel Read, the distinguished singing master from New Haven, wrote his first instruction book specifically for children. Although no copies of this work are known to have survived, some knowledge of its contents may be gained from the advertisement for it which appeared in the *Connecticut Journal* for March 17, 1790.

An Introduction to Psalmody; or, the Child's Instructor in Vocal Music. Containing a Series of familiar Diologues, under the following heads, viz. Psalmody in General, Stave, Musical Letters and Cliffs, an Exercise for the Bass, an Exercise for the Tenor or Treble, an Exercise for the Counter, Tones, Semi-tones, Flats, Sharps and Naturals, Solfaing, Transposition, &c. The Several Notes and Rests, and their Proportion, the

Several Moods of Time, Several other Characters used in Music, Key Notes, &c. Pitching Tunes &c. Graces. Illustrated with Copper Plates. By D. Read. Printed for, and sold by the Author, New Haven, 1790.[82]

Solomon Howe wrote instruction books with the children of farmers and mechanics principally in mind. Both his *Farmer's Evening Entertainment* (Northampton, 1799) and his *Worshipper's Assistant* (Northampton, 1804) contain useful suggestions to their parents concerning the best way to train them in the art of psalmody.

The Reverend William Bentley, who faithfully recorded vital statistics of all of the singing schools which he sponsored, was particularly meticulous in chronicling the one taught by a Mr. Groce in 1792. The entries in his *Diary* concerning this school demonstrate that it was designed for "Young Masters and Misses" of twelve years of age and older.

> Dec. 14, 1791. A contract with Mr. Groce, to attend & lead in the public singing of the East Meeting House for which he is to receive of the Proprietors from free contribution, subscription, or donation to the amount of three shillings per Sunday, and I am to make it equal to £9 s0 d0.
>
> By an after agreement he is to keep a School, & be paid upon the advice of the Committee, annually 12, 0, 0.[83]
>
> Jan. 8, 1792. Notified publickly the intention to open a new Singing School on Wednesday for young persons from 12 years & upwards.[84]
>
> Jan. 9, 1792. Went about to induce parents to send their young children to the Singing School. There was a plausible reception, which at least was flattering.[85]
>
> Jan. 11, 1792. This evening for the first time our new Singing School was opened. 40 youths of both sexes appeared, & with the addition of some old scattered singers a good prospect opens.[86]
>
> Jan. 12, 1792. We had our singers' meeting at Capt. Becket's.[87]
>
> Jan. 13, 1792. A Singing School again this evening. Prospect yet good, tho' the weather very unfavourable to the meeting of young people.[88]
>
> Jan. 15, 1792. Sunday, A most delightful & pleasant day. The sun clear, houses full, singing good.[89]
>
> Jan. 20, 1792. ...very pleasant day. No bad news yet from the effects of the storm in our neighborhood. No damage in the harbour. The Snow lays in vast drifts of eight to ten feet, against houses,

> fences, &c. Market well supplied. A List of the Young Masters & Misses at the Singing School this evening...[90]
>
> (Editor's note: 45 names, 27 males and 18 females, follow.)
>
> Mar. 23, 1792. Our School for singing goes on, the bass, & the young school alternately.[91]
>
> Aug. 29, 1792. My Singers made some new arrangements, & meet at Le Fevre's & soon to meet in turn throughout the parish...[92]
>
> Sept. 17, 1792. In attempts to settle with Groce, who disingenuously left us without notice, I find that his first school was opened on 18 Dec. ult. & his Letter resigning the School Aug. 5.[93]
>
> Dec. 25, 1792. Delivered to Wm. King 9 shillings for Wood. Statement of Singing School Account for 1792.

For Books of Music	£	1	10	0
Psalm Books dozen		1	16	0
For Candles		1	5	0
For Groce, services		6	4	5
For Seats, Groce's Bill		7	0	7
For King's Bill on Seats		2	2	3
	£	19	13	3[94]

Of the many interesting entries that of March 23, 1792, is especially pertinent to the present discussion, since it supplies additional proof that children and youth were taught separately in the singing school.

Bentley's records are also useful in establishing the democratic nature of the singing school. His list of scholars for the singing school of 1789 serves to elucidate this point.

> (p. 47) Mar. 23, 1789. Mr. B. Babbidge brought the following List of persons disposed to enter a *New School*, proposed to fill the Singing Seats, &c.
>
> Miss Betsey Philips, on the Common.
> Miss Sally Chever, _____.
> Miss Sally Phippen, Hardy's-Lane.
> Miss Polly Herrick, New Street.
> Miss Sally Becket, Becket's Lane.
> Miss Lydia Herrick, New Street.
> Miss Nabby Swasey, Daniel's Lane.
> Mr. John Duncklee, App: of A. Manning, Smith.
> John Trask,_____.
> Andover Ward, App: of R. Becket, Shipwright.
> Luke Heard, App: of B. Chever, Cordwainer.
> Samuel Leach, App: of J. Becket, Boatbuilder.
> Ebenezer Phelps, Baker.
> Mr. Samuel Chever, S. of Capt. S. Chever.
> Ebenezer Leach, App: of Mr. Fowler, Cordwainer.
> Jonathan Webb, Cooper.

Thomas Palfrey, Cooper.
Joseph Vincent, S. of J. Vincent, Ropemaker.
Miss Hannah Swasey, Daniel's Lane.
Priscilla Webb, On the Common.
Peggy Chever, On the Common.[95]

Apr. 3, 1789. On Friday opened a *New School* for singing at my own house. Present at the first meeting were Misses Phillips, S. & P. Chever, S. Phippen, & P. Webb. The men were Messieurs Luke Heard, S. Leach, B. Hutcheson, & J. Becket. New names added to page 47.

Mr. Benjamin Hutcheson, a Smith, apprentice.
John Becket, a miner.
Benja. Dean, a miner.
Miss Polly Bowditch.
Betsey Bowditch.
Sukey Dean.
Polly Emerton.[96]

Apr. 7, 1789. Added to *New Singers,* Miss Hannah Beadle.[97]

The youth of both the great and the humble families of Salem are represented in this list, as are many of the most important trades of this thriving seaport town.

The discussion of the democratic nature of the singing school would not be complete without some consideration of the place which it occupied in the lives of the youth who attended it. Evidently, its place was an important one, since it is mentioned frequently in the diaries written by young people during this period. Two diaries, one by a fifteen-year-old country parson's daughter, the other by a nineteen-year-old farm boy, supply a much needed human dimension to the preceding recital of facts and figures.

Elizabeth Fuller, who was born in 1776 in Princeton, Massachusetts, was introduced at an early age to the necessary round of chores that made up the woman's world of her day. Like so many others[98] of her sex, she found her chief recreation in attending the local singing school.

Dec. 4, 1790. I minced the Link meat.[99]

Dec. 6, 1790. Timmy has gone to singing meeting.[100]

Dec. 11, 1790. Sabbath. David Perry here to borrow our singing book.[101]

Dec. 16, 1790. John Brooke here killing our sheep. Severe snow storm.[102]

Dec. 17, 1790. Very cold. I made sixteen dozen candles.[103]

Dec. 22, 1790. David Perry here to get Timmy to go to the singing school with him.[104]

Dec. 24, 1790. I scoured the pewter. Pa went to Fitchburg.[105]

Jan. 21, 1791. I am writing Grammar today. Pleasant weather. Nathan Perry put our Horse into their sleigh and carried me to the singing school and back again. I had a fine ride and a fine evening; they sung a great many Tunes, I sang with them.[106]

Mar. 31, 1791. Fast. I went to Meeting all day. Mr. Rolph preached half of the day & Mr. Sanders the other half. Mr. Sanders is a very good Preacher & a handsome Man. David Perry here this evening to sing with us.[107]

April 25, 1791. Leonard Woods here all this forenoon, brought Holyoke's Singing Book, left it here.[108]

April 28, 1791. I spun five skeins of linnen yarn. Pa went to Sterling.[109]

April 29, 1791. I pricked some Tunes out of Holyoke's Singing Book. I spun some.[110]

Caleb Jackson, who was born in 1786 in the town of Rowley, Massachusetts, also learned the meaning of work at an early age. A tiller of the soil by summer and a maker of shoes by winter, he was nonetheless an imaginative and perceptive youth who delighted in writing pastoral poetry and in recording scientific observations in his diary. Like his contemporary Elizabeth Fuller, he found his chief recreation in attending the local singing school.

Dec. 10, 1805. A very cold and windy day. Sir went to Mr. Stickney and Mr. Joseph Sander, took up goods, these to the amount of $14.93 which I am to pay for this winter in making shoes.

Dec. 12, 1805. Cloudy more moderate. I went to (the) Mill &c. In the evening I went to the Schoolhouse to consult about having a singing school. We agreed to have it twice a week and to have it kept by Thomas Howe. This night was the first.

Dec. 16, 1805. Something pleasant cool wind. I went to Mr. Solo. Stickney's and get 70 pare of upper leather and 60 pares of sole leather to make into shoes.

Dec. 17, 1805. Pleasant. In the evening Sally, Sam and I went to the singing school.

Dec. 20, 1805. Cloudy day, clear and pleasant evening. We had our 3rd sing. meeting.

Dec. 25, 1805. Cold. I made shoes. Samuel closed 11 pares.

Dec. 26, 1805. Warm sun cold wind. Sam and I went to the singing meeting in the evening. There were about a dozen. We sing out of Kimball's Essex Harmony.

Dec. 28, 1805. Dull and cloudy. We finished threshing rye by noon. Mr. Pingrey helped. We had a good crop of winter rye. Sir got home wood &c. In the evening it began to rain, wind in the south.

Dec. 31, 1805. Very cold. I made 5 shoes and Samuel 4 and we went to Singing School in the evening. There were about 20 of us to sing and 14 or 15 spectators from old Rowley & Byefield.[111]

Elizabeth Fuller's and Caleb Jackson's accounts about the singing schools which they attended provide valuable, though limited insight into what such schools meant in the lives of the youth of New England. Broader insight into the same subject may be gained from the writings of later-day singing masters, such as Lowell Mason and Thomas Hastings, provided due allowance is made for their not always unbiased points of view. Influenced, perhaps, by the same spirit of reform which was then directed towards the establishment of temperance and the abolition of slavery, they went out to eradicate what they considered to be deplorable practices in the handling of singing schools.

In 1826 Mason in an address[112] on church music decried the "unrestrained levity and folly" of the young persons who attended singing schools. In 1854 Hastings in a book about choral problems repeated and elaborated upon Mason's charges in a chapter entitled, "Fun at Singing Schools."

As often as once in two years, a regular singing school was maintained during the winter months, for three afternoons and evenings in a week. Afternoons were devoted to children. Two of the evenings were spent at different districts in school houses. The third was devoted to a general meeting in the village ball-room, on Sabbath evenings, which were not then regarded as holy time. What could be more suitable than to "follow up" the last hours of the holy day with the practice of psalmody? The young people were in their best dress. They were not fatigued with labor; and a little recreation appeared quite reasonable after the "confinements and restraints" of the day. All who could "raise the eight notes" were "natural singers," entitled to the privileges of the school; the rest were "spectators." None but special geniuses would learn to read music. That was the business of teachers and choristers. The pupils sought amusement, and paid as little attention to the rules as possible.

The school had nothing to do with religious order. It was usually opened by the odd canon—

"Welcome, welcome every guest,

Welcome to our music fest,

Music is our only cheer, etc."

Then there was a catechetical exercise upon the sixpenny gamut. Then a few tunes were sung; commencing separately with the several parts of the score, led off by the uproarious intonations of the teacher, while other portions of the school were whispering, "making faces," or "cutting up": sly tricks of merriment, till a signal was given for a general rush of a hundred harsh voices, sufficiently loud to make the "foundations tremble." Several tunes, all taken up in the same manner, would occupy the first half of the allotted season.

Then came the greatest charm of the evening— a long and merry recess, to be spent variously, according to the pleasure of individuals. Some, if the evening was pleasant, would "start off on a sleigh ride," and be seen no more. Some would retire to the bar-room to "clear their throats of cobwebs." Others would be talking nonsense or romping or dancing, or joining in loud laughter or merry songs. At length a loud stamp of the foot, with a vociferating call for "silence," would be the signal for the gradual termination of the uproar. The remainder of the evening, on account of the many absentees, would drag heavily; the parts would be ill-sustained and the performances would close in a languid and listless manner.[113]

Perusal of the remainder of this chapter and of the rest of the book reveals Hastings to have been a pious, humorless "Victorian," who was determined to make the world of church music over in his own image. However, once the polemical intent of his statement is understood, it is apparent that he succeeded not only in describing the type of singing schools which Elizabeth Fuller and Caleb Jackson attended but also in demonstrating that these schools fulfilled what now would be called perfectly legitimate recreational needs.

A very important conclusion may be drawn from the preceding study of the singing scholars. Although organized for the purpose of studying sacred music, the singing school was not an institution which was characterized by a pious, dignified, other-worldly atmosphere. Rather it was an institution which was characterized by the enthusiasm and vitality of youth. As the traditional agency for bringing the younger persons of the community together for wholesome recreation, it was in fact a kind of youth movement in which both sacred and secular purposes were realized.

The manner in which the dual purposes of the singing school were realized is best described by dividing the story of the singing school proper into two pairs of sub-topics which bear a significant relationship to one another. The promotion and organization of the singing school constituted important first steps in the realization of these purposes. For this reason they will be examined first.

Singing Schools—Promotion and Organization

Two patterns of promoting singing schools may be discerned from existing sources. The first pattern was that of the independently sponsored singing school and the second pattern was that of the parish-sponsored singing school.

The first pattern came about as the result of the singing master's efforts on his own behalf. Usually, he would insert an advertisement in a local newspaper stating intention to start a school in the near future and soliciting the patronage of the members of all of the religious societies of the town. Various particulars such as the time and place of meeting, the hoped-for size of enrollment, the length of the term, and the tuition fee were given and the advertisement was reprinted in succeeding issues of the newspaper until such a time as the enrollment was complete. An advertisement inserted by Samuel Holyoke, author of *The Harmonia Americana* (Boston, 1791), in the *Salem Gazette* for December 6, 1803, was a typical advertisement[114] for an independently sponsored singing school.

NOTICE

A Suitable room having been conditionally engaged by the subscriber, he proposes to open a SINGING SCHOOL, in this town for the term of three months provided sixty names can be obtained. The times for meeting to be in each week, on Thursday and Friday evening. The price to each scholar to be Two Dollars. The expenses of room, wood, candles, &c. to be defrayed by the scholars.

S. HOLYOKE

N.B. The number of scholars is not limited to sixty, but all who may wish to attend from the several societies may have an opportunity by sending their names to Cushing and Appleton's Bookstore or to the store of Messrs. S. and J. Peabody.[115]

From this brief announcement a number of facts may be gleaned. The term was to be of the usual length, i.e., one quarter or three months. The master was confident that he could handle an unusually large group of scholars. The customary number of meetings per week, which was two, were to be held. The tuition was no more than what a competent master had the right to request. The scholars were responsible for all incidental expenses such as rent, heat, and light. The school was open to the members of all religious societies. Subscription papers were conveniently at hand in two local stores.

The last two items of the above list of particulars were the most important aspects of the independently sponsored singing school. The school had no ties with any particular society or denomination and the cost was borne by those who benefited directly from the instruction offered. These aspects are clearly seen in a subscription paper circulated by Elisha West, the author of *The Musical Concert* (Northampton, 1807), in the town of Woodstock, Vermont, during the early part of his career as a singing master.

To regulate harmony in the religious societies in this town—and to encourage youth and others who wish to gain knowledge in the pleasing Art of Psalm singing—We, the subscribers, voluntarily agree to pay the sums we hereunto annex with our names, to Mr. Elisha West, for his services in the instruction of said art and the intervening charges,—At a price as shall be agreed on betwixt a Committee of the Subscribers and said West.— Said parties are to agree on the place where said services are to be performed—and the time when to begin them. Dated Woodstock, Dec. 17th, 1794.

Dolls.

A. Baker	2
J. Richardson	3
B. Swan	3
S. Day	2
Abr'm Hedge	1
Nathaniel Smith	1
Timothy Stevens	$\frac{1}{2}$
Moses Osgood	1
Josiah Taylor	1
Charles Marsh	2
Samuel Sherman	1
Rufus Carpenter	1
Samuel Fuller	1
Jesse Williams	2[116]

This paper was thus a contract between the singing master and his patrons which served to bind each to their respective obligations.

As is evident from the many advertisements quoted in the present dissertation, the advertising pages of the newspapers of the day have furnished invaluable information about the singing school. Indeed, these pages rank next to singing books and the diaries of singing scholars in their capacity to evoke within the modern reader a feeling for the singing school and the place which it occupied in the life of the community. A page reproduced from a later edition of the *Salem Gazette (Figure 12)* testifies to this fact and provides insight into the second pattern by means of which singing schools were promoted.

The advertisement at the top of the page is but one of many such advertisements which Samuel Holyoke inserted in the papers of Salem to assist in the promotion of his own singing schools. The advertisement immediately below it, that by Mr. Towne, is clearly of another sort because it announces a school which was open free of charge to the members of a particular religious society. Mr. Towne's school was obviously of the parish-sponsored type and for this reason the history of its formation, though unknown, can be reconstructed from our knowledge about similar schools.

The typical parish-sponsored singing school came about as the result of the desire on part of the congregation to improve the musical aspects of the divine service. In most parishes this meant the revitalization of the choir through the recruitment and training of new singers. Usually a committee of interested persons would be formed and entrusted with the responsibility of circulating a subscription paper, the purpose of which was to raise through voluntary contribution a sum sufficient to hire a singing master to conduct a school for aspirants from within their own membership.[117] A subscription paper which was circulated throughout the parish at Dorset, Vermont, in October 1797 is a typical example of this type of document.

> Sensible that it is the indispensable duty of all to be ready and cheerful to support the public worship of God in its primitive order & beauty: and sensible that singing the praises of God with musical harmony & decency is a pleasant & important branch of public worship enforced by divine

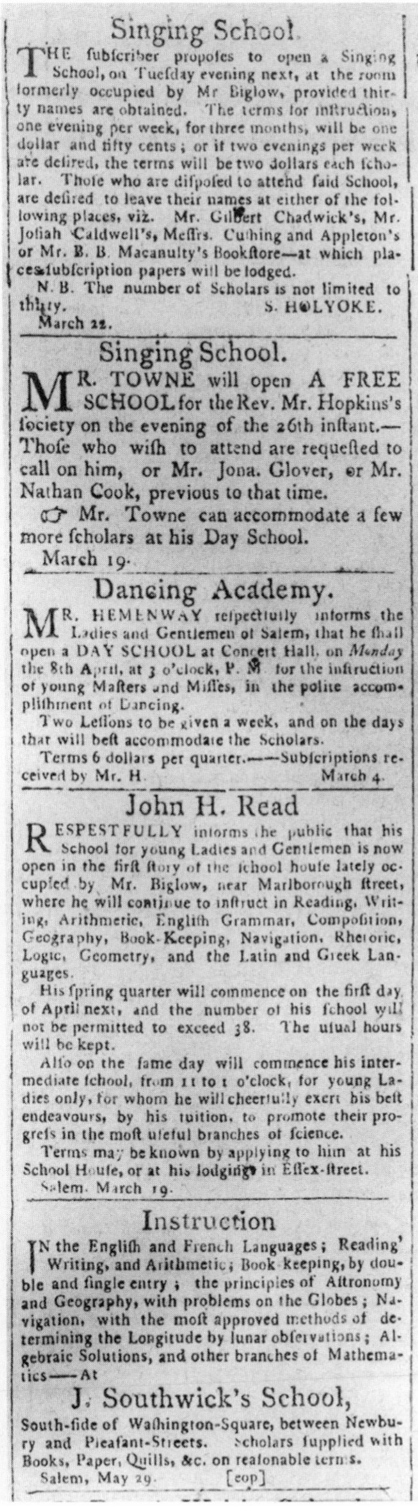

Figure 12. A portion of a page of advertisements from the *Salem Gazette* 19, no. 1419, Tuesday, April 2, 1805 (Salem: Printed by Thomas C. Cushing) which included advertisements for two singing schools, one taught by Samuel Holyoke, the other by Mr. Towne. Courtesy, American Antiquarian Society.

authority & viewing it as a hard & unequal that render themselves decent as the public organs of a worshipping assembly should be obliged to pay the expense of those necessary acquirements, we the subscribers do mutually covenant & bind ourselves in the manner following:

1st. That we will for the encouragement and promotion of singing, pay the sums annexed to our several hands in cash or grain to a committee hereafter to be chosen by the subscribers for the disposal of the same.

2nd. That a meeting of the subscribers shall be holden on Monday the 6th day of Novem. next at Justus Holley in this town for the purpose following—1st to choose a moderator of said meeting. 2. To choose by ballot a committee as above mentioned to dispose of the money raised by this instrument for the promotion of singing in public worship in this place, to procure a singing master & books for the use of a singing school if judged necessary. 3rd to see if the subscribers will adopt any other measures for a more uniform & permanent encouragement of singing in this place. In testimony of the above agreement we hereunto subscribe our names. Dorset, Oct. 24, 1797

Justus Holley	0-6-0
Joseph Holley	0-3-0
Eliphalet Farwell	0-6-0
Abram Underhill	0-6-0
Chauncey Stannard	0-3-0
Foster Paddock	0-6-0
Wm. Farnsworth	0-6-0
B. B. Downs	0-9-0
Wm. Martindale, Jr.	0-3-0
Isaac Farwell, Jr.	0-3-0
Elephalet Townsley	0-2-0
Titus Kellogg	0-2-0
Guy C. Baldwin	25¢
Solomon Collins	0-6-0
Wm. Jackson	0-6-0
John Manly, Jr.	0-9-0
Alpheus Morse	0-6-0
Cephas Kent, Jr.	0-6-0
John Manly	0-1-6
Peter P. Nott	25¢
Chester Southworth	0-1-6
David E. Crain	0-3-0
Josiah Southworth	0-3-0
David Sherman	0-1-6
Elijah Fore, Jr.	0-3-0
Moses Robinson	0-1-0
Isaiah Gray	25¢
Samuel Collins	0-9-0
Isaac K	0-6-0
Daniel Gray	0-3-0

Ashbel Sykes, Jr.	0-2-0
Samuel Read	0-2-0
Alex Kent	0-1-0
Barzilla Hudson	0-3-0
John Gray	0-5-0
Richard Dunning	0-3-0
Sylvanus Sikes	0-3-0
Lemuel Stannard	0-3-0
Thompson	0-3-0
John Manly, 3rd.	0-3-0
James Stewart	0-1-6
Reuben Bloomer	0-4-0
James Underhill	0-3-0
John Cook	0-4-0
Joseph Sheldon	0-4-0
Ebenezer Morse	0-3-0
David Townsley	0-3-0
Ira Sears	0-3-0
Amos Field	0-3-3
Reuben Harmon	0-2-0
Jeduthan Farwell	0-6-0
Thomas Dunton	0-3-0
Moses Kent	0-5-0
Lewis Dunning	0-3-0
Abigail M. Kent	0-1-0
John Farwell	0-4-0
Asa Farwell	0-6-0
Gershon Martindale	0-2-0
Noah Fuller	0-6-0
Stephen Martindale	0-9-0
Noah Fuller	0-3-0

We the subscribers bind ourselves by the within written instrument provided the master employed to instruct in singing do not belong to the United Society of Dorset and Rupert but is procured from abroad—

Enos Harmon	0-6-0
Martin Kent	0-10-0
Cephas Kent	0-6-0
John Farwell, Jr.	0-3-0
Shubael Cook	0-3-0
Joseph Paddock	0-3-0
Z. Huggins	0-6-0
Titus Sikes	0-4-0
Reuben Post	0-3-0
David Dunnell	0-1-6
Zadock Morne	33¢
Underhill	0-4-0
John Rose	33¢
Titus Sikes Jr.	0-4-0
Jonathan Church	0-3-0

Errors excepted the subscription seems to amt. to
s 317 - d 6 + 16
5283 + 1.16   53.99
£ 16. 4. 6 N.E. Currency.[118]

Many particulars of this document, such as the declaration that the choir should not have to pay for its own training and the statement that all subscribers would have an equal voice in the allocation of the money pledged, are of interest.

The virtues and the defects of the system of support through subscriptions are obvious. On the one hand, the members of the choir, who did not receive any remuneration for their services, could look forward periodically to the assistance of a "trained musician" to aid them in carrying out their duties without having to contribute to the cost of such assistance. On the other hand, because subscription was voluntary, the cost of the singing school was borne unequally by the congregation. The "lovers of harmony" gave generously, while those without an ear for music or children to send to the school gave very little or nothing at all. To make matters worse, the sum collected did not always match the sum subscribed because not everybody could be counted upon to honor their pledges when they became due. In such cases the committee which was elected to oversee the school usually had to make up the difference between the amount collected and the amount promised to the singing master out of their own pockets.

For these reasons the method of raising money for a singing school by means of subscription was often an inefficient one. William Pynchon, a conservative lawyer from Salem, commented wryly upon a subscription situation in which he found himself involved in 1782.

Oct. 1, 1782. Tuesday. Rain. Singing-school house goes on heavily; some withdraw their subscriptions.[119]

Oct. 15, 1782. Tuesday. Fair and cool. It is said the singing-school will be raised this week, and the 74-gun ship at Portsmouth on Wednesday, next week.[120]

Oct. 22, 1782. Tuesday. The singing-school raised.[121]

This situation, if not completely typical, was at least representative of the discouragement experienced by the supporters of the singing school when things weren't going well.

Three solutions to the subscription problem seem to have been tried with varying decrees of success. In William Bentley's congregation it was the custom apparently to designate the offering contributed on a particular date as being specifically for the support of the singing school.

Jan. 10, 1808. This evening was a contribution to aid the singing. It fell greatly short of the sum we wished, amounting to 52 dollars & only three bills above one Dollar. We have agreed to spend 70 Dollars upon Mr. Davis at the rate of one and a half each School night. This Sum is not sufficient to pay him. But we must remember the oppression which is felt from the Embargo. The Tabernacle are to give Holyoke 100 D. a quarter, & find, as we do, everything. Dr. Barnard's North Meeting are tired of the attempts & have purchased a very expensive organ which is every day expected from Philadelphia.[122]

This method,[123] which was fairly common, had the same defect as the subscription system in that the members of the congregation could and probably did contribute unequally. This defect was eliminated in the plan adopted by the congregation of the First Church in Hartford in 1783.

Voted that the sum of three farthings on the pound be laid on the Polls and Rateable Estate of the inhabitants of this Society for the purpose of hiring a suitable person for teaching psalmody in the Society.[124]

This plan is of interest because it anticipates a practice which became fairly general throughout New England a few years later.

Although Oliver Noble had advocated the opening of "schools for psalmody upon a generous plan, free for all denominations without distinction" as early as 1774, the practice of appropriating public funds for the instruction of youth in music seems to have originated, not in the visionary pronouncements[125] of one man, but in the need to provide the singing school, which was a truly popular institution, with a better financial foundation. That such a solution was possible was due to the curious relationship which existed between church and state in New England at the beginning of the nineteenth century. In Massachusetts the town in its corporate capacity exercised the functions of a parish.[126] "In the settlement and dismissal of a minister the church had a concurrent vote, but the control and repair of the meeting house, the salary of the minister, and all other parochial affairs were debated and determined in open town meeting."[127] Thus, the need to distribute the burden of financing the singing school equally among all members of the congregation was properly the subject for action by the town as a whole.

The deliberations of the Town of Sudbury, Massachusetts, provide an excellent example of how the citizens, who had granted the singers of their community the honor of being seated together in the gallery of the meeting house as a choir in 1796, went about securing public funds for the support of a singing school the following year. In accord with the usual custom an article was inserted in the Town Warrant for October 19, 1797.

> 8th. To see, if the Town, will Grant a Sufficient Sum of Mony to hire some suitable person, to teach a Singing School in said Town, for one Month, Agreeable to the Petition of Samuel Puffer, Jun. & others, Reference being had to the said petition.[128]

On October 30, 1797, at a "Legal Town Meeting," the article was considered and passed in the affirmative.

> 8th. Granted, the sum of $30 for the purpose Express in this Article also Appointed a Committee for the purpose of procuring a Singing Master & providing a suitable place to keep said School in. Committee chosen were Mr. Samuel Puffer, Jun. & Mr. John Maynard, Jun.[129]

Such action meant that every taxpayer in the community regardless of whether he was a member of the church or not shared equally in financing the singing school.

Actions such as this one were no more arbitrary from a non-church member's point of view than any of the other actions taken by towns, such as paying the ministers' salaries out of public funds. Furthermore, as long as the communities remained nearly one hundred percent Congregationalist in their makeup no problems of discrimination between sects arose. In the few towns in which there was more than one sect, as there was in Chelmsford, Massachusetts, the townspeople had the good sense to provide instruction for each in equal proportion.[130]

The practice of allocating public funds for the support of musical instruction in Massachusetts, which began about 1790, became fairly general by 1800 and continued sporadically until about 1833 when the "legislators of Massachusetts confirmed the Eleventh Amendment to the Constitution of the Commonwealth which made a complete separation between the parish and the town."[131] By projecting the information preserved in town histories (Table 2) a reasonable estimate of the scope and importance of this method of financing singing school may be made. A conservative estimate is that about a third of the towns in the state underwrote the cost of their singing schools at one time or another in this manner.

Of the various ways of financing the singing school, the above practice seems to have been the most successful, though it was, by no means, perfect. The solvency of the town played an important part in determining whether a singing master would be hired and if so whether he would be paid. In at least one instance a master had to bring suit through the courts to receive payment from a town that was in arrears not only with regard to its obligation to him but also with regard to its minister as well.[132] "With potatoes ten cents per bushel and lumber two dollars a thousand" hard cash was not easy to come by in the seventeen nineties.[133] The citizens of one town solved this problem with considerable ingenuity. In Framingham, Massachusetts, the town voted in 1798 to appropriate $30 to hire a singing master and stipulated that this sum was to come from the proceeds of the alewife fishery in Cochituate Brook. This action created what came to be known as the singers' fish privilege, a right which was renewed annually for several years.[134]

Once the question of financing the singing school had been settled, the next problem which those responsible for its establishment had to face was housing. This problem was solved in one of three ways.

According to Nathaniel Gould, a later-day singing master, the most popular place to hold the singing school during pre-temperance times was the local tavern.[135] Most taverns of this period included among their public rooms a multi-purpose hall, which was rented to the sponsors of the singing school on easy terms, "for it was well understood by all parties that the profits arising from the sales in the bar-room to scholars and spectators" would more than compensate for the modest rental fee. The popularity of the tavern was not due entirely to the availability of "ardent spirits." The atmosphere of the place was such that those singing masters "who could sing a good song and play the viol" could give free reign to their talents.[136] During the recess and after the school was over for the evening, they were frequently the center of convivial groups, since it was not considered indecorous for the scholars to invite their masters, particularly those who were adept on the violin, to play tunes "while they used their feet instead of their hands, to beat time to the measure of the music."[137]

Although Gould's assertions[138] are borne out in general by the researches of at least two town historians,[139,140] relatively few singing masters made specific reference in their advertisements to the tavern as a place of meeting. One who did was a Mr. Attwill, who inserted the following advertisement in a Boston newspaper in 1793.

SINGING ACADEMY

MR. ATTWILL respectfully informs the young Ladies and Gentlemen of this metropolis that he proposes opening a SINGING SCHOOL in the Hall of the Green Dragon, where he will give Lessons of Vocal Music two evenings in a week, from 6 to 9 o'clock P.M., on the following terms. lst. Each Scholar will pay Six Shillings at the expiration of three months,—2nd. The Hall will be lighted and prepared for the reception of the School at the expense of the Instructor.

Those who please to favor him with their encouragement may depend on his utmost exertions to render it deserved.

He will attend in person at the Green Dragon Hall next Monday evening, and each succeeding Monday, Wednesday, and Friday evenings, from 4 to 9 o'clock, P.M. until a sufficient number of Scholars presents to render it an object to open the school.

A Subscription Paper will be left at Messrs. Thomas and Andrew's Bookstore, and another in the hands of Mr. Bowman, at Messrs. Bond and Bryant's Store, where any inclined to subscribe may have an opportunity.

He will also attend in private families (if requested) at such hours as will be most agreeable, to instruct such as are inclined to employ him in that way.

It is at the request and promised patronage of a number of respectable gentlemen in this town that he has been induced to make the foregoing proposals. —From the usual readiness of the inhabitants of this town to encourage and promote all useful and improving institutions, he flatters himself that in the present undertaking he shall not fail of success.

N.B. After a sufficient number of Scholars have made application, Public notice will be given in the *Centinel* when the School will commence.[141]

That a singing master could with complete propriety hold a school for youth in a tavern such as "The Green Dragon" may seem strange to the modern reader. This paradox arises quite naturally from the fact that the character of the tavern has changed considerably over the years. As one social historian[142] has remarked, the New England inn or tavern was an institution, not a mere incident of travel and wayfare. Frequently placed near the meeting house so that it could provide a place in which the worshippers could thaw out and partake of the ever-comforting flip between services, the tavern was the social center of the community. It was only natural, therefore, that both the committees in charge of parish-sponsored singing schools and the singing masters themselves chose the tavern as a place for holding the singing school.

The school house, while perhaps not as popular as the tavern, is mentioned far more frequently in the literature as the place for holding a singing school. The advertisement which two enterprising singing masters from Salem inserted in a local newspaper in 1772 is typical of many which designate the school house as the place of meeting.

BENJAMIN WILLIAMS & SAMUEL WADSWORTH

Propose to open a SINGING SCHOOL next Monday Evening, at the Town School-House, to be kept on Monday and Thursday Evenings in each Week, from 6 to 9 o'Clock, where all Persons, who are desirous of being instructed in the divine Art of Psalmody may be taught by the newest and best Method.[143]

Although the manner in which Messrs. Williams and Wadsworth went about obtaining the use of the school house has not come to light, it is reasonably certain that permission to use a public building for that which was essentially a private enterprise came about as the result of formal action by the town.

Such at least was the case in other New England communities which realized that the singing school whether independently sponsored or parish sponsored benefited the majority of the youth of the community and therefore deserved public assistance. Thus, in the town of Sudbury when the citizens inserted an article in the Town Warrant for September 28, 1801, to see if the town would hire a singing master, they also inserted an article to see if the town would let him use several of the school houses for his various classes.

> 16th. To see if the Town will grant a Suitable Sum of Money for the further Encouragement of hiring a Master to teach a Singing School in said Town the present year Agreeable to the request of Lt. Hopestill Willis...[144]

> 17th. To see if the Town will give liberty to their Singing Society to Occupy the several School Houses in said Town during the term of time they shall have a Singing School in said Town the present fall...[145]

On October 12, 1801, at a Town Meeting both articles were considered and passed in the affirmative.

> 16th. Then the Town by their Vote took up this 16th Article & Granted the sum of $10 for the purpose of enabling their Committee appointed for the purpose of procuring a teacher of a Singing School in said Town to provide a teacher of said School.[146]

> 17th. The Town by their Vote gave liberty to the Singing Society in said Town that they have the privilege of Occupying the several School Houses in said Town during the term of time said School shall be kept provided said School does not interfere with the Reading and Writing Schools, also that the teacher of said School shall be directed to pay strict attention that there shall be no damage done to any of the School houses during the time they shall occupy them.[147]

In so doing the citizens of the town were merely following a practice of long standing.[148]

Mentioned less frequently as places for holding singing schools are the homes of church officials and parishioners. Many deacons, because of their particular responsibilities for the musical aspect of the service, opened their doors to the youthful singers of their congregations. Deacon Jewett of Rowley was typical of those who did. In his "Diary" he noted:

> Oct. 29, 1799. Very pleasant. Singing school in ye house.[149]

Impractical for large groups, the homes of parishioners were especially suitable for small schools whose membership was largely made up of scholars of tender age. William Bentley of Salem noted in his *Diary* the initial meeting of one of the many singing schools which he sponsored for the "Young Masters and Misses" of his parish.

> Nov. 10, 1797. Opened for the first time our Singing School in part of Mrs. Hutchinson's House in Turner Street. A young band was present in the evening.[150]

Information concerning the financial arrangements, if any, which were made for these and other such occasions, is lacking. One scrap of evidence suggests that the householders involved may not always have been motivated by a spirit of altruism in making their homes available to the singing school. In the account book of one sturdy New Englander the following entry may be found.

> 1801 to one third my house for Singing School 0-12-0.[151]

Once the question of housing the singing school was settled, the last problem which those responsible for its establishment had to solve was that of organizing the school. This problem was usually solved in cooperation with the singing masters themselves since they often had their own ideas on the subject.

Every school presented slightly different problems. Of these, the related problems of the size of the enrollment and the ratio between the untrained and the partially trained scholars were the most pressing. While relatively little first-hand information concerning the size of enrollment has survived, it is possible to estimate in a general way how large the singing school classes were and how the singing masters made provision for the different degrees of previous training found among their scholars. Samuel Holyoke indicated through his advertisements in the *Salem Gazette* on two different occasions that he desired an enrollment of sixty and thirty scholars, respectively.[152] Sewall Short indicated through his advertisements in the *Nantucket Inquirer* that he desired an enrollment of fifty scholars.[153] Lemuel Badcock reported an actual enrollment of forty-six scholars (thirty-four males, twelve females) in the singing school which he taught at Westborough, Massachusetts, in the winter of 1778.[154] William Bentley recorded in his *Diary* that the total enrollment of the singing school taught by a Mr. Groce for his congregation in 1792 was forty-three scholars (twenty-five males, eighteen females) not counting the old singers in attendance.[155]

By today's standards these groups were considerably larger than what is considered an optimum size for classes. The figures mentioned, however, may be misleading, since there is reliable evidence that the singing masters did not always try to handle the entire enrollment in one class. As was noted in the discussion of the singing scholars, the masters regularly scheduled classes for children who possessed little or no training in the rudiments of music in the afternoon and for their older brothers and sisters who possessed some knowledge of the fundamentals in the evening. Some masters, such as Mr. Claggett of Salem, added a further refinement by scheduling classes for young adults on alternate evenings of the week so that the advanced singers constituted one group and the beginners another.[156] Such refinements of scheduling were, of course, less feasible in the smaller rural singing schools such as those which Moses Cheney attended in his youth. It may reasonably be assumed that the masters of these schools had of necessity learned the fine art of handling successfully with the same class students with marked differences in ability and training.

William Billings, who was one of the first to codify instructional practice, included in his second opus a set of instructions designed to help the singing scholars in regulating their conduct in the singing school.

Observe these Rules for regulating a Singing School

As the well being of every Society depends in a great measure upon GOOD ORDER (I have heard it remarked that Order was the first thing that took place in Heaven), I here present you with some general rules to be observed in a Singing School.

1st. Let the society be first formed, and articles signed by every individual; and all those who are under age should apply to their parents, masters or guardians to sign for them: the house should be procured before the arrival of the Master, to prevent his being unnecessarily detained.

2nd. The Members should be very punctual in attending at a certain hour or minute, as the master shall direct, under the penalty of a small fine, and if the master should be delinquent, his fine to be double the sum laid upon the scholars — Said fines to be appropriated to the use of the school in procuring *wood, candles,* &c. N.B. The fines to be collected by the Clerk, so chosen for that purpose.

3rd. All scholars should submit to the Judgement of the master, respecting the part they are to sing;

and if he should think fit to remove them from one part to another, they are not to contradict, or cross him in his Judgement; but they would do well to suppose it is to answer some special purpose because it is morally impossible for him to proportion the parts properly, until he has made himself acquainted with the strength and fitness of the pupils' voices.

4th. No unnecessary conversation, whispering, laughing to be practised; for it is not only indecent, but very impolitic; it being a needless expense of time, and instead of acquiring to themselves respect, they render themselves ridiculous and contemptible in the eyes of all serious people; and above all, I enjoin you to refrain from all levity, both in conduct and conversation, while singing sacred words; for where the words *God, Christ, Redeemer,* &c. occur, you would do well to remember the third Commandment, the profanation of which, is a heinous crime, and God has expressly declared he will not hold them guiltless who take his name in vain; and remember that in so doing you not only dishonor God and sin against your own souls; but you give occasion and very just ground to the adversaries or enemies of music, to speak reproachfully. Much more might be said; but the rest I shall leave to the Master's direction and your own discretion, heartily wishing you may reap both pleasure and profit in this your laudable undertaking.[157]

These instructions provide insight into some of the more subtle aspects of the way in which the singing school was organized.

Billings's first and second rules appear to refer not to the subscription papers, which were circulated in advance of the school, but to a set of bylaws by means of which singing groups governed themselves. An early example of what he had in mind is the following document which was found among some old deeds belonging to John Lee (1717–1761), a blacksmith active in Boston around 1750.

Articles of Agreement

We whose names are underwritten do mutually agree to abide by, comply with, and conform ourselves in every respect to the articles within mentioned.

First: We do agree to put ourselves under the tuishion and instruction of Mr. Saml Holbrook to be by him instructed in the Rules of Psalmody.

2ly, We do agree (in order to be tought the above Rules) to meet once a week at the house of Mr.

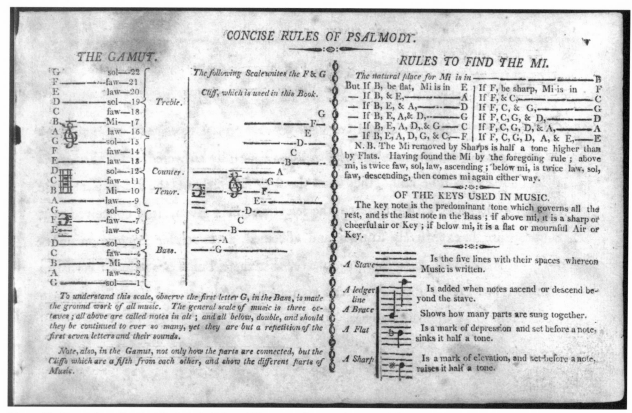

Figure 13. A page from Stephen Jenks's *Delights of Harmony* showing his use of the gamut and Thomas Walter's "Short Scheme" for finding and transposing the *mi*. Eda Kuhn Loeb Music Library of the Harvard College Library.

Sam'l Pitcher and we do appoint the time for this Quarter to be thursday at seven a Clock in the evening and so to alter the time Each Quarter as the Company shall think Proper.

3ly, That if any one of us is Absent after said hour he shall forfit the sum of one shilling ould tennor.

4ly, We do agree to chuse a Clark to Receive such fines as may be Du as afor'd and Render an Acct. of the same an all other money that he shall Receve of the Company for the Maintainance of the Society once every three months.

5ly, We do agree not to sing after the houer of nine and then that who Ever is so minded may withdraw and that if aney are inclined to stay longer they may not exceed the houer of ten.

6ly, We do agree thet no person be Invited or admitted as a member with oute the Consent of the Maj'r part of the Society.

7ly, We do agree that Every Person upon his Entrance shall pay to the Clarke ten shill'n Old tennor that so the stock is kept good.

8ly, We do agree to Conforme ouer selves with Regard to all the Clauses of Each of the Above Articals to the maj'r Vote of ye Com'y.

Sam'l Holbrook
Sam'l Pitcher
William Beairsto
David Wheeler
John (mark) Lee
Joseph (mark) Lawrence
Caleb Eddy
Nath'l Caton (?)
Nathaniel Walker
Thomas Baker[158]

These articles, which are not unlike some of those governing present-day choral organizations, are yet another example of the way in which New Englanders expressed their passionate concern for self-government during the colonial period.

Billings's third rule refers to the all important and occasionally heart-rending task of testing and classifying the scholars' voices. This task, which was the principal activity associated with the opening exercises of the school, was accom-

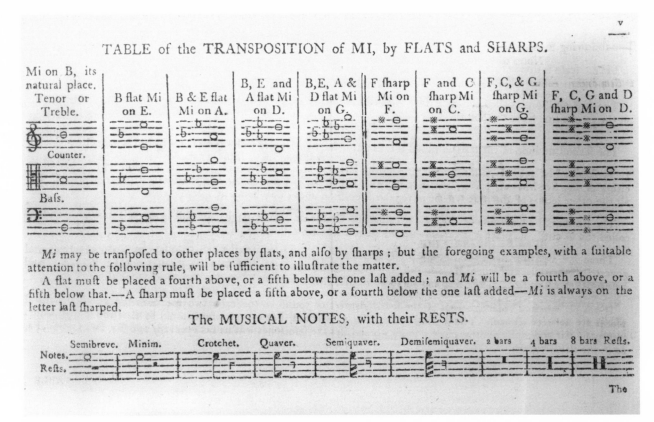

Figure 14. A page from Jacob Kimball's *Rural Harmony* (Boston, 1793) showing his use of musical charts to illustrate the transposition of the *mi*. Courtesy, American Antiquarian Society.

plished by having each scholar in turn attempt to raise the eight notes, i.e., sing the scale, by imitating the voice of the master. Those who could do this satisfactorily were accepted and those who could not were rejected, the decision of the singing master being, as Billings states, final. This meant that the so-called "monotones" or "weak singers" left the classroom with "blasted hopes" and were henceforth denied "the amusements and comforts anticipated from the social interviews of the school."[159] It could not have been otherwise for the minority who were not accepted. Scientific knowledge about the nature of their disability was as sparse then as it is now. Furthermore, the large classes and the circuit riding itinerary followed by most singing masters were not conducive to the institution of remedial measures for their benefit. The majority, of course, could raise the eight notes and thus were ready for the real work of the singing school, namely, the mastery of the art of solmization, or *faw-sol-law*, which was the royal road to the choral music of their day.

Singing Schools—Materials, Methods, and Objectives

In the educational parlance of our day the words in the phrase, "materials, methods, and objectives," are customarily used in reverse order because teachers are trained to consider their objectives first, then to create appropriate methods, and finally to select the necessary materials. Although the singing masters were just as concerned about these matters as their present-day counterparts, as a group they were not given to the modern proclivity for drawing up elaborate courses of study or curriculum statements. Instead, they made their concern manifest through the manner in which they wrote their instruction books. For this reason, if the historian is to reconstruct their methods and objectives he must begin with their teaching materials.

The materials by means of which the singing scholars received their introduction to the mysteries of solmization were of three types. The simplest were the manuscript tune books which

LESSONS for TUNING the VOICE.

Leſſon in the major key.

N. B. This leſſon ſhould be well learned, and the relative diſtance of each note from the key note, (as diſtinguiſhed by the figures placed over them) underſtood ſo as to be ſounded readily, before tunes in the major key are attempted.

Leſſon in the minor key.

N. B. This leſſon alſo ſhould be well underſtood before tunes in the minor key are attempted.

Whichever of theſe leſſons a teacher chuſes his pupils ſhould firſt attend to, it is recommended that they be made to practiſe upon tunes in the ſame key, before they endeavour to acquire a knowledge of the other, &c.

Figure 15. A page from Jacob Kimball's *Rural Harmony* (Boston, 1793) showing his incorporation of the concept of mode, i.e., major-minor, in the lessons for tuning the voice. Courtesy, American Antiquarian Society.

contained little more than a gamut, or table for solmization, and such tunes as the master and the scholar felt were worth preserving. Somewhat more pretentious but still quite rudimentary were the printed "Gamuts" which contained in addition to a brief summary of the rules of music a few standard practice pieces and a large number of blank pages for manuscript tunes. The most complete were characteristic oblong tune books which not only contained a thorough introduction to the rudiments but also an extensive collection of printed music.

The importance of the manuscript tune books has generally gone unrecognized by the authors of secondary works dealing with church music in America, presumably because so few of these books have survived to the present day. Evidence preserved in contemporary accounts suggests that these crude, homemade productions were widely used by beginners and masters who could not afford to purchase the more elegant printed tune books.[160] Some scholars, such as Hannah Boldery,[161] made their own books by sewing together the single stave voice parts copied out for them by their singing master.[162] Other scholars, such as George Newberry, made their books by taking blank commonplace books and copying into them such directions and tunes as they thought necessary.[163] Still others had recourse to enterprising bookbinders such as the sons of the Reverend Ebenezer Parkman, who made a business of turning out inexpensive manuscript tune books.

Feb. 27, 1778. My Sons are both of them much engaged in making Singing Books & pricking out Tunes.[164]

Mar. 10, 1778. Breck makes a Business of Bookbinding; but also by Singing Books. The Singing School is still kept at Mr Tim. Warren's, under the Instructions of Mr. Jonathan Batherick.[165]

Tunebooks such as these were often used and added to by successive generations of the same family.[166]

The need for inexpensive printed materials for use in singing schools was first met by Nathaniel Patten who created what came to be known as the "four penny gamut." In an issue of the *Connecticut Courant* for February 11, 1788, he announced:

Just printed, and now selling by NATHANIEL PATTEN, Ten rods north of the Court-house, and

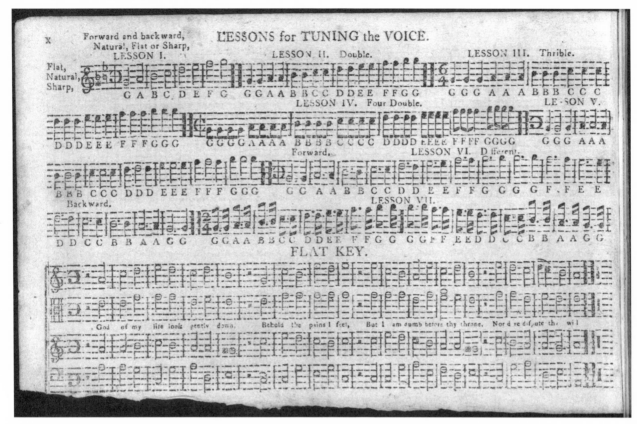

Figure 16. A page from Jacob French's *Harmony of Harmony* (Northampton, 1802), showing his incorporation of the concept of rhythm and meter in the lessons for tuning the voice. Eda Kuhn Loeb Music Library of the Harvard College Library.

directly opposite the North Meeting House, Hartford, THE GAMUT OR SCALE OF MUSIC, containing all the necessary rules for young beginners. Price 4d, single, and 3 s. per dozen.[167] Patten's creation was evidently a great success for six more gamuts were published before the century was over. Unfortunately, no copies of the original four penny gamut and its successors are known to have survived.[168]

Some idea of their contents may be gained from perusal of the later-day gamuts[169,170] published by Oliver Cooke, who may have been Patten's successor at Hartford. Cooke's gamuts are of unique proportion, being oblong in shape, $3\frac{1}{2}$ high by $9\frac{1}{2}$ long. Within their covers the rudiments of music are presented in the briefest possible manner. The treble, tenor, counter, and bass clefs, the solmization syllables, the rules for finding the mi, the names of the notes, the moods of time, the sharp and flat keys are all explained. In addition, there are a few lessons for tuning the voice, a collection of easy psalm tunes in three and four parts, and a number of blank pages for manuscript music.

The characteristic printed tune books are more useful in establishing the methods and objectives of the singing school than the manuscript singing books and the four penny gamuts for two reasons. First, almost every tunebook contains an introduction to the rudiments of music which reflects the author's best thinking about these subjects. Second, nearly all of the major singing master-composers produced one or more works in this genre; thus there is a wealth of original material available for study.

The analysis of the introductions[171] contained in a selected bibliography of tune books (see *Table 3*) reveals that although the singing masters of the periods from 1770 to 1800 had minor differences of opinion about specific matters, they did have one major objective in common, namely, the production of musically literate choral singers. That this was the object of their instruction becomes apparent when the introductions to their tune books are compared with Tufts's

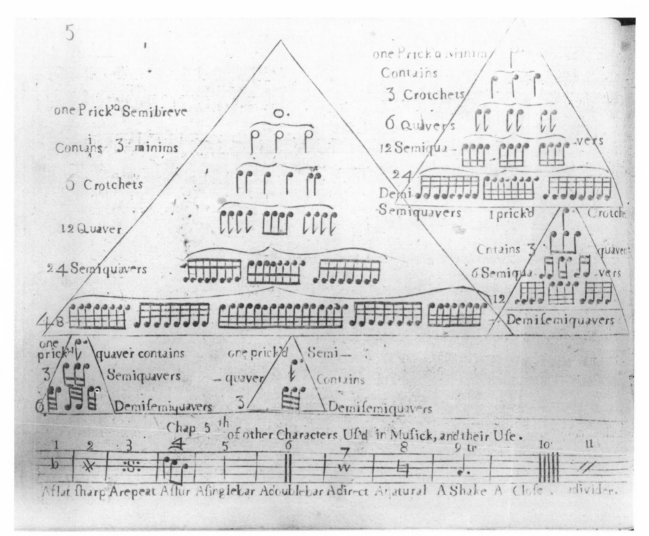

Figure 17. A page from William Billings's *New England Psalm Singer* (Boston, 1770) showing his use of pyramid-shaped tables of rhythmic values in the different "Moods of Time." Courtesy, American Antiquarian Society.

Introduction and Walter's *Grounds and Rules.* Every topic covered by Tufts and Walter has been expanded in terms of the higher degree of musical literacy and vocal skill demanded by the choral music. A systematic comparison between the tune books of the two eras serves to clarify this point.

Study of the gamut continued to be the principal learning activity of the chorally oriented singing school. Most masters, such as Stephen Jenks, retained Walter's "Short Scheme" for finding and transposing the mi (see *Figure 13*). Others, such as Jacob Kimball, abandoned it and substituted complete charts showing the actual transposition of the mi on musical staves (see *Figure 14*). Relatively few masters retained the table of solmization wherein the application of the remaining syllables

to the notes in a given key was plotted, presumably because such tables were too complicated for most beginners.

Belief in the utility of Walter's lessons for tuning the voice varied from master to master. Some masters, such as the anonymous editor of the popular tune book *Laus Deo!*, did not bother to include such lessons in their introductions, preferring perhaps to teach them by rote. Other masters either retained them in approximately their original form as interval drills or expanded their function to include the concept of mode (see *Figure 15*) and the concept of rhythm and meter (see *Figure 16*).

One of the great charms of the new choral music was its rhythmic and metric complexity. The masters were unanimous in their concern that the choral singer understand not only the relationships between the notes but also the conventions involved in the "Moods of Time." William Billings made the relationships between the notes clear by expanding Walter's schemes of common and triple time (see *Figure 9*) into the now familiar pyramid-shaped tables of note values (see *Figure 17*). Stephen Jenks similarly clarified the metric picture by compiling a table which showed how the time signatures then in use indicated definite meters and tempos (see *Figure 18*).

The establishment of a proper tempo depended as much upon the singer's ability to beat time correctly as upon his understanding of the moods of time. Jacob Kimball's remarks on the subject of beating time reveal that he subscribed to the conventional beat patterns of his day.

> BEATING time is an artificial way of measuring the proportionate duration of the notes; the common methods of doing which, are as follow, viz. For the two first modes of common time which have four beats in a bar, lst, let the ends of the fingers fall; 2nd, the heels of the hand; 3rd, raise the heel of the hand; 4th, throw up the ends of the fingers, and the bar will be finished. For the third and fourth modes of common time, and for the 6/4 and 6/8 modes of compound time, which have only two beats in a bar, lst, let the hand fall; 2nd, raise it, and the bar will be completed. For treble time, all the modes of which have three beats in a bar, lst, let the ends of the fingers fall; 2nd, the heel of the hand; 3rd, throw up the ends of the fingers, &c.[172]

Whether he also subscribed to the practice of having every scholar beat time for himself is not known. Daniel Read was of the opinion that masters who did not do so were not fulfilling their obligations.[173]

The training given to choral singers of Read's time included much more than instruction in the rudiments of music. They were expected to master all of the basic vocal techniques by means of which choral music is given its proper expression. This meant that their attention was directed toward producing the best possible tone with their voices and toward singing with good diction.

The masters were in complete agreement in urging them to learn the art of singing "softly," which was their way of describing what would now be called singing with a light, resonant, well-supported "head tone." Daniel Read instructed them to begin by imitating their masters.

The method of singing in a soft and easy manner is very advantageous to learners; it gives them an opportunity of hearing the master's voice and imitating him; it is the best way to cultivate their own, and some times causes those voices which are harsh and unpleasant to become musical.[174]

Simeon Jocelin warned them about four of the most common faults of untutored singers, namely, "nasal tone," "rigid jaw," "excessive vibrato," and "scooping."

Of Tuning and Forming the Voice

> Let the voice be clear and smooth as possible, neither forcing the sound through the nose, nor blowing through the teeth with the mouth shut; —a trembling in the voice is also carefully to be avoided. All high notes should be sounded soft, but not faint; the low notes full but not harsh; and let all be done with ease and freedom, endeavouring to cultivate a musical voice; observing for imitation, the sweet sound of the violin, the soft melody of the flute, and the tuneful notes of the nightingale.[175]

> In singing the notes should not be struck and ended abruptly, like the report of a smith's hammer; nor yet in a dull and heavy manner, by beginning half a tone under, and painfully arriving at the true sound:—The low notes, indeed, should be sounded full, but the others ought to be struck and ended soft, swelling each sound as the air of the tune may require.[176]

John Stickney pointed out to them the consequences of employing a forced "chest tone."

> A Person should never exert all the strength of his voice, as if he aimed to sing as loud as he could; this destroys the Musick of the voice; and makes it impossible to pass on with sufficient swiftness; where the Notes are short, catching at a Note and Jerking along, are likewise disagreeable; there is a kind of ease and seeming negligence in which consists the beauty of singing.[177]

Oliver Holden endeavored to show them how to avoid the bad effects of loud, thoughtless singing.

Of Soft Singing

> In a school, or choir, where soft music is successfully inculcated, it would be difficult for an attentive observer to point out many imperfections. Soft music is always accompanied with graceful motion, just expression, proper accent, and captivating harmony. On the other hand, harsh singing is attended with convulsive motion, bad pronunciation, misapplied accent, and a disgustful jarring. The latter is too just a description of the present mode of singing, occasioned in a great

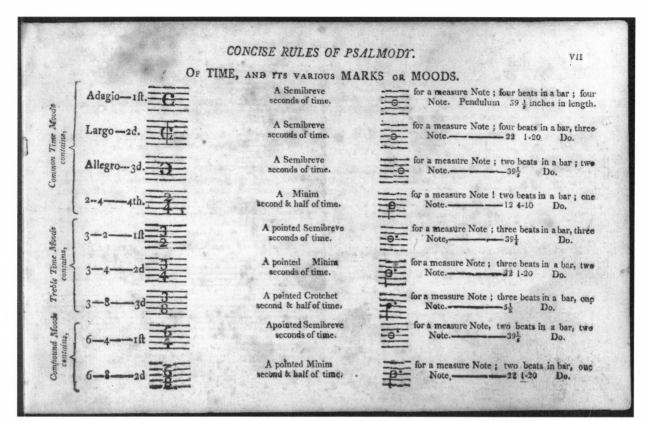

Figure 18. A page from Stephen Jenks's *Delights of Harmony* (Dedham, Mass.: H. Mann, 1805) showing his table of the "Moods of Time." Interesting differences between the way the conventional time signatures were used in Jenks's day and our own may be observed. Also, the specification of a definite tempo for each by means of the singing master's metronome, the pendulum, reveals that the singers of his day could always establish the correct tempo in spite of the fact that Italian terms for tempo were but infrequently used in the music which they sang. Eda Kuhn Loeb Music Library of the Harvard College Library.

measure by a mistaken idea, which many entertain, that good music consists principally in singing loud; but the reverse of this is the case. In performing *fortes* and *fortissimos*, the voice should not be extended beyond its natural elevation; in performing *pianos* the voice should be reduced to as small a degree of sound as will just admit intelligible pronunciation.[178]

William Billings astutely summarized for them the several advantages which would accrue from "soft singing".

GOOD singing is not confined to great singing, nor is it entirely dependent on small singing. I have heard many great voices, that never struck a harsh Note, and many small voices that never struck a pleasant one; therefore, if the Tones be Musical, it is not material whether the voices be greater, or less; yet I allow there are but few voices, but what want restraining, or softening upon high notes, to take off the harshness, which is disagreeable to a delicate ear, as a wire-edged raisor to a tender face, or a smoaky House to tender eyes. It is an essential thing in a master, to propagate soft singing in the school; because soft musick, has a great tendency to refine the ears of the performers, and I know by experience, that a new piece may be learned with more ease to the master and scholars, where they practice soft singing, and in less than half the time, it would otherwise require.[179]

The singing masters were also unanimous in urging the choral singers to learn the art of communicating the meaning of the texts through proper "pronunciation" of the words. John Stickney, prompted no doubt by the speech habits of New Englanders, cautioned them to beware of both poor pronunciation and poor diction.

Many good singers have an unhappy way of pronouncing the words, some mumble so as scarce to make any articulate sound; some have an awkward, vulgar pronunciation, and others, through inattention, continually put one word for

David's Lamentation.

David the King was grieved & moved He went to his Chamber his Chamber & wept :S: and as he went he wept & said

O my Son. O my Son would to God I had died would to God I had died would to God I had div'd for the O Absalom my Son. my Son.

Figure 19. "David's Lamentation" by William Billings has been reproduced from the third edition of his *Singing Master's Assistant* (Boston: Draper and Folsom, 1781), p. 22. Courtesy, American Antiquarian Society.

DAVID'S LAMENTATION
David, the King, was grieved & moved; / He went to his Chamber & wept.
And as he wept, he wept & said: / O my Son, O my Son. / Would to God I had died for thee, / O Absalom, my Son.

another; these faults should be early and carefully guarded against.[180]

Chauncey Langdon begged them to consider not only the importance of proper pronunciation but also the relationship which it bore to the accent of the music.

> It adds much to the Beauty of Singing to pay a careful Attention to the *Accent* of the Music, and the Pronunciation of the Words. Words in general ought to be pronounced as Grammarians pronounce them in common Conversation, and so distinctly articulated, that whatever is sung may be perfectly understood.[181]

Stephen Jenks introduced a third and final dimension of good singing for their consideration, namely, the "swell." The nearest modern equivalents for this general term appears to be "articulation" and "management of the breath," since it clearly refers to the manner of articulating, sustaining, and concluding the notes of the musical phrase.

A genteel pronunciation is one of the principal beauties of singing;—every word should be spoken as clear and distinct as possible;—it is that which gives vocal music the preference to instrumental, by affording at the same time the sweets of harmony with the sense of what is expressed in those harmonious strains.

The accent is another very important part of music;—it is a certain stress or emphasis of the voice upon particular notes or parts of the bar. It is inseparably connected with good pronunciation, and in a great measure distinguishes one mood of time from another: the first part of the bar is the accented part in all moods of time.

A swell is an essential beauty in singing; it should be applied by striking the notes soft; and gradually increasing the sound to the center; then diminishing in the same proportion. All notes should have their swell gently as the air of the tune requires.[182]

Taken together, the three dimensions of vocal technique mentioned by Jenks prove that the more distinguished singing masters of his day had an excellent understanding of both the theory and practice of choral music.[183]

Additional proof of the singing masters' grasp of the essentials of their craft is found in their handling of the voices of their singers. The four-part music of their day was scored for bass, tenor, counter, and treble. It was their ideal to have "the Bass be sung grave and majestic, the Tenor steady and engaging, the Counter soft and delicate, and the Treble shrill and melodious."[184] They sought to implement this ideal by assigning "the deepest men's voices" to the bass, "the highest men's voice" to the tenor, "the lowest women's voices" and the voices of boys to the counter, and "the highest voices of women" to the treble.[185] In so doing they were following commonly accepted practices of voice-part assignment.

In making these assignments the singing masters paid particular attention to the quality of the voice, its overall range, and the physical maturation of the singer. This was especially true where the boys were concerned because most of them could be expected to experience voice change during the period in which they attended singing schools. In accordance with the best modern principles of handling the changing voice, the masters believed in helping them sing all through the periods of change. Thus, instead of assigning them to the treble part and keeping them on that part until their voices "broke," they assigned them to the lower, more comfortable counter part, which was ideally suited to the narrow range of the typical "alto-tenor."[186] In time, as the boys entered the final phases of voice change, they assigned them to the tenor part, which was suited to the latent tenor, or to the bass part, which was suited to the "boy baritone."

Confirmation of these conclusions about the masters' skill in handling the boys' voices may be found in the ranges of the voice parts of the music, in the directions given by specific masters concerning voice assignment, and in reminiscences of those who attended their schools.

Consider for a moment Billings's "David's Lamentation" (see *Figure 19*) and Kimball's "Woburn" (see *Figure 20*). It will be at once obvious to those who have worked with youth that these pieces, unlike so much of the standard SATB repertory, are perfectly suited to the strange aggregate of unchanged, changing, and changed voices found in the junior and senior high school choirs of today. The range of each part is adapted to the working range of each voice type. Thus the treble parts never exceed the second F above middle C, which is about the top note for the immature high school soprano; the counter parts never exceed the limited range of the "alto-tenor," which is generally from the F below middle C to the B Flat above middle C; the tenor parts never enter the upper tenor range required of adult tenors; and the bass parts, which again are not excessive as to range, provide for both the "boy baritone" and the mature bass by means of the ingenious "chusing notes" (octaves) that occur at various places in the music.

There were, of course, differences of opinion among the singing masters concerning voice assignment. Most masters followed the "alto-tenor" counter plan, but there were exceptions. In the directions for singing in his *Responsory* (Worcester, 1795), Amos Bull noted that he had scored his music for treble I, treble II, tenor, and bass because he had found it difficult to get a sufficient number of boys to sing counter. Solomon Howe, in the introduction to his *Farmer's Evening Entertainment* (Northampton, 1804), advised other singing masters to restrict the counter to the unchanged voices of children of both sexes.

> ...the Teacher (should) be very careful to get the highest and clearest voices, at 7, 8, or 10 year's age, males or females, for Counter; which should always be sung, with what is call'd a child's voice, viz., as little children naturally sing at 7, &c. before they learn to imitate a woman's voice; for it spoils a tune to have both Treble and Counter sung with feminine voices. There should be an almost inexpressible delicacy in pronouncing, accenting, emphasizing, and cadecizing the Counter: a strong harsh Counter, especially in flat key'd Tunes, destroys the whole beauty in the Music.[187]

He expressed no opinion one way or the other concerning the handling of those whose voices were changing. The process of elimination suggests that he probably assigned them to the tenor part since it rarely goes too low for the changing voice. Other masters who used his book were free to make whatever voice assignments they thought proper.

Of the many persons who recorded their reminiscences of the singing school, Samuel Preston of

Figure 20. "Woburn" by Jacob Kimball has been reproduced from his *Rural Harmony* (Boston: Isaiah Thomas and Ebenezer T. Andrews, 1793), p. 33. Like so many tunes of the period it is named after a New England town and is constructed in the usual AABB form. Courtesy, American Antiquarian Society.

WOBURN

Firm was my health, my day was bright, / And I presum'd 'twould ne'er be night. / Fondly I said within my heart, / Pleasure and peace shall ne'er depart.

Danvers was perhaps the most successful in describing what it meant to be a counter singer in a choir led by one of the foremost singing masters of the day. In 1805 when Preston was a boy of thirteen, he participated in the dedication of the new brick meeting house in his hometown.

There was an educated lawyer in Topsfield, who, after he had, as he said, plead one thief clear, left his profession and took up that of writing and teaching music. His name was Jacob Kimball. He was a tall, portly man, not quite faultless in his habits, and was employed to teach six months, which the brick house was building, with a view to having a well-drilled class ready to sing at the dedication. There were about half a dozen boys of nearly the same age, of whom Nathaniel Pope and myself alone now remain, who sang counter. Music has taken many new names since then. Fa, sol, la, and mi were all the names to notes that we knew in those days. Master Kimball had taken considerable pains to drill us for the dedication, as we had an important part to perform there. We were to sing on that day the old Selby anthem, "Behold God is my salvation, I will trust and not be afraid," in which there is a counter solo of some importance to the tune, and as it was to be the first time we ever sang in public, Mr. Kimball felt rather solicitous about our pluck, and I can see him now, partly turned around, for he had placed us near him, in his rear, his trembling hand beating time for us, while we performed the feat. I believe we did it to his entire satisfaction, as he called us "brave boys," when it was over.[188]

His pride in his accomplishment and his respect for his teacher are symptomatic of the good feeling which existed between the singing scholars and their masters in his day.

Jacob Kimball's success in working with boys such as Samuel Preston was based upon more than a profound knowledge about adolescent voices and adolescent psychology. It was founded upon a deep understanding of both the short-term and the long-term aspect of method, which he had inherited from previous singing masters.

The short-term method which was employed by the previous singing masters was essentially the same as that which was used in Walter's day. The rudiments of music were taught first. Then the lessons for tuning the voice were practiced. Finally, the knowledge and skill gained in the earlier stages were applied to the learning of simple tunes by note.

William Billings was the first to reduce the expanded body of rudiments to a systematic form. In his *Singing Master's Assistant* (Boston, 1778) they were presented as a series of eleven "lessons" or topics for study.

Lesson I.   The Gamut.
Lesson II.   On Transposition.
Lesson III.   On Cliffs.
Lesson IV.   On Characters.
Lesson V.   On Characters, continued.
Lesson VI.   An Explanation of the Several Moods of Time.
Lesson VII.   Syncope, Syncopation, Driving Notes.
Lesson VIII. The Grace of Transition.
Lesson IX.   (Concords and Discords)
Lesson X.   Two Natural Primitive Keys in Music.
Lesson XI.   Concerning Slurs.

He urged "the several teachers of Music, in this, and the adjacent States" to teach these lessons after the manner in which they were inserted, because he had found this sequence to be the best from long experience.

That most masters followed Billings's method of presenting the rudiments is apparent from their own treatments of the same subject in their tune books. This is not to say, however, that they imitated him slavishly or that they closed their minds to further innovations. Nearly every one of them added certain personal touches to their tune books. Also, a number of them, including Billings[189] himself, later abandoned the usual lessons and replaced them with the popular method of presenting information in the form of a dialogue between the master and his scholar.

Many examples of these personal touches might be given. One of the most interesting is Jacob French's method of illustrating the principles expounded in the rudiments. In his *Psalmodist's Companion* (Worcester, 1793) he included a set of nine, four-part lessons, or vocalises, each of which was written in a different key and in a different mood of time. Another interesting example is Walter Janes's method of illustrating the relationship between rhythm and meter. In his *Massachusetts Harmony* (Boston, 1803) he included no less than eighteen lessons, or vocalises, in unison and three-part settings, each of which is based upon a different meter and a different rhythmic pattern. Both French's and Janes's work in this area anticipate the solfeggio-methods of the present day.

The honor of having codified the singing masters' views on the long-term aspect of method belongs to Andrew Law. All of them, including French and Janes, believed that scholars should progress from rudiments to lessons, from lessons to simple psalm tunes, and from simple psalm tunes to difficult "set pieces." Most masters organized their tune books in precisely this fashion thereby guaranteeing the purchaser a complete library of music in one volume which ranged from the simplest to the most complex pieces. Law took this method, or mode of organization, and made it the basis for structuring most of his output. He divided his magnum opus, *The Art of Singing*, into three separate parts, each of which was designed to fill a specific purpose. The first part was called *The Musical Primer* and it served, as he said, to teach the singers "the ABC of their Art." The second part, which was issued in two volumes, was called *The Christian Harmony*, and it served to provide fledgling singers with "an assortment of music proper for practice as soon as they (had) attended to the rules and lessons comprised in *The Musical Primer*." The music in these volumes consisted chiefly of simple tunes in four-part settings which were equally appropriate for use in the church and the singing school. The third part was called *The Musical Magazine*, and it served to provide advanced singers with extended choral compositions in pamphlet form. In time, this part of *The Art of Singing* was issued in six different numbers. All three parts were available singly or in various combinations.[190]

Taken as a whole, *The Art of Singing* represents the high point of thoughtful concern for method both in its short-term and long-term aspects. As such, it was probably ahead of its time, because the conditions that prevailed in the singing school were not conducive to the systematic study of a single, comprehensive method. The ever-changing procession of masters meant an ever-changing emphasis in books and methods. The short time available to them in any one school meant that, even where a comprehensive method was available, only beginners' topics and music would be covered. Indeed, the typical master had no sooner gotten his scholars well started on the long road to Parnassus than he had to bid them farewell at a singing lecture or singing exhibition.

Singing Lectures and Exhibitions

The successful conclusion of educational endeavor has by long tradition been marked by public ceremony wherein the achievements of teachers and pupils are acknowledged. In the case of the New England singing school, the end of the agreed term of study was marked by the presentation either of a singing lecture or of a singing exhibition, whichever was most appropriate to the situation.

The singing lecture, which was most characteristic of the parish-sponsored singing school, combined the best features of a choral concert, a formal lecture, and a graduation exercise. The chronicles of a singing school taught by Lemuel Badcock in Westborough, Massachusetts, in 1779 confirm this description and demonstrate that the singing lecture was a cooperative venture which involved the singing master, his singing scholars, and their minister.

Jan. 18, 1779. N.B. Mr. Badcock keeps a singing school at Mr. Barn. Newton's. Elias and Timothy go to it to hear.[191]

Jan. 25, 1779. Being at ye Shop, Capt. Fisher and Mr. Badcock were there and acquainted me with the Desire of ye Singing School to have a Lecture preached to ym, and though (as they say) they would be glad if Mr. P. would himself preach, yet because of the disquietment among ye people, it was mentioned to ask one of the neighboring Ministers, particularly Mr. Sumner to preach it. I replied with Consent....[192]

Jan. 30, 1779. N.B. Mr. Badcock has been with me to speak about ye Singing, viz., how many times, and what times they desire to sing on the proposed Lecture Day. At eve Mr. Elisha Parker here, to let me know yt Mr. Sumner will come (extras accepted) to preach ye proposed Lecture, & askes me to his on Wednesday.[193]

Feb. 2, 1779. I preached at Mr. Barnabas Newton's on Ps. 44.15 to p. 73rd. N.B. We Sung twice, because ye Singing School was there, and I tarried to hear ym Sing after my Exercise.[194]

Feb. 4, 1779. A Singing Lecture at ye Request of ye Singing School. Mr. Sumner preached. His text was Ps. 149.1. It was conducted thus. After Dinner (at which besides Mr. Sumner & Col. Job Cushing yt came with him, and Mr. Stone of Southboro) when we first went into ye Meeting House, an Anthem was sung. Then Mr. Stone made a short Prayer. After which I appointed and read Ps. 149 which was sung without Reading the Lines by the Deacon. Then Mr. Sumner prayed after which we sung Ps. 113, Deacon reading as usual, & ye Sermon next followed. Mr. Sumner prayed again and we sung ye 5th Hymn without reading over ye whole. In conclusion of the Exercise, I pronounced the Blessing. But then Mr. Badcock began an exercise of Singing —Anthems and Tunes— which was very grateful, and may God graciously condescend to accept ye Sacrifice![195]

Feb. 10, 1779. P.M. went up to ye Singing School (by desire) to hear ye Singing. This is Mr. Badcock's last day.[196]

Feb. 11, 1779. Mr. Badcock leaves us.[197]

Few of the lectures delivered on occasions[198] such as the one described above have survived the ravages of time. This fact is explained by the not unreasonable assumption that in reality the lectures were sermons, and thus were subject to the same conditions which governed the production and preservation of sermons. Most of the sermons produced during this period were not written down, but were delivered extemporaneously, the speaker being guided only by the inspiration of a short Biblical text. A few sermons, especially those in a more learned style, were delivered from manuscript notes. Some of these were submitted for publication, there being a lively market for religious tracts in New England. In this manner thirteen singing lectures (see *Table 4*) found their way into print and thus were preserved for scholarly consideration.

As literary productions these lectures have much in common with the tracts of Tufts's era. The standard scriptural admonitions concerning the duty and manner of singing divine praise are quoted and developed at length. Regular singing, however, receives scant attention because it had become a dead issue by this time. In its place a number of problems associated with the development of singing schools and village choirs, such as the emancipation of female singers, and the abandonment of lining-out are discussed.

As *pièces d'occasion* these lectures have much in common with the addresses delivered at high school commencement exercises of the present day. The ministers, having developed their topics to the fullest extent, almost invariably bring their remarks to a conclusion by addressing the youthful singers assembled before them. The concluding section of a singing lecture delivered by Charles Stearns at Lincoln, Massachusetts, in 1792 is typical of the gracious way in which the achievements of the singing masters and their scholars were acknowledged.

> Brethren and Sisters of the Choir
>
> With pleasure we beheld your zeal, and the animated diligence of your teacher. We have often had our ears refreshed by your agreeable performances. Your attention to speaking your words plain, and full; to avoiding uncouth and vulgar strains, according to the matter of the song; to express grief, joy, wonder, &c, by natural tones, has given you this acceptance. Nature is the standard of taste, and what is truly natural, will always please.[199]

Such acknowledgement of worth not only served to express the community's willingness to reengage the master on future occasions but also to certify the admission of his scholars to the choir.

How the scholars felt about their admission to the choir is not revealed by the singing lectures. To obtain insight into their feelings in this matter, one must turn to their diaries. Jonathan Hayward of Danvers, Massachusetts, kept a diary that was typical of those kept by youths of his age. He recorded everything that touched upon his existence: local fires, regimental training, and beating his friends at checkers. When he was twelve, he made two entries which show that attending the singing school and admission to the "singers' seats," or the choir, were important events in his life.

> June __ 1800. Mr. Kimball begins to keep a Singing School, of which School I am a Scholar.[200]
>
> April Fast, 1801. This day was the first I Set in the Singers' Seat.[201]

Whether the latter occasion was marked by a singing lecture is not known because Jonathan was not given to overlong statements about anything. The chances are that it was, and if the fact

of his admission looms larger than the lecture itself in his diary, it was because he was only human.

The singing exhibition, which was most characteristic of the independently sponsored singing school, was a more informal affair than the singing lecture, because it did not customarily include the lecture-sermon among its features and it did admit on occasion to the use of secular music. As such it seems to have been closer to a choral concert than to a graduation ceremony or a religious rite. Indeed, in the usage of the day the terms "exhibition" and "concert" were practically synonymous. This fact is apparent in the way in which two diarists recorded the various public performances given in Salem by Andrew Law and his scholars during the spring of 1796. The always observant William Bentley noted:

> March 24, 1796. Mr. Law has notified me of his intention to have Singing Exhibition at Dr. Barnard's Meeting House on the morrow evening.[202]
>
> March 25, 1796. Mr. Law had his singers in the Front of the North Church gallery. There was a large collection of people on the occasion.[203]
>
> June 25, 1796. Had a Card for Law's Music School Exhibition in the Concert Hall this evening.[204]

The last-named event, which was held on the second floor of the Market House, was also attended by Mrs. Mary Holyoke, who noted:

> June 25, 1796. I was at Singing Concert.[205]

Unfortunately, other writers of the period were not so consistent as Mr. Bentley in using the term "exhibition," some even going so far as to describe exhibition-like events without assigning any name whatsoever to them. In this category was an anonymous writer who reviewed three musical events which took place in Salem nearly a generation before those noted above. Some insight into the nature and importance of typical singing exhibitions may be gained by analysis of his review.

The first paragraph suggests that in their simplest form the singing exhibitions were not unlike the choral concerts given periodically by present-day high school choirs for the edification of their parents and friends.

> On Tuesday last a considerable Number of Youth of both Sexes, who have been under the Tuition of Mr. Ripley, met at one of the Meeting Houses, and entertained a large Assembly by singing a Number of Anthems, &c. to general Acceptation.[206]

The second paragraph suggests that in their more complex form they were not unlike modern choral festivals wherein high school choirs from several communities are brought together to experience the joy of singing great music under the direction of a distinguished conductor.

> On Wednesday last a much greater Number of Youth selected from Mr. Munson's Scholars in this and several neighboring Towns, met at another of the Meeting Houses, and performed their several Parts in Psalmody, particularly in singing a Number of Anthems, to the general Approbation of the Audience.[207]

The third paragraph, because it discusses an entirely different type of concert in juxtaposition with the two preceding exhibitions, suggests that these youthful enterprises were considered to be as important as any adult production by the people of that day.

> On Thursday Evening a Concert of Vocal and instrumental Musick was performed in the Assembly Room before a large Company of Gentlemen and Ladies of the Town who were highly pleased with the Entertainment. The several Parts in the Concert were performed by a Number of Gentlemen of this Place, who, the Winter past, spent their leisure Hours in perfecting themselves, for their own Amusement, in the most approved Branches of that noble Science.[208]

Additional insight into the singing exhibition, both as a ceremony which led to membership in the village choir and an event which aroused community-wide interest, may be gained through the examination of a diary kept by a nineteen-year-old shopkeeper's clerk, who resided in New Mills, now Danvers, Massachusetts, in the days of the young republic. In this diary amidst entries about Jefferson's re-election, British high-handedness on the seas, and "party rage" over the choice for governor, there are to be found the chronicles of two rival singing schools kept by two of the foremost singing masters of the day, Samuel Holyoke and Jacob Kimball.

> April 27, 1806. Sent flaxseed to Boston, price there 9/. The singing school kept by Mr. Holyoke begins this evening.[209]
>
> March 8, 1806. Proposals for an Instrumental School. I am not determined about joining it.[210]
>
> March 9, 1806. Spent the evening at Grandsir's. Mr. Holyoke being there, we sang a number of new tunes.[211]

> March 15, 1806. Last evening made choice by written votes of 3 leaders in each part., viz., tenor, treble, & bass. But I am confident that they have made choice of an Incapable one as the 2nd leader of the Bass.[212]
>
> March 16, 1806. Last evening had open doors in our singing school for spectators & there appeared a large number & we believe that we gave them tolerable satisfaction. I went to meeting & sat in the singing seats for the first time.[213]
>
> March 23, 1806. Mr. Holyoke finished his school last evening and by the desire of his scholars gave his answer to keep a month more.[214]
>
> March 28, 1806. I, with Mr. Stearns & Doke, went over to Kimball's singing school last evening.[215]
>
> April 28, 1806. Mr. Kimball's singing at Mr. Felton's, it being the last evening there were a good many spectators. I was perfectly satisfied that ours was its equal without any prejudice.[216]
>
> May 4, 1806. Last evening we had a general assemblage of spectators at our singing school. The performance lasted from 7 to half past 10 o'clock in which we hope we gratified their curiosity. Our scholars propose meeting together every Saturday evening for a term.[217]

The only thing lacking in Putnam's account is a description of the music which was sung at the exhibitions given by the two singing schools. Since it was customary for singing masters to promote the sale of their singing books by using them almost exclusively in their schools, it may reasonably be assumed that the major portion, if not all, of the music performed at these events consisted of psalm tunes, fuging tunes, and anthems found in Holyoke's and Kimball's books. Although both of these men were among the most conservative of the singing master-composers (Holyoke especially disliked the fuging tune), it does not follow that the music which was sung on these and other occasions was exclusively sacred in nature or that the atmosphere which prevailed was completely serious in character. Even these conservatives had their lighter moments which found expression in a few secular and quasi-secular pieces, such as Holyoke's ode to spring, "Brandon" *(Figure 21)* and Kimball's ode to love, "Invitation" *(Figure 22)*. Furthermore, it must not be forgotten that many singing schools were held in taverns which were conducive to the performance of the type of music which would have been inappropriate to the meeting house.

Figure 21. "Brandon" by Samuel Holyoke has been reproduced from his *Harmonia Americana* (Boston: Isaiah Thomas and Ebenezer T. Andrews, 1791), pp. 43–45. Courtesy, American Antiquarian Society.

BRANDON
The Scatter'd clouds are fled at last, / The rain is gone, the winter's past
The lovely vernal flow'rs appear, / The feather'd choirs invite our ear.
Now with sweetly pensive moan, / Coos the turtle dove alone.

The amount of secular music which was performed and the degree of levity which prevailed at an exhibition were largely determined by the outlook of the particular singing master. Some masters, such as French, whose ode to the joys of the cup, "Fly" *(Figure 23)*, was bound cheek to jowl with sacred tunes, and Billings, whose ode to discord, "Jargon" *(Figure 24)*, was designed to provoke a smile, had a decided proclivity for the secular, which could only find expression in the singing exhibition.

It was the irrepressible Billings who seems to have been the first to capitalize upon the singing exhibition as an outlet for this proclivity. In his hands it became not only one of the principal forms of public entertainment, but also one of the principal vehicles for the public expression of the political and religious sentiments current in his day.[218] Although detailed records of his exhibitions have not survived, this conclusion may be easily established by reference to his printed works.

The text of his concert anthem, "Modern Musick," supplies as good a description of his exhibitions as may be found anywhere.

Modern Musick

N.B. After the Audience are seated and the performers have taken the pitch slyly from the leader the Song begins:
We are met for a Concert of modern invention;
To tickle the Ear is our present intention.

The Audience are seated,
expecting to be treated
to a piece of the Best;
And since we all agree
to set the tune on E
the Author's darling Key
he prefers to the Rest.

Let the Bass take the Lead
and firmly proceed

Figure 21.

Figure 22. "Invitation" by Jacob Kimball has been reproduced from the second edition of Thomas Attwill's *New York and Vermont Collection* (Albany: Printed by the Proprietor, 1804), p. 58. Reprinted many times, it was a great favorite of New England singers. "Stafford," a fuging tune by Read, also appears in this reproduction. Courtesy, American Antiquarian Society.

INVITATION

Come my beloved, haste away, / Cut short the hours of thy delay, / Fly like a youthful hart or roe, Over the hills where spices grow.

to fugue away.
Let the Tenor succeed
and follow the Lead
till the parts are agreed
to fugue away.
Let the Counter inspire
the rest of the choir,
inflam'd with desire
to fugue away.

Let the Treble in the rear
no longer forbear
but expressly declare
for a fugue away.

Then change to brisker time
and up the ladder climb
and down again,
Then mount the second time
and end the strain.

Then change the Key to pensive tones
and slow in Treble time the Notes.
Exceeding low keep down a while,
then rise by degrees,
The process surely will not fail to please.

Thro' Common and Treble we jointly have run,
we'll give you their Essence compounded in one:
Altho' we are strongly attach'd to the rest,
six four is the movement which pleases us best.

And now we address you as Friends to the cause
(performers are modest and write their own laws):
Altho' we are sanguine and clap at the Bars,
'tis the part of the Hearers to clap their Applause.[219]

This glorious piece of doggerel, which served to open his exhibitions, was but a prelude to better things to come.

Figure 22.

CONCLUDING REMARKS: In Billings's day no formal evaluations of the master's work or of his scholars' achievements were made at the close of the singing school. For his contemporaries it was enough that a given master had succeeded in keeping his scholars profitably occupied during the term and that he had produced creditable singing at the lecture or exhibition. For this reason it is difficult to determine in a precise way the extent to which the masters succeeded in accomplishing their major objective, that is, the training of musically literate choral singers.

The phrase "musically literate choral singers" suggests that a twofold evaluation is in order. It may be asked, how successful were the singing masters in teaching their scholars to read music, and how successful were the singing masters in teaching their scholars the vocal techniques associated with good choral expression?

The answer to the first question appears to be that the singing masters, like the music educators of today, were able to make those possessing a modicum of talent literate enough to read music of the order of difficulty encountered in their tune books. This does not mean, however, that most scholars mastered the rudiments and became fluent readers as the result of attendance at a single school. The typical term of three months was simply not long enough for the accomplishment of this formidable task. Furthermore, the singing scholars were just as impatient with the drier, more technical aspects of music and just as eager to get to music itself as the youth of today.

The latter point is particularly germane to the determination of the extent to which the singing masters succeeded in teaching their scholars to be musically literate. John Stickney warned those who planned to use his book in their singing schools:

Let not a Learner covet to run on too fast; but make himself perfect in rising and falling by

Figure 23. "Fly" by Jacob French has been reproduced from his *Harmony of Harmony* (Northampton; Printed by Andrew Wright, 1802), p. 73. Eda Kuhn Loeb Music Library of the Harvard College Library.

FLY

Busy curious thirsty fly, / Drink with me & drink as I, / freely welcome to my cup, / Couldst thou sip & sip it up.
Make the most of life you may, / Life is short and wears away.

---

degrees and intervals; and each Tune both as to air and time, before he proceeds further.[220]

Daniel Read carried Stickney's injunction further by showing that the scholars' penchant for learning music by ear would defeat the master's purposes if he indulged them in it.

> ... it may be proper for anyone, while learning the rules, to endeavor to cultivate his voice, having a master to instruct him; but it is as inconsistent for one to attempt singing any tune, till acquainted with the rules, as for a child ignorant of the alphabet to think of reading the Bible with propriety. Some, I am sensible, who are unacquainted with the rules, have, by hearing others, learnt to sing a tune nearly right; so a child unable to read a single word, may, by observation, joined with a strong memory, repeat several pages from an author; but as the latter cannot justly be called a reader; so neither can the former justly claim the title of singer. After acquiring a good

understanding of the rules, the learner may proceed to some plain tune, or the eight notes, if the master directs, but should not attempt to sing any tune in words till he has first perfectly learned it by note.[221]

Solomon Howe commented in a similar vein and in so doing confirmed that many masters did in fact indulge their scholars in their desire to learn their music by ear.

> The Master should *never* let his scholars sing a tune, by word 'till they can sing the Notes accurately from memory. N.B. Many masters ruin their schools by such foolish license.[222]

It is, of course, impossible to state with confidence how many masters actually "ruined their schools" by indulging their scholars. Certainly, the charges made by Mason,[223] Gould,[224] and Hastings[225] to the effect that few scholars learned to read music in the singing schools of Howe's day

Figure 24. "Jargon" by William Billings has been reproduced from his *Singing Master's Assistant*, 3rd ed. (Boston: Draper and Folsom, 1787), p. 102. Courtesy, American Antiquarian Society. The composer left specific directions for its performance in a witty reply to his critics, p. 29. "In order to do this piece ample justice, the concert must be made of vocal and instrumental music. Let it be performed in the following manner, viz. Let an Ass bray the bass, let the fileing of a saw carry the Tenor, let a hog who is extream hungry squeel the counter, and let a cart-wheel, which is heavy loaded, and that has been long without grease, squeek the treble; and if the concert should appear to be too feeble you may add the cracking of a crow, the howling of a dog, the squalling of a cat; and what would grace the concert yet more, would be the rubbing of a wet finger upon a window glass. This last mentioned instrument no sooner salutes the drum of the ear, but it instantly conveys the sensation to the teeth; and if all these in conjunction should not reach the cause, you may add this most inharmonical of all sounds, 'Pay me that thou owest.'"

JARGON
Let horrid Jargon split the Air, / And rive the Nerves asunder; / Let hateful Discord greet the Ear, / As terrible as Thunder.

---

must be dismissed as being too biased to warrant serious consideration. It is clear from the memoirs of those who attended singing schools that most singing masters were forced to make a compromise between their own interest in teaching the rudiments and their scholars' interest in learning tunes "by word." This compromise meant that mastery of the rudiments and fluency in reading came about only as the result of attendance at a number of singing schools held over a period of several years. Such was true in the case of Moses Cheney and such was probably true in the case of most others,[226] since musical literacy is something which is usually achieved only after a long period of study and practice. It may be concluded, therefore, that those with sufficient musi-

cal ability and ample opportunity for study became musically literate and that those who lacked one or the other of these prerequisites did not.

Two developments which occurred toward the end of the period under consideration suggest that the singing masters were anxious to find better methods of teaching those who failed to learn to read music by means of the traditional system of solmization.

The first of these developments was the introduction by Hans Gram, Samuel Holyoke, and Oliver Holden of the seven-syllable system of solmization which eliminated the confusing repetition of syllables in the four-syllable system. In 1793 these men pointed out in a book written

Figure 25. A page from William Little and William Smith's *Easy Instructor* (Albany: Printed by Webster & Skinner, and Daniel Steele, 1811), p. 51, containing two psalm tunes in shape note notation, "Brookfield" by William Billings and "Warren." Courtesy, American Antiquarian Society.

BROOKFIELD
Look down in pity Lord and see / The mighty woes that burthen me; / Down to the dust my life is brought
Like one long buried and forgot.

chiefly for the edification of their fellow singing masters that:

> In the German schools, the notes are named by seven different letters, viz. C, D, E, F, G, H, &c. The Italian schools make use of seven syllables, viz. *do, re, mi, fa, sol, la, si.* The French adopt the same method, excepting that in the place of *do,* they use the syllable *ut.*[227]

Unfortunately, the hold of tradition[228] was so strong, that an entire generation elapsed before the manifold advantages of a seven-syllable system[229] were commonly recognized.

The second of these developments was the invention of shape notes, which were designed to remedy one of the principal difficulties inherent in the four-syllable system, namely, the problem of assigning the proper syllables to the notes by inspection once the key had been determined by locating the *mi.* This problem was solved by altering the shape of the notes to conform to the sylla-bles involved.[230] Thus, in Little and Smith's *Easy Instructor* (Albany, 1798, and many later editions) the *mi* is shaped like a diamond, the like *fa* a tri-angle, the *sol* like a circle, and the *la* like a square (see *Figure 25*).[231, 232] In the later editions of Law's *Christian Harmony* (Windsor, 1805) the same shapes are used, but they are assigned to the sylla-bles in a different manner. The *mi,* as above, is shaped like a diamond; the *fa* is shaped like a square; the *sol,* as above, is shaped like a circle, and the *la* is shaped like a triangle (see *Figure 26a* and *b*).[233] The great advantage of the shape notes was that unlike the letter notation of Tufts's *Introduction,* both the names of the syllables and the duration of the notes were indicated by single characters.

Shape notes, or "buckwheat notes" as they were disdainfully called by the partisans of the new taste in music, did not come into their own until the following era, 1805–1860.[234] Their history[235] is, therefore, beyond the scope of the present book. They are mentioned here because they formed the basis for a vigorous choral tradition in the South,[236] which preserved the music of the New England singing master-composers long after it had been forgotten by their compatriots, and because they seem to have been the solution to the methodological problems which plagued the singing schools of the previous era. The fact that many singers of the previous era were presumably no more than semi-literate before the advent of shape notes must not be taken to mean that they were unable to participate successfully in the singing schools and choirs which they attended. Both the music, which was performed by these groups, and the vocal techniques, which were associated with its proper expression, were things which could be learned entirely by ear, if necessary. For this reason it is not surprising to find that most singing masters could and did turn out creditable performances with their groups in spite of the handicaps already mentioned. William Bentley, who was as astute an observer of the musical scene as the times afforded, recorded in his *Diary* a conversation with Samuel Holyoke concerning the latter's success in achieving perfect tonal homogeneity and perfect ensemble in the school which he taught in Newbury, Massachusetts.

> May 15, 1796....I went up to the South Parish in Boxford, & preached for Mr. Holyoke who has suffered & is impaired by a paralytic stroke. His Son Samuel who is eminent for his Musical publications, & his talents in the Instruction of Musical Companies was with us. His success was great in Newbury, in the society under Mr. Spring. He says that he rendered them so perfect, as to make

90 scholars sing in such harmony as that the parts could not be distinguished when intermixed, & that the voices of each part were sounded so as to be exactly the same. He shewed me beside his first Compositions, in 4to the *Massachusetts Compiler*, of which he & Hans Gram & Oliver Holden are the professed Editors.[237]

Bentley also recorded his impressions of an exhibition given by Andrew Law a week later in Salem.

> May 23, 1796. Mr. Law had a Musical Exhibition this evening, & persons were introduced only as they had tickets to be delivered at the door. He aims to have his music very soft, the Treble is the leading part, not one note of Tenour was heard through the Evening. The greatest good order prevailed, & the visiting Company was respectable. In their attempts to sing soft, many of the Voices do not accent the notes so as to enable the ear to distinguish the strains from soft murmurs. He must have had above one hundred Scholars.[238]

Taken separately or together these entries suggest that the better masters were quite skillful in obtaining the effects[239] which they desired from their singers.

In the final analysis the evaluation of an educational institution is best made, not in terms of the achievements of specific men who are active in its behalf, but in terms of the contributions which it makes to the society that sponsors it. The singing school played a vital role in the great flowering of choral music which took place in New England between 1760 and 1800. The final evaluation of the singing school as an educational institution will, therefore, be deferred until that role has been described.

Figure 26a. This is a reproduction of the psalm tune, "Stamford," taken from the first volume of Andrew Law's *Christian Harmony* (Cheshire, Conn.: Printed and sold by William Law, 1794), p. 48, where it appears in conventional notation. Its composer is unknown. Courtesy, American Antiquarian Society.

Original text:

STAMFORD

Love divine, all love excelling, / Joy of heaven to earth come down! / Fix in us thine humble dwelling,
All thy faithful mercies crown; / Jesus! thou art all compassion, / Pure unbounded love thou art; / Visit us with thy salvation,
Enter ev'ry trembling heart!

Alternate text:

Saviour, visit thy plantation, / Grant us, Lord, a gracious rain! / All will come to desolation, / Unless thou return again:
Keep no longer at a distance; / Shine upon us from on high; / Lest, for want of thine assistance, / Every plant should droop and die.

Figure 26b. A reproduction of the psalm tune, "Stamford," taken from the fourth edition of Andrew Law's *Christian Harmony* (Windsor, Vermont: Printed by Nahum Mower, 1805), p. 109, where it appears printed upon a "new plan," i.e., Law's shape note notation. Courtesy, American Antiquarian Society.

STAMFORD

1. Love divine, all love excelling, / Joy of heaven, to earth come down! / Fix in us thy humble dwelling,
All thy faithful mercies crown; / Jesus! thou art all compassion, / Pure, unbounded love thou art; / Visit us with thy salvation,
Enter every trembling heart!

2. Breathe, O breathe thy loving spirit, / Into every troubled breast! / Let us all in thee inherit, Let us find thy promis'd rest.
Take away the love of sinning, / Alpha and Omega be, / End of faith as its beginning, / Set our hearts at liberty.

3. Come, almighty to deliver, / Let us all thy life receive! / Suddenly return, and never, / Never more thy temples leave!
Thee we would be always blessing, / Serve thee as thine hosts above; / Pray and praise thee without ceasing;
Glory in thy precious love.

IV
The Golden Age of Choral Music

NATHANIEL GOULD, a later-day singing master, was of the opinion that the period from 1760 to 1800 should be characterized as a "dark age" in the history of church music because the works which were sung were "destitute of correct harmony."[1] In expressing this opinion, he was merely reiterating the criticisms which had been made earlier in the nineteenth century by the apostles of the new taste in religious music who insisted upon judging the homespun creations of the New England singing master-composers in terms of European art music. He no doubt felt these criticisms were well taken since the music of his predecessors contained demonstrable ineptitudes such as parallel fifths and octaves which were strictly forbidden by the rules of classical harmony. Furthermore, he probably found the imitative writing, the vigorous rhythms, and the melodic charm of their music alien to the ideal of congregational music which prevailed in his day.

The appreciation of the primitive in art is a twentieth-century phenomenon which has come about as the result of the deeper understanding which exists today concerning the nature of art and the relationship which it bears to the cultures which produce it. For this reason it is not surprising to find that those scholars who have examined the music of the "dark age" thoroughly have come to rather different conclusions regarding its worth. They have found that the so-called ineptitudes of this music have been so consistently used that they constitute the hallmarks of a genuine primitive style which is notable for its simplicity and expressiveness.[2] They have also come to realize that the place of this music in the life of the community far transcended the narrow implications of the word "psalmody." Allen P. Britton, who has studied all of the tune books published up to 1800, has noted this music was the product of "a vital musical culture" which had come into being during the closing years of the eighteenth century.[3] Richard Franko Goldman, who has compiled and published a modern edition[4] of selected works by Billings and his contemporaries, has concluded that this music was "the popular art of

New England; the folk song, the community singing material, the educational music of its time and place, the truly democratic art-form of a whole society."

Both Britton's and Goldman's conclusions have of necessity been based upon the music itself, because no detailed studies have been made to date of the social history associated with this music. The present chapter, which is devoted to the choirs and musical societies that were brought into being as the result of the singing schools, will serve to corroborate their conclusions and to demonstrate that the "dark age" was in reality a golden age of choral music.

The Establishment of Choirs

The establishment of choirs is a subject that is best introduced by picking up the threads of the historical discourse which was used to introduce the previous chapter. It will be recalled that it was the importation of two English tune books, William Tans'ur's *Royal Melody Compleat* (London, 1755, 1760, 1764–66) and Aaron Williams's *Universal Psalmodist* (London, 1763, 1764, 1765, 1770), which provided the impetus for the great flowering of a choral music that took place in New England between 1760 and 1800. *The Royal Melody Compleat*, which was republished eleven times between 1767 and 1774, was issued separately at first under its own title and later in combination with *The Universal Psalmodist* under the title, *The American Harmony*.[5] Of the two works, *The Royal Melody Compleat* (see *Figure 27*) was the most influential in introducing American singers to the beauties of choral music.

Some measure of the influence which Tans'ur's work had may be seen in three entries from a diary kept by John Tileston (1735–1826), who was the principal instructor at the North Writing School in Boston.

> Nov. 16, 1763. The Tans'ur Singers at my House.[6]
>
> Aug. 9, 1763. The Singers at my House.[7]
>
> Feb. 23, 1764. Singers at my House.[8]

Tileston was evidently a member of one of the first of many such groups of devoted amateurs who banded together to sing music composed by an important musician.

Those who enjoyed performing the new choral music at home soon found that they were severely handicapped in their singing on the Sabbath because they were dispersed throughout the meeting house. One of the prerequisites for successful part-singing is that the singers must be placed close enough to one another to ensure the proper coordination of their respective parts. Thus it is not surprising to find that during the years when *The Royal Melody Compleat* had its greatest influence those who sang "by Rule" began agitating for the right to sit together in order that they might receive "the Benefit of helping Each other in said Rule."[9]

The regular singers of the First Church in Boston were the first to receive permission to sit together as a choir. At the annual meeting of the church in 1758, the parish clerk noted in the records:

> It being suggested that a number of the Brethren, who were skillful singers, sitting together in some convenient place, would greatly tend to rectify our singing on the Lord's day, and render that part of Divine Worship more agreeable, it was Voted that the Committee appoint the Persons and Place.[10]

For reasons that went unrecorded the singers did not actually begin sitting together until 1761 when they were specifically directed to do so as a part of a larger plan "to encourage and revive the Spirit of Singing" in church.

> Voted, that a number of the best Singers among us be desired to sit together in some convenient place in the Meeting House; that the reading of the Psalms on the Sabbath day be omitted; that a committee be appointed to confer with the pastor as to the introduction of a new version of the Psalms.[11]

While the place assigned to the singers was also unrecorded, it may be assumed that they probably were seated downstairs, since this location was the one which was most often selected for the singers in other communities at this time.

The practice of seating the singers downstairs was a satisfactory one as long as they remained small in number. Once their ranks had been enlarged by the admission of additional singers from the singing school, the problem of seating them became acute.

Further expansion of the space allotted to them downstairs was usually out of the question because all of the remaining space was devoted to the pews of socially prominent members of the congregation. The only suitable place open to them was the gallery upstairs, which in some cases was reserved for the boys and the tithing man and in others for men and women of lesser social rank.[12]

The appropriation of part of the gallery for the choir, or "singing society" as it was most often called, was considered a serious matter. It meant that those who would be displaced by this move would have to be reseated elsewhere in the building and that additional money would have to be found for the necessary alteration of the seats. In Massachusetts the control and repair of the meeting house were matters which could only be settled by formal action of the town. The vote of the Town of Brookline concerning the seating of its choir is typical of many taken at this time.

> Thursday, Jan. 1, 1778. At a Meeting of the Inhabitants of the Town of Brookline, warned and assembled according to Law at the Meeting House....upon the Petition of the Singing Society, that they may be allowed to form certain Seats in the front gallery of the Meeting House, into a Pew for their better Accomodation, at their own Expense: Voted, that the Town will allow the Singing Society leave to form the requested Seats in the Gallery into a Pew for their better Accomodation, they making the desired Alteration at their own expense; reserving to the Town the absolute Right to alter or dispose of the same, whenever they think proper, the proposed Alteration to be under the Direction of the Selectmen, who are appointed a Committee for that Purpose.
>
> Voted, that this meeting be adjourned without day.
>
> Attest. William Thompson, Town Clerk.[13]

This vote not only meant that the singers of this town had secured a suitable location for themselves in the meeting house but also that they had achieved full recognition as a group to be reckoned with in future deliberations about the musical portion of the divine service.

The tabulation of the many town votes with regard to the seating of choirs provides valuable insight into the way in which choral music flowered in New England. From *Table 5* it is apparent

Figure 27. The frontispiece and title page of the second edition of William Tans'ur's *Royal Melody Compleat* (Newburyport, Mass.: Daniel Bayley, 1768). Courtesy, American Antiquarian Society.

that the first flowering took place in eastern Massachusetts at about the time when *The Royal Melody Compleat* made its first appearance on these shores. By the end of the first decade (1760–1770), at least ten,[14] and probably many more, choirs had been established and the first tune book[15] containing original music by a New England singing master-composer had been published. By the end of the second decade (1770–1780), the flowering of choral music was well underway in most areas. Choirs had been established in most of the larger towns of Connecticut and in many of the smaller towns of Massachusetts and New Hampshire. Furthermore, during this period many of the original choirs in Massachusetts, such as those of the towns of Beverly,

Essex, Ipswich, and Lincoln, were rejuvenated by the addition of new singers from the singing schools and reseated in the galleries of their respective meeting houses. By the end of the third decade, the flowering of choral music was complete in that choirs had been established even in the outlying areas of Maine and New Hampshire.

The establishment of choirs constituted an important turning point in the history of church music in New England for two reasons. First, the choirs succeeded in having lining-out abolished and in having the ban against the use of musical instruments in the meeting house removed. Second, the choirs enriched both the religious and civic observances of the community through the

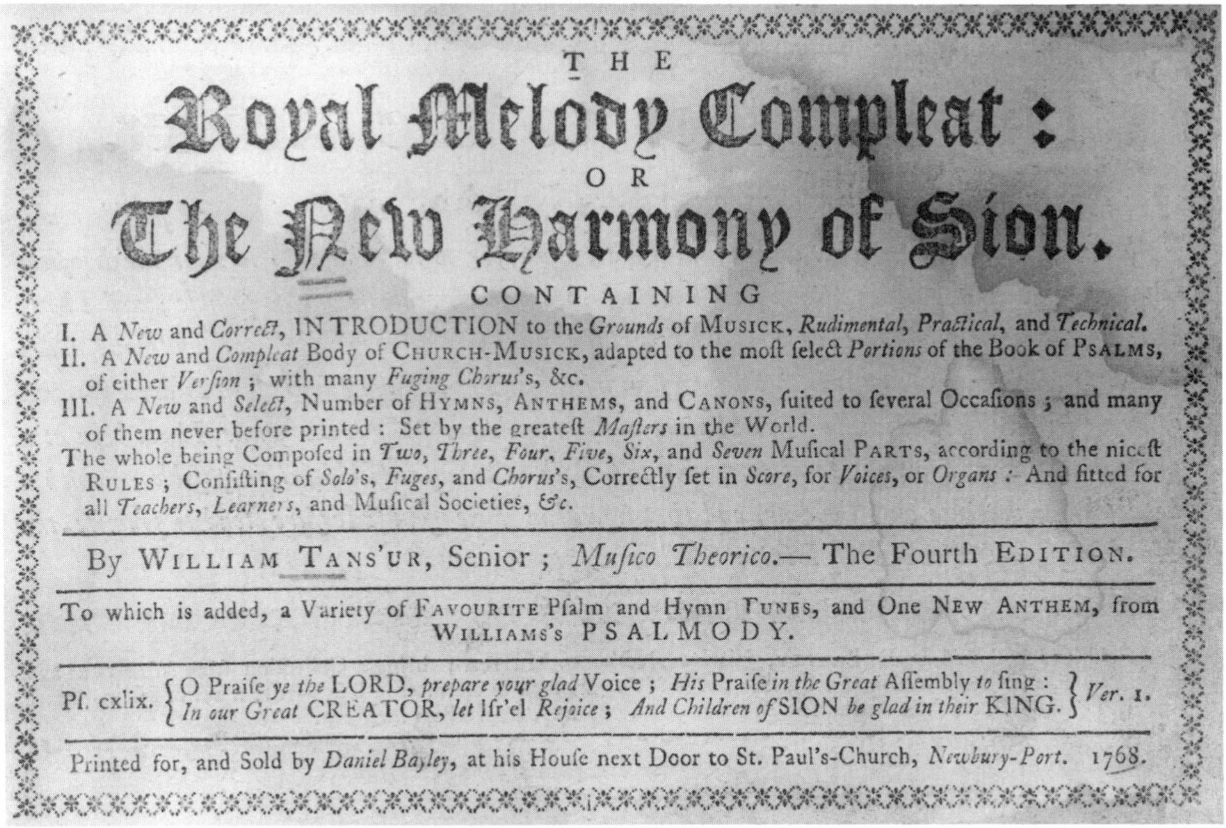

THE

Royal Melody Compleat:

OR

The New Harmony of Sion.

CONTAINING

I. A *New* and *Correct*, INTRODUCTION to the *Grounds* of MUSICK, *Rudimental*, *Practical*, and *Technical*.
II. A *New* and *Compleat* Body of CHURCH-MUSICK, adapted to the moſt ſelect *Portions* of the Book of PSALMS, of either *Verſion*; with many *Fuging Chorus's*, &c.
III. A *New* and *Select*, Number of HYMNS, ANTHEMS, and CANONS, ſuited to ſeveral Occaſions; and many of them never before printed: Set by the greateſt *Maſters* in the World.
The whole being Compoſed in *Two*, *Three*, *Four*, *Five*, *Six*, and *Seven* Muſical PARTS, according to the niceſt RULES; Conſiſting of *Solo's*, *Fuges*, and *Chorus's*, Correctly ſet in *Score*, for *Voices*, or *Organs*: And fitted for all *Teachers*, *Learners*, and Muſical Societies, *&c.*

By WILLIAM TANS'UR, Senior; *Muſico Theorico*.— The Fourth EDITION.

To which is added, a Variety of FAVOURITE Pſalm and Hymn TUNES, and One NEW ANTHEM, from WILLIAMS's PSALMODY.

Pſ. cxlix. { O Praiſe *ye the* LORD, *prepare your glad* Voice; *His* Praiſe *in the Great* Aſſembly *to* ſing: / *In our Great* CREATOR, *let* Iſr'el *Rejoice*; *And Children of* SION *be glad in their* KING. } *Ver.* 1.

Printed for, and Sold by *Daniel Bayley*, at his Houſe next Door to St. Paul's-Church, *Newbury-Port*. 1768.

Figure 27.

performance of a distinctive body of choral music composed by the singing masters.

In the days of unison congregational singing, the chief difficulty associated with the practice of lining-out was that of sustaining the pitch throughout the many antiphonal interchanges between the deacon and the congregation. This difficulty was compounded in the days of chorally supported congregational singing by virtue of the fact that instead of a unison pitch, three or four harmony parts had to be resumed each time after the deacon had read the line.

The earliest attempts to solve this difficulty involved having two parts sustain what must have been the final notes of their particular lines throughout the reading of the next line by the deacon. Both the advantages and the disadvantages of this solution were clearly set forth in a singing lecture delivered by the Reverend Lemuel Hedge at Warwick, Rhode Island, in 1772.

> But some may say, that they should not so strongly object against the practice of singing without reading, if it was not for the continuing the *Bass* and the *Treble* between the Lines, but this is so much sound without substance, and sounds so oddly and uncouthly to them, that they cannot away with it:—But such should know and consider that this *continuing* has its advantages; it keeps the musick alive, stretches the tune, and helps the better to strike into the same pitch again—and therefore ought not to be found fault with.[16]

The disadvantages evidently outweighed the advantages of this solution for shortly thereafter considerable clamor arose for the most logical solution of all, namely, dispensing with reading altogether. William Billings summarized the principal arguments in favor of this solution in his usual witty fashion.

> The practice* of retailing the psalm line by line was introduced so long ago was when very few people had the knowledge of reading; therefore a reader was substituted for the whole congregation, who was called a Clerk; but at this time when every man is capable of reading, for himself; and when we consider the confusion that is

caused in the music by reading the lines, and the destruction it occasions to the sense of the psalm, I see no reason for keeping up so absurd a practice. Consider further, that according to the practice in country churches the psalm is three times repeated. First the minister reads it audibly alone, secondly the clerk, or deacon, line by line, and thirdly, it is sung by the congregation; now if we are obliged to repeat the psalm three times over, why are we not obliged to repeat our prayers as often before they would be deemed to be acceptable.

* Whatever Mr. Clerk, or Mr. Deacon, or Mr. Anybody-else, who sustains the office of retailer may think; I shall take the liberty to tell them, I think it is a very gross affront upon the audience, for they still go by the old supposition, viz. the congregation in general cannot read; therefore they practically say, *we man of letters*, and *you ignorant creatures.*[17]

Those who advocated abandoning lining-out had not reckoned with the hold which tradition had upon the minds of their fellow parishioners. The best that they could achieve initially was a compromise whereby half of the psalms sung were to be lined out and half were to be sung "without reading." An account of a singing lecture given at Westborough in 1778 shortly after a sizable group of singers had graduated from the singing school into the choir serves to illustrate how this compromise was put into practice.[18] The Reverend Ebenezer Parkman noted:

Mar. 31, 1778. The Snow is so deep, that though a Lecture is appointed, I am in doubt whether the Preacher can get to us. Therefore I prepare myself. After Dinner the Storm being much abated, Mr. Foster, & Capt. Joseph How from Marlboro came. The former preach'd ye Singing Lecture from 1 Cor. 14.15. N.B. We sung at Entrance two staves of Hymn 80, 4 v. without *Reading*—after prayer—Sung Ps 57 from verse 5, 3 st. and the Deacon (Bond) read as usual line by line. The last Singing was Ps. 148, 6 stanzas to end of 12 v. After the Blessing, The Singers (who were increased in strength by some number from Marlboro (Dr. Curtis) & from Northboro (Capt. Sam Wood, his Daughter, & Sister, &c.) went on in Singing some tunes.

N.B. Old Mr. Hardy fell into an unhappy Frame, about ye Singers. Said their Behavior was abominable![19]

Although there were always a few reactionaries who refused to go along with agreements of this type, the majority of congregations seem to have been well satisfied with them, since they were put into effect in other towns such as Ashfield,[20] Beverly,[21] and Dracut[22] during this period.

This compromise was actually a victory for the more progressive elements of the congregations, because it gave them an opportunity to demonstrate the obvious advantages of "singing without reading" to one and all. The singers in Westborough thus succeeded in winning their congregation over to the newer way within two years after they had agreed to compromise.[23] Although the records of the actions taken by the towns mentioned above are incomplete on this point, it is likely that they followed the same pattern as Westborough. The movement to abandon lining-out struck at one of the deacons' most cherished rights and privileges. Some deacons gave up this right gracefully. Others, such Deacon Chamberlain of Worcester, attempted to stave off the inevitable by open defiance to the people's expressed wishes. In Worcester the congregation voted on August 5, 1779:

...that the singers in the front seats in the front gallery, and that those gentlemen who have hitherto sat in the front seats in said gallery have a right to sit in the front and second seat below, and that said singers have said seat appropriated to said use. Voted, that said singers be requested to take said seats and carry on the singing in public worship. Voted, that the mode of singing in the congregation here be without reading the Psalms line by line to be sung.[24]

On the Sabbath following this vote the singers proceeded to put these resolutions into effect knowing full well that the stage was set for combat with the conservative deacon who up until this time had ruled the musical destinies of the congregation.

...after the hymn had been read by the minister, the aged and venerable Deacon Chamberlain, unwilling to desert the custom of his fathers, rose and read the first line according to the usual practice. The singers, prepared to carry the alteration into effect, proceeded without pausing at the conclusion. The white-hatted officer of the church, with the full power of his voice read on, until the louder notes of the collected body overpowered the attempt to resist the progress of improvement, and the deacon, deeply mortified at the triumph of musical reformation, seized his hat, and retired from the meeting house in tears. His conduct was censured by the church, and he was for a time deprived of its communion, for absenting himself from the public services of the Sabbath.[25]

Battles[26] such as this one were not always so easily won by the progressive elements, but in time the deacons' power to control the singing was broken everywhere, leaving the choirs fully in command.

Once the deacons were in full retreat, the choirs next turned their attention toward having the ban against the use of musical instruments in divine service removed. They had excellent reasons for doing so. Experience in the singing school had taught them that a pitch pipe was an absolute essential for successful part-singing. Furthermore, they had come to enjoy and rely upon the support of such string and wind instruments as were available to them in the various singing schools which they had attended. The lack of these instruments made their singing on the Sabbath unnecessarily hazardous.

They began by agitating for the right to use the pitch pipe.[27] Where opposition was encountered it was used furtively at first and later more openly as more and more people in the congregation came to understand the necessity for its employment.[28]

Long used to the support of the "bass viol"[29] in the singing school, the choirs next sought its admission to the galleries of the meeting houses. Here they ran into stiff opposition from the conservative elements in the congregations, since the viol, unlike the innocuous pitch pipe, was clearly an instrument which was designed for extensive music making. The pros and cons of this move were debated endlessly in terms of Scriptural admonitions. The conservative elements quoted the Book of Amos, "Take thou away from me the noise of thy songs; for I will not hear the melody of thy viols." The progressive elements quoted other bits of Scripture in reply to show that various string and wind instruments had been used in Biblical times. The conservatives, ever-mindful of the Puritan prohibition against the use of musical instruments in the divine service, saw the introduction of the viol as the work of the Devil and proceeded to call the instrument the "Devil's fiddle." The progressives, well aware of the tonal support which the instrument lent to the singing of the Lord's praises, found no evil in its use and countered by naming it the "Lord's fiddle."[30]

As is usually the case in debates of this type, neither side succeeded very often in convincing the other as to the correctness of its position. In many instances the impasse was broken by the singers' decision to bring the viol to the meeting house regardless of the consequences. When the "Devil's fiddle" was played for the first time in the First Church in Roxbury (Thomas Walter's parish) in 1788, the "old pious people were horror-struck at what they considered a sacrilegious innovation and went out of the meeting in high dudgeon. One old church member stood at the church door and showed his contempt for the music by making a sort of caterwauling noise, which he called 'mocking the banjo.'" As the result of this episode, a meeting of all members of the church was called to discuss what action ought to be taken with regard to the viol. The progressive element succeeded in preventing the matter from ever coming to a vote, and the viol was used henceforth at all services.[31]

Once the bass-viol had been admitted to the meeting house, it was just a matter of time before other musical instruments were pressed into service. William Bentley, who was a conservative when it came to the "Catholic use" of the organ,[32] chronicled in his *Diary* the steps taken by the singers in his congregation to provide a satisfactory substitute for that instrument.[33]

> Dec. 25, 1792. For the first time in this place the Clarionet, & violin, introduced into Church Music. There is now no ground of complaint against the Catholics.[34]

> Oct. 28, 1795. Sent & purchased at Boston a Bass Viol for 21 dollars. The fondness for Instrumental Music in Churches so increases, that the inclination is not to be resisted. I have applied to Mr. Gardner to assist the Counter with his German Flute.[35]

The "fondness for instrumental music," which Bentley noted, increased not only in his own congregation[36] but also in most others to the point where gallery orchestras similar to the one described in the previous chapter became commonplace throughout New England.

The establishment of gallery orchestras opened up a whole new range of musical possibilities for the singing masters and their choirs. The masters saw at once that the instruments would be useful in supporting the weaker singers in their choirs when they negotiated the more difficult passages in the music. The choirs perceived their public appearances were greatly enhanced by presence of the instruments.

A review of a dedication service, which William Bentley attended, serves to demonstrate both the characteristic instrumentation of the gallery orchestras and the major contribution which they made to the music performed on special occasions.

Jan. 1, 1805. This day was appropriated for the dedication of the New South Meeting House at Salem. A large Band of music was provided & Mr. Holyoke took the direction. A double bass, 5 bass viols, 5 violins, 2 clarionets, 2 bassoons, & 5 german flutes composed the Instrumental music. About 80 singers, the greater part males, composed the vocal music. It could not have the refinement of taste as few of the singers were ever together before & most were instructed by different masters. But in these circumstances it was good. The House was crowded & not half that went were accomodated. Mr. Hopkins, the Pastor, performed the religious service of prayer & preaching, & Mr. Emerson of Beverly made the last prayer. The music had an excellent dinner provided for them at the Ship [tavern] & the 16 ministers present dined in elegant taste at Hon. Jno. Norris, Esq. the principal character in the list of the Proprietors of the new Meeting House.[37]

How the Puritan fathers would have reviewed the same service is best left to the imagination. The only thing lacking was the organ, that "Devil's box of whistles," and it too would one day grace the meeting houses of New England.

The Choir and Community Life

At the same time that the typical choir was correcting the unfortunate malpractices associated with the Puritan ideal of congregational music, it was building an important place for itself in the life of the community which it served. This life was centered around the meeting house where the Sabbath and the principal religious and civic holidays were observed.

"Church attendance on the Sabbath by no means turned out to be the chore that some historians of our godless age imagine it to have been."[38] The rural New Englander after a week of hard work tilling the soil on his farm looked forward to "goin' to meetin'" at the village because it meant an opportunity to greet his friends and neighbors, to discuss the events of the day, to receive intellectual and spiritual sustenance, and, after the choir had entered the picture, to satisfy his craving for musical beauty.

Attendance at the meeting house on religious and civic holidays was looked forward to with even greater pleasure by the rural New Englander because of the pomp and circumstance which always accompanied such observances. The pious sermons of the ministers, the inspiring speeches by the dignitaries, the colorful parades by the militia, the brilliant singing by the choir made these occasions the high points of an otherwise uneventful existence.

Before studying in detail the role played by the choir in some of these observances, it would be well to consider the choir as a musical association. The age groups which made up its membership, the persons who were responsible for its proper functioning after the singing master had left the community, the provisions which were made for its seating, and the music which was sung are pertinent topics for consideration.

Basically, the typical New England choir was a youth organization because it was succored by an institution which was dedicated to the education of youth through music. This point, which is made by all who wrote about New England music from the basis of their personal experiences, is clearly set forth in Harriet Beecher Stowe's description of the choir at Litchfield, Connecticut.

But the glory of our meeting-house was its singers' seat, that empyrean of those who rejoiced in the mysterious art of fa-sol-la-ing. There they sat in the gallery that lined three sides of the house, treble, counter, tenor, and bass, each with its appropriate leader and supporters. There were generally seated the bloom of our young people, sparkling, modest and blushing girls on one side, with their ribbons and finery, making the place as blooming and lively as a flower garden, and fiery, forward, confident young men on the other.[39]

It would be a simple matter to dismiss Mrs. Stowe's description as being as much the product of poetic license as of reality but for the fact that her assertions are faithfully born out by other documents.

William Bentley's "List of Intended Singers in 1792,"[40] which provides insight into the size of such organizations, proves that the membership of the typical choir included children, youth, and young adults. The fifty-eight persons whose names appear in this list range in age from five to thirty years. Their median age is seventeen and they are divided, statistically at least, into three

Figure 28. The title page of Oliver Brownson's *Select Harmony* (New Haven, 1783) contains the only contemporary picture extant of a New England choir performing in the gallery of the meeting house. The chorister may be faintly seen at the center near the top of the page holding a long pitch-pipe. Arrayed on either side of him in the men's and women's wings of the gallery are the members of the choir. A few parishioners may be seen in the pews below. The idea of placing a canon printed in oval form is obviously derived from Tans'ur's *Royal Melody Compleat.* The canon here, "Welcome, Welcome Ev'ry Guest," was a great favorite of New England singers who used it to open their singing meetings.

WELCOME, WELCOME EV'RY GUEST

Welcome, welcome ev'ry guest, / Welcome to our musick feast. / Musick is our only cheer, / Fills both soul and ravish'd ear. Sacred Nine teach us the mood, / Sweetest notes explor'd. / Softly moves the trembling air / To complete our concert fair.

---

subgroups: five to twelve years, fourteen to twenty-two years, and twenty-four to thirty years. Half of the total group are males and half are females. Curiously enough, no one over thirty years of age is listed. It can only be concluded that middle-aged and older persons, many of whom would have been styled as "heads of families," apparently were content to leave the choral singing to the younger generation.

The person who was chiefly responsible for the proper functioning of the choir in the absence of the singing master was the man who held the position of "chorister," or leading singer. Both he and the assistant leaders of each voice part were recruited from the ranks of the choir and were elected to their posts by popular vote. The Reverend E. H. Sears wrote that which is probably the most sympathetic description of the chorister ever to be penned by an alumnus of the singing

school. In his semi-fictional account of the choir at the town of "Oxford" he recalled:

The leading chorister was a tall, bilious, wiry-looking person by the name of Peter Bettis. You should have seen him in his glory, especially in the full tide of one of the "fuging tunes." His forces marshaled on each side of him, he would bend his lithe figure, now this way, now that way, throwing his voice into the bass and into the treble alternately, as if rolling a volume of song on each side out of his own inexhaustible nature. It really seemed, sometimes, as if all the other voices were touched off by his singing, like a row of gas lights breaking out in long lines of splendor by the touch of a single flambeau. Especially when they sang, as they very often did, the 122nd Psalm, proper meter:

"How pleased and blest was I
To hear the people cry,…"

you should have witnessed the strophes and anti-strophes, sometimes in jets and jahs, sometimes in billows, which the bass rolled back and forth and the treble rolled back again, and which then three living sides of the quadrangle would all take up anew, and bring down in one tremendous crash of harmony—Peter Bettis as the central figure, swaying with the inspirations riding on the whirlwind and directing the storm.[41]

Again, it would be an easy matter to dismiss this kind of account because of the excesses of the writer's style. In reality, Sears's account is correct in every respect. The choristers, unlike the choral conductors and choir masters of the present day, did sing along with their choirs while they performed. Furthermore, the music did roll and thunder back and forth in the manner described, because of the unique seating arrangement which was employed in the meeting house.

The typical gallery where the choir was seated was a "U-shaped" affair in which the chorister was placed at the bottom of the "U." From this position he could direct both the singers who were immediately before him and the singers in the two wings of the gallery by pivoting right and left. Some idea of this seating arrangement may be gained by perusal of the title page of Oliver Brownson's *Select Harmony* (New Haven, 1783) which is reproduced in *Figure 28*. To those who were seated downstairs facing the pulpit the sound appeared to come from three different directions: from behind, from the right, and from the left. This auditory impression was vastly magnified by the imitative writing employed in fuging tunes such as "Psalm 122" (see *Figure 29*), which caused the text to be tossed back and forth between the four voice parts. Only a Billings could do justice to the effect thereby achieved. In referring to the fuging tune he wrote:

> ...each part seems determined by dint of harmony and strength of accent to drown his competitor in an ocean of harmony, and while each part is thus mutually striving for mastery, and sweetly contending for victory, the audience are most luxuriously entertained and exceedingly delighted....their minds are surprisingly agitated and extremely fluctuated; sometimes declaring in favor of one part, and sometimes another. Now the solemn bass demands their attention, now the manly tenor, now the lofty counter, now the volatile treble, now here, now

there, now here again. O enchanting! O ecstatic! Push on, push on ye songs of harmony, and
Discharge your deep mouth'd canon,
 full fraught with Diapasons;
May you with Maestoso, rush on to
 Choro-Grando,
And then with Vigoroso, let fly
 your Diapentes
About our nervous system.[42]

The stirring fuging tunes which Billings described so enthusiastically formed but one part of the choirs' repertories. Short, straightforward psalm and hymn tunes in familiar style and long, through-composed odes, set-pieces, and anthems formed the remainder of the literature which they performed.

The titles of the odes, set-pieces, and anthems are of particular interest because they reveal the many ways in which the choirs enhanced the religious and civic observances of their respective communities. Odes for dedications and ordinations; set-pieces for Election Day and Independence Day; and anthems for Thanksgiving, Easter, Fast Day, and for funerals may be found in greater or lesser numbers in almost all of the important tune books written by the singing master-composers.

In New England, extraordinary preparations were made for the observance of Thanksgiving, because the citizens considered it to be the most important holiday[43] of the year. Included among these preparations was the study of special pieces of music which were to be performed in the gallery of the meeting house. In 1798 William Bentley chronicled the unusual manner in which the members of the parish singing school and the parish choir assisted the congregation in observing this holiday during the height of the young republic's troubles with France.

> Sept. 25, 1798. The celebrated song, *Adams and Liberty*, was sung at the Singing School. I paid for a copy of the verses to all the singers. It was written by Thomas Paine.[44]

> Nov. 29, 1798. Thanksgiving Day. There was Rain in the Morning but soon afterwards it cleared off & tho' the walking was wet, yet it was a pleasant day. The fame of our *Music* attracted many persons, especially the young, & the house was unusually full, but it did not add to the whole amount of the Poor's Contribution five dollars. The order of service was:

Figure 29. The "Hundred and Twentysecond Psalm Tune," P.M., by Amos Bull has been reproduced from the second edition of *Laus Deo!* (Worcester, 1788), p. 46. Courtesy, American Antiquarian Society.

HUNDRED AND TWENTYSECOND PSALM TUNE

How pleas'd and blest was I / To hear the people cry, / Come let us seek our God today; / Yes, with a cheerful zeal
We'll haste to Zion's hill / And there our vows and honours pay.

Opening with Instrumental Music. Two bass viols, tenour viol, 3 violins, hautboy, 4 G. flutes & voices.

Introductory prayer. 42 Hymn set to Music vocal, accompanied. Lecture. Instrumental music. Prayer. Particular metre, Barbault's Hymn 15th, set to music by Mr. Palfrey. Sermon. Instrumental during the Contributions. Anthem on the occasion. Prayer & Blessing, The Song of the Day, *Adams and Liberty.*[45]

Religion and politics were never very far apart in the New England psyche; thus the inclusion of a political song (see *Figure 30*) along with the usual anthem for Thanksgiving in the divine service was a perfectly acceptable procedure.

The same mixture of religion and politics is to be found in other civic observances of this period. In New Haven the singing master, Daniel Read, was employed for two weeks in preparing the music for the Independence Day Celebration of 1798. His description of the program[46] on that occasion is unusually complete, with one exception.

> Wednesday, July 4, 1798, Was awaked about four o'clock by firing Guns and ringing of Bells. At 9 o'clock went to the Meeting House to lead in the singing. About 10 the procession, which was formed in the New Township, arrived; when, after singing "Ocean," Doctor Dwight made a prayer; we then sang "Triumph" and Dr. Dwight gave a sermon from Rev. After which we sung "Bristol," and Mr. Webster delivered an Oration; the assembly was then dismissed and a procession formed, which Moved to the State House, where an entertainment was provided by Mr. Miles, of which about 350 people partook. After the Toasts were drunk I withdrew.[47]

The thing which is lacking is some indication concerning the textual content of the pieces employed in the musical part of the celebration. Several of the works mentioned by Read were cast in a definite metrical form which would have permitted their performance with new texts based

Figure 30. "Adams and Liberty," the Boston patriotic song. Written by Thomas Paine, A.M. For the pianoforte, German flute or violin. Third edition, corrected. Boston: Printed & sold by P.A. von Hagen & Co. at their pianoforte warehouse, No. 3 Cornhill. Oscar Sonneck in his *Bibliography of Early American Secular Music* notes, p. 2, that this edition was issued between May 1799 and Nov. 1800. As in the previous editions Paine's text is set to the tune of Samuel Arnold's popular drinking song, "To Anacreon in Heaven," which was later used for "The Star-Spangled Banner."

…creafe, with the glory of Rome, and the wifdom of Greece; And ne'er may the fons of Columbia be

flaves while the earth bears a plant, or the fea rolls its waves.

2

In a clime, whofe rich vales feed the marts of the world
Whofe fhores are unfhaken by Europe's commotion,
The Trident of Commerce fhould never be hurl'd
To incenfe the legitimate powers of the ocean.
But fhould Pirates invade,
Though in thunder array'd,
Let your cannon declare the free charter of Trade
For ne'er fhall the fons &c.

3

The fame of our arms, of our laws the mild fway,
Had juftly ennobled our nation in ftory,
Till the dark clouds of Faction obfcur'd our young day,
And envelop'd the fun of American glory.
But let TRAITORS be told,
Who their Country have fold,
And barter'd their God for his image in gold—
That ne'er will the fons &c.

4

While FRANCE her huge limbs bathes recumbent in blood,
And fociety's bafe threats with wide diffolution,
May PEACE, like the Dove, who return'd from the flood,
Find an Ark of abode in our mild CONSTITUTION.
But though PEACE is our aim,
Yet the boon we difclaim,
If bought by our Sov'reignty, juftice, or Fame.
For ne'er fhall the fons &c.

5

'Tis the fire of the flint, each American warms;
Let Rome's haughty victors beware of collifion!
Let them bring all the vaffals of Europe in arms,
We're a WORLD by ourfelves, and difdain a divifion.
While, with patriot pride,
To our Laws we're allied,
No foe can fubdue us — no faction divide.
For ne'er fhall the fons &c.

6

Our mountains are crown'd with imperial Oak,
Whofe roots, like our Liberties ages have nourifh'd;
But long ere our nation fubmits to the yoke;
Nor a tree fhall be left on the field where it flourifh'd
Should invafion impend,
Every grove would defcend,
From the hill-tops they fhaded, our fhores to defend.
For ne'er fhall the fons &c.

7

Let our Patriots deftroy Anarch's peftulent worm,
Left our Liberty's growth fhould be check'd by corrofion;
Then let clouds thicken round us, we heed not the ftorm,
Our realm fears nofhock, but the earth's own exploſion.
Foes affail us in vain,
Though their FLEETS bridge the main,
For our altars and laws with our lives we'll maintain.
And ne'er fhall the fons &c.

8

See the fierce ftorm of war Freedom's temple invade,
While a light breaks from heaven thro' clouds rent afunder,
On Glory's bright furlough, 'tis WASHINGTON'S fhade,
Defcends through the whirlwind to vanquifh the thunder
His fword from the fleep
Our foes long fhall keep,
And conduct, with its point, every flafh to the deep.
For ne'er fhall the fons &c.

9

Let Rome to the world found AMERICA'S voice fever:
No Intrigue can her fons from their Government;
Her pride is her ADAMS—his Laws are her Choice,
And fhall flourifh, till LIBERTY flumber forever.
Then unite, heart and hand,
Like Leonidas' band,
And fwear to the GOD of the ocean and land.
That ne'er fhall the fons &c.

Figure 30.

upon patriotic themes. The interchangeability of texts and tunes was one of the characteristic features of the sacred music of this period; thus it may be assumed that some of the favorite tunes such as "Ocean" were decked out with new texts appropriate to the day.

Some Independence Day celebrations were the occasion for the revival of the older patriotic hymns such as Billings's "Chester" (see *Figure 31*) which had achieved popularity as a marching tune during the Revolution. One such revival was noted by William Bentley in 1801 when he attended the Independence Day Celebration at Marblehead, Massachusetts.

> July 5, 1801. At the Celebration in Marblehead the public services were introduced by a New England Tune & Verses accomodated to it by Mr. Billings, who was the first man to introduce original composition in Church Music, & who composed several volumes, being self-taught. This man composed several pieces at the Commencement of the War & among other compositions was Chester, which still continues in common use. This was sung at Marblehead as appropriate, & in Billings' own verses. This was as appropriate as the Marseilles Hymn or the French *Ça ira*.[48]

Other revivals may well have included his psalm tune "Columbia,"[49] and his anthems, "Retrospect"[50] and "Independence."[51]

The custom of celebrating Election Day in New England by means of a combined religious and musical service seems to date to Walter's day. In 1724 Hugh Adams made reference to "the so Noble Singing Lecture at the New North Brick House of Prayer in Boston, yearly on the Day after Election of Councillors."[52] This custom seems to have spread to other communities throughout the region during the years which followed. In 1772 the Reverend John Ballantine preserved in his journal the details of a singing lecture held on Election Day in Westfield, Massachusetts.

> May 27, 1772. Election Day. Rev. Mr. Lathrop dined here. Singing Lecture, Mr. Lathrop preached. Very well attended. Tunes sung: Dalton, Landaff, Stevenson, 15th Psalm Tune, 2 Anthems. The whole service performed with decency and to general satisfaction.[53]

A few years later Noah Webster recorded his attendance at the "Public Singing" held in Hartford, Connecticut.

> Sept. 5, 1784. Heard Mr. Strong AM and Mr. Boardman PM. Attended Public Singing in the evening.[54]
>
> April 4, 1787. Public Singing at West-division. Music very good.[55]

It is not known whether these sessions, which were held on the eve of Election Day, included a singing lecture as part of the program.[56]

Interest in celebrating through music the successful functioning of the process of self-government seems to have reached its peak in the work of the singing master Jeremiah Ingalls of Newbury, Vermont. Ingalls included in his *Christian Harmony* (Exeter, 1805) an "Election Hymn" (see *Figure 32*) and an "Election Ode," the first of which celebrated the national elections and the second of which celebrated the state elections. These two works, which are so far removed from the artistic ideals of present-day composers, are best understood as heartfelt expressions of a youthful nation that was still mindful of the sacrifices which it had made to obtain the blessings of autonomy.

Many more public occasions associated with the religious life of the congregations might be cited. Ordinations, dedications, funerals, and even public spinning bees were enhanced by the singing of the choir. The last-named occasion is especially interesting because it shows how completely the choirs had been accepted by the congregations. A spinning bee, sponsored in 1788 by the parishioners of the First Church in Portland, Maine, a few years after the singing master Isaac Gage had set the town "in a blaze about singing," serves to elucidate this point.

> On the lst instant, assembled at the house of the Rev. Deane of this town, more than one hundred of the fair sex, married and single ladies, most of whom were skilled in the important art of spinning. An emulous industry was never more apparent than in this beautiful assembly. The majority of fair hands have motion to not less than sixty wheels. Many were occupied in preparing the materials, besides those who attended to the entertainment of the rest—provision for which was mostly presented by the guests themselves, or sent in by other generous promoters of the exhibition, as were also the materials for the work. Near the close of the day, Mrs. Deane was presented by the company with two hundred and thirty-six knotted skeins of excellent cotton and linen yarn, the work of the day, excepting about a dozen skeins which some of the company

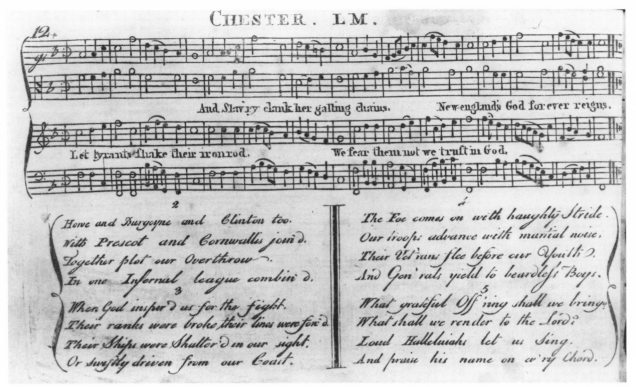

Figure 31. "Chester" by William Billings has been reproduced from the third edition of *The Singing Master's Assistant* (Boston, 1781). Billings first published this tune with the first verse only in his *New England Psalm Singer* (Boston, 1770). The remaining verses were added in 1778 when the first edition of *The Singing Master's Assistant* was published. Courtesy, American Antiquarian Society.

CHESTER

Let tyrants shake their iron rod / And slav'ry clank her galling chains, / We'll fear them not, we trust in God, / New-england's God forever reigns.

Howe and Burgoyne and Clinton, too, / With Prescot and Cornwallis join'd, / Together plot our overthrow, / In one infernal league combin'd,

When God inspir'd us for the fight, / Their ranks were broke, their lines were forc'd, / Their Ships were Shatter'd in our sight, / Or swiftly driven from our coast.

The Foe comes on with haughty Stride, / Our troops advance with martial noise, / Their Vet'rans flee, before our youth, / And Gen'rals yield to beardless boys.

What grateful Off'ring shall we bring, / What shall we render to the Lord? / Loud Halleluiahs let us Sing, / And praise his name on ev'ry Chord.

brought in ready spun. Some had spun six, and many not less than five skeins apiece. She takes this opportunity of returning thanks to each, which the hurry of the day rendered impracticable at the time. To conclude, and crown the day, a numerous band of the best singers attended in the evening, and performed an agreeable variety of excellent pieces of psalmody.[57] This spinning bee, like most others, was held in order to raise money for the Reverend Deane's salary, and, since hard cash was very difficult to come by, he was paid directly in the skeins that were spun that day. The picture of these good women of Portland dressed in their characteristic costumes, spinning away, chatting amicably with one another, preparing and serving refreshments, enjoying a choral concert at the close of the day is one that is not easily forgotten.

The Choir and Family Life

The members of the New England choirs appear to have been unable to get their fill of singing through ordinary means. To their performances at the morning and afternoon services on the Sabbath and their appearances on special occasions they added informal singing meetings

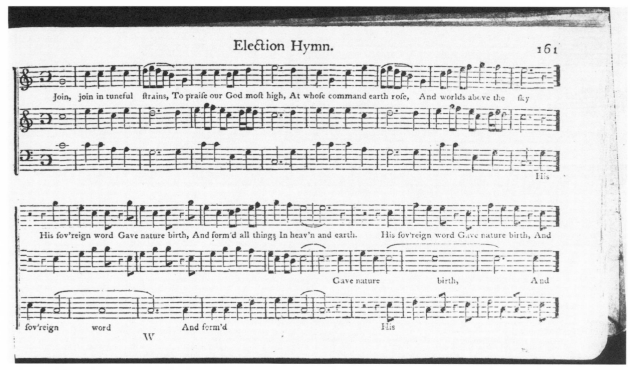

Figure 32. "Election Hymn" by Jeremiah Ingalls has been reproduced from his *Christian Harmony* (Exeter, 1805).

ELECTION HYMN

Verses

1–5. (See the musical pages.)

6. Quincy's illustrious Sage, / Wisdom's immortal friend, / May peace, a good old age, / And happiness attend; / And when from earth he wings his way, / Meet Washington in realms of day.

7. May Jefferson, our Chief, / In Cabinet and Field, / Check vice and party feud, / Be Order's friend and shield; / In virtue great, as in command, / Deal justice with impartial hand.

8. Lord, our Republic's Chief, / And Council; with thou guide; / In wisdom keep the House, / And over them preside; / May justice rule the public cause, / Example's aid enforce the laws.

9. To God let paeans rise, / His goodness loud proclaim, / Who, in this wilderness, / Rear'd Temples to his name; / Made Freedom's sons and Christians dwell, / Where late was heard the savage yell.

---

which took place in their own homes and in those of their friends.

Samuel Gilman in his semi-fictional account of a typical New England village choir notes that its members "when passing an evening with a few musical friends...preferred extracting an hour of rational pleasure from *The Village Harmony* to the frivolous entertainments of cards, coquetry, and scandal."[58] Gilman's observation about the choir of his youth is confirmed by entries from two diaries that were kept by two persons who were widely separated as to time and place. In 1778 the Reverend Ebenezer Parkman of Westborough, Massachusetts, chronicled the part-singing which took place under the guidance of the singing master Lemuel Badcock at his home one evening after the family religious exercise.[59]

> Mar. 29, 1778. This Eve. *Breck* and *Suse* & their *Billy Spring*, & with them, came *Mr. Badcock, Luke Wilder, Elisha Parker, & Sam'l Fisher*, to attend our Family Exercise and to Sing in which we spent the Evening.[60]

In 1797 the Reverend Paul Coffin of Buxton, Maine, recorded the part-singing which took place under the guidance of Mr. Smith, the local singing master, one evening at the home of Major Coburn in Pittston.

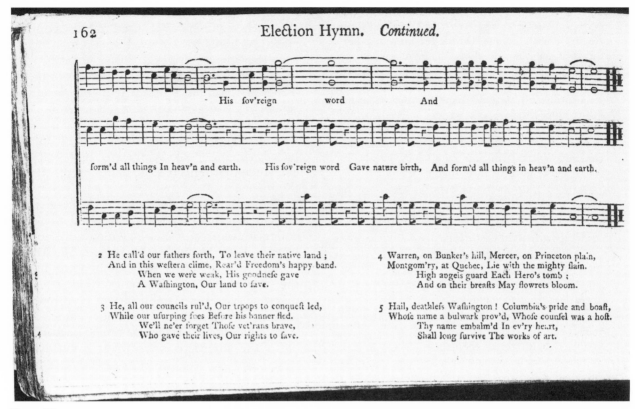

Election Hymn. *Continued.*

His fov'reign word And

form'd all things In heav'n and earth. His fov'reign word Gave nature birth, And form'd all things in heav'n and earth.

2 He call'd our fathers forth, To leave their native land ;
And in this weftern clime, Rear'd Freedom's happy band.
When we were weak, His goodnefs gave
A Wafhington, Our land to fave.

3 He, all our councils rul'd, Our troops to conqueft led,
While our ufurping foes Before his banner fled.
We'll ne'er forget Thofe vet'rans brave,
Who gave their lives, Our rights to fave.

4 Warren, on Bunker's hill, Mercer, on Princeton plain,
Montgom'ry, at Quebec, Lie with the mighty flain.
High angels guard Each Hero's tomb ;
And on their breafts May flowrets bloom.

5 Hail, deathlefs Wafhington ! Columbia's pride and boaft,
Whofe name a bulwark prov'd, Whofe counfel was a hoft.
Thy name embalm'd In ev'ry heart,
Shall long furvive The works of art.

Figure 32.

Oct. 21, 1797. Sabbath. Pittston. Major Coburn. Preached from Mark 16: 15–16 and Mark 12: 34. The hearers gave good attention. I believe they were satisfied. Had good singing. In the evening Major Coburn, Mr. Smith, singing master, his son-in-law, his daughters and their cousin Sally Coburn sang some excellent tunes.[61]

Some idea of the music which was sung on these musical evenings may be gained from the tune books which were employed by the singers. Ebenezer Parkman's manuscript singing book, which he had begun in the days of the Society for Promoting Regular Singing and which he had given to his daughter Sophia at the time of Mr. Badcock's arrival in the community, has survived to the present day. Preserved within its pages is a collection of the most popular sacred and secular music of his time. Psalm tunes like "St. Martin's" and "Mear," drum and fife tunes like "To Arms" and "Britons Strike Home," jig tunes like "The Jolly Young Swain" and "Rigadoon," and ballads like "Love Triumphant" are ingenuously placed side by side without the slightest concern for their diverse character.[62]

The printed tune books, which were presumably used by Paul Coffin's friends, also provide insight into the music which was sung and played during these musical evenings at home. These books contained in addition to the usual psalm tunes, fuging tunes, and anthems a considerable number of delightful quasi-religious pieces which, while not suitable for employment in the meeting house on the Sabbath, were ideal for use in a family setting. Among these pieces were canons like Billings's "Wake Every Breath" (see the frontispiece), carols like Billings's "Judea" (see *Figure 33*) and glees like Maxim's "Machias" (see *Figure 34*).

Many more recorded instances of family music-making might be cited to show how the choirs were instrumental in bringing about a rich musical life within New England households.[63, 64] Indeed, the "musical families of Billings's day were those which participated in and enjoyed to the utmost the homespun choral music that was all about them. William Bentley has left a charming description of one such family in his *Diary.*

Jan. 20, 1798....the Son plays well on a Bass Viol, & the g. daughter sings well, while the Father retains a sweet voice, even after fifty, and performs in the Meeting House. They had made the largest collection of Music I had ever seen in private hands; entirely church music & all American publications. It is to be regretted that America has produced so few good writers of Music; when there is so ready sale for all works which pretend to the name. To love to sing & the readiness to continue without disgust or apology, speaks in favour of the best music of the heart.[65]

This family, like so many others, seems to have realized the singing masters' ideal which Solomon Howe enunciated so beautifully in his *Farmer's Evening Entertainment.*

> When lab'rers quit their cares for rest,
> With calm content and friendship blest;
> They may their ev'ning hours employ
> In gratitude and social joy.
>
> Sweetly their tuneful voices join,
> To show their Maker's praise divine;
> Sincere delight attends their songs,
> In their united hearts and tongues.
>
> Domestic Pleasures cheer their mind,
> While male and female voices join'd;
> Attract the heart and charm the ear,
> And GOD supreme delights to hear!
>
> Thus let our tuneful voices prove,
> The means of friendship, peace and love;
> Improved to serve and honor GOD,
> Prepared for His sublime abode.[66]

The Establishment of Collegiate Musical Societies

The singing schools and choirs played such an important role in the lives of New England youth that when they attended the college of their choice they sought ways in which they might continue to enjoy the pleasures of music. Some, like Robert Treat Paine (Harvard A.B., 1749), enrolled in local singing schools in the college town where they lived.

> Feb. 7, 1749. I joined myself to a Singing Society taught by Mr. Edward Manning.[67]

Others, such as the eighteen members of the Class of 1787 at Yale College who joined together in their sophomore year under the sponsorship of Tutor Baldwin,[68] formed singing schools of their own within the college walls and engaged one of their more musical fellow students to instruct them.[69]

While little specific information concerning the method and materials used in these collegiate singing schools has survived, it is reasonably certain that they employed the same ones which were used in the other singing schools of the day. Three of the more prominent members of these schools, Chauncey Langdon (Yale A.B., 1787), Samuel Holyoke (Harvard A.B., 1789), and Andrew Law (College of Rhode Island A.B., 1775) published singing books early in their respective careers which reflected the common practices of their time.

The most important outcome of these singing schools was that they led to the foundation of the collegiate musical societies which are known to have been active during this period. The Musical Society of Yale College is a case in point. In 1786, the year after Tutor Baldwin's singing schools, this society attracted public attention through the medium of an advertisement for Daniel Read's *American Musical Magazine* which mentioned as one of the conditions governing its publication:

> *Secondly*, No Pains will be spared in procuring and selecting a variety of the newest and most approved Pieces of Musick, both from British Authors, and American Composers; and no Piece will be published, without being previously examined and approved by the *Musical Society of Yale College.*[70]

In the same year it attracted further attention through another advertisement, which announced the publication of Langdon's tune book.

> Beauties of Psalmody
> a new
> SINGING BOOK
>
> Compiled by a Member of the Musical Society of Yale College. Price Two Shillings and Six-pence.
>
> To be Sold by Amos Doolittle, at his House in College Street; by Mr. Chauncey Langdon, Member of the Musical Society of College; by Mr. Hitchcock, Singing Master, at the House of Mr. John Pierpont.
>
> The Book is calculated one purpose for the Use of Singing Schools; and contains (besides a Selection of the most approved Psalm-Tunes and Anthems) the necessary Rules of Music, so that Learners may, with a little attention, make great Proficiency in that Noble Art.[71]

Harvard also had a musical society at about this time and knowledge of its existence similarly may be derived from an advertisement for a tune book published by one of its members.

Figure 33. "Judea" by William Billings has been reproduced from the third edition of *The Singing Master's Assistant* (Boston, 1781). Courtesy, American Antiquarian Society. It is typical of the many Christmas pieces written by the singing master-composers who, along with their singing scholars, did not subscribe to the Puritan belief that Christmas was a Popish holiday and should therefore not be observed. Pieces such as "Judea" were sung at home instead of at the meeting house.

JUDEA

A Virgin unspotted ye Prophet foretold / Should bring forth a Sav'our which we now behold /
To be our Redeemer from Death, Hell, & Sin / Which Adam's transgression involved us in. /
Then let us be merry put Sorrow away / Our Sav'our Christ Jesus was born on this Day.

SACRED MUSICK PROPOSAL

For Printing (typographically) by Subscription, an Original composition Entituled,

HARMONIA AMERICANA

Containing a Variety of Airs, suitable for Divine Worship, and the use of Musical Societies; consisting of Three and Four Parts. by

SAMUEL HOLYOKE.

Student at the University, Cambridge.

RECOMMENDATION

Ever desirous of encouraging a taste for the pleasing and improving art of Musick, we are happy in having an opportunity to recommend to the world the "Harmonia Americana." Having perused the composition, and heard a number of pieces performed, we most cheerfully recommend it to the publick. We think the Musick far more expressive of the sentiment it attempts than any American composition now extant. It indicates ingenuity in the Author and is worthy the patronage of every friend of genius. Should this original composition meet with encouragement, we think it may be a means of reforming the present taste for musick, and of promoting an important part of divine worship. We esteem it an honour to patronize so valuable a work, which we flatter ourselves will meet the generous encouragement of the musical world.

From the Singing Club of the University,

J. D. Dunbar, Secr'y.[72]

Perusal of the list of subscribers to this book reveals that its author received in addition to the support of his fellow students the backing of the President (Willard), the Hollis Professor of Divinity (Wigglesworth), the Hollis Professor of Natural Philosophy (Webber), and the Professor of Orien-

Figure 34. "Machias" by Abraham Maxim has been reproduced from the fifth edition of *The Village Harmony* (Exeter, 1800), a tune book which was a great favorite of those who sang at each other's homes in the evenings. The text of "Machias," which expresses the fellowship of small-group singing so well, was common property among the singing master-composers at this time. Examination of other tune books reveals that nine out of ten of them contain one or more musical settings of this text.

MACHIAS

How pleasant 'tis to see / Kindred and friends agree, / Each in their proper station move; / And each fulfill their part / With sympathizing heart / In all the cares of life and love.

---

tal Languages (Pearson), as well as that of students at Dartmouth College and several of the more prominent singing masters, such as Ichabod Johnson and Abraham Wood.

These two tune books supply a partial index to the repertories of the Musical Society of Yale College and the Singing Club of the University. Chauncey Langdon's *Beauties of Psalmody* is one of the most aesthetically pleasing compilations of early American music ever made. Included within its covers are such works as Swan's "Rainbow," Edson's "Lenox," Billings's "Maryland," and Read's "Amity." Holyoke's *Harmonia Americana* is fine in its own way too, since it contains a large number of solidly constructed pieces in a conservative style.

It appears unlikely that the repertory of either organization was restricted to the psalm tunes, fuging tunes, and anthems in the tune books published by their respective members. Langdon also compiled a delightful little songster which covered the subjects of wine, women, and song very thoroughly. Yale men who sang from this book were familiar with drinking songs such as "The Flowing Bowl" and "The Tipler's Defence"; love songs such as "The Despairing Damsel" and "The Disappointed Lover"; and ballads such as "The Frog and Mouse" and "The Death of General Wolfe."[73] Harvard men were also probably well acquainted with music dealing with these subjects but no direct evidence to this effect has survived other than the cryptic reference to undergraduate singing made by John Quincy Adams (Harvard A.B., 1787). While in Newburyport he noted in his diary:

Jan. 3. 1788. Pass'd the evening at Little's in Newbury. A Mr. Coffin, who graduated two years ago at Harvard, was there. We spent our time in sociable chat and in singing; not such unmeaning, insignificant songs as those with which we killed our time last evening, but good, jovial, expressive songs such as we sang at College, "when mirth and jollity prevail'd." One evening of this kind gives me more real satisfaction than fifty pass'd in a company of girls. (I beg their pardon.)[74]

Considering the scope of musical activity at these and other colleges, it is not surprising to find that collegiate ceremonies were often enriched by the performance of musical compositions written by the students themselves. Morison has noted that the Harvard commencement program for 1771 included "an Anthem, composed, set to music and performed by some of the Students."[75] Lord has found that the Dartmouth commencement program for the same year included an anthem which was "composed and set to music by the young gentlemen, candidates for a degree."[76]

That Yale also had student composers is attested to by an entry from President Ezra Stiles's diary.

Dec. 17, 1783. Quarter Day. For the first time I admitted a Flute in Chapel with the vocal music. The Exercises thus performed by the Senior Class:
Music—Psalm Tune "Stratford." Lat. Orat. by Prentice. 5'
Music—Poem by Col. Humphry. Tune. "Washington." Dialogue by Cone, Fowler, Hinman Roe. 33' Eng. Orat. by Basset. 9'
Music—Poem by Marsh, a Sen. Soph. Set to music by a Sen'r.
Begin III h 15 PM, End IV h 31.[77]

The identity of the composer in question is, as in the case of the Harvard student mentioned above, unknown.

The significance of these collegiate singing schools and musical societies is twofold. First, they supplied informally many of those things which are provided by present-day college music departments and singing clubs.[78] Second, they were instrumental in training and sending back to the communities from which they came, men who organized singing schools and musical societies that played an important role in the history of American church music.

The societies which these college-trained men founded were largely responsible for the reforms that brought about profound changes in the public taste during the years from 1803 to 1825. The first of these societies was the Essex Musical

Association which was established in 1797 in Boxford, Massachusetts, by Samuel Holyoke. The chief objective of this group according to Jacob Kimball (Harvard A.B., 1780), was "the ameliorating and refining the Taste for Music in this Country."[79]

The Association sought to achieve its objective by three means. First, it encouraged the production of tune books written in a conservative style. Both Kimball and Holyoke assisted them in this good work by writing a tune book apiece along the lines suggested by the group.[80] Second, they gave yearly exhibitions[81] at which prominent men spoke about the need to reform the public's taste in church music. Third, they limited their membership to the singing masters and choristers from Essex County. This last-named restriction made their group in effect the first bona fide music teachers' organization in America.[82]

The changes in taste promulgated by the Essex Musical Association meant the abandonment of the primitive style of traditional New England music. This style of music was not without its champions, fortunately. Elijah Dunbar (A.B., 1760) who "learned while going through Harvard in addition to his Latin and Greek the art of reading music," returned upon his graduation to his home town, where he commenced teaching singing and common schools. In time, as the result of efforts and those of other singing masters such as John Stickney and William Billings, the community of Canton became alive with music. People held singing meetings at each other's homes and sang from the new singing books which they introduced. Eventually an interested group of singers formed the Stoughton Musical Society which drew its membership from Canton and Stoughton. Dunbar, who was elected its first president in 1786, made it into one of the staunchest defenders of the primitive New England style of music during the twenty-one years that he held that office.[83]

The story of the reform of church music during the period from 1803 to 1825 is beyond the scope of the present book. When it is told, it will be found that the graduates of Dartmouth College, which had supported a musical society from 1785 onward, played a very important role in the reformation. The same pattern of making music at college, teaching singing schools after graduation, and founding musical societies was followed by

John Hubbard, Asa McFarland, and others. Dartmouth also trained several of the most important reform-minded divines such as Worcester, Dana, Palmer, and Parish.

The chronicle of the collegiate musical societies brings the story of the singing school back to the scenes of its birth and early childhood. Brought into being by musically literate college men, it served during its infancy to introduce the people of New England to the world of choral music. Later when it was full-grown, it returned to the colleges where it was given redirection and sent back to serve the people once again.

The significance of the contributions made by the choirs and the musical societies to the musical life of New England may be estimated in two ways. First, the richness of musical life which existed in Bentley's day after the establishment of choirs and societies might be compared with the drabness of musical life which existed in Sewall's day before the advent of regular singing. Second, the musical life of New England in Bentley's day might be compared with the musical life of the rest of the nation.

The first comparison is so easily made from the materials which have been presented thus far and the conclusions which might be drawn are so obvious that it will not be undertaken here. The second comparison is not so easily made because of the many aspects of music involved and because of the lack of a suitable yardstick by means of which measurements might be obtained. In spite of these difficulties the second will be undertaken here because it will serve to confirm the hypothesis that the period from 1760 to 1800 was a golden age of choral music in New England.

The musical life of a nation may for convenience be studied in terms of the two basic categories of music, i.e., sacred and secular music. The comparison of the musical life of different regions within a nation ideally ought to include consideration of music in both categories. In the present study an all-inclusive examination of musical activity is impractical because the magnitude of the task is so great and because the scholarly studies of related topics are not complete enough to ensure that valid conclusions have been reached. For these reasons the second comparison will be restricted to a consideration of the area of sacred music with special reference to the manner in which it was practiced by the various denominations.

A future president of the United States, John Adams, unwittingly provided the musical historian with that which is probably the best single yardstick for measuring the musical life enjoyed by the various denominations in America. A great traveler and a faithful diarist, Adams recorded in his diary his impressions of all the places that he visited on the several journeys which he made in pre-revolutionary days. While on these journeys he made it a practice to attend the religious services of other denominations as well as those of his own. Since he was both a musical[84] and a pious man, he often included his impressions of the sacred music which was sung, along with his reactions to the sermons which were preached at these services. The entries in his *Diary* concerning two journeys which he took long before he became president contain some of the most penetrating observations on the congregational music of this period that were ever written.

In the spring of 1771 Adams journeyed to Stafford Springs, Connecticut, to partake of the waters there. A side journey to Hartford by way of Somers and Windsor found him one Sabbath in the village of Middletown.

> June 9, 1771. Went to meeting in the morning, and tumbled into the first pew I could find. Heard a pretty sensible Yalensian Connecticutsian preacher. At meeting I saw Dr. Eliot Rawson, an old school-fellow; he invited me to dine....Went to meeting with him in the afternoon, and heard the finest singing that ever I heard in my life; the front and side galleries were crowded with rows of lads and lasses, who performed all their parts in the utmost perfection. I thought I was rapt up; a row of women all standing and playing their parts with perfect skill and judgment, added a sweetness and sprightliness to the whole which absolutely charmed me.[85]

On this occasion he was privileged to hear a New England youth choir at its very best.

In the summer of 1774 Adams journeyed to Philadelphia, Pennsylvania, to attend the Continental Congress. This trip, which was made by way of New York and New Jersey, permitted him to compare the music and theology of New England with that which was found in some of the other colonies at this time.

While in New York City he visited the Old Presbyterian Society, which still sang in the unreformed way.

> Aug. 21, 1774....in the afternoon we...heard Mr. Treat from "These shall go away into everlasting punishment."...the psalmody is an exact contrast to that of Hartford; it is in the *old way*, as we call it—all the drawling, quavering, discord in the world.[86]

A few days later he stopped at Princeton, New Jersey, where he found that the scholars at Nassau Hall College sang in the same manner as the rest of their denomination.

> Aug. 27, 1774....by this time the bell rang for prayers; we went into the chapel; the President soon came in, and we attended. The scholars sing as badly as the Presbyterians at New York.[87]

After he arrived in Philadelphia, he proceeded to visit a different church each Sabbath. On the first Sunday he visited both the Presbyterians and the Anglicans and compared them with the Congregationalists at home.

> Sept. 4, 1774. Went to the Presbyterian meeting, and heard Mr. Sprout in the forenoon. He uses no notes;...opens his Bible and talks away. Not a very numerous nor very polite assembly....Went in the afternoon to Christ Church and heard Mr. Coombe. This is a more noble building, and a genteeler congregation. The organ and a new choir of singers were very musical. Mr. Coombe is celebrated here as a fine speaker; he is sprightly, has a great deal of action, he speaks distinctly. But I confess I am not charmed with his oratory; his style was indifferent; his method confused. In one work, his composition was vastly inferior to the ordinary sermons of our How, Hunt, Chauncy, Cooper, Eliot, and even Stillman.[88]

In the evening of the second Sunday, he attended the Moravian church where he heard German congregational music for the first time.

> Sept. 11, 1774....we drank coffee, and then Reed, Cushing, and I strolled to the Moravian evening lecture, where we heard sweet music, and a Dutchified English prayer and preachment.[89]

The third Sunday evening he visited the Quaker meeting house but found no music there.

Two weeks after his visit to the Quakers he put aside his New Englander's fear of popery and visited the Catholic chapel, where he heard Gregorian chant for the first time.

> Oct. 9, 1774. Went in the afternoon to the Romish chapel and heard a good discourse upon the duty of parents to the children, founded in justice and charity. The scenery and the music are so calculated to take in mankind, that I wonder the Reformation ever succeeded. The paintings, the bells, the candles, the gold and silver; our Saviour on the Cross, over the altar, at full length, and all his wounds bleeding. The chanting is exquisitely soft and sweet.[90]

Four weeks after his visit to the Quaker meeting he attended the Baptist church in the afternoon and heard a genuine backwoods preacher but no music worthy of notice. In the evening of the same day he attended the Methodist meeting, where he heard the Wesleyan congregational hymns for the first time.

> Oct. 23, 1774....I went to the Methodist meeting and heard Mr. Webb, the old soldier, who first came to America in the character of quarter-master under General Braddock....the singing here is very sweet and soft indeed; the first music I have heard in any society, except the Moravians, and once at church with the organ.[91]

Adams's observations concerning the state of music in the various denominations in New York and Philadelphia indicate that each one sang in accord with its own traditions. Of these denominations only the Anglicans, the Moravians, and the Methodists seem to have been successful in developing good congregational singing. Some of the others, of course, did not approve of singing and only later included it in their religious services.

Of those which did develop good congregational singing, only the Anglicans seem to have also developed a choir that was worth mentioning. However, even after due allowance is made for manifestations of regional pride in Adams's observations, it is apparent that this choir was nowhere near being the equal of the choir of "lads and lasses" at Middletown.

Now the crux of the matter is simply that the excellence of these lads and lasses was not in any way unique. Their successes were repeated again and again by other groups of young people throughout the whole of New England as the singing masters made their way from town to town.

That their region was well ahead of the rest of the country in the area of church music was a fact that was fully appreciated by New Englanders at this time. In 1785 Noah Webster[92] found the singing in Baltimore congregations woefully underdeveloped and the choral music in Charleston hopelessly under the spell of the Handelian style. In 1793 Daniel Read[93] advised a young singing master to go to the South where his services and his singing books would be very much in demand because the area was practically virgin territory, musically speaking. In 1792 Andrew Law belittled Philadelphia's first important institution devoted to instruction in church music, the Uranian Academy, which had been founded in 1785 by Andrew Adgate. Law said that it was really no more than a common singing school and that there were "a thousand schools of equal importance in the United States," i.e., chiefly in New England.[94]

In the final analysis the number of singing schools is not sufficient in itself to prove that the period from 1760 to 1800 was a golden age of choral music in New England. The ultimate proof lies in the extent to which the singing schools had enabled the average person to make music a part of his life. The New Englander, who had attended singing schools in his youth, sent his own children to them that they too might profit from the instruction which was offered. He graced the singing lectures and singing exhibitions which were given at the close of the school with his presence. He participated in their singing at home. He assisted them when they were in the choir by voting in favor of all of the various projects necessary for its proper operation. He acknowledged the leadership of their collegiate musical societies. He encouraged their singing masters by purchasing their tune books and by engaging them to write occasional music for civic observances. In short, he and his children, no less than the musical amateurs of Elizabethan England, made their age a golden age of choral music.

CONCLUDING REMARKS: The history of education in America should be regarded as more than the mere record of men and events; rather, it ought to be interpreted as the chronicle of a new society striving to provide educational opportunities commensurate with the needs of a growing nation. In the early days of the Republic, opportunities for an extended, formal education were available to very few, the great majority of people receiving no more education than that which was offered by the common school and the grammar school. By modern standards the offerings of these schools were very limited in scope because they encompassed no more than the "three R's" and a little Latin. As a result of this fact, when the need for special education arose, various private agencies were set up to meet the demand. Among these agencies were the countless little schools taught by individuals who made a living by offering instruction in those branches of learning in which they possessed special competency. In this manner modern languages, navigation, law, bookkeeping, dancing, drawing, and other subjects were made available to those who desired to improve their educations.

In the narrowest sense the Yankee singing school, which was held in the evening like the above-named schools, was just another private tutorial venture. In the broadest sense, however, it was much more important than these undertakings. Instituted to achieve narrowly defined objectives in the areas of congregational music, it was endowed with much wider aims by the singing scholars and the singing masters. The former transformed it into a thing of their own making, a veritable youth movement, which filled valid recreational needs. The latter also made it serve their own purposes in that it was at once the stimulus of and the outlet for the original music which they were wont to write. Thus, it may be concluded that the singing school far transcended the other types of evening schools which only occasionally captured the public imagination and which rarely were the stimulus for creative activity. Furthermore, because it helped to raise the general level of American culture when few had access to intellectual or artistic disciplines, the singing school ought to be included with the Lyceum as one of the major movements in popular education.

The history of early American music, like the history of early American education, should be regarded as more than the mere record of men who labored blindly, but nobly, outside the mainstream of Western music. Rather, it should be interpreted as the chronicle of a society which had to forge a musical life for itself out of the materials at hand and which would in due time build a musical culture that would be the equal of any in the Western world.

As the creation of a provincial society, the singing school inevitably reflected the values of those who brought it into being. As their values changed, it changed; and as the cultural conditions changed, it was re-oriented towards the further development of those benefits which had accrued from its operation. Thus, once a musical culture consisting of a goodly number of musically literate amateurs and a small number of semi-professional music teachers had come into existence, it was inevitable that the advent of an appropriate stimulus would cause the singing school to develop still further. This development was characterized by the establishment of choirs in nearly every village and town in New England and by the production of a great many original choral compositions, both of which were symptomatic of a burgeoning choral tradition.

This tradition, which placed New England in the musical vanguard of Federalist America, in turn formed the foundation for still later developments in the history of music in America. Public school music, which was the creation of a later-day New England singing master, might well have died stillborn but for the comparatively high level of musical culture which prevailed in New England at the time of its birth. The singing school had taught the people to know and love music; thus the extension of music instruction to all children enrolled in the public schools was no more than the logical extension of existing practice. The amazing survival of the singing school and its music to modern times in parts of the South, a development which was studied by George Pullen Jackson, becomes more credible when it is viewed in terms of the hardiness of the parent institution and the affection with which it was held by the common people.

The true significance of the Yankee singing school did not escape the attention of the more thoughtful New Englanders of the mid-nineteenth century. A contributor to *Dwight's Journal of Music* noted in 1853 that "Psalm tunes are worth attending to. They have their influence, and a mighty influence over the nation. It was Billings and Psalm-singing that prepared, in the course of years, this Yankee people for the *Messiah*,...the *Creation*, and the *Mount of Olives*."[95] The editor of another journal had made the same point even more succinctly two years earlier in a eulogy to the Yankee singing master. With deep insight he wrote, "The singing master of old time will soon be obsolete, having had his day and his influence. Without his labors, rude and unscientific though they were, we should be a great way behind our present work of progression. His efforts awoke a taste for music in the abstract, and his methods afford a suggestive experience to those who follow him. He was the pioneer of future Mozarts and Mendelssohns, and they who would sneer at his crudities are such as would ridicule the pan-pipe because it is not the organ. The teacher who is to come may or may not be more successful; but one thing is certain—he will scarcely accomplish more with smaller means than his predecessors."[96]

The singing master and the singing school were, of course, the two sides of a coin, since the one controlled the destinies of the other. Thus, the latter statement applies equally well to the singing schools. Important, necessary, vigorous, creative institutions that they were in their own day, their greatest significance lay in the foundations which they laid for the future generations of a musical people.

Appendixes

Appendix A. Musical Theses Included in the Commencement Broadsides of Harvard College, 1711–1730

The following list of thirty-two musical theses that were included in the commencement broadsides of Harvard College has been compiled from the collection entitled, "Harvard College Theses and Quaestiones," Vol. 1 (1642–1736) and Vol. 2 (1737–1800), HUC 6642 in the Harvard Archives. Translations, which endeavor to reconcile the not-so-pure Ciceronian Latin and the not always consistent terminology of the eighteenth-century Harvard undergraduate with present-day usages, have been supplied for each. The writer wishes to acknowledge the kind assistance of Miss Mary M. Meehan of the above department in accomplishing this task.

Theses Mathematicae, 1711.
No. 10. Musica est sonus modulatus ad temporis et soni quantitatem.
(trans.) Music is sound properly measured as to duration and pitch.

No copies of the theses for the years from 1712 to 1716 are known to have survived.

Theses Mathematicae, 1717.
No. 17. Musica est Ars Tonus modulandi secundum Quantitatem et Qualitatem.
(trans.) Music is the art of regulating a tone according to duration and pitch.

No. 18. Ut Quantitas respicit Tempus, ita Qualitas Gravitatem et Acutionem Soni.
(trans.) As quantity is concerned with time, so quality is concerned with depth and height of sound (pitch).

No. 19. Unisoni sunt Elementa Musicae.
(trans.) Unisons are elements of music.

No. 20. Harmonia est Conventia Sonorum bene proportionatorum.
(trans.) Harmony is the combination of well-proportioned sounds.

No copy of the theses for the year 1718 is known to have survived.

Theses Mathematicae, 1719.
No. 18. Dias et Trias harmonia sunt fundamenta contrapuncti Musici.
(trans.) The harmonious dyad (the interval of two notes) and triad (the common chord) are the foundations of part music.

No. 19. Bassus in sede gravissimarum, semper tenet Basin Triadis.
(trans.) The bass, which is the lowest part, always forms the foundation of the triad.

No. 20. Coeunt Melodiae motu graduali, non Saltatorio.
(trans.) Melodies move gradually, not abruptly.

No. 21. Diades sunt Consonantes simplices.
(trans.) Dyads are simple consonants.
No theses dealing with music were included in the broadside for 1720.

Thesis Musica, 1721.
No. 22. Partes Musicae tantum sunt tres revera distinctae.
(trans.) There are only three truly distinct parts to music.

Theses Musicae, 1722.
No. 20. Musica es Ars, qua e congrua Sonorum Mixtione Harmonia producitur.
(trans.) Music is the art whereby Harmony is produced from the proper mingling of various sounds.

No. 21. Soni sunt graves vel acuti secundum Celeritatem vel Tarditatem Vibrationum.
(trans.) Sounds are low or high in pitch according to the swiftness or slowness of the vibrations of the air.

Theses Musicae, 1723.
No. 23. Partibus absque quatuor Musica non est perfecta.
(trans.) Music is not complete without four parts.

No. 24. Sonorum Differentia ex diversis aeris Vibrationibus Oritur.
(trans.) Variations in sounds arise from different vibrations in the air.

No. 25. Musicae partis sunt, vel Εὐφωηια vel ξυμφωηια.
(trans.) The elements of music are euphony and harmony.

Thesis Musica, 1724.
No. 20. Musica materialiter in Sono, Formaliter vero in Sonorum Harmonia, consistit.
(trans.) The substance of music is sound, but the true nature of music consists of the harmony of sounds.

Theses Musicae, 1725.
No. 23. Musica est Ars Sonos modulandi.
(trans.) Music is the art of regulating sounds.

No. 24. Quoties Toni septem harmoniace varientur, tot Partes distinctas Musica agnoscit.
(trans.) Music recognizes as distinct elements, the seven tones harmoniously varied (the scale).

No. 25. Quo majus Coincidentiae Intervallum, eo ingratior est Dissonantia, et vice versa.
(trans.) The nearer that two tones coincide, the greater the dissonance, and vice versa.

Thesis Musica, 1726.
No. 23. Musica est Ars, son Quantitatem, Melos et Tonum, in Harmoniae Productionem modulandi.
(trans.) Music is the art of regulating the duration, the quality and the pitch of sound for the production of harmony.

Theses Musicae, 1727.
No. 23. Musica est Ars Soni Melodiam et Harmoniam apte modulandi.
(trans.) Music is the art of skillfully regulating the melodic and harmonic properties of sound.

No. 24. Nullae, praeter Octavam, Consonantiae duplicatae, Consonantiam efficiunt.

(trans.) No repeated consonant interval, except the octave, produces a similar consonance.

No. 25. Consonantiarum prima, gratissimaq; est Octava.
(trans.) The principal and most pleasing of the consonances is the octave.

Theses Musicae, 1728.
No. 24. Musica est Ars harmonice Vocem et Instrumenta modulandi.
(trans.) Music is the art of modulating voices and instruments harmoniously.

No. 25. Quanto brevior est Chorda, (Aeteris. . .paribus) tanto velociores sunt ejus Vibrationes.
(trans.) The shorter the string, the more rapid are its vibrations (the air similarly agitated).

No. 26. Ex Chordiae Fidis primariae percussione, producitur eadem alterius Chordae, si sit Unisona, Vibratio.
(trans.) From the striking of a given gut string, the same vibration is produced in another string, if they are in unison.

Theses Musicae, 1729.
No. 23. Musica est Ars, varias Sonorum modifcationes docens.
(trans.) Music is the art which teaches various modifications of sounds.

No. 24. Corpora majora graviorem, minora acutiorem, producunt Sonum.
(trans.) Large bodies produce a deeper tone, small bodies a higher one.

No. 25. Soni collati certas proprietates habent, quibus seorsim considerati, distinguunter.
(trans.) All sounds have certain properties by which they are distinguished when they are considered separately.

No. 26. Sonus gravis ex tardioribus, acutus ex velocioribus Motibus oritur.
(trans.) A deep tone arises from slower motions (vibrations), and a high tone arises from more rapid motions.

Theses Musicae, 1730.
No. 25. Musica est Ars sonos Voce et Instrumentis modulandi.
(trans.) Music is the art of regulating sounds by means of voices and instruments.

No. 26. Tonus a Soni intensione non pendet.
(trans.) Pitch in not dependent upon intensity of sound.

1731–1800.
Musical theses do not appear during the remainder of the century, the single exception being the year 1741 when two ostensibly musical theses dealing with the science of sound appear under the heading "Theses Physicae."

Appendix B. The Great Awakening and the Establishment of Regular Singing

The authors of standard works[1,2] on church music have held that the Great Awakening, which was the first religious revival to sweep across America, was a positive factor in the development of sacred music during the eighteenth century. They have noted that this revival was responsible for renewed interest in singing and for the wide-spread introduction of hymnody. By way of illustration, they have drawn upon a statement made by one of the principal leaders of the revival, Jonathan Edwards, concerning the singing in his own congregation at Northampton, Massachusetts, in 1736.

> Our public praises were then greatly enlived: God was then served in our psalmody, in some measure in the *beauty of Holiness*. It has been observable, that there has been scarcely any part of Divine worship, wherein good men amongst us have had grace so drawn forth, and their hearts so uplifted in the ways of God, as in singing his praises. Our congregation excelled all that I ever knew in the externall part of the duty before, generally carrying regularly and well, *three parts* of music, and the women a part by themselves. But now they were evidently wont to sing with unusual elevation of heart and voice, which made the duty pleasant indeed.[3]

They have also utilized a letter[4] by Edwards in which he reported that his congregation had begun singing Watts's hymns to the exclusion of the Psalms while he was away on a journey in 1742. They have endeavored to show that the events which he described were representative of events elsewhere in New England at this time by referring the reader to the annals and commentaries written by his fellow divines.

Unfortunately, they have not carried their researches much further than this point. From the material which they have presented, it would not be illogical to conclude that the Great Awakening was also a positive factor in the establishment of regular singing. This conclusion would be in accord with another important piece of evidence, namely, that George Whitefield, the instigator of the revival, was both a regular singer[5] and partisan of Watts's hymns.[6]

Further research proves the above conclusion to be erroneous for two reasons. First, closer examination of Edwards's statement about the singing in his congregation suggests that the revival was not responsible for the introduction of regular singing, but only for its improvement. Second, careful analysis of the annals of the revival reveals that only one other congregation among those described sang in a demonstrably regular manner.

The best single source of information about the effects of the Great Awakening upon the congregations of New England is Thomas Prince's two-volume set of annals, which contains reports made by the ministers of thirty-six towns. Of these reports only that by the Reverend John White of Gloucester contains a specific incident in which instruction in music is linked with the expression of revivalistic sentiment.

> ...and on Monday Morning in the School of Mr. Moses Parsons; a Man disposed zealously to serve the best Interests of all he has to do with: and being hired by a Number of Gentlemen to train up their Children in religious Exercises, and Singing as well as other useful Knowledge; the Spirit of God came so powerfully upon the School, so that they could not attend the ordinary School Exercises. But with their joyful Master (with whom I had left the Care of my Flock while I went on a Journey, which I was necessitated to take) and a Multitude of Spectators, they prayed to, and praised God by singing spiritual Hymns.[7]

The remaining reports contain references to singing, but these references are too brief for the determination of the type of singing which prevailed.

The next best source of information about the effects of the Great Awakening upon the congregations of New England is Charles Chauncey's *Seasonable Thoughts*, which contains eyewitness accounts of religious gatherings held during the revival. One of Chauncey's reporters described a series of such meetings held in one town as follows:

> They had a publick Exercise *every Day*, and for *nine Nights* successively. Numbers of the People continued the greatest Part of the Night, in the utmost Disorder. They were *groaning, crying out, fainting, falling down, praying, praying, exhorting, singing, laughing, congratulating* each other, which they did by *shaking Hands* and *Embraces*. The latter was commonly practiced by *different Sexes*. And by the *fifth* Night, there were almost Three Hundred thus affected, who were acting their different Parts at the *same* Time.[8]

This description reveals that the behavior which was prompted by the Great Awakening was very much like the mass hysteria which was observed at the camp meetings on the frontier sixty years later.

The crux of the matter is that, while this type of behavior was not consistent with the performance requirements of the carefully measured, precisely harmonized psalm tunes in Tufts's and Walter's books, it was in keeping with the free and untrammeled mode of expression associated with the common way of singing. Another account by one of Chauncey's reporters serves to illustrate this point.

> Many of the *young Women* would go about the House *praying* and *exhorting*; then they would separate themselves into a Corner of the House to *sing* and *rejoice* together; and then they would break forth into *as great a Laughter as could be*, to think, as they expresst it, that they should go Hand in Hand to Heaven. Then they would speak it over again, and shout out into a *great Laughter, laughing*, and *singing, jumping up and down*, and *clapping their Hands* together; and some would be so filled with *Joy*, as they pretended, that they could not *stand* or *walk....*[9]

Only by the wildest stretch of the imagination could the singing described in this account be interpreted as being regular in nature. In all likelihood it was very similar to the ecstatic, but untutored religious singing of the camp meetings.[10]

Tabulation of all of the data pertaining to the spread of regular singing suggests that the common way of singing had not been completely discarded by the time the Great Awakening occurred. This suggestion seems to be confirmed by Edwards's censure[11] of those congregations which indulged in disorderly singing during the height of the revival.

When all of the evidence is considered, it is apparent that the Great Awakening was characterized by both the common way of singing and the regular way of singing. It is also apparent that the Great Awakening probably did little to advance the cause of regular singing in those communities that had been untouched by the first efforts at reform, because the revivalistic fervor which it generated was closer to the spirit of the old way of singing than to the spirit of the new.

Appendix C. A Country Parson and the Singing Schools of Westborough, Massachusetts

The Reverend Ebenezer Parkman (1703–1782) had the distinction of witnessing and participating in many of the musical events associated with the development of singing schools and village choirs in New England during his lifetime. As a member[12] of the class of 1721 of Harvard College, and later as a resident of Boston, he witnessed the first efforts at musical reform, the publication of the first singing books, and the establishment of the Society for Promoting Regular Singing.

These events apparently had a great impact upon him for shortly after he graduated from college he made himself quite an elaborate manuscript singing book[13] into which he copied a gamut and psalm tunes taken from Thomas Walter's *Grounds and Rules*. Armed with this little book and filled with the spirit of reform, he made the adoption of regular singing one of the first items of business when he was called to the newly formed parish of Westborough in 1724. Like so many of his fellow reformers, he encountered considerable opposition to his plans; and it was not until 1731 that he succeeded in having regular singing adopted by his congregation.[14] A genial, sensible man, Parkman soon found that he liked Westborough and the life of a country parson very much. Each year found him more deeply involved in the affairs of his community with the result that by common consent he remained the minister of the parish until his death at the age of seventy-nine.

In 1778 when Parkman was seventy-five, an itinerant singing master named Lemuel Badcock appeared on the scene at Westborough. As might be expected, the staunch believer in regular singing did everything he could to assist this teacher of choral music. He provided Badcock with room and board, and he sent his own children to the singing school which Badcock taught. He encouraged his son, Breck, who was a bookbinder by trade, to make manuscript singing books for Badcock's scholars. He entertained him and other musical friends by holding singing parties at the parsonage. He helped him and his scholars practice the difficult task of sustaining the pitch of the music while the psalm was lined out. When the singing school was almost over, he arranged for another friend, the Reverend John Foster, to give a singing lecture. And after Badcock had left, he used his influence to see that the singers whom he had trained received their just reward, that of being allowed to sit together in the gallery of the meeting house as a full-fledged choir.

Both Ebenezer Parkman and his daughter, Sophia, who attended Badcock's singing school with her beau, Elijah Brigham, were indefatigable diarists. When selected entries from their diaries for the year 1778 are placed in juxtaposition with each other, a fascinating picture of what the singing school meant in the lives of the citizens of a small New England town emerges. In the following compilation, entries from Ebenezer's diary[15] have been denoted by the letter "E," and entries from Sophia's diary[16] have been denoted by the letter "S."

S: Dec. 31, 1777. I card Wool for Molly to spin and knit some. Mother is knitting Gloves for Patty Miller. –'tis Extream cold weather very good sleighing.

E: Jan. 12, 1778. This Day Mr. Lemuel Badcock opens a Singing School at Capt. H. Fishers. *Breck* & his Wife, also *Sophy* attend there, V.M. & Eva. He asks two Dollars a month of each Person.

E: Jan. 13, 1778. . . . the Singing School increases greatly.

E: Jan. 14, 1778. Elias goes to Singing School. 38 at School at Evening. Miss Mindwell Brigham attending ye Singing School.

E: Jan. 15, 1778. The Singing School is so attended, yt it causes Drury Fairbank to range about for singing Books. *Mr. Badcock* came at Eve and drank Coffee here.

E: Jan. 17, 1778. My Sons & their Wives, tho' it is a Snow Storm, return to *Concord.* Neither Elias nor Sophy go to Singing School to Day.

S: Jan. 20, 1778. I spin. p.m. go to Singing School at evening. Mr. E. B. here and spend the evening. He is just home from College.

E: Jan. 21, 1778. Very difficult . . . ing, yet ye Singing School they attend.

S: Jan. 21, 1778. I spin. Mr. Br. goes away p.m. Go to school . . .

E: Jan. 22, 1778. Town Meet'g to consider ye Articles of Confederation of ye United States. A Committee meet here for my advice.

S: Jan. 25, 1778. I go to meeting at evening. Mr. B. here to spend evening.

E: Jan. 27, 1778. Returned home at Eve. *Col. Baldwin* from *Brookfield* and Mr. Badcock, ye Singing Master—both lodge here.

E: Jan. 28, 1778. Mr. *Badcock* boards with us.

E: Jan. 29, 1778. *Mr. Badcock* was detained from us last night—is also today.

E: Jan. 30, 1778. *Mr. Badcock* dined here. He gave me a List of his Singing Scholars. They are 46—34 males—ye rest Women & Girls. *Mr. Badcock* sups and lodges here.

S: Jan. 30, 1778. I sew in the forenoon—p.m. go to school. Mr. E. B. at school came home with me and spend the evening here.

E: Jan. 31, 1778. It being a very rainy Season *Sophy* dined at D___ Wood's, and *Mr. Badcock* came not either to dine or to lodge here.

S: Jan. 31, 1778. I go to School all day. Mr. B. goes away in the morning. I gave him my Singing Book to Prick some tunes into it, while I was gone to School.

E: Feb. 1, 1778. *Mr. Badcock & Bradshaw* came & lodged here. Our Evening was spent very much in Singing.

E: Feb 2, 1778. NB. *Mr. Badcock* dines at Capt. Morse's, & at night goes to Mr. Tainbery.

E: Feb. 4, 1778. Samuel Brigham dined here. P.M., He, Elias, & Sophy attend ye Singing School at Deacon Wood's, as usual. *Mr. Badcock* at night, he lodged here.

E: Feb. 5, 1778. In the forenoon a No. of Singers were here, with *Mr. Badcock* and desired me to meet with them tomorrow in ye Meeting House, to pray & preach to ym. They Sing here till noon. Mr. Badc. & Mr. Batherick dine here. I consent to go to the Meeting House tomorrow. Their Motive is to try their skill in Singing there & with Reading ye Line, which they hadn't been used to. *Mr. Badcock* came not at night.

E: Feb. 6, 1778. Mr. Badc. & Sam. Brigh. break. & dine here. P.M. The Singers meet at ye Meeting House. We began with Singing—Sang Dr. Watt's Hymn, *Te Deum,* inst. St. Martyn's. Then I prayed — Sang Ps. 113. Preached on Ps 47.6. a Collection out of Various Setts of Sermon(s) on ye Subject. The last Singing before ye Blessing was ye 95th Hymn, & Gloria Patris. After my Exercise was over, they Sung some No. of tunes, & tarried a while to hear. Mr. Badc. returning to my House. He, with Bradshaw & Brigham here at Tea.

E: Feb. 7, 1778. Miss Mindwell Brigham was able to come to lodge here last night (as she has done for sometime) but is forced by ye Storm to continue in ye morning with us somewhat longer: but p.m. She & ye rest went in ye sleigh to Singing School. NB. Capt. Fisher came at ye Desire of ye Singers, and in their name thank'd me for my Sermon to them yesterday.

E: Feb. 8, 1778. *Mr. Badcock* & his Singers sat in the Front on the Women's Side & rose up to Sing— Sung m.m. p.m. I preach'd a.m. again on Ps. 77. 13.14. p.m. on Col. 3.16 from page 17 omitting p. 23 to 26 thence to p. 28. Mr. Badcock dined here, returned after meeting & tarried over night.

S: Feb. 8, 1778. I go to meeting. Set in the gallery with the Singers. Mr. Badcock and Mr. Bradshaw here after meeting and Sing in the Evening.

E: Feb. 9, 1778. Mr. Badc. here thro' the day. & lodged here at night. I went up to his School, p.m. At Eve I returned to ye Singing School & tarried 'till 9 when Elias came home with me in the sleigh. *Mr. Badcock* & Cons. Bradshaw came & lodged here. NB. Today was the first time of my going to hear ye Singing. They performed to good Acceptance. May it bless the Glory and Honour of God.

S: Feb. 9, 1778. I am very poorly. Mollie washed. I go in the sleigh to School. At evening Mr. Bradshaw here to Lodge. I rec'd a letter from Mr. Brigham.

E: Feb. 11, 1778. This Evening, *Mr. Badcock's* Singing School finishes.

S: Feb. 11, 1778. I spin. p.m. this day Mr. Badcock finish[es] his school and we settled with him. My part of School expenses is 18/10.

E: Feb. 13, 1778. The Four Singers meet . . . at Deacon Wood's to Sing & Settle all Accts.

E: Feb. 14, 1778. *Mr. Ezra Ripley* from *Framingham* & going to Barre accompanied by Mr. Packard, a Candidate going to Pelham call here, but do not stay to dine. *Mr. Luke Wilder* of *Lancaster* din'd. & afterwards, with Messrs. John Batherick and Winslow Brigham, sang several Tunes with us. Mr. Daniel Stockwell present to hear the Singing.

E: Feb. 27, 1778. My Sons are both of them much engaged in making Singing Books & pricking out Tunes.

E: Mar. 10, 1778. Breck makes a Business of Book-binding; but also by Singing Books. The Singing School is still kept at Mr. Tim Warren's, under Instructions of Mr. Jonathan Batherick.

E: Mar. 19, 1778. Several young women, viz. Miss Hephz. Parker & Miss Lydia Batherick, came after Lecture & begin their Boarding & Lodging here, that they may go to School to Mr. Badcock.

E: Mar. 23, 1778. Mr. Badcock, Breck & Six Women Sing a.m.

E: Mar. 27, 1778. Mr. Badcock & Sam'l Brigham ask for a Singing Lecture & that Mr. Foster may preach it.

E: Mar. 29, 1778. P.M. I mentioned to ye Congregation the Request of ye Singers to have a Sermon next Tuesday . . . This Eve. *Breck* and Suse & their *Billy Spring*, & with them, came Mr. *Badcock, Luke Wilder, Elisha Parker*, & *Sam'l Fisher*, to attend our Family Exercise and to Sing in which way we Spent the Evening.

E: Mar. 31, 1778. The Snow is so deep, that though a Lecture to appointed, I am in doubt whether the Preacher can get to us. Therefore I prepare myself. After Dinner the Storm being much abated, Mr. Foster, & Capt. Joseph How from Marlboro came. The former preach'd ye Singing Lecture from 1 Cor. 14.15. N.B. We sung at Entrance two staves of Hymn 80, 4 v. without *Reading*—after pray'r Sung Ps. 57 from verse 5, 3 st[anzas] and the Deacon (Bond) read as usual line by line. The last Singing was Ps. 148. 6 stanzas to end of 12 v. After the Blessing, (who were increased in strength—by some number from Marlboro (Dr. Curtis) & from Northboro (Capt. Sam. Wood, his Daughter, & Sister &c) went on in Singing some tunes. N.B. Old Mr. Hardy fell into an unhappy Frame, about ye Singers—Said their Behavior was abominable!

E: Apr. 1, 1778. The Singing Scholars (tho' the roads are bad) meet at Deacon Woods, as they have been wont, this Second Term, for a fortnight, which finishes this Evening, for another Dollar a piece to Mr. Badcock.

E: Apr. 2, 1778. With Difficulty I obtain an Horse (my Son gone with his to Worcester) and go to Southboro (bad Riding) to preach his both Sacramental & Singing Lecture. Mr. Badcock Returning to Wrentham.

E: Oct. 23, 1778. The People had a Town Meeting in which they are to reconsider a vote of April the 16 last concerning the Singers sitting in the Meeting House: Now it is recommended to them to sit, the Males in the Front Gallery on the Men's Side, and the Females in the Front Gallery on the Women's.

E: Oct. 25, 1778. NB. The Singers chiefly are in the Front today & Sing again.

E: Nov. 1, 1778. NB. The Singers more generally sat today in ye Front, & some no. stood up. Mr. Lemuel Badcock was among ym. We were not so happy as to have any singing in Family today—not in ye Evening.

E: Nov. 21, 1778. Mr. Joseph Harrington came to see me & talked about ye late Grant of ye Town and about ye Singing. He bro't an extraordinary Present of Butter.

E: Nov. 28, 1778. *Thanksgiving*. I had prepared in part, but could not finish it. I improved part of sermon Ps. 147.1.7. to page 7 and wrote additions on loose papers. Breck and all his were at ye Entertainment, also Sr. Brigham. May ye Lord accept our gratulations, and bless the Holy Word dispensed!—had excellent singing.

E: Dec. 1, 1778. I preached at Liut. Levi Warren's, a third Exercise on Rev. 2.10. May God be graciously pleased to add His own efficacious Blessing! N.B. Mr. Daniel Hardy was at Mr. Warren's before ye Exercise began and manifested his Disgust at my sermon on ye late Thanksgiving. He found fault with my saying so much about Singing ye praises of God. I replied yt it was the very Business of the Day. —the present Truth— yt if he was dissatisfied with it, he had need ask himself whether it was not because he *himself was out of Tune*. After ye Exercises, Mr. Badcock and his Scholers sang a number of good Tunes, in Parts. We had also a plentiful Table Spread and agreeable Entertainment.

Appendix D. Suggestions for Further Research

The history of the first half of the singing school's life span carries it to the peak of the golden age of choral music. All was not well at the summit, however, and the history of the second half of its life span begins, not as might be supposed with the adoption of Pestalozzian principles, but with the reform of musical taste which took place between 1800 and 1825. This period of reform, like the one during which regular singing was promulgated, was characterized by the rise of musical crusaders who organized musical societies, delivered singing lectures, and published new singing books to accomplish their ends.

The new spirit of reform does not seem to have appeared upon the scene as something that was spontaneous and without any cultural precedent. Rather, it appears to have been the logical outgrowth of the strong streak of conservatism which was nurtured throughout the golden age by certain singing master-composers, who, if not totally absorbed in European church music, at least had little sympathy for certain American musical forms such as the highly popular fuging tune. Andrew Law, Oliver Holden, Samuel Holyoke, and Elias Mann with more or less success advocated and adhered to an austere style in which the texts were set syllabically instead of melismatically. They objected to the alleged jargon produced by the simultaneous sounding of the text which occurs normally in music which has been written in contrapuntal style. Mann summarized the feelings of this group when he wrote in the introduction to his *Massachusetts Collection of Sacred Harmony* (Boston, 1807):

> In this collection will be found none of those wild fugues, and rapid and confused movements which have so long been the disgrace of congregational psalmody and the contempt of the judicious amateur.[17]

Mann's attack upon the fuging tune, which was but one of many such attacks made during this period, was symptomatic of a much larger cultural revolution which was taking place at this time. Intellectual leaders had begun to fall hopelessly under the spell of imported European church music, which to their minds was written in a far more correct style than native American music. Daniel Dana's thinking on this matter was typical of this new generation of reformers who were bound to save Americans from themselves. In addressing the Essex Musical Association in 1803, he observed:

> To speak of the existing state of music in our own country, is a difficult and delicate task. Indeed, our character, in this respect, is scarcely formed. Our music, whether considered an art or a science, is still in its Infancy. Nor do we seem, as yet, to have agreed on any standard by which the merit of compositions is to be tested. The state of society among us being so little advanced, few of our composers have been enabled, like the great masters of Europe, to devote their lives to the object. The consequence is, that our country has been for years overflowing with productions, not destitute of sprightliness perhaps, nor, in every instance of gleams of genius, but composed on no plan, conformed to no principles, and communicating no distinct or abiding impression—fugitive, unsubstantial things which fill the ear and starve the mind.[18]

The complete story of the reform of musical taste would make a sizable monograph if all of the principals, all of the societies, and all of the singing books are accounted for. Research into this topic properly should begin with the singing lectures delivered by the principals before the reforming musical societies. No bibliography of these works exists anywhere, to the writer's knowledge; thus, *Table 6* (A List of Singing Lectures and Musical Essays Published in New England from 1800 to 1826), is offered as a point of departure for those who would seek to understand this obscure, yet important episode in American cultural history.

Tables

Table 1. The Establishment of Regular Singing in New England.

The manner in which regular singing spread throughout New England may be roughly gauged by the record of its adoption in the twenty-seven towns listed here. It is at once obvious that Boston was the radiant point for a movement that eventually reached the most distant communities in Connecticut and New Hampshire. It is less clear why the provinces of Rhode Island, Maine, and Vermont are not represented. Rhode Island, long a haven to dissenting groups, such as the Baptists, seems to have been by-passed completely by that which was essentially a Congregationalist concern. That the Baptists were concerned about religious music at this time is apparent from the publication of two tracts, Valentine Wightman's *Letter to the Elders* (1725) and John Hammett's *Promiscuous Singing* (1739). Members of this sect were, however, more concerned about whether it was proper to sing at all than whether to sing in the new or the old way. The view that it was improper to sing in the meeting house seems to have carried the day, for it was not until 1775 that music was admitted to the divine service of the First Baptist Church in Providence. Regular singing was no longer an issue anywhere by that date and the Baptists merely adopted all the paraphernalia of Congregationalist music, i.e., the singing school and the gallery choir. See William Dineen, *Music at the Meeting House, 1775–1958* (Providence: Privately printed for the First Baptist Church in America, 1958). Large portions of Maine, New Hampshire, and Vermont were still virgin territory at the time when reform was initiated. Some appreciation of this fact may be gained from Adams's unpublished "Narrative of Remarkable Instances of a Particular Faith and Answers to Prayers," wherein a victory over the troublesome Indians at Norridgwock is ascribed to the adoption of regular singing by the parish at Dover.

Place	Date	Source
I. Massachusetts		
Boston	by 1723	Thacher et al., *Cases*, p. 7.
Roxbury	by 1723	Thacher et al., *Cases*, p. 7.
Dorchester	by 1723	Thacher et al., *Cases*, p. 7.
Cambridge	by 1723	Thacher et al., *Cases*, p. 7.
Taunton	by 1723	Thacher et al., *Cases*, p. 7.
Bridgewater	by 1723	Thacher et al., *Cases*, p. 7.
Charlestown	by 1723	Thacher et al., *Cases*, p. 7.
Ipswich	by 1723	Thacher et al., *Cases*, p. 7.
Newbury	by 1723	Thacher et al., *Cases*, p. 7.
Andover	by 1723	Thacher et al., *Cases*, p. 7.
Reading	by 1723	Walter, *Sweet Psalmist*, Preface
Weston	1723	Russel, "The First Parish," p. 139.
Needham	by 1730	Clarke, *History*, p. 308.
Beverly	1730	Stone, *History*, p. 265.
Westborough	1731	Deforest et al., *History*, p. 115.
Franklin	1739	Blake, *History*, p. 31.
Hanover	1742	Briggs, *History*, p. 58.
Mattapoisett	1744	(Anon.), *Mattapoisett*, p. 197.
II. Connecticut		
E. Windsor	1727	Stiles, *History*, p. 730.
Wallingford	1731	Davis, *History*, p. 403.
Hartford	1733	Walker, *History*, p. 228.
Glastonbury	1733	Hibbard, *History*, p. 77.
Canaan	1739	(Anon.), *Readings*, p. 136.
Windsor	1740	Stiles, *History*, p. 273.
Eastbury	1740	Chapin, *History*, p. 78.
Stamford	1747	Huntington, *History*, p. 298.
III. New Hampshire		
Dover	1724	Adams, "Narrative."

Table 2. Town-supported Singing Schools in Massachusetts and New Hampshire, 1788–1831.

Town	Date	Amount	Source
I. Massachusetts			
Acton	1807	$40	Phalen, *History*, p. 124.
Arlington	1799	$50	Cutter, *History*, p. 109.
Berlin	1804	$30	Houghton, *History*, p. 55f.
	1809	$30	Ibid.
	1819	$30	Ibid.
Brimfield	1789		Hyde, *Town of Brimfield*, p. 128.
Brookline	1801	$35	*Muddy River*, vol. I, p. 438.
	1831	$100	Ibid., p. 580.
Chelmsford	1800	$40	Waters, *History*, p. 681.
	1826	$150	Ibid.
Framingham	1798	$30	Temple, *History*, p. 338.
	1803	$60	Barry, *History*, p. 122.
	1824	$100	Temple, *History*, p. 338.
Greenfield	1793	£6	Thompson, *History*, p. 291.
Hadley	1792	$13	Judd, *History*, p. 409.
	1796	$20	Ibid.
	1799	$50	Ibid.
	1807	$80	Ibid.
Hubbardston	1799	$9	Stowe, *History*, p. 82.
Ludlow	1791	£6	Noon, *History*, p. 56.
Northfield	1800	$50	Temple, *History*, p. 354.
Northampton	1791	£3	Small, *Early N.E. Schools*, p. 375.
	1795	$26	Trumbull, *History*, vol. II, p. 589.
	1798	$50	Trumbull, *History*, vol. II, p. 589.
Palmer	1797	$40	Temple, *History*, p. 211.
	1800	$30	Temple, *History*, p. 211.
Shirley	1808	$30	Bolton, *Shirley*, p. 129.
Sudbury	1797	$30	"Records," n.p.
	1801	$10	"Records," n.p.
	1803	$30	"Records," n.p.
Sutton	1825	$40	Benedict, *History*, p. 149.
Wayland	1795	£30	Hudson, *Annals*, p. 213.
Weston	1802	$60	*Town Records*, vol. I, p. 517.
	1803	$60	*Town Records*, vol. II, p. 22.
	1815	$70	*Town Records*, vol. II, p. 168.
II. New Hampshire			
Dublin	1819	$50	*History*, p. 197.
Keene	1820	$50	Griffin, *History*, p. 377.
New Ipswich	1802	$40	Gould, *History*, p. 262.
	1803	$40	Ibid.
	1807	$40	Ibid.
	1808	$40	Ibid.
Temple	1799	$30	Blood, *History*, p. 154.
	1800	$30	Ibid.
	1801	$30	Ibid.
	1803	$30	Ibid.
	1805	$30	Ibid.
	1807	$30	Ibid.
Walpole	1788	£15	Aldrich, *Walpole*, p. 153.

Table 3. Fifty Tune Books by New England Authors.

The following list constitutes a representative sampling of some of the most important tune books produced by New England singing masters, compilers, composers, and publishers, 1764–1808. The conclusions expressed in the present chapter concerning the methods and objectives of the chorally oriented singing school have been based in large measure upon the careful analysis of the introductions to these works. The reader is referred to Metcalf's *American Writers and Compilers of Sacred Music* (New York: Abingdon Press, 1925) for information concerning where these works fitted into a particular composer's output and to the "Bibliography" of the present book for complete information about each title.

Author	Short Title	Place and Date of Publication
Bayley	*New and Compleat Introduction*	Newburyport, 1764
Flagg	*Collection of the Best Psalm Tunes*	Boston, 1764
Billings	*New England Psalm Singer*	Boston, 1770
Tans'ur	*American Melody, Part I*	Newburyport, 1773
Williams	*American Melody, Part II*	Newburyport, 1773
Stickney	*Gentleman and Lady's Companion*	Newburyport, 1774
Billings	*Singing Master's Assistant*	Boston, 1776
Law	*Select Harmony*	New Haven, 1779
Jocelin	*Chorister's Companion*	New Haven, 1782
Brownson	*Select Harmony*	New Haven, 1783
Law	*Rudiments of Music*	Cheshire, 1783
Langdon	*Beauties of Psalmody*	New Haven, 1786
Thomas	*Laus Deo!*	Worcester, 1788
French	*New American Melody*	Boston, 1789
Norman	*Federal Harmony*	Boston, 1790
Holyoke	*Harmonia Americana*	Boston, 1791
French	*Psalmodist's Companion*	Worcester, 1793
Kimball	*Rural Harmony*	Boston, 1793
Read	*American Singing Book*, 4th ed.	New Haven, 1793
Read	*Columbian Harmonist*	New Haven, 1793
Stone and Wood	*Columbian Harmony*	Boston, 1793
Belcher	*Harmony of Maine*	Boston, 1794
Billings	*Continental Harmony*	Boston, 1794
Law	*Art of Singing*	Cheshire, 1794
Babcock	*Middlesex Harmony*	Boston, 1795
Bull	*Responsory*	Worcester, 1795
Gram et al.	*Massachusetts Compiler*	Boston, 1795
Holden	*Union Harmony*	Boston, 1795
Benham	*Social Harmony*	Wallingford, 1793
Howe	*Worshipper's Assistant*	Northampton, 1799
Belknap	*Evangelical Harmony*	Boston, 1800
Jenks	*New England Harmonist*	Danbury, 1800
Kimball	*Essex Harmony*	Exeter, 1800
Ranlet	*Village Harmony*, 5th ed.	Exeter, 1800
Swan	*New England Harmony*	Northampton, 1801
French	*Harmony of Harmony*	Northampton, 1802
Holyoke	*Columbian Repository*	Exeter, 1802
Mann	*Northampton Collection*	Northampton, 1802
Janes	*Massachusetts Harmony*	Boston, 1803
Attwill	*N.Y. and Vt. Collections*, 2nd ed.	Albany, 1804
Howe	*Farmer's Evening Entertainment*	Northampton, 1804
Ingalls	*Christian Harmony*	Exeter, 1805
Jenks	*Delights of Harmony*	New Haven, 1805
Forbush	*Psalmodist's Assistant*	Boston, 1806
Law	*Harmonic Companion*	Philadelphia, 1807
Holyoke	*Vocal Companion*	Exeter, 1807
Little and Smith	*Easy Instructor*	Albany, 1807
Mann	*Massachusetts Collection*	Boston, 1807
West	*Musical Concert*	Northampton, 1807
Maxim	*Northern Harmony*	Exeter, 1806

Table 4. A List of Singing Lectures Published in New England from 1770–1800.

Author	Short Title	Place and Date of Publication
Clarke, J.	Use and Excellency	1770 Lexington, Mass.
Adams, Z.	Nature, Pleasure,...	1771 Lancaster, Mass.
Hedge, L.	Duty and Manner	1772 Warwick, R.I.
Mellen, J.	Religion Productive	1773 Marlborough, Mass.
Strong, J.	Duty of Singing	1773 Simsbury, Conn.
Noble, 0.	Regular and Skilful	1774 Newburyport, Mass.
Mills, S.	Nature and Importance	1775 Litchfield, Conn.
Symmes, W.	A Discourse	1779 Andover, Mass.
Weld, E.	A Sermon	1789 Braintree, Mass.
Stearns, C.	A Sermon	1792 Lincoln, Mass.
Skinner, I.	A Discourse	1796 North Bolton, Mass.
Langdon, T.	Pleasures and Advantages	1797 Danbury, Conn.
Kinne, A.	Alamoth	1798 Groton, Conn.

Table 5. The Establishment of Choirs in New England.

The following table summarizes the findings of an exhaustive survey of existing secondary sources which contain material pertinent to the establishment of gallery choirs in New England during the period 1760–1800. In those entries in which two dates are given, the first represents the year in which the choir was formed and the second represents the year in which it was seated in the gallery of the meeting house. A specific reference to, or a quotation of, a town or parish vote is implied by the entries in most instances.

Place	Date	Source
I. Massachusetts		
Andover	1782	Mooar, *Historical Manual*, p. 56.
Arlington	1775	Cutter, *History*, p. 49.
Beverly	1764–74	Stone, *History*, p. 255.
Boston	1761	Ellis, *History of the First Church*, p. 205.
Boxford	1782	Perley, *History*, p. 248.
Brookline	1778	*Muddy River and Brookline Records*, vol. 1, p. 274.
Chelmsford	1776	Waters, *History*, p. 679.
Concord	1774	Hudson, *History*, vol. I, p. 250.
Dedham	1766	Smith, *History*, p. 56.
Dover	1770	Smith, *History*, p. 180.
Essex	1768–85	Crowell, *History*, p. 234.
Framingham	1768	Temple, *History*, p. 337.
Greenfield	1784	Thompson, *History*, vol. I, p. 286.
Hardwick	1779	Paige, *History*, p. 189.
Harvard	1779	Nourse, *History*, p. 207.
Haverhill	1769	Chase, *History*, p. 552.
Ipswich	1763–81	Felt, *History*, p. 212.
Leicester	1768–80	Washburn, *Historical Sketches*, p. 109.
Lincoln	1765–70	*Proceedings*, p. 26.
Methuen	1776	Currier, "Music of Other Days," p. 11.
Needham	1778	Clarke, *History*, p. 213.
Newbury	1761	Currier, *History*, p. 340.
Northfield	1770	Temple, *History*, p. 318.
Princeton	1787	Blake, *History*, p. 134.
Randolph	1778–86	Mann, "History of Psalms," p. 93.
Rowley	1773	Jewett, *Rowley*, p. 110.
Shirley	1786	Chandler, *History*, p. 227.
Sudbury	1796	*Records.*
Sturbridge	1768	Haynes, *Historical Sketch*, p. 57.
Wenham	1770	Allen, *History*, p. 200.
Westborough	1778	Deforest, *History*, p. 157.
Westford	1767	Hodgman, *History*, p. 79.
Weston	1772	Russell, "The First Parish," p. 139.
Worcester	1773–79	Lincoln, *History*, pp. 178–79.
II. Connecticut		
Bethlehem	1774	Cothren, *History of Ancient Woodbury*, p. 249.
Goshen	1777	Hibbard, *History*, p. 86.
Farmington	1773	Gay, "Church Music," p. 38.
Hartford	1773	Parker, *History of the Second Church*, p. 143.
New Haven	1771	Blake, *Chronicles*, p. 110.
Norfolk	1774	Gay, "Church Music," p. 38.
Simsbury	1773	Gay, "Church Music," p. 38.
Torrington	1786	Orcutt, *History*, p. 32.
East Windsor	1776	Stiles, *History*, vol. I, p. 730.
III. New Hampshire		
Bedford	1790	Woodbury, *History*, p. 200.
Chester	1765	Chase, *History*, p. 323.
Concord	1784	Bouton, *History*, p. 581.
Hampstead	1775	Noyes, *A Memorial History*, p. 167.
Hollis	1767–88	Worcester, *History*, p. 73.
Jaffrey	1787–91	Cutter, *History*, p. 154.
Lyndeborough	1779	Donovan, *History*, p. 157.
New Ipswich	1780	Gould, *History*, p. 192.
Rindge	1782	Stearns, *History*, p. 164.
Temple	1790	Blood, *History*, p. 154.
IV. Province of Maine		
North Yarmouth	1783	Rowe, *Ancient North Yarmouth*, p. 138.
Wells	1787–96	Bourne, *History*, p. 625.

Table 6. A List of Singing Lectures and Musical Essays Published in New England from 1800 to 1826.

Although not published in New England, Andrew Law's *Essays on Music* (Philadelphia: Printed for the Author, 1814) belongs among the works listed herein because its author was one of the most influential men in the movement to reform American church music.

Author	Short Title	Place and Date of Publication
Emerson, S.	*Oration*	1800
Dana, D.	*Discourse*	1803 Essex Musical Assoc.
Woods, L.	*Discourse*	1804 Essex Musical Assoc.
Emmons, N.	*Discourse*	1806
Hubbard, J.	*Essay*	1807 Middlesex Musical Soc.
Emerson, C.	*Discourse*	1808 Handelian Musical Soc.
Livermore, S.	*Practice*	1809 Middlesex Musical Soc.
Brown, F.	*Address*	1809 Handel Society
Parish, E.	*Eulogy*	1810
Worcester, S.	*Address*	1810 Handel Society
Crane, J.	*Discourse*	1811
Willard, S.	*Use*	1811
Foster, J.	*Discourse*	1811
Bray, O.	*Oration*	1811 Hans Gram Musical Soc.
Dana, D.	*Address*	1813 Rockingham Sacred Music Soc.
Emerson, R.	*Oration*	1814 Handel Society
Coffin, C.	*Address*	1815 Rockingham Sacred Music Soc.
Willard, S.	*Expediency*	1816
Williams, T.	*Discourse*	1817
Gould, N. D.	*Address*	1818 Hubbard Musical Soc.
Mason, L.	*Address*	1826

Notes

Chapter I

1. Thomas Symmes, *The Reasonableness of Regular Singing* (Boston: Printed by B. Green for S. Gerrish, 1720), p. 3.

2. Cotton Mather, *The Accomplished Singer* (Boston: Printed by B. Green for S. Gerrish, 1721), pp. 22–23.

3. Ibid.

4. Ibid.

5. One of the principal points made by Percy A. Scholes in his book *The Puritans and Music in England and New England* (London: Oxford University Press, 1934) is that the Puritans were not against music *per se*, but rather against indecent secular music and the musical trappings of the established church. Scholarly reaction to Scholes's book has on the whole been very favorable. See K. B. Murdock's review of it in the *New England Quarterly 8*, pp. 433–37. See also S. E. Morison's *Harvard College in the Seventeenth Century* (Cambridge: Harvard University Press, 1936), pp. 113–14, in which he states, "Dr. Percy A. Scholes has demolished the ancient superstition that the English Puritans were opposed to vocal and instrumental music." Similarly, H. W. Foote states in *Three Centuries of American Hymnody* (Cambridge: Harvard University Press, 1940), p. 76, that "Mr. Scholes has completely demolished the myth that the Puritans hated music, for all who will take the trouble to read his masterly book." The recent attack by Cyclone Covey in the *William and Mary Quarterly*, "Puritanism and Music in Colonial America," 8, no. 3 (July, 1951) upon Scholes as an apologist for the Puritans has been brilliantly answered by Clifford K. Shipton and Walter Muir Whitehill in succeeding issues: 9, no. 1 (January, 1952) and 9, no. 2 (April, 1952).

6. Edward Johnson, *A History of New England from the English Planting In the Yeere 1628 until the Yeere 1652* (London: Printed for Nath. Brooke, 1664), p. 83.

7. Thomas Sternhold and John Hopkins, *The Whole Booke of Psalmes* (London: Printed by John Day, 1562).

8. Cotton Mather, *Magnalia Christi Americana* (London: Printed for Thomas Parkhurst, 1702), Book 3, p. 100.

9. *The Whole Booke of Psalmes faithfully Translated into English Metre* (Cambridge: Printed by Stephen Daye, 1640).

10. Henry Wilder Foote, *Three Centuries of American Hymnody* (Cambridge: Harvard University Press, 1940), chap. 2, "The Reign of the Bay Psalm Book," pp. 34–73.

11. Zoltan Haraszti, *The Enigma of the Bay Psalm Book* (Chicago: University of Chicago Press, 1956).

12. Irving Lowens, "The Bay Psalm Book in 17th Century New England," *Journal of the American Musicological Society* 8, no. 1 (Spring, 1955), pp. 22–29.

13. John Cotton, *Singing of Psalms a Gospel Ordinance* (London: Printed for M.S. for Hannah Allen, 1647).

14. Quoted by Charles Burney, *A General History of Music* (London: Printed for the author, 1776–1789), 3:433.

15. Among the fourteen queries addressed by Samuel Hicks to the Church at Plymouth in 1637 is a question concerning the lawfulness of singing psalms in the meeting house. See *Plymouth Church Records, 1620–1859* (Publications of the Colonial Society of Massachusetts; Boston: Published by the Society, 1920), vol. 1, part 1, pp. 92–96.

16. Cotton, *Singing of Psalms*, p. 2.

17. Ibid., p. 2.

18. Ibid., pp. 5–6.

19. It is interesting to note that in another context he made it clear that the ban against instruments in church music did not extend to private worship provided that attention to the instrument did not divert the heart from attention to the matter of the song.

20. Cotton, *Singing of Psalms*, p. 15.

21. Ibid., p. 41.

22. Ibid., p. 43.

23. Ibid., p. 48.

24. Ibid., p. 62.

25. Thomas Lechford, *Plain Dealing, or News from New England*, 1641. Reprinted with an introduction and notes by J. Hammon Trumbull (Boston: J. K. Wiggin & Wm. Parsons Lunt, 1867), p. 137.

26. Henry Ainsworth, *The Book of Psalmes: Englished both in prose and metro…By H.A.* (Amsterdam: Giles Thorp, 1612).

27. Daniel Appleton White, *Early Records of the First Church in Salem* (Salem: n. p., 1861), p. 72.

28. Edward Winslow, *Hypocrisie Unmasked* (Reprinted from the original edition issued in London, 1646; Providence: Club for Colonial Reprints, 1916), p. 90. Proof for his assertion that many of the Pilgrims were "very expert in musick" may be seen in the fact that included in William Brewster's library was a copy of Richard Allison's *Psalms of David In Meter* (London, 1599), a psalter which stands as one of the most musical and sophisticated works of its type.

29. *Plymouth Church Records. 1620–1859*, vol. 1, part 1, pp. 156–57.

30. Ibid., p. 257.

31. Ibid., vol. 2, part 2, p. 171.

32. Ibid., p. 178.

33. Thomas Lechford, *Plain Dealing*, p. 137.

34. *New England Courant*, no. 134 (Feb. 17–24, 1724).

35. Ibid.

36. Ibid.

37. The writers of most secondary sources have been content to define lining-out simply as a sequence of reading and singing. They have not attempted to clarify the relationship between reading, setting, and singing. The singing master William Billings makes it very clear in the introduction to his tune book, *The Continental Harmony* (Boston, 1794), that in country congregations the text was presented three times, more or less in the manner described above. In his day, however, it was the custom of the minister to read the psalm through in its entirety; thus lining-out was essentially a two-step process, i.e., setting and singing.

38. Thomas Mace, *Musick's Monument* (Cambridge, England: Printed by T. Ratcliffe, 1676), pp. 5–9.

39. Ibid., p. 40.

40. John Playford, *Psalms and Hymns in Solemn Musick of Foure Parts on the Common Tunes to the Psalms in Metre* (London: Printed by W. Godbid, 1671), preface.

41. John Playford, *The Whole Book of Psalms* (London: Printed by W. Godbid, 1677), preface.

42. Samuel Sewall, "Letter to Mr. Burbank, the son; Boston, N.E., July 22, 1695," *Letterbook* (Collections of the Massachusetts Historical Society, 6th ser.; Boston: Published by the Society, 1886), vol. 1, p. 155.

43. *The Psalms, Hymns and Spiritual Songs of the Old & New Testament*, 9th edition (Boston: Printed by B. Green and J. Allen for Michael Perry, 1698), pp. 419–20.

44. Samuel Sewall, *Diary* (Collections of the Massachusetts Historical Society, 5th ser., vols. 5–7; Boston: Published by the Society, 1879), 6:151.

45. Ibid., 6:391.

46. Ibid., 5:460 and 479; 6:403–4: psalm singing at a picnic, during a social visit, and at the provincial wedding, respectively.

47. Sewall, *Diary*, 7:39.

48. Peter Thacher, John Danforth, and Samuel Danforth, *An Essay: Cases of Conscience Concerning the Singing of Psalms* (Boston: Printed by S. Kneeland for S. Gerrish, 1723), p. 13.

49. Josiah Dwight, *An Essay to Silence the Outcry* (Boston: Printed for John Eliot, 1725), p. 11.

50. Thomas Walter, *The Grounds and Rules of Musick Explained* (Boston: Printed by J. Franklin for S. Gerrish, 1721), p. 4.

51. Mather, *The Accomplished Singer*, p. 23.

52. Symmes, *The Reasonableness of Regular Singing*, pp. 3–4.

53. Nathaniel Chauncey, *Regular Singing Defended* (New London: Printed by T. Green, 1728), p. 10.

54. Gilbert Chase, presumably acting upon a suggestion made by Allen P. Britton in his "Theoretical Introductions to American Tune Books to 1800" (Ph.D. diss., University of Michigan, 1949, p. 87), was the first to define systematically the common way of singing in New England and to hypothesize that it was similar to the folk psalmody which prevailed in rural parishes in England and Scotland during the eighteenth century. The above discussion of the common way of singing and the discussion of the folk psalmody hypothesis which follows are based in part upon the ideas and sources incorporated by him in chap. 2, "The New England Reformers," in his book, *America's Music* (New York: McGraw-Hill, 1955). Additional sources not employed by Chase have been utilized in both discussions. Confirmation of the folk psalmody hypothesis through analysis of psalm-tune variants is the present writer's solution to the problem.

55. Thacher et al., *Cases of Conscience*, p. 6.

56. Walter, *The Grounds and Rules*, p. 2.

57. Chauncey, *Regular Singing Defended*, p. 48.

58. James Grassineau, *A Musical Dictionary, being a Collection of Terms and Characters* (London: Printer for J. Wilcox, 1740), p. 225.

59. Ibid., p. 192.

60. Symmes, *The Reasonableness of Regular Singing*, p. 10.

61. Walter, *The Grounds and Rules*, p. 4.

62. Ibid., pp. 4–5.

63. *Pacificatory Letter about Psalmody, or Singing of Psalms* (Boston: Printed by J. Franklin for John Eliot, 1725), p. 6.

64. Thacher et al., *Cases of Conscience*, pp. 13–14.

65. Ibid., p. 14.

66. See footnote 54 for a discussion of the origin of this phrase.

67. Chauncey, *Regular Singing Defended*, p. 48.

68. Thomas Symmes, *Utili Dulci, or a Joco-Serious Dialogue concerning Regular Singing* (Boston: Printed by B. Green for S. Gerrish, 1723), pp. 44–45.

69. Walter, *The Grounds and Rules*, p. 4.

70. Ibid., p. 3.

71. Symmes, *The Reasonableness of Regular Singing*, p. 8.

72. Chauncey, *Regular Singing Defended*, p. 3.

73. Symmes, *The Reasonableness of Regular Singing*, p. 15.

74. Walter, *The Grounds and Rules*, p. 3.

75. Millar Patrick, *Four Centuries of Scottish Psalmody* (London: Oxford University Press, 1949), pp. 45–104.

76. Ibid., p. 105.

77. John Spencer Curwen, *Studies in Worship Music*, 1st ser., 2nd ed. (London: J. Curwen and Sons, 1888), p. 138.

78. Ibid., p. 142.

79. Patrick, *Four Centuries of Scottish Psalmody*, p. 110.

80. Ibid., p. 111.

81. Ibid., pp. 130–31.

82. Ibid., chapter 14, "The Rise of the Choir Movement," pp. 149–63.

83. Curwen, *Studies in Worship Music*, pp. 148–52.

84. Quoted by Patrick, *Four Centuries of Scottish Psalmody*, pp. 139–40.

85. Ibid., p. 139.

86. Curwen, *Studies in Worship Music*, p. 145.

87. Mainzer's example presumably represents a time when the tunes were so well known to the congregation that the setting of the tune could be dispensed with and the reading combined directly with the singing by reciting the text in a sing-song manner at a definite pitch.

88. Thomas Symmes, *The Reasonableness of Regular Singing*, p. 20.

Chapter II

1. *Collections of the Massachusetts Historical Society* (2nd ser.; Boston: Printed by John Eliot, 1816), 4:301.

2. *Records of the Church in Brattle Square* (Boston: Benevolent Fraternity of Churches, 1902), p. 98. The fact that the date of his admission to the church is considerably later than the dates of his apprenticeship does not invalidate the account as a whole. As an apprentice from a neighboring village, he was probably considered to be a member of the congregation from which he came. His formal admission into the Brattle Square Church was, in all likelihood, deferred until he had become of age and had taken his place in the community as a master of his trade. That Mr. Burbank resided in Plymouth for much of his life is proven by nine entries about him and his family between the years of 1730 and 1793 in *The Plymouth Church Records, 1620–1859* (Publications of the Colonial Society of Massachusetts; Boston: Published by the Society, 1920). That he was a chorister, or leading singer, is not confirmed by the

records of the Plymouth church, but again, this does not preclude the possibility that he was a chorister, since the deliberations about the appointment of minor figures often went unrecorded in the church records.

3. *Records of the Church in Brattle Square*, p. 5.

4. *Boston News Letter*, Feb. 23–Mar. 2, 1713 (Boston: Printed by H. Green in Newbury Street for John Campbell, Post-Master, 1713).

5. *Boston News Letter*, April 12–19, 1714.

6. *Boston News Letter*, April 16–23, 1716.

7. Cotton Mather, *Diary* (Collections of the Massachusetts Historical Society, 7th ser., vols. 7–8; Boston: Published by the Society, 1912), 8:373.

8. Ibid., p. 560. In the same year he delivered to the press a work entitled, *Psalterium Americanum*, which was an attempt to create versifications of the psalms that were closer to the Hebrew than those which were then in use.

9. Thomas Symmes, *The Reasonableness of Regular Singing* (Boston: B. Green for S. Gerrish, 1720), pp. 3–5.

10. The musical content of the chief singing book available, the Bay Psalm Book (Boston, 1698), was too limited in scope to be the basis for systematic training in the rudiments of music. Masters and scholars may have been able to count upon a little known American reprint of *A New Version of the Psalms* by Tate and Brady (Boston, 1713) for guidance in technical matters. Certain English editions of the *New Version* contained an extensive musical supplement designed to teach the rules of psalmody. That the American reprint also included this musical supplement is a moot question, since no copy of this book has survived to the present day. See Allen P. Britton and Irving Lowens, "Unlocated Titles in Early Sacred American Music," *Music Library Association Notes* 11 (December 1953), p. 37.

11. *Boston News Letter*, Jan. 2–9, 1721.

12. Credit for solving one of the most difficult problems in the field of early American music, i.e., the bibliographical history of the unlocated editions of Tufts's Introduction, belongs to Irving Lowens who has summarized his findings in "John Tufts's Introduction to the *Singing of Psalm Tunes* (1721–1744): The First American Music Textbook," *Journal of Research in Music Education* 2, no. 2 (Fall 1954), pp. 89–102.

13. John Tufts, *An Introduction to the Singing of Psalm-Tunes*, 5th ed. (Boston, 1726). Facsimile Reprint for Musical Americana (Harry Dichter) by Albert Saifer, Publisher, Philadelphia, 1954. Foreword by Irving Lowens.

14. Thomas Walter, *The Grounds and Rules of Musick Explained: Or, an Introduction to the Art of Singing by Note* (Boston: Printed by J. Franklin, for S. Gerrish, near the Brick Church in Cornhill, 1721).

15. *Boston News Letter*, May 15–22, 1721.

16. Lowens, "John Tufts's Introduction to the Singing of Psalm Tunes," pp. 89–102.

17. Matt B. Jones, "Bibliographical Notes on Thomas Walter's *Grounds and Rules of Music Explained*," reprinted from the *Proceedings of the American Antiquarian Society* for October 1932 (Worcester: Published by the Society, 1933). It should be noted that in addition to the six editions mentioned above, Walter's book was issued three times more between 1764 and 1768 in an abridged form that included material taken from Tans'ur's *Royal Melody Compleat* (London, 1755).

18. Thomas Walter, *The Grounds and Rules of Music Explained: or, an Introduction to the Art of Singing by Note. Fitted to the Meanest Capacities. By Thomas Walter, M.A.*

Recommended by several Ministers. The Second Edition (Boston: Printed by B. Green, for S. Gerrish, near the Brick Meeting House in Cornhill, 1723), p. 14.

19. Walter, *The Grounds and Rules*, 2nd ed., p. 20.

20. Ibid., p. 21.

21. Ibid., p. 18.

22. Ibid., pp. 18–19.

23. Ibid., pp. 22–23.

24. Ibid., p. 24.

25. Tufts, *An Introduction*, 5th ed., p. 8.

26. Peter Thacher, John Danforth, and Samuel Danforth, *An Essay: Cases of Conscience concerning the Singing of Psalms* (Boston: Printed by S. Kneeland for S. Gerrish, and Sold at his Shop in Cornhill, 1723), p. 9.

27. Samuel Sewall, *Diary* (Collections of the Massachusetts Historical Society, 5th ser., vols. 5–7; Boston: Published by the Society, 1879), 7:284–85.

28. Ibid.

29. Mather, *Diary*, 8:608.

30. *New England Courant*, no. 20, Dec. 11–18, 1721. The advertisement is unsigned; thus the identity of the "Moderator" remains a mystery.

31. Ibid., 25, Jan. 15–22, 1722.

32. *New England Courant*, no. 31, March 5–12, 1722.

33. Their reaction to this lecture as well as the avowed purpose of their society is revealed in the title page: The *Sweet Psalmist of Israel*, a Sermon preach'd at the Lecture held in Boston, by the SOCIETY for promoting REGULAR & GOOD SINGING, and for reforming the Depravations and Debasements our PSALMODY labours under, in order to introduce the proper and true OLD WAY of SINGING. Now published at the desire of several ministers that heard it, and at the request of the Society aforesaid. By Thomas Walter, M.A. Boston: Printed by J. Franklin, for S. Gerrish, near the Brick Meeting-house in Cornhill, 1722.

34. Brown's own summary of his musical activities may be found in E. K. Shipton, *Sibley's Harvard Graduates*, vols. 4–9 (Cambridge: Harvard University Press, 1933–1956), 4:140.

35. *New England Courant*, no. 33, March 19–26, 1722.

36. In this connection it should be noted that the youthful Ben Franklin was in charge of the *Courant* during much of this period because his older brother James to whom he had been apprenticed had been jailed for publishing materials critical of the government. Ben's predilection for music is well known (see William Lichtenwanger, "Benjamin Franklin on Music," *Church Music and Musical Life in Pennsylvania*, vol. 3, Part 2, pp. 449–72). It is not unreasonable to assume, therefore, that many if not all of the *Courant*'s reviews about the singing lectures were his work. If this premise be accepted, the title, "America's first music critic," must be added to the already extensive roster of appellations applied to him.

37. *New England Courant*, no. 41, May 7–14, 1722.

38. Henry W. Foote, *Three Centuries of American Hymnody* (Cambridge: Harvard University Press, 1940), pp. 156–57.

39. *New England Courant*, no. 44, May 28–June 4, 1722.

40. Joseph Green, "A Letter for the Rev'd. Mr. Stephen Williams, Pastor of ye Church of Christ att Longmeadow in Springfield, dated Boston, Oct. 1, 1722," *Transactions*, Publications of the Colonial Society of Massachusetts, vol. 46, pp. 391–92.

41. Jeremiah Bumstead, "Diary," *New England Historical and Genealogical Register* 15:196.

42. In this connection it should be noted that the German religious societies which settled in Germantown in 1694 and in Ephrata in 1720 are also legitimate contenders for this title, since they regularly performed choral music in their respective churches. See Gilbert Chase, *America's Music* (New York: McGraw-Hill, 1955), pp. 54–61. The basis for conferring this title upon The Society for Promoting Regular Singing is the fact that its activities approximated those of present-day choral societies far more closely than those of the German sects. Not only was its membership drawn from the community as a whole, but also its aims and activities were community-wide in scope.

43. Bumstead, "Diary," pp. 198–99.

44. *New England Courant*, no. 95, May 27–June 3, 1723, and no. 113, Sept. 23–30, 1723.

45. Peter Thacher et al., *Cases of Conscience*, p. 7.

46. Walter, who contracted consumption in the winter of 1723–24, experienced increasing "Languishments" from that dread disease during 1724. The course of his final illness may be traced in his uncle's diary. See Cotton Mather, *Diary*, 8:710, 716, 718, 725, 727, 748, 760, 766, 770, 773, 780, 782, 783, and 790.

47. The *Courant*, which noted his passing on Jan. 10, 1725, restricted its announcement to the barest essentials. Mather, who eulogized him in a funeral sermon entitled, "Christodulus," did not comment upon his musical activities. Chauncey, who praised his intellectual powers in a letter to Dr. Stiles dated May 6, 1768, ignored his musical achievements entirely.

48. H. W. Foote has elucidated this point admirably in his *Three Centuries of American Hymnody*. On page 97 of that work he notes, "The widespread belief that the Puritan ministers were harsh, narrow-minded, and bigoted persons who held in check their more broad-minded congregations is a gross perversion of the truth. They were the best educated persons in the community and the natural leaders in intellectual and social matters. They led in the revival of singing; in the introduction of innoculation for smallpox; in the movement for political freedom which culminated in the Revolution; and some of them kept in touch to a remarkable degree with scientific progress in Europe. With few exceptions they were well in advance of the laity in these and kindred matters."

49. S. E. Morison, *Harvard College in the Seventeenth Century* (Cambridge: Harvard University Press, 1936), 1:113.

50. Ibid., pp. 115–16.

51. Ibid., p. 117.

52. The above form of the "Account" has been copied form Arthur O. Norton's "Harvard Text-books and Reference Books of the Seventeenth Century," *Publications of the Colonial Society of Massachusetts, Transactions, 1930–1933*, 28 (April 1933), p. 365.

53. Symmes, *The Reasonableness of Regular Singing*, p. 6. Symmes elaborated this point two years later in another tract, *Utili Dulci* (Boston: Printed B. Green, 1723). On page 38 of that work he noted, "My father learnt it at College; and I can Sing a Tune he learnt me by Note, when I was a Child; and I have now in my Study, Tunes prick'd with his own Hand, and I can't be more sure of any thing of that nature, than of *this*, That he highly approv'd of it, & greatly delighted in it." Symmes's father, Zechariah Symmes, was a member of the Class of 1657.

54. Samuel Sewall, *Diary*, 7:159. That singing "in Consort" meant more than merely singing in concert, or together, is seen in a passage from Symmes's *Utili Dulci*, p. 19, "Now there is no man can judge aright of the Melody of Singing by Note, that has not heard Tunes sung in the several Parts or in Consort."

55. S. E. Morison, *Harvard College*, 2:580, Appendix B.

56. "Harvard College Theses and Quaestiones," vol. 1 (1642–1736) and vol. 2 (1737–1810). HUC 6642.

57. This thesis and those which follow have been taken from the above-named collection in the Harvard Archives.

58. A list of all musical theses written during this period and a discussion of the problems involved in translating them may be found in *Appendix A* (Musical Theses Included in the Commencement Broadsides of Harvard College, 1711–1730).

59. This thesis literally echoes the definition of music given by Walter in his *Grounds and Rules* (see *Figure 5*).

60. Johann Heinrich Alsted, *Johannis-Henrici Alstedii Encyclopedia*; Vol. I Praecognita disciplinarum, Vol. II Philologia, Vol. III Philosophia theoretica, Vol. IV Philosophia practica, Vol. V Tres superiores facultates, Vol. VI Artes mechanicae, Vol. VII Farragines disciplinarum (Herborn, 1630).

61. The topic headings given above are those found in John Birchensha's translation of Alsted's chapter which was published separately as *Templum Musicum* (London, 1664). The summaries of content are the present writer's.

62. Walter, *Grounds and Rules*, 2nd ed., p. 22.

63. Compare for example:
Theses Mathematicae, 1719.
No. 19. Bassus in sede gravissimarum, semper tenet Basin Triadis. (trans.) The bass, which is the lowest part, always forms the foundation of the triad.
Alsted, *Encyclopedia*, 3:1204.
Bassus in sede gravissimarum semper teneat imam seu basin Triadis harmonica. (trans.) Let the Bass always take the lower part or foundation of the harmonical Triad in the place of the gravest.

64. Walter, *Grounds and Rules*, 2nd ed., p. 22.

65. Lowens, "John Tufts's Introduction to the *Singing of Psalm Tunes*," pp. 97–100.

66. There is a definite similarity between their rules for tuning the voice and the vocal exercises found in Playford's *Introduction*.

67. Messrs. Ellis (Booksellers, London), *Playford's "Brief Introduction to the Skill of Musick,"* an Account with Bibliographical Notes of an Unique Collection comprising all the editions from 1654 to 1730 in the possession of Messrs. Ellis (London: Messrs. Ellis, 1926).

68. The eighteenth-century English musical historian, Charles Burney, noted in his *General History of Musick* (London, 1776–1789, 3:417–18) that Playford's introduction was "more generally purchased and read than any elementary musical tract that ever appeared in this or any other country."

69. Alsted, *Encyclopedia*, 3:1195.

70. Morison, *Harvard College*, 1:208–10.

71. Before 1721 propositions in the area of arithmetic, geometry, and music were classified together under the general heading, Theses Mathematicae. Thereafter they were classified separately under the specific headings Theses Arithmeticae, Theses Geometriae, and Theses Musicae.

72. Charles Morton, *Compendium Physicae*, Publications of the Colonial Society of Massachusetts 33 (Boston: Published by the Society, 1940), chap. 24, "Of Hearing," pp. 163–73.

73. Compare for example: *Theses Musicae*, 1728. "No. 26. Ex Chordiae Fidis primariae percussione, producitur eadem alterius Chordae, si sit Unisona, Vibratio."(trans.) From the striking of a given gut string the same vibration is produced in another string, if they are in unison.

Morton, *Compendium Physicae*, p. 170. "Hence 'tis found that 2 strings of the Same Length, thickness, and tension will yield exactly the Same Sound, or tone, and if one be Struck the other will Shake, these are called Unisons..."

74. Cotton Mather, *Manuductio ad Ministerium*, Directions for a Candidate of the Ministry, Wherein, First a Right Foundation is laid for his Future Improvement; and, the Rules are offered for such a Management of his Academical & Preparatory Studies... as may Render him a Skilful and Useful Minister of the Gospel (Boston: Printed for Thomas Hancock, 1726). Section 10 The MATHEMATICS, p. 57.

75. Cotton Mather, "A Letter to Thomas Hollis, dated Nov. 5, 1723," *Collections of the Massachusetts Historical Society*, 7th ser., 8 (Boston: Published by the Society, 1912), p. 693.

76. Two other tracts upon religious music, Wightman's *A Letter to the Elders*, which was published in 1725 and Hammett's *Promiscuous Singing* which was published in 1739, have been omitted from this list because they are not technically part of the immediate reform picture.

77. Symmes, *Utili Dulci*, p. 17. The abbreviations "N." and "M." stand for "Neighbor" and "Minister," respectively, the "Neighbor" being the country bumpkin described in an earlier paragraph.

78. Symmes, *Utili Dulci*, p. 18.

79. Symmes, *Utili Dulci*, p. 19.

80. *New England Courant*, no. 36, April 2–9, 1722.

81. This furor was covered in its entirety by the *Courant* in the issues for Sept. 9–16, 1723; Sept. 23–30, 1723; and Feb. 10–17, 1724.

82. *New England Courant*, no. 69, Nov. 19–22, 1722.

83. Ibid., no. 86, Mar. 18–25, 1723.

84. Ibid., no. 134, Feb. 10–17, 1724.

85. Walter, *Grounds and Rules*, 1st ed., the preface.

86. Thacher et al., *Cases of Conscience*, p. 5.

87. Nathaniel Chauncey, *Regular Singing Defended* (New London: Printed and Sold by T. Green, 1728), p. 49.

88. Symmes, *Monitor for Delaying Sinners*: A Sermon studiously adapted to the meanest capacities, published by the desire of a society of Young Men to whom it was preached Lord's Day Evening, Dec. 7, 1718. With a Preface by Increase Mather, D.D. Reprinted in *Memoirs of the Rev. Mr. Symmes* (Newburyport: Printed by W. D. Allen, 1816).

89. Symmes, *The Reasonableness of Regular Singing*, p. 20.

90. Walter, *The Sweet Psalmist of Israel*, p. 6.

91. Mather, *Diary*, 8:242.

92. Thacher et al., *Cases of Conscience*, p. 5.

93. (Anon.), *A Brief Discourse concerning Regular Singing, Shewing from the Scriptures, the Necessity and Incumbency thereof in the Worship of God* (Boston: Printed by B. Green, jun. for John Eliot at his Shop at the South End of the Town, 1725), p. 16.

94. Walter, *The Sweet Psalmist of Israel*, p. 26.

95. Arthur Bedford, *The Great Abuse of Musick* (London: J. H., 1711).

96. George Lavington (L.L.B., Canon of the Church of Worcester), *The Influence of Church Musick*, a Sermon preach'd in the Cathedral-Church of Worcester, at the Anniversary Meeting of the Choirs of Worcester, Hereford, and Gloucester, Sept. 8, 1725 (London, 1725).

97. Peter Senhouse, *The Right Use and Improvement of sensible Pleasures, and more Particularly of Musick*, a Sermon preach'd in the Cathedral of Gloucester at the Anniversary Meeting of the Choirs of Gloucester, Hereford, and Worcester, Sept. 20, 1727 (London, 1727).

98. Bedford, *The Great Abuse of Musick*, p. 64.

99. Ibid., p. 265.

100. Timothy Woodbridge, *The Duty of GOD's Professing People* (New London, 1727), the Introduction.

101. Such was apparently the case in Westborough, Massachusetts, which adopted regular singing in 1731 shortly after the arrival of its new minister, the Rev. Ebenezer Parkman, who was a very musical man. See H. P. Deforest and E. E. Bates, *History of Westborough, Massachusetts* (Westborough: Published by the Town, 1891), p. 115.

102. The earliest reference to a specific master may be found in the account book kept by the Rev. Timothy Edwards of East Windsor, Connecticut. Quotations from this book covering the activities of a Mr. George Beale and his son in Hartford, Springfield, Willington, and Windsor have been included in Henry R. Stiles, *The History of Ancient Windsor*, 1:273–75.

103. Quoted by David N. Camp, *History of New Britain,1640–1889* (New Britain: William B. Thomson & Co., 1889), p. 87.

104. Quoted by George L. Walker, *History of the First Church in Hartford, 1633–1833* (Hartford: Brown & Gross, 1884), p. 228.

105. Quoted by Rockwell Harmon Potter, *Hartford's First Church* (Hartford: Published by the First Church of Christ, 1932), p. 79.

106. Quoted by John S. Barry, *Historical Sketch of the Town of Hanover, Massachusetts* (Boston: Published for the Author by Samuel G. Drake, 1853), p. 61.

107. Quoted by Charles Henry Davis, *History of Wallingford, Connecticut* (Meriden: Published by the Author, 1870), p. 403.

108. Quoted by Alonzo B. Chapin, *Glastonbury for Two Hundred Years* (Hartford: Press of Case, Tiffany and Co., 1853), p. 77.

109. Quoted by (Anon.), *Mattapoisett and Old Rochester, Massachusetts* (New York: Grafton Press, 1907), pp. 196–97.

Chapter III

1. This conclusion, which is somewhat at odds with the tacit assumption made by the authors of most secondary works, i.e., that the Great Awakening was a positive factor in the further development of the singing school, is the outcome of an analysis of all existing primary sources. See *Appendix B* (The Great Awakening and the Establishment of Regular Singing).

2. Irving Lowens and Allen P. Britton, "Daniel Bayley's *The American Harmony*, a Bibliographical Study," reprinted from the *Papers of the Bibliographical Society of America* 49, Fourth Quarter 1955, pp. 340–54.

3. See *Appendix D* (Suggestions for Further Research).

4. Solomon Kidder Livermore, *On the Practice of Music*, a Discourse pronounced at Pepperell, Massachusetts, May 17th, 1809, before the Middlesex Musical Society. By Solomon Kid-

der Livermore, Attorney-at-Law (Amherst, N.H.: Printed by Joseph Cushing, 1809).

5. Oliver Bray, *An Oration on Music:* Pronounced at Fryeburg before the Hans Gram Musical Society on their First Anniversary, October 10, 1811 (Portland: Printed by Arthur Shirley, 1812).

6. The evaluation of these and similar utterances will not be undertaken in this book because they are properly the subject of studies dealing with the later-day singing school and with the profound changes in musical taste which banished all things American from polite society after 1820.

7. This set of recollections is unique in the annals of the singing school for three reasons. First, it is one of the few statements extant concerning the training undergone by the singing masters which is based upon first-hand experience. Second, it is one of the few statements issued during the nineteenth century in which the subject is treated in non-polemical terms. Third, no writer of that period succeeded better than Cheney did in describing the impact which the singing school had upon the youth of rural New England. For these reasons this set is quoted, contrary to accepted conventions of dissertation style, in nearly complete form.

8. Charles Henry Pope, *The Cheney Genealogy* (Boston: Published by Charles H. Pope, 1897), notes on pp. 305–6 and pp. 377–78 that Cheney, who was a Baptist minister as well as a singing master, was born in Haverhill, Massachusetts, in 1776. He became a resident of Derby, Vermont, in 1824 and died in Sheffield, Vermont, in 1856. He was the head of a musical family which toured as the Cheney Family Singers from 1845–1847. His four sons, Nathaniel, Simeon Pease, Moses Ela, and Joseph, all became singing masters, and a daughter named Elizabeth Ela was noted as a vocal soloist. Simeon Pease Cheney achieved the distinction of compiling *The American Singing Book* (Boston: White, Smith & Co., 1879), which was one of the last oblong tune books to be published and one of the few tune books of the later period which included works by Billings and his contemporaries.

9. Moses Cheney, "Letter to Friend Mason," *Musical Visitor* 2, no. 17 (Dec. 1, 1841), pp. 132–33 and no. 18 (Jan. 1, 1842) (Boston: Published by an Association of Gentlemen, Kidder & Wright, Printers, 1841–1842), pp. 139–40.

10. Perhaps the best illustration of the way in which the musical tools of the trade were passed from master to "apprentice" is to be found in the life of William Billings. Frank J. Metcalf notes in his *American Writers and Compilers of Sacred Music* (New York: Abingdon Press, 1925), on pages 42, 83, 161, respectively, that Billings directly influenced John Stickney, Supply Belcher, and Abraham Maxim, all of whom became eminent singing master-composers in their own right. The total number of masters whom he influenced, either personally or through his music, is, of course, much larger. The comparative scarcity of primary source material prevents the compilation of a more detailed list.

11. A copy in Read's own hand is included in his "Letterbook," a manuscript in the possession of the New Haven Historical Society. Read refers to this letter as a "certificate."

12. *Nantucket Inquirer*, Sept. 10, 1822. Published by Samuel H. Jenks.

13. William Bentley, *Diary,* 4 vols. (Salem: Essex Institute, 1911), 3:17.

14. Ibid., 3:342.

15. See *Appendix C* (A Country Parson and the Singing Schools of Westborough, Massachusetts).

16. Although "union singing schools" seem to have been quite common, the term itself does not seem to have had currency. Its use in the present discussion is justified by Frank Smith's forthright description of such schools in his *History of Dover, Massachusetts* (Dover: Published by the Town, 1897), p. 242. "We think of the women of that period as spending their days in spinning, weaving, or knitting; but they had much recreation in public balls, quilting parties, and singing schools which were the beginning of many a courtship in the early time. Union singing schools, which were very enjoyable, were often held at the tavern, the singing master inviting the members of his several schools in other towns to unite for the evening."

17. Mrs. Augusta Harvey Worthen, *History of Sutton, New Hampshire* (Concord: Printed by the Republican Press Assoc., 1890), part 1, p. 538.

18. Quoted by Henry M. Brooks, *Olden Time Music, a Compilation from Newspapers and Books* (Boston: Ticknor and Co., 1888), p. 51.

19. Aaron Kinne, *Alamoth,* an Address delivered to the Singing Schools in the First and Second Societies in Groton (New London: Printed by S. Green, 1798), p. 15.

20. Metcalf, *American Writers and Compilers of Sacred Music,* p. 42.

21. Ibid., p. 66.

22. Ibid., p. 80.

23. Ibid., p. 84.

24. Ibid., p. 87.

25. Ibid.

26. Ibid., p. 93.

27. Ibid., p. 95.

28. Ibid., p. 103.

29. "Jacob Kimball," *Historical Collections of the Topsfield Historical Society* (Topsfield: Published by the Society, 1907), vol. 12, p. 96.

30. Metcalf, *American Writers and Compilers of Sacred Music,* p. 122.

31. Ibid., p. 125.

32. Ibid., p. 162.

33. Quoted by Robert Francis Seybolt, *The Private Schools of Boston* (Cambridge: Harvard University Press, 1935), p. 31.

34. Quoted by Harry R. Warfel, *Noah Webster, Schoolmaster to America* (New York: Macmillan Co., 1936), p. 40.

35. Seybolt, *The Private Schools of Boston,* p. 32, has noted that Holbrook, who regularly kept school in Boston from 1741 until his death in 1789, was permitted by the town authorities to "improve" the South Writing School as a private school after hours.

36. E. E. F. Ford, *Notes on the Life of Noah Webster* (New York: Privately printed, 1912), vol. 1, p. 45, states that Webster kept a singing school one evening a week to supplement his day school in Sharon.

37. In this connection it should be noted that James Fenimore Cooper also made use of the Yankee singing master as a character in a literary work. In the *Last of the Mohicans* (New York: George P. Putnam, 1850) a singing master, appropriately named David Gamut, supplies comic relief from the many serious episodes of derring-do on the frontier.

38. Washington Irving, "The Legend of Sleepy Hollow," *The Sketch Book of Geoffrey Crayon, Gent.* (London: John Murray, 1821), p. 263.

39. Ervin C. Shoemaker, *Noah Webster, Pioneer of Learning* (New York: Columbia University Press, 1936), p. 32, notes an apocryphal story about Webster to the effect that he became so attached to one of the girls who attended his singing school in Sharon that he left town after losing her hand to a rival, just as Ichabod did after losing Katrina to Brom Bones.

40. Irving Lowens, "Daniel Read's World: The Letters of an Early American Composer," *Music Library Association Notes,* Second Series 9, no. 2 (March 1952), pp. 241–42.

41. Warwick Palfray, *The Evangelical Psalmodist:* An original work; consisting of Plain Tune Fuges, and Set Pieces, in Three and Four Parts; Suitable for Schools and Singing Societies (Salem: Printed by Joshua Cushing for the Author, 1802).

42. Bentley, *Diary,* 2:20.

43. Ibid., 3:258.

44. Allen P. Britton, "Theoretical Introductions in American Tune Books to 1800," Unpublished doctoral dissertation, University of Michigan, 1949, p. 127. Information used by permission of the author.

45. Allen P. Britton and Irving Lowens, "Unlocated Titles in Early Sacred American Music," *Music Library Association Notes* 11 (December 1953), p. 33. "For some time now, the writers have been investigating, both as individuals and as a team, the nature and backgrounds of sacred music in eighteenth and early nineteenth century America. Their researches have led them to a heightened appreciation of the important role played by the tune book in young America's cultural development, a role far transcending the narrow implications of the term 'psalmody' with which the tune book is almost invariably damned. For, in reality, these humble collections of hymn tunes, fuguing tunes, set pieces, and anthems are among the most significant early monuments of music in this country. They are eloquent testimony to a society in which music was perhaps as integral a part of daily life as it had been in England during Elizabethan days. They are our first music textbooks, products of the New England singing school, a dominating force in American music for well over a century. In their omnipresent introductions to 'grounds of music' can be read the full story of music pedagogy in colonial and post colonial days. They supply us with detailed, authentic information about the vocal performance practices of the period. And thousands of compositions in a striking native idiom to be found in their pages are the fruit of a great flowering of musical creativity, the first to occur on American soil."

46. Bentley, *Diary,* 2:192.

47. Ibid., 2:296.

48. No further mention of Law's "Music School" is made in the Bentley *Diary.* The entry for Nov. 21, 1797, quoted above suggests that he had left Salem by 1798; thus it could not have been in existence for more than a year or two.

49. Bentley, *Diary,* 2:247.

50. Ibid., 2:292.

51. The imprecise way in which the words *society, school,* and *club* were used, as well as the complex interlocking of the membership of the groups which they were intended to describe, prevents a more positive identification.

52. *Salem Gazette* 19, no. 1419, April 2, 1805 (Salem: Published by Thomas C. Cushing).

53. Samuel Holyoke, *The Instrumental Assistant.* Containing instructions for the Violin, German-Flute, Clarionet, Bass-Viol, and Hautboy. Compiled from late European publications. Also a Selection of favorite Airs, Marches, &c. Progressively Arranged, and adapted to the use of Learners by Samuel Holyoke, A.M. Vol. 1 (Exeter, N.H.: H. Ranlet, 1800).

54. Samuel Holyoke, *The Instrumental Assistant.* Containing a Selection of Minuets, Airs, Duettos, Rondos and Marches: with Instructions for the French-Horn and Bassoon. Compiled by Samuel Holyoke, A.M. Vol. 2 (Exeter, N.H.: Printed and sold by Ranlet and Norris, 1807).

55. Nathaniel D. Gould, *Church Music in America* (Boston: A. N. Johnson, 1853), p. 73.

56. Francis G. Butler, *A History of Farmington, Franklin County, Maine, 1776–1885* (Farmington: Press of Knowlton, McLeary and Co., 1885), p. 379.

57. Metcalf, *American Writers and Compilers of Sacred Music,* p. 161.

58. August A. Gould and Frederic Kidder, *History of New Ipswich* (Boston: Gould and Lincoln, 1852), pp. 263–64.

59. Bentley, *Diary,* 3:253. Note: the man identified as "Farmington" was probably Mr. Farrington who taught a singing school for Bentley's singers in 1793. See 2:15, of the Bentley *Diary* for this correction.

60. Ibid., 3:389.

61. Ibid., 3:414.

62. Metcalf, *American Writers and Compilers of Sacred Music,* p. 66.

63. Ibid., p. 91.

64. Frederick P. Wells, *History of Newbury, Vermont* (St. Johnsbury, Vt.: The Caledonian Co., 1902), p. 178.

65. Francis G. Butler, *History of Farmington,* p. 379.

66. Metcalf, *American Writers and Compilers of Sacred Music,* p. 69.

67. Bentley, *Diary,* 2:350–51.

68. Gould, *Church Music in America.*

69. Ibid., p. 234.

70. Edward Bailey Birge, *The History of Public School Music in the United States* (Philadelphia: Oliver Ditson Co., 1937), pp. 35–56.

71. Arthur Lowndes Rich, *Lowell Mason, "The Father of Singing Among the Children"* (Chapel Hill: University of North Carolina Press, 1946).

72. Peter Thacher et al., *Cases of Conscience* (Boston, 1723), pp. 16–17.

73. Thomas Symmes, *The Reasonableness of Regular Singing* (Boston, 1720), p. 2.

74. It will be recalled that Tufts's "plain and easy Method" was advertised as being specially designed "for the ease of Learners, whereby even Children, or People of the meanest Capacities, may come to Sing" by rule.

75. Quoted by Seybolt, *The Private Schools of Colonial Boston,* p. 27.

76. The meager number of advertisements of this sort is not a good measure of the probable number of singing masters who taught singing schools for children during this period since many singing masters dealt directly with particular congregations and did not, therefore, have to advertise their services.

77. Seybolt, *Private Schools of Colonial Boston,* p. 31.

78. Ibid., p. 56.

79. *Essex Gazette* 6, no. 268, Sept. 14, 1773 (Salem: Printed by Samuel and Ebenezer Hall).

80. Henry Swan Dana notes on page 221 of his *History of Woodstock, Vermont* (Boston: Houghton, Mifflin and Co., 1889) that Elisha West, a singing master who was active in Woodstock from 1791 until 1807, taught his younger pupils in the afternoon and his older ones in the evening.

81. Worthen notes on page 538 of her *History of Sutton, New Hampshire*, that Captain Buell, a singing master who was active in Sutton and Newport from about 1790 onward, regularly taught singing school classes in the afternoon and in the evening.

82. Quoted by Charles Evans, *American Bibliography* (Chicago: Blakely Press, 1903–1955), no. 22829.

83. Bentley, *Diary*, 1:2.

84. Ibid., 1:337.

85. Ibid.

86. Ibid., 1:338.

87. Ibid.

88. Ibid.

89. Ibid.

90. Ibid., 1:340.

91. Ibid., 1:341.

92. Ibid., 1:357.

93. Ibid., 1:389.

94. Ibid., 1:2.

95. Ibid., 1:119.

96. Ibid., 1:119.

97. Ibid.

98. See also the extracts from Sophia Parkman's "Diary" which are quoted in *Appendix C* (A Country Parson and the Singing Schools of Westborough, Massachusetts).

99. Elizabeth Fuller, "Diary Kept by Elizabeth Fuller, Daughter of Rev. Timothy Fuller of Princeton," quoted by Francis Everett Blake, *History of Princeton, 1759–1915* (Princeton: Published by the Town, 1915), vol. I, chap. 12, p. 304.

100. Ibid.

101. Ibid.

102. Ibid.

103. Ibid.

104. Ibid.

105. Ibid.

106. Ibid., p. 305.

107. Ibid., p. 308.

108. Ibid., p. 309.

109. Ibid.

110. Ibid.

111. Caleb Jackson, Jr., "Daily Journal, 1802–1805," a manuscript diary in the Library of the Essex Institute, Salem, Massachusetts. Pages not numbered.

112. Lowell Mason, *Address on Church Music* (Boston: Hilliard, Gray & Co., 1826).

113. Thomas Hastings, *The History of Forty Choirs* (New York: Mason Brothers, 1854), pp. 176–77.

114. Other examples may be found in Brooks, *Olden Time Music: A Compilation from Newspapers and Books*, and in Seybolt, *The Private Schools of Colonial Boston*.

115. *Salem Gazette* 17, no. 1281, Dec. 6, 1803.

116. Quoted by Dana, *History of Woodstock, Vermont*, p. 221.

117. Gould, *Church Music in America*, pp. 79–84.

118. Quoted by Zephine Humphrey, *The Story of Dorset* (Rutland, Vt.: Tuttle & Co., 1924), pp. 102–4.

119. William Pynchon, *Diary*, edited by F. E. Oliver (Boston: Houghton, Mifflin & Co., 1890), p. 134.

120. Ibid., p. 135.

121. Ibid.

122. Bentley, *Diary*, 3:338.

123. S. Leroy Blake, *The Later History of the First Church of Christ, New London, Connecticut* (New London: Press of the Day Publishing Co., 1900), p. 230 notes, "In 1804 the society instructed its committee to 'agree with Asa Dutton to teach a Singing School in this Society the year ensuing, and that the Society Committee make a Collection in the usual way in the Meeting House once in each month for the support of Psalm Singing.'"

124. Quoted by Rockwell Harmon Potter, *Hartford's First Church* (Hartford: Published by the First Church of Christ, 1932), p. 79.

125. Oliver Noble, *Regular and Skillful Music in the Worship of God* (Boston: Printed by Mills and Hicks for Daniel Bayley in Newburyport, 1774), p. 40.

126. Abijah P. Marvin, *History of the Town of Winchendon* (Winchendon, Mass.: Published by the Author, 1868), chap. 9, "The Town as a Parish," p. 145.

127. Ezra S. Stearns, *History of Ashburnham, 1734–1886* (Ashburnham, Mass.: Published by the Town, 1887), p. 287.

128. "Sudbury, Massachusetts, Records of the Town," manuscript records on file in the office of the town clerk, n.p.

129. Ibid.

130. Wilson Waters, *History of Chelmsford* (Lowell, Mass.: Printed for the town by Courier-Citizen Co., 1917), pp. 682 notes, "In 1826 the Town appropriated $150 for a singing school for the benefit of the three religious societies: the First Parish and the Baptists, and the Second Parish at Middlesex Village."

131. *History of Bolton, 1736–1938* (Bolton, Mass.: Privately published, 1938), p. 72.

132. Herbert Collins Parsons, *A Puritan Outpost, a History of the Town and People of Northfield, Massachusetts* (New York: Macmillan & Co., 1937), p. 198, discusses the case of *Sever vs. Northfield* in great detail but fails to give the exact date, which appears to have been about 1790.

133. Alfred Noon, *History of Ludlow* (Springfield, Mass.: Springfield Printing and Binding Co., 1912), p. 56.

134. J. H. Temple, *History of Framingham, Massachusetts, 1640–1880* (Framingham: Published by the Town, 1887), p. 338.

135. Gould, *Church Music in America*, p. 82.

136. Ibid., p. 81.

137. Ibid., p. 83.

138. Gould's assertions also raise the interesting question, did the singing and playing of secular music have a regular place in an institution ostensibly devoted to the cultivation of sacred music? The answer appears to be that it did and that the

degree to which it was indulged in depended upon the talents and attitudes of particular masters. At least two of them, Chauncey Langdon and Timothy Swan, individually published songsters (Metcalf, *American Writers and Composers of Sacred Music,* p. 103) containing a wide variety of political songs, drinking songs, amatory songs, sea songs, patriotic odes, and ballads, which were the popular music of their day. E. H. Sears in his fictionalized account of "The History of the Oxford Singing School" (*Dwight's Journal of Music* 18, no. 15, p. 332) relates how the singing master Solomon Huntington entertained his scholars with "battle pieces" on his violin. Samuel Gilman in his "Memoirs of a New England Village Choir" (*Contributions to Literature,* 1856, p. 14) tells how the youthful chorister, Charles Williams, would play "The Devil's Dream" and other dance tunes on the bass viol for his friends. William Bentley in an entry in his *Diary* for May 21, 1809, speaks of how he had to reprimand his singers for "playing and singing to the Bass Viol before service began." Ebenezer Parkman and his daughter, Sophia, included many love songs and dance tunes along with the gamut and psalm tunes in their manuscript singing book (*Appendix C*). Thomas Hastings in his *Forty Choirs,* p. 177, admits that during the singing school recess periods many "scholars would be talking nonsense, or romping, or dancing, or joining in loud laughter or merry songs."

139. Frank Smith, *History of Dover, Massachusetts* (Dover: Published by the Town, 1897), p. 242.

140. Worthen, *History of Sutton,* part 1, p. 538.

141. *Columbian Centinel* 19, no. 25 (Whole No. 9611), June 5, 1793 (Boston: Printed by Benjamin Russell).

142. Mary Caroline Crawford, *Social Life in Old New England* (Boston: Little, Brown, and Co., 1914), p. 384.

143. *Essex Gazette* 5, no. 226, Nov. 24, 1772.

144. "Sudbury, Massachusetts, Records of the Town."

145. Ibid.

146. Ibid.

147. Ibid.

148. See Pauline Holmes, *A Tercentenary History of Boston Public Latin School, 1635–1935* (Cambridge: Harvard University Press, 1935), pp. 502–4 for a list of the various singing masters who were granted permission to use the Boston Latin School for their singing school classes. See also the entries in the Bentley *Diary* for April 25, 1804, and Nov. 17, 1807 (3:82 and 3:329, respectively), which note the use of the Eastern Public School House in Salem for singing schools.

149. A. E. Jewett and E. Y. A. Jewett, "The Diary of Deacon Joshua Jewett," *Rowley, Massachusetts, Mr. Ezechi Rogers Plantation, 1639–1850* (Rowley: Published by the Jewett Family in America, 1946), p. 276.

150. Bentley, *Diary,* 2:245.

151. Jewett and Jewett, "The Accompts of Benjamin Todd of Rowley," *Rowley, Massachusetts, Mr. Ezechi Rogers Plantation, 1639–1850,* p. 266.

152. *Salem Gazette* 17, no. 1281, Dec. 6, 1803, and 19, no. 1419, April 2, 1805.

153. *Nantucket Inquirer* 3, no. 38, Sept. 16, 1823.

154. Bentley, *Diary,* 1:2–3.

155. See the entry in Ebenezer Parkman's "Diary" for Jan. 30, 1778, which is quoted in *Appendix C* (A Country Parson and the Singing Schools of Westborough, Massachusetts).

156. See Claggett's advertisement in the *Salem Gazette* 39, New Series vol. 3, no. 17, March 1, 1825.

157. William Billings, *The Singing Master's Assistant,* or Key to Practical Music. Being an Abridgement from the New England Psalm-Singer; together with several other Tunes, never before published (Boston: Printed by Draper and Folsom, 1778), pp. 16–17.

158. Quoted by Dr. William Lee, "Instructions in Psalmody in Boston Before 1750," *New England Historical and Genealogical Register* 42, pp. 197–98.

159. Gould, *Church Music in America,* p. 91.

160. It will be recalled that Moses Cheney in his "Letter to Friend Mason," reported that the singing master and many of his fellow scholars used manuscript materials in the singing school which he attended in 1788. Peter Woodbury et al., *History of Bedford, N.H.* (Boston: Printed by Alfred Mudge, 1851), p. 200, reported a similar occurrence which took place in their community in 1782.

161. Hannah Boldery, "Her Book," a manuscript singing book made up almost entirely of single stave voice parts to the standard New England psalm tunes. In the possession of Mr. Irving Lowens, Hyattsville, Md.

162. Metcalf notes in his *American Writers and Compilers of Sacred Music,* p. 42, that it was the custom of John Stickney to write as many as sixty copies a day of the music which he wished his scholars to learn.

163. George Newberry, "(Singing) Book," a manuscript tune book with music from the Tufts period. In the possession of Mr. Irving Lowens, Hyattsville, Md.

164. Ebenezer Parkman, "Diary, 1777–1778," a manuscript in the possession of the Massachusetts Historical Society.

165. Ibid.

166. An excellent example would be the one which Parkman made for himself in 1721 while residing in Boston. His daughter, Sophia, took it up again in 1778 and added many new tunes. See *Appendix C* (A Country Parson and the Singing Schools of Westborough, Massachusetts).

167. Quoted by Brooks, *Olden Time Music, a Compilation from Newspapers and Books,* p. 256.

168. See the following numbers in Evans's *American Bibliography* for a complete description of the gamuts published between 1788 and 1800: no. 21103 (1788), no. 25525 (1793), no. 28724–25 (1795), no. 30470 (1796), no. 32173 (1797), no. 33778 (1798), and no. 35532 (1799).

169. *A Gamut, or Scale of Music. To which Is added Blank Lines for Favorite Music* (Hartford: Published and Sold by Oliver D. Cooke, 1807).

170. *A Gamut, or Scale of Music. To which is added Blank Lines for Favorite Music* (Hartford: Published and sold by Oliver D. Cooke, 1811).

171. Readers who desire a different and considerably more extensive treatment of this subject are referred to Britton's "Theoretical Introductions in American Tune books to 1800."

172. Jacob Kimball, *The Rural Harmony* (Boston: Isaiah Thomas and Ebenezer T. Andrews, 1793), p. xi.

173. Daniel Read, *The American Singing Book,* 4th ed. (New Haven: Printed for the Author, 1793), p. 24.

174. Ibid., p. 23.

175. Simeon Jocelin, *The Chorister's Companion* (New Haven: Printed for and Sold by Simeon Jocelin and Amos Doolittle, 1782), p. 13.

176. Ibid., p. 14.

177. John Stickney, *The Gentleman and Ladies Musical Companion* (Newburyport: Printed and Sold by Daniel Bayley, 1774).

178. Oliver Holden, *The Union Harmony*, 2nd ed. (Boston: Isaiah Thomas and Ebenezer T. Andrews, 1796).

179. William Billings, *The Singing Master's Assistant*, 3rd ed., p. 15.

180. Stickney, *Gentleman and Ladies Musical Companion*.

181. Chauncey Langdon, *The Beauties of Psalmody* (New Haven: Printed by Daniel Bowen, 1786).

182. Stephen Jenks, *Delights of Harmony* (New Haven: Printed and Engraved for the Purchaser, 1805).

183. It is a most enlightening exercise to compare the pronouncements made by eighteenth-century singing masters with those made by twentieth-century choral conductors such as A. T. Davison, whose *Choral Conducting* (Cambridge: Harvard University Press, 1940) is a standard work on that subject. For example, Davison's statement about dynamics (p. 69) has much in common with Holden's remarks about "soft singing," which are quoted above. "It goes without saying that a wide dynamic range is essential; but for once that a conductor feels obliged to ask for more volume, he will on twenty occasions ask for less. A fine pianissimo which is maintained at pitch requires mainly a controlled tone and full breathing, and that pianissimo is much easier to produce than a fine fortissimo. Just how loud a chorus may sing without offense is a question each conductor must decide for himself.... [There] is, after all, a point at which choral singing ceases to be music and becomes plain natural undisciplined sound. Forte and piano are relative, not abstract terms, and sheer volume is not, in itself, a desideratum."

184. Stephen Jenks, *Delights of Harmony*.

185. Samuel Holyoke, *The Columbian Repository* (Exeter, 1802), chap. 1.

186. Duncan McKenzie, *Training the Boy's Changing Voice* (New Brunswick, N.J.: Rutgers University Press, 1956), p. 3.

187. Solomon Howe, *Farmer's Evening Entertainment* (Northampton: Printed by Andrew Wright, 1804).

188. Samuel Preston, "Recollections by Samuel Preston written for the *Salem Village Gazette*, Dec. 8, 1869," reprinted in *Historical Collections of the Danvers Historical Society* (Danvers: Published by the Society, 1919), vol. 7, pp. 125–30.

189. William Billings, *The Continental Harmony* (Boston: Isaiah Thomas and Ebenezer T. Andrews, 1794).

190. A complete bibliography of the bewildering array of editions resulting from Law's manner of issuing *The Art of Singing* may be found in Joyce Ellen Mangler's unpublished master's thesis, "Andrew Law, Musical Reformer," Department of Music, Brown University, 1956.

191. Ebenezer Parkman, *The Diary of the Rev. Ebenezer Parkman, 1737 and 1778–1780* (Westborough: Westborough Historical Society, 1899), p. 86.

192. Ibid., p. 88.

193. Ibid., p. 94.

194. Ibid., p. 95.

195. Ibid., p. 96.

196. Ibid., p. 97.

197. Ibid., p. 97.

198. For another example of a singing lecture, see the entry for Mar. 31, 1778, in the Parkman diary which is quoted in *Appendix C* (A Country Parson and the Singing Schools of Westborough, Massachusetts).

199. Charles Stearns, *A Sermon, preached at an Exhibition of Sacred Musick in Lincoln on the nineteenth of April, 1792* (Boston: Isaiah Thomas and Ebenezer T. Andrews, 1792), p. 13. Isaac Lane, a singing master from neighboring Bedford, was the teacher mentioned in the sermon.

200. Jonathan Hayward, "Diary, 1800–1808" (extracts), *Historical Collections of the Danvers Historical Society* (Danvers: Published by the Society, 1915), vol. 3, p. 53.

201. Ibid., p. 58.

202. Bentley, *Diary*, 2:175.

203. Ibid.

204. Ibid., 2:190.

205. Mary Holyoke, "Diary, 1760–1800," *The Holyoke Diaries, 1709–1856* (Salem: The Essex Institute, 1911), p. 134.

206. *Essex Gazette* 6, no. 300, April 19–26, 1774, p. 154.

207. Ibid.

208. Ibid.

209. Archelaus Putnam (1787–1818), "A Journal and Diary of Foreign and Domestic Intelligence, or Remembrancer of Remarkable Days, Weather, etc., commenced at Danvers, Massachusetts, Jan. 1. 1805," *Historical Collections of the Danvers Historical Society* (Danvers: Published by the Society, 1916), vol. 4, p. 64.

210. Ibid. Holyoke was also well known as a teacher of instrumental music; thus his entry may be interpreted to mean that he attempted to broaden the scope of his work in Danvers by setting up such a school.

211. Ibid.

212. Ibid., p. 65. It was the custom during this period to choose the leaders of the various voice parts by democratic means. See Gould, *Church Music in America*, p. 103.

213. Ibid., p. 65.

214. Ibid., p. 66.

215. Ibid., p. 67.

216. Ibid., p. 68.

217. Ibid., p. 68.

218. Henry Wilder Foote, *Three Centuries of American Hymnody* (Cambridge: Harvard University Press, 1940), pp. 118–20.

219. William Billings, *The Psalm Singer's Amusement* (Boston: Printed and sold by the Author at his House near the White Horse, 1781).

220. Stickney, *The Gentleman and Ladies Musical Companion*.

221. Read, *The American Singing Book*.

222. Solomon Howe, *The Farmer's Evening Entertainment* (Northampton: Printed by Andrew Wright, 1804).

223. Mason, *Address on Church Music*, p. 27.

224. Gould, *Church Music in America*, p. 96.

225. Thomas Hastings, *The History of Forty Choirs* (New York: Mason Brothers, 1854), p. 176.

226. The reader is referred to the charming autobiographical account, "Incidents in the First Seventeen Years of the Life of Robert Rhythm," *Musical Gazette* 1, no. 15 (August 17, 1846), pp. 113–15, which describes the day-to-day progress of the typical singing school and the year-to-year progress of the anonymous narrator toward musical literacy.

227. Hans Gram, Samuel Holyoke, and Oliver Holden, *The Massachusetts Compiler of Theoretical and Practical Elements of Sacred Vocal Music. Together with a Musical Dictio-*

nary and a Variety of Psalm Tunes, Choruses, &c. Chiefly Selected from Modern European Publications (Boston: Isaiah Thomas and Ebenezer T. Andrews, 1793), p. xxix.

228. Samuel Holyoke's retention of the four-syllable system in his magnum opus, *The Columbian Repository* (Exeter, 1802) suggests that he was unwilling to risk losing his patrons by using an unfamiliar method of solmization.

229. The seven-syllable system advocated by Andrew Adgate in his *Rudiments of Music* (Fourth edition, Philadelphia, 1793) was ignored by New England singing masters with the exception of Andrew Law, who made it the subject of ridicule in the first issue of his *Musical Magazine* (Cheshire, 1792).

230. Scholars are not in complete agreement as to which credit should be given for the invention of shape notes. No attempt will be made here to resolve their differences because no new information concerning this highly complicated point was uncovered during the course of the present investigation. The reader should consult the works listed in the footnotes which follow for their views on this matter.

231. Frank J. Metcalf, "The Easy Instructor," *Musical Quarterly* 23, no. 1 (January 1937), pp. 89–97.

232. Irving Lowens and Allen P. Britton, "The Easy Instructor, (1798–1831); a History and Bibliography of the First Shape Note Tune Book," *Journal of Research in Music Education* 1, no. 1 (Spring 1953), pp. 30–55.

233. Mangler, "Andrew Law, Musical Reformer," pp. 30–39.

234. George Pullen Jackson, "Buckwheat Notes," *Musical Quarterly* 19, no. 4 (October 1933), pp. 393–400.

235. George Pullen Jackson, *White Spirituals in the Southern Uplands* (Chapel Hill: The University of North Carolina Press, 1933).

236. Irving Lowens has traced the fascinating story of how the music of New England singing master-composers came to be transmitted to the South in his monograph, "John Wyeth's Repository of Sacred Music, Part Second: A Northern Precursor of Southern Folk Hymnody," *Journal of the American Musicological Society* 5, no. 2 (Summer 1952), pp. 114–31.

237. Bentley, *Diary*, 2:183.

238. Ibid., 2:185.

239. It should be noted that Law was not only a staunch advocate of "soft singing" but also an advocate of the modern practice of assigning the "air" or principal melody to the highest part, the soprano. Most of the other singing master-composers continue Walter's practice of giving the melody to the tenor. Thus, in the entry quoted above, when Bentley states that "not one note of Tenour was heard through the evening" he means that the melody was no longer found in the tenor, but in the soprano.

Chapter IV

1. Nathaniel D. Gould, *Church Music in America* (Boston: A. N. Johnson, 1853), p. 58.

2. Allen P. Britton, "The Musical Idiom in Early American Tune Books," an abstract of a paper read in St. Louis on April 14, 1950, at a meeting of the Midwestern Chapter. *Journal of the American Musicological Society* 3, no. 3 (Fall 1950), p. 286.

3. Allen P. Britton, "Theoretical Introductions to American Tune Books to 1800," (doctoral diss., University of Michigan, 1949), p. 122. Quoted by permission of the author.

4. Richard Franko Goldman and Roger Smith, *Landmarks of Early American Music, 1760–1800* (New York: G. Schirmer, 1943), p. 8.

5. Irving Lowens and Allen P. Britton, "Daniel Bayley's *The American Harmony*, a Bibliographical Study," reprinted from the *Papers of the Bibliographical Society of America* 49, Fourth Quarter 1955, pp. 340–55.

6. John Tileston, "Diary," quoted by D. C. Colesworthy, *John Tileston's School* (Boston: Antiquarian Bookstore, 1887), p. 74.

7. Ibid., p. 75.

8. Ibid., p. 76.

9. This phrase is taken from the wording of a vote taken in 1765 by the congregation at Old Chester, N.H., who agreed to let the singers of the parish sit together in the gallery of the meeting house. See Benjamin Chase, *History of Old Chester* (Auburn: Published by the Author, 1869), p. 323.

10. Arthur B. Ellis, *The History of the First Church in Boston, 1630–1880* (Boston: Hall and Whiting), p. 204.

11. Ibid., p. 205.

12. Alice Morse Earle, *The Sabbath in Puritan New England* (New York: Charles Scribner's Sons, 1891), Chapter V, "Seating the Meeting," pp. 45–65.

13. *Muddy River and Brookline Records, 1634–1838* (Brookline: J. E. Farwell and Co., 1875), p. 274.

14. *Table 5* represents a very limited sampling of that which was a widespread phenomenon, because of the conservative manner in which it was compiled. Knowledge about the period in general suggests that the figure of ten might well be multiplied by a factor of two, or even of three, and still not be seriously in error.

15. The work referred to is William Billings, *New England Psalm Singer* (Boston: Edes and Gill, 1770). Josiah Flagg's *A Collection of the Best Psalm Tunes* (Boston: Engraved By Paul Revere, 1764) does not qualify because it is chiefly a compilation "from the most approved Authors." James Lyon's *Urania* (Philadelphia: Printed by William Bradford, 1761), though full of original material, does not qualify either because its author was a New Jersey man who emigrated to New England ten years after its publication in Philadelphia.

16. Lemuel Hedge (A.M.), *The Duty and Manner of Singing in Christian Churches*, considered and illustrated in a Sermon preached at a Singing Lecture in Warwick, January 29, 1772. By Lemuel Hedge, A.M., Pastor of the Church there. Published at the Request of the Singers. (Boston: Printed by Richard Draper, 1772), pp. 34–35.

17. William Billings, *The Continental Harmony*, containing a Number of Anthems, Fuges, and Choruses, in several Parts. Never before published. Composed by William Billings, Author of various Music Books (Boston: Isaiah Thomas and Ebenezer T. Andrews, 1794), p. xviii.

18. The complete sequence of events leading up to this lecture may be found in *Appendix C* (A Country Parson and the Singing Schools of Westborough, Massachusetts).

19. Ebenezer Parkman, "Diary, 1777–1778," a manuscript journal in possession of the Massachusetts Historical Society.

20. Frederic G. Howe's, *History of the Town of Ashfield, 1742–1910* (Ashfield: Published by the Town, 1910), p. 159.

21. Edwin Stone, *History of Beverly, 1630–1842* (Boston: James Munroe and Company, 1843), p. 255.

22. Silas R. Colburn, *History of Dracut, Massachusetts* (Lowell: Press of Courier-Citizen Co., 1834), p. 192.

23. H. P. Deforest and E. C. Bates, *History of Westborough, Massachusetts* (Westborough: Published by the Town, 1891), p. 157.

24. William Lincoln, *History of Worcester to 1836* (Worcester: Moses D. Phillips and Company, 1837), p. 178.

25. Ibid., p. 179.

26. The wrangling between Deacon Warriner and the singers of the town of Wilbraham would be a case in point. See Rufus Stebbins (D.D.), *An Historical Address delivered at the Centennial Celebration of the Incorporation of the Town of Wilbraham, June 15, 1863* (Boston: George O. Rand & Avery, 1864). pp. 84–91. See also Ezra Barker, "A Letter to Moses Stebbins dated Wilbraham, Massachusetts, August 30, 1780," quoted in full by Frances Grace Smith, "The American Revolution Hits Church Music," *New England Quarterly* 4, no. 4 (1931), pp. 783–88.

27. The typical pitch pipe was an instrument which worked on the same principle as the penny whistle. It consisted of an elongated wooden tube, square in cross-section, with a recorder-like mouthpiece at one end and a draw slide marked with the pitches of the scale at the other. The Essex Institute possesses a collection of six pitch pipes which the writer has personally examined. Of these, five are of the shape described, being eight to twelve inches in length, and one is shaped like a psalm book. None are in working condition. The book-shaped pitch pipe seems to have been an attempt to disguise the true nature of this instrument so as not to offend those who still subscribed to the Puritan prohibition against the use of instruments in the divine service. The Massachusetts Historical Society possesses a book-shaped pitch pipe which is in working condition.

28. "W.E.B.," "The Old Pitch-pipe," *Dwight's Journal of Music* 17, no. 20 (August 11, 1860), p. 157.

29. As Gould, *Church Music*, p. 168, states the so-called "bass viol" was not a viol at all, but a cello. It possessed neither the flat back nor the sloping upper bouts, or shoulders, of a true viol. The Essex Institute possesses a collection of three bass viols which the writer has personally examined. In his opinion they might best be called "folk cellos" because their humble American makers only approximated the classical proportions and the usual dimensions employed by the best European makers.

30. Walter Eliot Thwing, *History of the First Church in Roxbury, Massachusetts, 1630–1904* (Boston: W. A. Butterfield, 1908), p. 337.

31. Ibid., p. 339.

32. William Bentley, *The Diary of William Bentley, D.D.* (Salem: Essex Institute, 1911), 1:214.

33. Leonard Ellinwood, *The History of American Church Music* (New York: Morehouse-Gorham Co., 1953), notes, p. 57, "By 1800 there were approximately twenty organs throughout New England, mostly in Episcopal churches due to the prejudices which still lingered in most Puritan congregations. A notable exception was in the First Congregational Church at Providence, which in 1770, after considerable hesitation and debate, acquired the first 'dissenting' organ in New England."

34. Bentley, *Diary*, 1:412.

35. Ibid., 2:163.

36. See Chapter III, footnote 49.

37. Bentley, *Diary*, 3:181.

38. Carl Bridenbaugh, "The New England Town: A Way of Life," *Proceedings of the American Antiquarian Society for April, 1946*, vol. 56, p. 33 (Worcester: Published by the Society, 1947).

39. Quoted by Alain C. White, *The History of the Town of Litchfield, Connecticut, 1720–1920* (Litchfield: Compiled for the Litchfield Historical Society, 1920), p. 29.

40. Bentley, *Diary*, 1:2.

41. Rev. E. H. Sears, "History of the Oxford Singing School," *Dwight's Journal of Music* 18, no. 15 (January 12, 1861), pp. 331–32 and no. 16 (January 19, 1861), pp. 340–41.

42. Billings, *The Continental Harmony*, p. xxviii.

43. Contrary to present custom, the Puritans did not observe Christmas because they believed it to be a Popish holiday. The children of the Puritans, the Congregationalists, subscribed to this belief until the middle of the nineteenth century at which time they too began to celebrate it in their religious services. Mary Crawford, *Social Life in Old New England* (Boston: Little, Brown, and Company, 1914), pp. 494–505.

44. Bentley, *Diary*, 2:283.

45. Ibid., 2:290.

46. For another detailed Independence Day program see Bentley, *Diary*, 3:96.

47. Daniel Read, "Diary, 1796–1806," a manuscript journal in the possession of the New Haven Historical Society.

48. Bentley, *Diary*, 2:378.

49. William Billings, *The Singing Master's Assistant* (Boston: Printed by Draper and Folsom, 1778), p. 56.

50. Ibid., pp. 81–90.

51. Ibid., pp. 91–99.

52. Hugh Adams, "A Narrative of Remarkable Instances," a manuscript dated Dec. 7, 1724 – Mar. 27, 1725, in the possession of the Massachusetts Historical Society.

53. John Ballantine, "Journal, 1737–1774," a manuscript diary in the possession of the Westfield Athenaeum, transcribed and annotated by Joseph D. Bartlett, 1886.

54. Noah Webster, "Diary," quoted in full by E. E. F. Ford, *Notes on the Life of Noah Webster*, vol. 1 (New York: Privately printed, 1912), p. 62.

55. Ibid., p. 438.

56. N. H. Allen, "Old Time Music and Musicians," *Connecticut Quarterly* 3, no. 1 (Jan., Feb., Mar., 1897), p. 69.

57. *Cumberland Gazette*, May 8, 1788. Quoted by William Willis, editor of *Journals of the Rev. Thomas Smith and the Rev. Samuel Deane* (Portland: Joseph S. Bailey, 1849), p. 362.

58. Samuel Gilman, "Memoirs of a New England Village Choir," *Contributions to Literature* (Boston: Crosby, Nichols, and Co., 1856), p. 77.

59. For the complete sequence of entries including that for Feb. 14, 1778, which tells of another evening of singing in the family circle, see *Appendix C* (A Country Parson and the Singing Schools of Westborough, Massachusetts).

60. Ebenezer Parkman, "Diary, 1777–1778."

61. Paul Coffin, "Journal, 1797," *Collections of the Maine Historical Society*, vol. 4, p. 354.

62. Ebenezer Parkman, "Singing Book," a small manuscript music book dated July 17, 1721, in the possession of the Massachusetts Historical Society.

63. See Frank Metcalf, *American Writers and Compilers of Sacred Music* (New York: The Abingdon Press, 1925), p. 123, for an amusing anecdote about the singing master, Jeremiah

Ingalls, and the music-making indulged in by his family on the Sabbath.

64. See also Amos Kendall, *Autobiography*, p. 2.

65. Bentley, *Diary*, 2:254.

66. Solomon Howe, *Farmer's Evening Entertainment* (Northampton: Printed by Andrew Wright, 1804).

67. Robert Treat Paine, "Journal, 1749," a manuscript diary in the possession of the Massachusetts Historical Society.

68. Simeon E. Baldwin, *Life and Letters of Simeon Baldwin* (New Haven: The Tuttle, Morehouse & Taylor Co., 1919), p. 187.

69. Another example would be the singing school which Andrew Law (A.B., 1775) taught at the College of Rhode Island in 1772. See: Joyce Ellen Mangler, "Andrew Law, Class of 1775: the Contributions of a Musical Reformer," *Books at Brown* 18, no. 2 (January, 1957), p. 61.

70. *Connecticut Journal*, no. 961 (March 29, 1786) (New Haven: Printed by Thomas and Samuel Green).

71. Ibid., no. 995 (Nov. 22, 1786).

72. *Massachusetts Spy, or Worcester Gazette* 18, no. 846 (June 25, 1789). Printed by Isaiah Thomas.

73. Chauncey Langdon, *The Select Songster, or a Collection of Elegant Songs with Music prefixed to each.* Compiled by Philo Musico (New Haven: Printed by Daniel Bowen, 1786).

74. John Quincy Adams, *Life in a New England Town: 1787–1788, the Diary of John Quincy Adams, while a Student in the Office of Theophilus Parsons at Newburyport* (Boston: Little, Brown, and Co., 1903), p. 79.

75. Samuel Eliot Morison, *Three Centuries of Harvard, 1636–1936* (Cambridge: Harvard University Press, 1942), p. 144.

76. John King Lord, *A History of Dartmouth College, 1815–1909* (Concord: The Rumford Press, 1913), p. 552.

77. Ezra Stiles, *Literary Diary of Ezra Stiles, President of Yale College*, edited by F. B. Dexter, vol. 3 (New York: Charles Scribner's Sons, 1901), p. 102.

78. If the inclusion of musical theses in the commencement broadsides is accepted as a reliable indicator of the presence of music in the curriculum, it is apparent from the list of theses given in *Appendix A* (Musical Theses Included in the Commencement Broadsides of Harvard College, 1711–1730) that music was not included in the curriculum of Harvard College after 1730. Its deletion from the curriculum coincides with the acceptance of the singing school in Cambridge and Boston; thus, it may be concluded that the colleges delegated the teaching of music to the singing schools for the remainder of the century.

79. Jacob Kimball, *The Essex Harmony* (Exeter: Printed for T. C. Cushing and T. Macanulty, 1800), the preface.

80. Both Kimball and Holyoke dedicated their respective books, *The Essex Harmony* and *The Columbian Repository*, to the Essex Musical Association.

81. See *Appendix D* (Suggestions for Further Research), for a list of these exhibitions.

82. There appears to have been a short-lived association of singing masters in Connecticut as early as 1769. Edwin Pond Parker, *History of the Second Church of Christ in Hartford, 1670–1892* (Hartford: Belknap and Warfield, 1892), p. 135 notes, "A company of singing masters, organized in Wallingford for the encouragement of psalmody in the government, arranged to come to Hartford in October 1769 and hold a meeting or convention in the South Church. They tried 'several pieces of music with instruments' and a sermon was preached on the occasion."

83. Daniel T. V. Huntoon, *History of the Town of Canton* (Cambridge: John Wilson and Son, 1893), pp. 306–9.

84. That the singing school was part of John Adams's childhood experiences is seen in the following entry from his *Diary* (vol. 2 of *The Works of John Adams*, edited by C. F. Adams [Boston: Little and Brown, 1850], p. 86). "May 31, 1760. Saturday. ...drank tea with Zab; ran over the past passages of my life; —little boats, watermills, windmills, whirligigs, bird's eggs, bows and arrows, guns, singing, pricking tunes, girls, &c.; ignorance of parents, masters Cleverly, Marsh, tutors Mayhew, &c. By a constant dissipation among amusements in my childhood, and by the ignorance of my instructors in the more advanced years of my youth, my mind has laid uncultivated; so that, at twenty-five, I am obliged to study Horace and Homer! —proh dolor!"

85. Adams, *Diary*, p. 275.

86. Ibid., p. 348.

87. Ibid., p. 356.

88. Ibid., p. 364.

89. Ibid., p. 379.

90. Ibid., p. 395.

91. Ibid., p. 401.

92. Noah Webster, "Diary," quoted in full by Ford, *Notes on the Life of Noah Webster*, 1:135–41.

93. Irving Lowens, "Daniel Read's World: The Letters of an Early American Composer," *Music Library Association Notes*, Second Series, 9, no. 2 (March 1952), p. 238.

94. Andrew Law, *Musical Magazine*, no. 1 (Cheshire, 1792), p. 1.

95. "H. T.," *Dwight's Journal of Music* 3, Sept. 24, 1853, p. 198.

96. *The Message Bird*, a Literary and Musical Journal, Feb. 1, 1851.

Appendixes

1. Louis F. Benson, *The English Hymn* (London: Hodder & Stoughton, 1915), chap. 8.

2. Henry Wilder Foote, *Three Centuries of American Hymnody* (Cambridge: Harvard University Press, 1940), pp. 138–48.

3. Jonathan Edwards, *A Faithful Narrative of the Surprising Work of God in the Conversion of Many Hundred Souls in Northampton and the Neighboring Towns and Villages of the County of Hampshire in the Province of the Massachusetts Bay in New England*, 3rd ed. (Boston: Printed by S. Kneeland and T. Green, 1738), p. 10.

4. Letter by Edwards in *Proceedings of the Massachusetts Historical Society*, 2nd ser., vol. 10, p. 429.

5. John S. Curwen, *Studies in Worship Music*, 1st ser., 2nd ed. (London: J. Curwen & Sons, 1888), p. 52.

6. Benson, *The English Hymn*, p. 163.

7. Thomas Prince, *The Christian History*, containing Accounts of the Revival and Propagation of Religion in Great Britain and America for the Year 1744, Vol. 2 (Boston...N.E.: Printed by S. Kneeland and T. Green, 1745), p. 44.

8. Charles Chauncey, *Seasonable Thoughts on the State of Religion in New England* (Boston: Printed by Rogers and Fowle, 1743), p. 240.

9. Chauncey, *Seasonable Thoughts*, p. 240.

10. Gilbert Chase, *America's Music* (New York: McGraw-Hill, 1955), pp. 207–31.

11. Jonathan Edwards, *Some Thoughts Concerning the Present Revival of Religion in New England* (Boston, 1742), p. 316.

12. Clifford K. Shipton, *Sibley's Harvard Graduates* (Cambridge: Harvard University Press, 1942), 6:511–27.

13. Ebenezer Parkman,"Singing Book," a small manuscript music book dated July 17, 1721, in the possession of the Massachusetts Historical Society.

14. H. P. Deforest and E. C. Bates, *History of Westborough, Massachusetts* (Westborough: Published by the Town, 1891), p. 115.

15. Ebenezer Parkman, "Diary, 1777–1778," a manuscript journal in the possession of the Massachusetts Historical Society.

16. Ann and Sophia Parkman, "Diary," quoted by H. M. Forbes, *The Hundredth Town, a Glimpse of Life in Westborough, 1717–1817* (Boston: Press of Rockwell and Churchill, 1889), pp. 86–87.

17. Elias Mann, *The Massachusetts Collection of Sacred Harmony* (Boston: Printed by Manning and Loring, 1807).

18. Daniel Dana, *A Discourse on Music, addressed to the Essex Musical Association at their Annual Meeting at Boxford, Sept. 12, 1803* (Newburyport: Edmund M. Blunt, 1803).

Bibliography

Over four hundred seventy sources were consulted in writing the present dissertation. These sources have been listed according to their essential nature as either primary or secondary sources. Included among the two hundred fifty primary sources are some ninety singing books, fifty-five tracts upon church music, twenty-four diaries or journals, and eleven newspapers contemporaneous to the singing school period. The remaining primary sources include miscellaneous psalters, letters, town and church records, songsters, and single pieces of choral music used in singing schools and choirs. Included among the two hundred twenty secondary sources are one hundred town and church histories, thirty scholarly monographs, and twenty works upon various aspects of the history of music in America, England, and Scotland. The remaining secondary sources include miscellaneous bibliographies, dissertations, and works about New England customs and institutions.

Not included in the bibliography are one hundred additional town and church histories which were examined and found wanting in terms of modern standards of historiography. They are mentioned here in spite of their failings because they did serve to confirm the ubiquitousness of the singing school throughout New England. For the sake of simplicity, manuscript diaries, tracts, and singing books, which technically do not belong under the heading "bibliography," have been included in this list of published works.

I. PRIMARY SOURCES

ADAMS, HUGH. "A Narrative of Remarkable Instances of a Particular Faith and Answers of Prayers . . . by Hugh Adams, A.M., Pastor of a Church in Dover in the Province of New Hampshire alias Piscataqua. Recollected by Him (in the Strength of that Promise in John xiv. 26) at his Spare Hours from December 7, 1724 to March 27, 1725 . . ." A manuscript in the possession of the Massachusetts Historical Society.

ADAMS, JOHN. *Diary, Vol. 2 of The Works of John Adams,* edited by Charles Francis Adams. Boston: Little and Brown, 1850.

ADAMS, JOHN QUINCY. *Life in a New England Town: 1787–1788; the Diary of John Quincy Adams, while a Student in the Office of Theophilus Parsons at Newburyport.* Boston: Little, Brown, and Co., 1903.

ADAMS, Z. *The Nature, Pleasure and Advantages of Church Musick, a Sermon preached at a Lecture in the First Parish of Lancaster on Thursday, April 4th, 1771.* Published at the request of the Choir. Boston: Printed by Richard Draper, 1771.

ADGATE, ANDREW. *Rudiments of Music.* By Andrew Adgate, P.U.A. The Fourth Edition. Philadelphia: Printed and sold by John McCulloch; and also sold by the Author, at No. 29, North Front-Street, 1791. (Note: This edition includes 24 pages of engraved music which presumably have been taken from the author's *Philadelphia Harmony.*)

AINSWORTH, HENRY. *The Book of Psalmes: Englished both in Prose and Metre.* With Annotations, opening the words and sentences, by conference with other Scriptures. By H. A. Amsterdam: Imprinted by Giles Thorp, Ao. Di., 1612.

ALSTED, JOHANN HEINRICH. *Johannis-Henrici Alstedii Encyclopaedia. I. Praecognita disciplinarum. II. Philologia. III. Philosophia theoretica. IV. Philosophia practica. V. Tres superiores facultates. VI. Artes mechanicae. VII. Farragines disciplinarum.* 7 vols. in 4. Engraved t.p. Herborn: 1630.

ALSTEDIUS, JOHANNES HENRICUS. *Templum Musicum, or the Musical Synopsis of the Learned and Famous Johannes-Henricus-Alstedius Being a Compendium of the Rudiments both of the Mathematical and Practical Part of Musick: . . .* Faithfully translated out of Latin by John Birchensha, Philomath. Imprimatur, Feb. 5, 1663. Roger L'Estrange. London: Printed by Will. Godbid for Peter Dring at the Sun in the Poultry next Dore to the Rose-Tavern, 1664.

The American Musical Miscellany, a Collection of the Newest and Most Approved Songs, set to music. Printed at Northampton, Massachusetts by Andrew Wright, for Daniel Wright and Company. Sold by them, and by S. Butler, in Northampton; by I. Thomas, Jun. in Worcester; by F. Barker, in Greenfield; and by the principal booksellers in Boston, 1798.

ATTWILL, THOMAS H. *The New York & Vermont Collection of Sacred Harmony.* Containing the necessary Rules of Music with a variety of Psalm & Hymn Tunes, Set-pieces & Anthems; many of which are original: Compiled for the Use of Worshipping Assemblies & Singing Societies, from the most approved Antient & Modern Authors. 2nd edition. Albany: Printed by the Proprietor, B. Buckley (1804).

BABCOCK, SAMUEL. *The Middlesex Harmony, being an Original Composition of Sacred Music in Three or Four Parts.* Boston: Printed by Isaiah Thomas and Ebenezer T. Andrews, 1795.

BALLANTINE, JOHN. "Journal, 1737–1774," a manuscript diary in the possession of the Westfield Athenaeum. Transcribed and annotated by Joseph D. Bartlett, 1886. References to the singing school extracted from the typewritten copy of Bartlett's notebooks (Nos. 2 and 7) in the possession of the American Antiquarian Society.

BARKER, EZRA. "A Letter to Moses Stebbins dated Wilbraham, Massachusetts, August 30, 1780," quoted in full by Frances Grace Smith, "The American Revolution Hits Church Music," *The New England Quarterly* 4, no. 4 (1931).

BAYLEY, DANIEL. *The New Universal Harmony, or a Compendium of Church Music.* Containing, a Variety of Favorite Anthems, Hymn-Tunes, and Carols. Composed by the greatest Masters. Carefully Set in score by Daniel Bayley, Philo Musico. Newburyport: Printed and Sold by the Author, 1773.

_____. *The Psalm Singer's Assistant;* containing, I. An Introduction, with such Directions for Singing as are necessary for learners. II. A Collection of Choice Psalm Tunes, suited to the several Measures both of the old and new Version; engraved in a correct Manner, and is designed for the Improvement of Psalmody in the Congregations, both in Town and Country: All being composed in three Parts, collected from the best Masters. By Daniel Bayley. Boston: Printed by W. McAlpine for the Author in Newburyport, 1767. Bound with A New Version of the Psalms of David, fitted to the Tunes used in Churches. By N. Brady, D.D., Chaplain in Ordinary, and N. Tate, Esq., Poet Laureat. Boston, N.E.: Printed for, and Sold by J. Perkins in Union Street near the Market, 1767.

_____, ed. *A New and Compleat Introduction to the Grounds and Rules of Musick.* In Two Books: Book I. Containing the Grounds and Rules of Musick; or an Introduction to the Art of Singing by Note, taken from Thomas Walter, M.A. Book II. Containing a New and Correct Introduction to the Grounds of Musick, Rudimental and Practical; from William Tans'ur's Royal Melody: The whole being a Collection of a Variety of the Choicest Tunes from the most approved Masters. Printed for and Sold by Daniel Bayley of Newbury, 1764.

BEDFORD, ARTHUR. *The Great Abuse of Musick.* In Two Parts containing an Account of the Use and Design of Musick among the Ancient Jews, Greeks, Romans, and others; with their Concern for, and Care to prevent the Abuse thereof. And also an Account of the Immorality and Profaness, which is occasioned by the Corruption of that most Noble Science in the Present Age. By Arthur Bedford, M.A. Chaplain to His Grace Wriothesly, Duke of Bedford, and Vicar of the Temple in the City of Bristol. London: Printed by J. H. for John Wyatt at the Rose in St. Paul's Churchyard, 1711.

BELCHER, SUPPLY. *The Harmony of Maine.* an Original Composition of Psalm Tunes and Hymn Tunes of various Metres, suitable for Divine Worship with a Number of Fuging Pieces and Anthems, together with a Concise Introduction to the Grounds of Musick, and Rules for Learners. By S. Belcher, of Farmington, County of Lincoln, District of Maine. Boston: Isaiah Thomas and Ebenezer T. Andrews, 1794.

BELKNAP, DANIEL. *The Evangelical Harmony.* Containing a great Variety of Airs, suitable for Divine Worship: besides a Number of Favourite Pieces of Music, selected from different authors, chiefly original, to which is prefixed a concise Introduction to the Grounds of Music. Boston: Isaiah Thomas and Ebenezer T. Andrews, 1800.

_____. *The Village Compilation of Sacred Music.* By Daniel Belknap. Boston: Printed for the Author by J. T. Buckingham, 1806.

BENHAM, ASAHEL. *Social Harmony:* Containing first, the Rudiments of Psalmody made easy, second, a Collection of Modern Music, calculated for the Use of Singing Schools and Worshipping Assemblies. Wallingford, Conn., 1798.

BENTLEY, WILLIAM. *The Diary of William Bentley, D.D. 4 vols.* Salem: Essex Institute, 1905–1914.

BILLINGS, WILLIAM. *The Continental Harmony, containing a Number of Anthems, Fuges, and Chorusses, in several Parts.* Never before published. Composed by William Billings, Author of various Music Books. Boston: Printed by Isaiah Thomas and Ebenezer T. Andrews, 1794.

_____. *Music in Miniature, containing a Collection of Psalm Tunes of Various Metres. Set in score by W. Billings.* Printed and sold by the Author at his house in Boston, N.E., 1779.

_____. *The New England Psalm-Singer: or, American Chorister.* Containing a Number of Psalm-Tunes, Anthems and Canons. In Four and Five Parts. (Never before Published.) Composed by William Billings, a Native of Boston, in New England. Boston: Printed by Edes and Gill, 1770.

_____. *The Psalm Singer's Amusement, Containing a Number of Fuging Pieces and Anthems composed by William Billings.* Printed & Sold by the Author at his House near the White Horse, Boston, 1781.

_____. *The Singing Master's Assistant or Key to Practical Music, being an Abridgement from the New England Psalm-Singer; together with several other Tunes, never before published.* Boston: Printed by Draper and Folsom, 1778.

_____. *The Suffolk Harmony, consisting of Psalm Tunes, Fuges, and Anthems. Composed by William Billings, Author of the Singing Master's Assistant.* Boston: Engraved and printed by J. Norman for the Author, and sold at his house near the Liberty-Pole, 1786.

BLANCHARD, AMOS. *The American Musical Primer; containing a correct Introduction to the grounds of music, rudimental, practical, and technical.* Together with a collection of tunes, of the various metres now in use in religious societies; and calculated for the improvement of youth, and the worship of God. The whole carefully selected from some of the most celebrated European writers, both ancient and modern. Exeter, N.H.: Printed by Norris & Sawyer, 1808.

BOLDERY, HANNAH. "Her Book." a manuscript singing book made up almost entirely of single stave voice parts to the standard New England psalm tunes. In the possession of Mr. Irving Lowens, Hyattsville, Md.

The Boston Gazette. Boston: Printed by S. Kneeland for Philip Musgrave, Postmaster at his Office in Corn-Hill, where Advertisements are taken in, and all Gentlemen and others may be supplied with this Paper. 1719–1726.

The Boston News Letter. Boston: Printed by B. Green in New-bury Street For John Campbell, Postmaster, 1704–1726.

BRADY, N. (D.D., Chaplain in Ordinary to her Majesty) and TATE, N. (Esq., Poet Laureat to her Majesty). *A New Version of the Psalms of David, fitted to the Tunes Used in Churches.* London: Printed by J. R. for the Company of Stationers, and are to be Sold at Stationers Hall, near Ludgate, and by most Booksellers. MDCCIII. Bound with this edition is: A Supplement to the New Version of Psalms by Dr. Brady and Mr. Tate; Containing, the PSALMS in Particular Measures; the usual Hymns, Creed, Lord's Prayer, Ten Commandments, for the Holy Sacrament, &c. with Gloria Patri's, and Tunes (Treble and Bass), proper to each of them, and all the rest of the Psalms. The Sixth Edition, Corrected; and much Enlarged: With the Addition of Plain Instructions for all those who are desirous to Learn or Improve themselves In Psalmody near 30 New Tunes, composed by several of the Best Masters; and a table of Psalms suited to the Feasts and Fasts of the Church, &c. With Tables of all the Psalms of the New, Old, and Dr. Patrick's Versions, directing what Tunes are fitted for each Psalm. The Whole being a Compleat PSALMODY. Useful for Teachers and Learners of either Version. In the Savoy: Printed by John Nutt; and Sold by James Holland, at the Bible and Ball, at the West End of St. Paul's. MDCCVIII.

BRAY, OLIVER. *An Oration on Music: Pronounced at Fryeburg before the Hans Gram Musical Society on their First Anniversary, October, 10, 1811.* Portland, Maine: Printed by Arthur Shirley, 1812.

A Brief Discourse concerning regular Singing Shewing from the Scriptures, the Necessity and Incumbency thereof in the Worship of God. Boston, N. England: Printed by B. Green, jun. for John Eliot at his Shop at the South End of the Town, 1725.

BROWN, BARTHOLOMEW. *Columbian and European Harmony: or, Bridgewater Collection of Sacred Music.* By Bartholomew Brown, A.M., and others. Boston: Isaiah Thomas and Ebenezer T. Andrews, 1802

BROWN, FRANCIS. *An Address on Music, delivered before the Handel Society, Dartmouth College, August, 1809.* Hanover: Printed by Charles and William S. Spear, 1810.

BROWNSON, OLIVER. *Select Harmony.* Containing the Necessary Rules of Psalmody Together with a Collection of approved Psalm Tunes, Hymns and Anthems, By Oliver Brownson. New Haven: Printed by Thomas & Samuel Green, 1783.

BULL, AMOS. *The Responsory;* containing a Collection of Church Musick, Set with Second Trebles, instead of Counters, and peculiarly adapted to the Use of the New England Churches. Together with a few Useful Rules of Psalmody. Printed at Worcester, Massachusetts by Isaiah Thomas, and sold by the Editor in Hartford, Connecticut, 1795.

BUMSTEAD, JEREMIAH. "Diary" (extracts), *New England Historical and Genealogical Register* (Boston: Samuel G. Drake, Publisher, 1861), XV, 194–204 and 309–310.

BURNEY, CHARLES. *A General History of Music.* 4 vols. London: Printed for the author, 1776–1789.

CHAUNCEY, CHARLES. *Seasonable Thoughts on the State of Religion in New England, a Treatise in Five Parts by Charles Chauncey, D.D., Pastor of the first Church of Christ in Boston.* Boston: Printed by Rogers and Fowle, for Samuel Eliot in Cornhill, 1743.

_____. "A Sketch of Eminent Men in New England. In a letter from the Rev. Dr. Chauncey to Dr. Stiles, Boston, May 6, 1768," reprinted in *Collections of the Mass. Hist. Soc.,* X, 154–165.

CHAUNCEY, NATHANIEL. *Regular Singing Defended and Proved to be the Only True Way of Singing the Songs of the Lord.* By Arguments from Reason and Scripture: Having been Heard and Approved of, by the General Association at Hartford, May the 12th, 1727 with their Recommendation of it to the Publick. New London: Printed and Sold by T. Green, 1728.

CHENEY, MOSES. "Letter to Friend Mason," *Musical Visitor 2,* no. 17 (Dec. 1, 1841), pp. 132–133, and No. 18 (Jan. 1, 1842), pp. 139–140. Boston: Published by an Association of Gentlemen, Kidder & Wright, Printers, 1841–42.

CLARKE, JONAS. *The Use and Excellency of Vocal Music in Public Worship, a Sermon preached at an occasional Lecture, in Lexington.* Appointed to promote and encourage the divine use of vocal Music, more especially in Public Worship on Wednesday, April 25, 1770. By Jonas Clarke, A.M., Pastor of the Church, in Lexington. Boston: Printed for Nicholas Bowes in Cornhill, 1770.

COFFIN, CHARLES. *An Address, before the Rockingham Sacred Music Society at Exeter, May 10, 1815.* Exeter: Printed by C. Norris & Co., 1815.

COFFIN, PAUL. "A Missionary Tour in Maine, 1800" (The journals of the Rev. Paul Coffin, D.D., a minister from Buxton, Maine), *Collections of the Maine Historical Society.* Vol. 4. Portland: Published by the Society, 1856.

Columbian Centinel 19, no. 25 (June 5, 1793). Boston: Printed and Published by Benjamin Russell.

Connecticut Journal. No. 961 (Mar. 29, 1786) and No. 995 (Nov. 22, 1786). New Haven: Printed by Thomas and Samuel Green.

Constitution of the Essex Musical Association, Established 28th March, 1797. Newburyport: Printed by Edmund M. Blunt, 1798.

COOPER, J. FENIMORE. *The Last of the Mohicans.* Author's revised edition. New York: George P. Putnam, 1850.

COTTON, JOHN. *Singing of Psalms a Gospel Ordinance, or a Treatise wherein are handled these four particulars.* 1. Touching the Duty it selfe. 2. Touching the Matter to be Sung. 3. Touching the Singers. 4. Touching the Manner of Singing. By John Cotton, Teacher of the Church at Boston In New England. London: Printed by M.S. for Hannah Allen, at the Crowne in Popes-Head Alley: and John Rothwell at the Sunne and Fountaine in Paul's Church-yard, 1647.

CRANE, JOHN. *A Discourse, delivered at Upton, March 15, 1810;* at Grafton, April 12, 1810; and at Sutton, March 13, 1811 at a public meeting of a number of Singers who had been improving themselves in Sacred Music. By John Crane, D.D., Pastor of the Church in Northbridge. Published at the particular request of the Singers in Sutton, North Parish. Sutton: Printed by Sewall Goodbridge, 1811.

DANA, DANIEL. *An Address on Sacred Music, delivered at a publick meeting of the Rockingham Sacred Music Society, in Hampton, Oct. 6th, 1813.* Exeter: Printed by Charles Norris & Co., 1813.

_____. *A Discourse on Music, addressed to the Essex Musical Association at their Annual Meeting at Boxford, Sept. 12, 1803.* Newburyport, Mass.: From the Press of Edmund M. Blunt, 1803.

DERRYFIELD, NEW HAMPSHIRE. *Early Records of the Town.* Vol. 2, 1782–1800. Manchester Historic Association Collections, vol. 9. Manchester, 1906.

DWIGHT, JOHN SULLIVAN, ed. *Journal of Music 1–41.* Boston, 1852–1881.

DWIGHT, JOSIAH. *An Essay to Silence the Outcry that has been in some Places against Regular Singing in a Sermon Preach'd at Framingham.* By the Reverend Josiah Dwight, Pastor of the Church of Christ in Woodstock. Boston: Printed for John Eliot, and Sold at his Shop at the South End of the Town, 1725.

EDWARDS, JONATHAN. *A Faithful Narrative of the Surprising Work of God in the Conversion of Many Hundred Souls in Northampton, and the Neighboring Towns and Villages of the County of Hampshire, in the Province of the Massachusetts Bay in New England.* In a Letter to the Reverend Dr. Benjamin Colman of Boston. Written by the Revd. Mr. Edwards, Minister of Northampton, Nov. 6, 1736. Published with a Large Preface by the Rev. Dr. Watts and Dr. Guyse of London: To which a Shorter is added by Some of the Reverend Ministers of Boston. Together with an attestation from some Reverend Ministers of Hampshire. The Third Edition. Boston: Printed & Sold by S. Kneeland, T. Green over against the Prison in Queen Street, 1738.

_____. *Some Thoughts Concerning the Present Revival of Religion in New England.* By Jonathan Edwards, A.M., Pastor of the Church of Christ at Northampton. Boston: Printed and Sold by S. Kneeland and T. Green in Queen Street, 1742.

EMERSON, CALEB. *A Discourse on Music, pronounced at Amherst, N.H. before the Handellian Musical Society, September 13, 1808.* Amherst, N.H.: Printed by Joseph Cushing, 1808.

EMERSON, REUBEN, A.M. *An Oration on Music, Pronounced before the Handel Society, Dartmouth University (sic) August 23, 1814.* Andover: Printed by Flagg and Gould, 1814.

EMERSON, SAMUEL (A.M.). *An Oration on Music, pronounced at Portland, May 28th, 1800.* Portland: From the press of E. A. Jenks, 1800.

EMMONS, NATHANAEL. *A Discourse, delivered April 11, 1806 at a Publick Meeting of a number of Singers who were improving themselves in Church Music.* Providence: Printed at D. Heaton's Office, by David Hawkins, Jun., 1806.

The Essex Gazette 5, no. 226 (Nov. 17–24, 1772) and no. 236 (Jan. 26–Feb. 2, 1773); 6, no. 268 (Sept. 7–14, 1773) and No. 300 (April 19–26, 1774). Salem: Printed by Samuel and Ebenezer Hall.

The Essex Journal & New Hampshire Packet. No. 279 (Nov. 4, 1789). Newburyport: Printed by John Mycall.

The Federal Harmony: In Three Parts. Containing, I. An Introduction to the Grounds of Musick. II. A large Collection of celebrated Psalm and Hymn Tunes from the most approved ancient and modern Authors: Together with several new ones, never before published: Suited to all Metres usually sung in Churches. III. Select Anthems, &c. Compiled for the Use of Schools and Singing Societies. Boston: Printed and Sold by John Norman at his Office No. 75 New-bury Street, 1790.

FLAGG, JOSIAH. *A Collection of the Best Psalm Tunes in two, three, and four Parts.* From the most approv'd Authors, fitted to all Measures and approv'd by the best Masters in Boston, New England; to which are added some Hymns and Anthems the greater part of them never before Printed in America. By Josiah Flagg. Engraved by Paul Revere: Printed and Sold by him and Josiah Flagg, Boston, 1764.

FORBUSH, ABIJAH. *The Psalmodist's Assistant:* containing an Original Composition of Psalm and Hymn Tunes; together with a Number of Favourite Pieces from different Authors, to which is prefixed, an Introduction to the Grounds of Music. Second Edition. Boston: Printed and sold by Manning & Loring, No. 2, Cornhill, 1806.

FOSTER, JOHN (A.M.). *A Discourse on Church Musick, delivered in Brighton, March 29, 1811.* Brighton, Mass.: Printed by D. Bowen, 1811.

FRANKLIN, BENJAMIN. *The Works of the Late Dr. Benjamin Franklin, consisting of his Life written by himself, together with Essays, Humorous, Moral & Literary, chiefly in the manner of the Spectator.* New York: Printed by Tiebout & Obrian, 1794.

FRANKLIN, JAMES, ed. *The New England Courant.* Boston: Printed and Sold by J. Franklin in Queen Street, over against Mr. Sheaf's School where Advertisements and Letters are taken in. 1721–1726.

FRENCH, JACOB. *Harmony of Harmony.* In Five Parts. Containing, I. The Ground Work, or Principles of Music, by way of Question and Answer. II. The Gamut, or Scale of Music, in a very Plain and Concise Method; together with Observations on Music. III. A Complete Set of Psalm Tunes, Adapted to all the different Metres and Keys usually sung in Churches. IV. A Number of Pieces Set to Particular Psalms and Hymns, together with Odes, Fuging and Flying Pieces. V. A Number of Anthems, Suitable for different occasions. By Jacob French, Musico Theorico. Author of the New American Melody, and the Psalmodist's Companion. Northampton: Printed by Andrew Wright for the Compiler, 1802.

———. *The New American Melody.* In Three Parts. Containing, I. An Introduction to the Grounds of Musick: or Rules for Beginners. II. A new and complete body of Church Musick suited to all Metres usually sung in Churches. III. A number of New Anthems adapted to several Occasions. The Whole entirely new and composed for the Use of Singing Societies. By Jacob French. Boston: Printed and Sold by John Norman, near Oliver's Dock and by Jacob French in Medway, Massachusetts, 1789.

———. *The Psalmodist's Companion.* In four parts, containing, I. The Rudiments of Musick, in a concise and easy method. II. A complete Collection of Psalm Tunes, suited to all Metres and Keys, usually sung in Churches. III. A number of favourite Choruses, Fuges, &c. suited to many occasions. IV. A number of Anthems. The whole in Alphabetical Order, in each Part. Many of the pieces never before published. By Jacob French, Philo Musicae, author of the New American Melody. Worcester: Isaiah Thomas, 1793.

FULLER, ELIZABETH. "Diary Kept by Elizabeth Fuller, Daughter of Rev. Timothy Fuller of Princeton," quoted in full by Francis

Everett Blake, *History of Princeton, 1759–1915.* Princeton: Published by the Town, 1915. Vol. 1, Chap. 12, pp. 302–323.

A Gamut, or Scale of Music. To which is added Blank Lines for Favorite Music. Hartford: Published and Sold by Oliver D. Cooke, 1807.

A Gamut, or Scale of Music. To which is added Blank Lines for Favorite Music. Hartford: Published and sold by Oliver D. Cooke, 1811.

A Gamut, or Scale of Music. To which is added Blank Lines for Favorite Music. Hartford: Published and sold by Cooke & Hale, 1816.

GILMAN, SAMUEL. "Memoirs of a New England Village Choir," Contributions to Literature. Boston: Crosby, Nichols, and Co., 1856, pp. 1–92. (First edition appeared separately in 1829 as *Memoirs of a New-England Village Choir, with Occasional Reflections.* By a member.)

GOULD, N. D. *An Address, delivered at New Ipswich, N. H., May 16, 1818 at the request of Bethel Lodge and the Hubbard Musical Society.* Amherst: Printed by R. Boylston, 1818.

GRAM, HANS; HOLYOKE, SAMUEL; HOLDEN, OLIVER. *The Massachusetts Compiler of Theoretical and Practical Elements of Sacred Vocal Music.* Together with a Musical Dictionary and a Variety of Psalm Tunes, Choruses, &c. Chiefly Selected from Modern European Publications. Boston: Isaiah Thomas and Ebenezer T. Andrews, 1795.

GRASSINEAU, JAMES. *A Musical Dictionary, being a Collection of Terms and Characters . . . of Music.* London: Printed for J. Wilcox, at Virgil's Head opposite the New Church in the Strand, 1740.

GREEN, JOSEPH. "A Letter for the Rev'd. Mr. Stephen Williams, Pastor of ye Church of Christ att Longmeadow in Springfield, dated Boston, Oct. 1, 1722," Transactions, Publications of the Colonial Society of Massachusetts 46, pp. 391–392.

HAMMETT, JOHN. *Promiscuous Singing, No Divine Institution.* Newport(?): Printed by the Widow Franklin, 1739. Evans 4365.

Harvard College Theses and Quaestiones. Vol. 1, 1642–1736, and Vol. 2, 1737–1810. Harvard University Archives. HUC 6642.

HASTINGS, THOMAS. *The History of Forty Choirs.* New York: Mason Brothers, 1854.

———. *Sacred Praise: an earnest appeal to Christian worshippers.* New York: A. S. Barnes & Co., 1856.

HAWKINS, SIR JOHN. *A General History of the Science and Practice of Music.* Five volumes. London: T. Payne & Son, at the Mews-Gate, 1776.

HAYWARD, JONATHAN. "Diary, 1800–1808" (extracts), *Historical Collections of the Danvers Historical Society* (Danvers: Published by the Society, 1915), III, 53–58.

HEDGE, LEMUEL (A.M.). *The Duty and Manner of Singing in Christian Churches, considered and illustrated in a Sermon preached at a Singing Lecture in Warwick, January 29th, 1772.* By Lemuel Hedge, A.M., Pastor of the Church there. Published at the Request of the Singers. Boston: Printed by Richard Draper, MDCCLXXII.

HOLDEN, OLIVER. *American Harmony:* containing a variety of Airs, suitable for Divine Worship, on Thanksgiving, Ordinations; Christmas, Fasts, Funerals, and other Occasions. Together with a Number of Psalm Tunes, in Three and Four Parts. The whole Intirely New. By Oliver Holden, Teacher of Music, in Charlestown. Boston: Isaiah Thomas and Ebenezer T. Andrews, 1792.

_____. *Plain Psalmody, or Supplementary Music.* An Original Composition, set in Three and Four Parts.

_____. *Sacred Dirges, Hymns, and Anthems, commemorative of the Death of General George Washington, the Guardian of his Country, and the Friend of Man.* An Original Composition by a Citizen of Massachusetts. Printed at Boston, by I. Thomas and E. T. Andrews, 1800.

_____. *The Union Harmony, or a Universal Collection of Sacred Music.* Vol. 1, containing: I. The Rudiments of Music laid down in a plain and concise manner. II. A large and valuable Collection of Tunes, suited to all the metres now used in the various worshipping Societies in America, many of which were never before published. 2nd edition. Boston: Isaiah Thomas and Ebenezer T. Andrews, 1796.

HOLYOKE, MRS. MARY. "Diary, 1760–1800," *The Holyoke Diaries, 1709–1856.* Salem: The Essex Institute, 1911.

HOLYOKE, SAMUEL. *The Columbian Repository of Sacred Harmony Selected from European and American authors, with many new Tunes not before published.* Including the whole of Dr. Watts' Psalms and Hymns, to each of which a Tune is adapted, and some additional Tunes to the particular Metres in Tate and Brady's, and Dr. Belknap's Collection of Psalms and Hymns. With an Introduction of Practical Principles. The whole designed for use of Schools, Musical Societies, and Worshipping Assemblies. By Samuel Holyoke, A.M. From the Music Press of Henry Ranlet. Exeter, New Hampshire, 1802.

_____. *Dedication Service, containing an Introductory Ode, Three Hymns, a Doxology, and a concluding Anthem, set to music by Samuel Holyoke, A.M.* Exeter, N.H.: Printed typographically by Henry Ranlet, 1801.

_____. *Exeter: for Thanksgiving.* By Samuel Holyoke, A.B. Exeter, N.H.: Printed by H. Ranlet, 1798.

_____. *Hark! from the Tombs, &c. and Beneath the Honors, &c.* Adapted from Dr. Watts, and set to music by Samuel Holyoke, A.M. Performed at Newburyport, 2nd January, 1800. The Day on which the Citizens unitedly expressed their unbounded veneration for the memory of our Beloved Washington. Exeter, N.H.: H. Ranlet, 1800.

_____. *Harmonia Americana.* Containing a concise Introduction to the Grounds of Music. With a Variety of Airs, Suitable for Divine Worship, and the Use of Musical Societies. Consisting of Three and Four Parts. By Samuel Holyoke, A.B. Boston: Printed by Isaiah Thomas and Ebenezer T. Andrews, 1791.

_____. *The Instrumental Assistant.* Containing Instructions for the Violin, German-Flute, Clarionett, Bass-Viol, and Hautboy. Compiled from late European publications. Also a Selection of favorite Airs, Marches, &c. Progressively Arranged, and adapted to the use of Learners. By Samuel Holyoke, A.M. Vol. 1. Exeter, N.H.: H. Ranlet, 1800.

_____. *The Instrumental Assistant;* containing a selection of Minuets, Airs, Duettos, Rondos and Marches: with Instructions for the French-Horn and Bassoon. Compiled by Samuel Holyoke, A.M. Vol. 2. Exeter, N.H.: Printed and sold by Ranlet and Norris, 1807.

_____. *Occasional Music;* consisting of an Anthem, a Lyric Poem, and a Doxology, suitable for Thanksgiving, Composed in a familiar Style. By Samuel Holyoke, A.M. From the Music Press of Henry Ranlet, Exeter, New Hampshire, 1802.

_____. *The Vocal Companion;* containing a Concise Introduction to the Practice of Music, and a Set of Tunes of Various Metres, arranged Progressively for the Use of Learners. Compiled by Samuel Holyoke, A.M. Exeter, N.H. From the Music-Press of Norris & Sawyer, 1807.

HOMER, GEORGE. "A Letter to Peter Teacher dated Boston, March 19, 1806," a manuscript concerning the supervision of a singing school taught by Elias Mann for the Society In Brattle Street. In the possession of the Massachusetts Historical Society.

HOWE, SOLOMON. *The Farmer's Evening Entertainment.* Containing, I. Characters, Rules and Directions for Vocal Music. II. A Number of New Tunes of as various Airs and Metres as the compass of the Book will admit. III. New Hymns, taken from sacred Writ, and adapted to the Tunes, Calculated for Social Worship. By Solomon Howe, A.M. Northampton: Printed by Andrew Wright for the Author, 1804.

_____. *The Worshipper's Assistant.* Containing the Rules of Music, and a Variety of Easy and Plain Psalm Tunes: Adapted to the weakest capacities, and designed for extensive utility, as an Introduction to more critical and curious music. By Solomon Howe, A.M. Northampton: Printed by Andrew Wright for the Author, 1799.

HUBBARD, JOHN. *An Essay on Music, pronounced before the Middlesex Musical Society, Sept. 9, A.D. 1807, at Dunstable, (Mass.).* By John Hubbard, Prof. Math, and Nat. Phil. Dartmouth College. Published at the Request of the said Society. Boston: Printed by Manning & Loring, No. 2, Cornhill, 1808.

_____. *A Volume of Sacred Musick, Containing Thirty Anthems, selected from the works of Handel, Purcell, Croft, and other eminent European authors.* Newburyport: Published by E. Little & Co., 1814.

INGALLS, JEREMIAH. *The Christian Harmony: or Songster's Companion.* By Jeremiah Ingalls. Exeter, N.H.: Printed by Henry Ranlet, for the compilers 1805.

IRVING, WASHINGTON. "The Legend of Sleepy Hollow," *The Sketch Book of Geoffrey Crayon, Gent.* London: John Murray, Albermarle St., 1821.

JACKSON, CALEB, JR. "Daily Journal, 1802–1805," a manuscript diary in the possession of the Essex Institute, Salem, Mass.

JANES, WALTER. *The Harmonic Minstrelsey.* Containing a New Collection of Sacred Music—in Three and Four Parts, Comprising Variety in Stile, Tune, Time and Measure; and well proportioned to all the different Metres and Keys commonly used in Churches. Together, with a number of Set-Pieces, Choruses and Anthems, appropriate to Ordination, Dedications, Thanksgiving, &c, —Chiefly Original. To which is prefixed the Necessary Rules for Learner. The whole being calculated and designed for the Use of Schools and Public Worship. Dedham: Printed by H. Mann and Sold at his Bookstore and the Various Booksellers in the United States, 1807.

The Massachusetts Harmony, in Four Parts. I. An Introduction to the Rudiments of Music, by way of Question and Answer. II. A variety of useful Lessons to exercise the Learner in the use of Notes, and for the Tuning of his Voice. III. A large number of Tunes, adapted to the various Metres and Keys usually performed in Churches. IV. A number of Pieces adapted to particular Hymns, together with Elegiac Pieces, Odes and Anthems. Designed particularly for the Use of Singing Schools and Musical Assemblies in the United States. Boston: Printed by Manning & Loring, 1803.

JENKS, SAMUEL H., ed. *Nantucket Inquirer.* Nantucket: 1821–1824.

JENKS, S(TEPHEN). *Delights of Harmony, or a choice Collection of Psalm and Hymn Tunes.* New Haven: Engraved and Printed for the Purchaser (1805).

JENKS, STEPHEN. *The Musical Harmonist.* Containing Concise and easy Rules of Music together with a Collection of the most approved Psalm and Hymn Tunes, fitted to the various Metres, most of which were never before Published. By Stephen Jenks, Author of the New England Harmonist. Engraved & Printed for the Author by Amos Doolittle, New Haven, 1800.

_____. *The New England Harmonist:* containing, concise and easy rules of music: together with a number of tunes adapted to public worship, most of which were never before published. By Stephen Jenks. Danbury: Printed by Douglas & Nichols, for the Author (1800).

JOCELIN, SIMEON. *The Chorister's Companion,* or Church Music Revised. Containing besides the Necessary Rules of Psalmody a Variety of Plain and Fuging Psalm Tunes. Together with a Collection of approved Hymns and Anthems, many of which, never before printed. New Haven: Printed for and Sold by Simeon Jocelin and Amos Doolittle, 1782.

JOHNSON, A. N., and J. C., eds. *The Musical Gazette* 1–3. Boston: Printed by Kimball & Butterfield, 1846–1848.

JOHNSON, EDWARD. *A History of New England, from the English Planting in the Yeere 1628 until the Yeere 1652.* London: Printed for Nath. Brooke at the Angel in Corn-hill, 1654.

KENDALL, AMOS. *Autobiography.* Edited by William Stickney. Boston: Lee & Shepard, Publishers, 1872.

KIMBALL, JACOB. *The Essex Harmony:* an original composition in three and four parts. Exeter, N.H.: Printed for T. C. Cushing and B. B. Macanulty, and sold at their book stores in Salem, 1800.

_____. *The Rural Harmony, being an original composition in three and four parts.* For the use of singing schools and musical societies. By Jacob Kimball, jun. A.B. Boston: Printed typographically by Isaiah Thomas and Ebenezer T. Andrews. Sold at their bookstore, No. 45, Newbury Street, by said Thomas in Worcester; and by booksellers in Boston and elsewhere. 1793.

KINNE, AARON. *Alamoth, an Address delivered to the Singing Schools in the First and Second Societies in Groton.* By Aaron Kinne, A.M. New London: Printed by S. Green. 1798.

LANGDON, CHAUNCEY. *The Beauties of Psalmody.* Containing concisely the Rules of Singing with a Collection of the most approved Psalm-Tunes and Anthems. By a member of the Musical Society of Yale College. New Haven: Printed by Daniel Bowen; Sold by Amos Doolittle, 1786.

_____. *The Select Songster, or a Collection of Elegant Songs with Music prefixed to each.* Compiled by Philo Musico. New Haven: Printed by Daniel Bowen, 1786.

LANGDON, TIMOTHY. *The Pleasures and Advantages of Church Music, a Sermon, preached at a concert of vocal and instrumental music in Danbury, on Wednesday, April 5. 1797.* By Timothy Langdon, A.M., Pastor of the First Church in Danbury. Danbury: Printed by Douglas and Nichols, 1797.

Laus Deo! The Worcester Collection of Sacred Harmony. In Three Parts. Containing, I. An Introduction to the Grounds of Musick: or, Rules for Learners, II. A large Number of celebrated Psalm and Hymn Tunes, from the most approved ancient and modern Authors; together with several new ones, never before published: The whole suited to all Metres, usually sung in Churches. III. Select Anthems, Fughes, and Favourite Pieces of Musick, with an Additional Number of Psalm and Hymn Tunes. The Whole compiled for the Use of Schools and Singing Societies. The Second Edition, with Large Additions. Worcester: Printed by Isaiah Thomas, 1788.

LAVINGTON, GEORGE (L.L.B., Canon of the Church of Worcester). *The Influence of Church Musick, a Sermon preach'd in the Cathedral-Church of Worcester, at the Anniversary Meet-*ing of the Choirs of Worcester, Hereford, and Gloucester, Sept. 8, 1725. London: 1725.

LAW, ANDREW. *The Art of Singing;* in Three Parts: viz., 1. The Musical Primer, II. The Christian Harmony in Two Volumes, III, The Musical Magazine—No. 1 and No. 2. Cheshire, Connecticut: Printed and Sold by William Law, 1794.

_____. *The Christian Harmony,* or the Second Part of the Art of Singing: Comprising a Select Variety of Psalm and Hymn Tunes: Calculated for Schools and Churches. Fourth Edition with Additions and Improvements. Printed upon a new plan. Printed at Windsor, Vermont by Nahum Mower, 1805.

_____. *A Collection of Hymn Tunes from the most modern and Approved Authors by Andrew Law, A.M.* Bound with A Collection of Hymns for Social Worship by Andrew Law, A.M. Printed by William Law, Cheshire, Connecticut (1782).

_____. *Essays on Music.* Philadelphia: Printed for the Author, 1814.

_____. *Harmonic Companion, and guide to Social Worship.* Being a choice selection of Tunes, adapted to the various Psalms and Hymns, used by the different Societies in the United States; Together with the Principles of Music, and Easy Lessons for Learners. By Andrew Law. Printed upon the Author's New Plan. Philadelphia: Printed for the author by William Carr, 1807.

_____. *The Rudiments of Music: or a Short and Easy Treatise on the Rules on the Rules of Psalmody.* To which are annexed a Number of Plain Tunes and Chants. By Andrew Law, A.M. Author of Select Harmony. Cheshire, Conn: Printed by William Law, 1783.

_____. *Select Harmony.* Containing in a plain and concise manner the Rules of Singing: Together with a Collection of Psalm Tunes, Hymns and Anthems. By Andrew Law, A.B. n.p.: n.d. [Note: This volume may possibly be the one described in Evans as being published in New Haven in 1779.]

LECHFORD, THOMAS. *Plain Dealing, or News from New England, 1641.* Reprinted with an introduction and notes by J. Hammond Trumbull. Boston: J. K. Wiggin & W. Parsons Lunt, 1867.

LITTLE, WILLIAM, and SMITH, WILLIAM. *The Easy Instructor, or a new method of teaching Sacred Harmony.* Containing, the Rudiments of Music on an improved Plan, wherein the Naming and Timing of the Notes are familiarized to the weakest Capacity. With a choice Collection of Psalm Tunes and Anthems from the most celebrated Authors, with a Number composed in Europe and America, entirely new; suited to the Metres sung in the different Churches in the United States. Published for the Use of Singing Societies in general, but more particularly for those who have not the Advantage of an Instructor. Albany: Printed by Websters & Skinner and Daniel Steele, Proprietors of the Copy-Right, 1807.

_____. *The Easy Instructor; or a new method of teaching Sacred Harmony.* Containing, I. The Rudiments of Music on an Improved Plan, wherein the Naming and Timing of the Notes are familiarized to the weakest Capacity. II. A choice Collection of Psalm Tunes and Anthems, from the most celebrated Authors, with a number composed in Europe and America, entirely new; suited to all the Metres sung in the different Churches in the United States. Published for the Use of Singing Societies in general, but more particularly for those who have not the advantage of an Instructor. Albany: Printed by Webster & Skinners and Daniel Steels, Proprietors of the Copyright, n.d. Note: This volume has been identified as Edition N 1815 as described in Lowens, Irving, and Britton, Allen P. "The Easy Instructor (1798–1831): A History and Bibliography of the First Shape Note Tune Book," *Journal for Research in Music Education* 1, no. 1 (Spring 1953), pp. 31–55.

LIVERMORE, SOLOMON KIDDER. *On the Practice of Music, a Discourse pronounced at Pepperell, Massachusetts, May 17th, 1809, before the Middlesex Musical Society.* By Solomon Kidder Livermore, Attorney-at-Law. Amherst, N.H.: Printed by Joseph Cushing, 1809.

LYON, JAMES. *Urania,* or a Choice Collection of Psalm-Tunes, Anthems, and Hymns from the most approv'd Authors with some Entirely New in Two, Three, and Four Parts—the whole Peculiarly Adapted to the use of Churches and Private families, To which are Prefix'd The Plainest & most Necessary Rules of Psalmody. By James Lyon, A.B. 1761. (Philadelphia: Printed by William Bradford.)

MACE, THOMAS. *Musick's Monument, or a Remembrancer of the Best Practical Musick both Divine, and Civil, that has ever been known, to have been in the World.* Divided into Three Parts. The First Part shews a Necessity of Singing Psalms Well, in Parochial Churches. The Second Part Treats of the Noble Lute (The Best of Instruments). In the Third Part the Generous Viol, in its Rightest Use is Treated upon. By Tho. Mace, one of the Clerks of Trinity College, in the University of Cambridge. London: Printed by T. Ratcliffe, and N. Thompson, for the Author, and are to be Sold by Himself at His House in Cambridge, and by John Carr, at His Shop at the Middle-Temple Gate in Fleetstreet, 1676.

MANN, ELIAS. *The Massachusetts Collection of Sacred Harmony.* Containing a plain and concise introduction to the grounds of music: also, a large number of psalm tunes, selected from the most approved and eminent Authors; adapted to the different Metres and Keys generally used in Churches. Together with a number of select pieces and anthems, suitable for various occasions. By Elias Mann. Boston: Printed by Manning and Loring, for the Author, 1807.

_____. *The Northampton Collection of Sacred Harmony, in Three Parts.* Containing: I. A Plain and Concise Introduction to the Grounds of Music; II. A large Number of Psalm Tunes, selected from the most approved and eminent Authors, and adapted by them to all the different Metres and Keys used in Churches; III. A Number of Pieces of several verses each, many of which are compositions never before publish'd and calculated for the use of Churches, and Extraordinary Occasions—with a number of universally approved Anthems. Printed, typographically, at Northampton by Andrew Wright for Daniel Wright, 1802.

MASON, LOWELL. *Address on Church Music.* Boston: Hilliard, Gray & Co., 1826.

_____. *Manual of the Boston Academy of Music, for Instruction in the Elements of Vocal music, on the System of Pestalozzi.* 2nd edition. Boston: J. H. Wilkins & R. B. Carter, 1836.

_____, ed. *The American Tune Book,* a complete collection of the tunes which are widely popular in America, with most popular anthems and set pieces, preceded by a new course of instruction for singing schools by Dr. Lowell Mason. The tunes and anthems selected from all sources by five hundred teachers and choir leaders. Boston: Oliver Ditson & Company, 1869.

Massachusetts Spy, or Worcester Gazette 18, no. 840 (May 14, 1789) and no. 846 (June 25, 1789). Printed at Worcester by Isaiah Thomas.

MATHER, COTTON. *The Accomplished Singer,* Instructions how the Piety of singing with a true Devotion, may be obtained and expressed; the Glorious God after an uncommon manner Glorified in it, and his People edified. Intended for the Assistance of all that would sing Psalms with Grace in their Hearts; but more particularly to accompany the Laudable Endeavours of those who are Learning to Sing by Rule, and seeking to preserve a Regular Singing in the Assemblies of the Faithful. Boston: Printed by B. Green for S. Gerrish, at his Shop in Cornhill, 1721.

_____. *Christodulus,* a good Reward of a good Servant, or, the Service of a Glorious Christ, Justly Demanded and Commended, from a View of the Glory with which it shall be Recompensed. With some Commemoration of Mr. Thomas Walter, Lately a Pastor to a Church in Roxbury. Boston: Printed by T. Fleet, for S. Gerrish, near the Brick Meeting-House in Cornhill, 1725.

_____. *Diary.* Collections of the *Massachusetts Historical Society,* 7th ser., vols. 7–8. Boston: Published by the Society, 1912.

_____. "A Letter to Thomas Hollis dated Nov. 5, 1723," *Collections of the Massachusetts Historical Society,* 7th ser., 7:693. Boston: Published by the Society, 1912.

_____. *Magnalia Christi Americana:* or the Ecclesiastical History of New England from its first planting in the year 1620 unto the year of Our Lord 1698. Part III. London: Printed for Thomas Parkhurst at the Bible and Three Crowns in Cheapside, MDCCII.

_____. *Manuductio ad Ministerium,* Directions for a Candidate of the Ministry, Wherein, First a Right Foundation is laid for his Future Improvement; and, then Rules are Offered for such a Management of his Academical & Preparatory Studies; and Thereupon for such a Conduct after his Appearance in the World, as may Render him a Skilful and Useful Minister of the Gospel. Boston: Printed for Thomas Hancock, and Sold at his Shop in Ann Street, near the Drawbridge, 1726.

_____. *Psalterium Americum The Book of Psalms in a Translation Exactly conformed unto the Original:* But all in BLANK VERSE, Fitted unto the Tunes commonly used in our Churches. Which Pure Offering is accompanied with Illustrations digging for Hidden Treasures in it; and Various Intentions of it. Whereto are added, Some other Portions of the Sacred Scripture, to Enrich the Cantional. Boston in N.E.: Printed by S. Kneeland, for B. Eliot, S. Gerrish, D. Henchman, and J. Edwards, and Sold at their Shops, 1718.

_____. *Ratio Disiplinae Fratrum Nov Anglorum.* A Faithful Account of the Discipline Professed and Practised; in the Churches of New England. With Interspersed and Instructive Reflections on the Discipline of Primitive Churches, Boston: Printed for S. Gerrish In Cornhill, 1726.

MAXIM, ABRAHAM. *The Northern Harmony,* being a collection from the works of many approved authors of Sacred Music; containing, 1. The Rudiments of Music, laid down in a plain and comprehensive manner. 2. Psalm and Hymn Tunes, adapted to the various metres, in common use, together with several anthems. Calculated for the use of singing schools and religious societies. 2nd edition. Exeter, N.H.: Printed by Norris & Sawyer, 1808.

MELLEN, JOHN. *Religion Productive of Music, a Discourse delivered at Marlborough, March 24th, 1773; at a Singing Lecture.* Published at the Desire of the Band and Friends of Music. Boston: Isaiah Thomas, 1773.

The Message Bird, a Literary and Musical Journal. Whole No. 25–41 (Aug. 1, 1850–Mar. 14, 1851). New York.

The Middlesex Collection of Church Music, or Ancient Psalmody Revived. Containing a Variety of Plain Psalm Tunes, the most suitable to be used in Divine Service; to which is Annexed, a Number of Other Pieces, of a more Delicate and Artificial Construction, Proper to be performed by a Choir of Good Musicians, in Schools and Public Religious Assemblies. 2nd edition. Boston: Printed and Sold by Manning & Loring, 1808.

MILLS, SAMUEL JOHN. *The Nature and Importance of the Duty of Singing Praise to GOD Considered, in a Sermon, delivered at Litchfield, March 22nd, 1775.* Occasioned by a Public Meeting of the Singers, in that Place; and published at their Desire. By Samuel John Mills, A.M., Pastor of the Church in Torringford. Hartford: Printed by Ebenezer Watson, near the Great Bird . . . (title page torn).

MOORS, HEZEKIAH. *The Province Harmony:* being an Original Composition of Airs. Consisting of Three and Four Parts. Adapted to all the Metres usually sung in Churches. Together with a brief Introduction to the Grounds of Musick. Calculated for the use of Singing Schools and Musical Societies. Boston: Printed for the Author by J. T. Buckingham, 1809.

MORTON, CHARLES. *Compendium Physicae.* Publications of the Colonial Society of Massachusetts 33. Boston: Published by the Society, 1940.

Muddy River and Brookline Records, 1634–1838. Brookline: J. E. Farwell and Co., Printers, 1875.

NEWBURY, GEORGE. "(Singing) Book." a manuscript tune book with music from the Tufts period. In the possession of Mr. Irving Lowens, Hyattsville, Maryland.

NOBLE, OLIVER. *Regular and Skilful Music in the Worship of God, . . .* shewn in a sermon preached at the North Meeting-House, Newbury-Port at the desire of the Church and Congregation, February 8th, 1774. Printed at the Desire of the Musical Society in Newbury-Port. Boston: Printed by Mills and Hicks, for Daniel Bayley, in Newbury-Port, 1774.

A Pacificatory Letter About Psalmody, or Singing of Psalms. Boston: Printed by J. Franklin for John Eliot, and sold at his Shop in Queen Street, 1724.

PAINE, ROBERT TREAT (Harvard A.B. 1749). "Journal, 1749." Manuscript diary in the possession of the Massachusetts Historical Society.

PAINE, THOMAS. *Adams and Liberty, the Boston patriotic song.* Written by Thomas Paine, A.M. For the pianoforte, German flute or violin. 3rd edition, corrected. Boston: Printed & sold by P. A. von Hagen & Co. at their pianoforte warehouse, No. 3 Cornhill. (Note: Sonneck, *Bibliography,* p. 2, states that this edition was published between May, 1799 and Nov., 1800.)

PALFRAY, WARWICK. *The Evangelical Psalmodist: an original work; consisting of Plain Tunes, Fuges, and Set Pieces, in Three and Four Parts; Suitable for Schools and Singing Societies.* Salem: Printed by Joshua Cushing for the Author, 1802.

PARISH, ELIJAH. *An Eulogy on John Hubbard, Professor of Mathematics and Natural Philosophy in Dartmouth College, who died Aug. 14, 1810.* Hanover: Printed by C. W. S. & H. Spear, 1810.

PARKER, JOHN, ed. *The Euterpeiad, or Musical Intelligencer, Devoted to the Diffusion of Musical Information and Belles Lettres.* Boston: Thomas Badger, 1820–1823.

PARKMAN, ANNA SOPHIA. "Diary," quoted by H. M. Forbes, *The Hundredth Town, a Glimpse of Life in Westborough, 1717–1817.* Boston: Press of Rockwell and Churchill, 1889.

PARKMAN, EBENEZER. "Diary, 1777–1778." A manuscript journal in the possession of the Massachusetts Historical Society.

PARKMAN, EBENEZER. *The Diary of the Rev. Ebenezer Parkman 1737 and 1778–1780.* Westborough: Westborough Historical Society, 1899.

_____. "Singing Book." a small manuscript music book dated July 17, 1721 in the possession of the Massachusetts Historical Society.

PLAYFORD, JOHN. *An Introduction to the Skill of Musick-plus-Psalms and Hymns to solemn musick, in foure parts, on the common tunes to the psalms in metre used in parish-churches.* London: Printed by W. Godbid, 1671.

_____. *Psalms & Hymns in Solemn Musick of Foure Parts on the Common Tunes to the Psalms in Metre: Used in Parish-Churches.* London: Printed by W. Godbid for J. Playford at his Shop in the Inner-Temple, 1671.

_____. *The Whole Book of Psalms, with the usual Hymns and Spiritual Songs; together with all the ancient and proper Tunes sung in Churches, with some of later Use.* Compos'd in Three Parts, CANTUS, MEDIUS, & BASSUS: In a more Plain and Useful Method, than hath been formerly published. By John Playford. London: Printed by W. Godbid for the Company of Stationers, and are Sold by John Playford near the Temple-Church. 1677.

_____. *The Whole Book of Psalms.* Seventeenth edition. London: Printed by W. Pearson, for the Company of Stationers and are to be sold by John and Benjamin Sprint at the Bell, in Little Britain, 1724.

Plymouth Church Records, 1620–1859. Publications of the Colonial Society of Massachusetts 23 and 24. Boston: Published by the Society, 1920.

PORTER, MOSES. "Diary, 1824." *Historical Collections of the Danvers Historical Society* (Danvers: Published by the Society, 1913), vol. 1, pp. 31–51.

PRESTON, SAMUEL. "Recollections by Samuel Preston, written for the Salem Village Gazette, Dec. 8, 1869," reprinted in *Historical Collections of the Danvers Historical Society* (Danvers: Published by the Society, 1919), vol. 7, pp. 125–130.

PRINCE, THOMAS. *The Christian History, containing Accounts of the Revival and Propagation of Religion in Great Britain & America for the Years 1743 and 1744.* Boston; N.E.: Printed by S. Kneeland and T. Green for T. Prince, junior, 1744 and 1745.

The Psalms, Hymns and Spiritual Songs of the Old & New Testament: Faithfully Translated into English Meetre. For the use, Edification and Comfort of the Saints in Publick and private, especially in New-England. Ninth edition. Boston: Printed by B. Green and J. Allen, for Michael Perry, 1698.

PUTNAM, ARCHELAUS (1787–1818). "A Journal and Diary of Foreign and Domestic Intelligence, or Remembrancer of Remarkable Days, Weather, etc., commenced at Danvers, Massachusetts, Jan. 10 1805," *Historical Collections of the Danvers Historical Society* (Danvers: Published by the Society, 1916). IV, 64–68.

PYNCHON, WILLIAM. *Diary.* Edited by F. E. Oliver. Boston: Houghton, Mifflin and Co., Riverside Press, Cambridge, 1890.

RAVENSCROFT, THOMAS. *The Whole Booke of Psalmes: with the Hymnes Evangelicall, and Songs Spirituall.* Composed into four parts by sundry Authors . . . Newly corrected and enlarged by Tho. Ravenscroft—Bachelor of Musicke. London, 1621.

READ, DANIEL. *The American Singing Book; or a new and easy guide to the art of Psalmody.* Designed for Use of Singing Schools in America. Containing in a plain and familiar Manner, the Rules of Psalmody, together with a Number of Psalm-Tunes, &c. To which is added a Supplement containing Twenty-Five approved Psalm-Tunes. By Daniel Read, Philo-Musico. 4th edition. New Haven: Printed for, and Sold by the Author, 1793.

_____. *The Columbian Harmonist, No. 1.* Containing, First. A Plain and Concise Introduction to Psalmody fitly calculated for the use of SINGING SCHOOLS. Second. A Choice Collection of New Psalm Tunes of American Composition. By Daniel Read. Author of the American Singing Book. New Haven: Printed for & Sold by the Editor, 1793.

_____. "Diary, 1796–1806." A manuscript journal in the possession of the New Haven Historical Society.

_____. *An Introduction to Psalmody; or, the Child's Instructor in vocal music.* Containing a Series of familiar Dialogues, under the following heads, viz. Psalmody in General, Stave, Musical Letters and Cliffs, an Exercise for the Bass, an Exercise for the Tenor or Treble, an Exercise for the Counter, Tones, Semitones, Flats, Sharps and Natural, Solfaing, Transposition, &c. The several Notes and Rests, and their Proportion, the Several Moods of Time, Several other Characters used in Music, Key Notes, &c. Pitching Tunes, &c. Graces. (Illustrated with Copper Plates.) By D. Read. Printed (by T. and B. Green) for, and sold by the Author, New Haven, 1790. Evans 22829.

READ, DANIEL. "Letterbook, 1829–1832," a manuscript collection of letters by the singing master, Daniel Read, in the possession of the New Haven Historical Society.

Records of the Church in Brattle Square. Boston: Benevolent Fraternity of Churches, 1902.

Salem Collection of Classical Sacred Musick; in three and four parts; consisting of psalm tunes and occasional pieces, selected from the most eminent composers; suited to all the metres in general use. To which is prefixed, a short introduction to psalmody. Salem, Mass: Printed by Joshue Cushing, and sold by Cushing & Appleton, at their bookstore in Salem, & by J. Sparhawk Appleton, No. 1. Cornhill, Boston. 1805.

The Salem Collection of Classical Sacred Musick; in Three and Four Parts: Consisting of Psalm Tunes and Occasional Pieces, Selected from the Works of the most eminent composers; Suited to all the metres in general use. To which is prefixed, An Introduction to Psalmody. 2nd edition, Improved and Revised. Boston: Printed by Manning & Loring, for Cushing & Appleton, 1806.

Salem Gazette 17, no. 1281 (Dec. 6, 1803), and 19, no. 1419 (April 2, 1805). Salem: Published by Thomas C. Cushing.

The Salem Register 3, no. 269, Dec. 6, 1802. Salem: Printed and Published by William Carlton.

SECCOMBE, JOSEPH. *An Essay to Excite a Further Inquiry into the Ancient Matter and Manner of Sacred Singing.* Boston: Printed by S. Kneeland and T. Green, 1741.

SENHOUSE, PETER. *The Right Use and Improvement of sensitive Pleasures, and more Particularly of Musick, a Sermon preach'd in the Cathedral Church of Gloucester at the Anniversary Meeting of the Choirs of Gloucester, Hereford, and Worcester, Sept. 20, 1727.* London: 1728.

SEWALL, SAMUEL. *Diary.* Collections of the Massachusetts Historical Society. 5th ser. vols. 5–7. Boston: Published by the Society, 1879–1882.

_____. "Letter to Mr. Burbank dated Boston, July 22, 1695," *Letterbook. Collections of the Massachusetts Historical Society.* 6th ser., 1, p. 155. Boston: Published by the Society, 1886.

SKINNER, ICABOD (A.B.). *A Discourse on Music, delivered February, 1796 at a Singing Lecture in North Bolton.* Hartford: Printed by Hudson and Goodwin, 1796.

SMITH, THOMAS, and DEANE, SAMUEL. *Journals of the Rev. Thomas Smith and the Rev. Samuel Deane.* Edited by William Willis. Portland: Joseph S. Bailey, 1849.

STEARNS, CHARLES. *A Sermon, preached at an Exhibition of Sacred Musick in Lincoln on the nineteenth of April, 1792.* Boston: Isaiah Thomas and Ebenezer T. Andrews, 1792.

STICKNEY, JOHN. *The Gentleman and Ladies Musical Companion; Containing a variety of Excellent Anthems, Tunes, Hymns, &c. Collected from the best Authors; with a Short Explanation of the Rules of Musick.* The Whole corrected and rendered Plain. By John Stickney, Printed and sold by Daniel Bayley, Newbury-port, 1774.

STILES, EZRA. *Literary Diary of Ezra Stiles.* President of Yale College. F. B. Dexter, editor. Vol. 3. New York: Charles Scribner's Sons, 1901.

STONE, JOSEPH, and WOOD, ABRAHAM. *The Columbian Harmony, Containing the Rules of Psalmody; together with a Collection of Sacred Music.* Designed, for the use of Worshipping Assemblies & Singing Societies. By Joseph Stone and Abraham Wood. (Boston: Printed by Isaiah Thomas and E. T. Andrews, 1793.)

STOWE, HARRIET BEECHER. *Old Town Folks.* Boston: Houghton, Mifflin and Company, 1897. (1st edition, 1869.)

_____. *Poganuc People.* Boston: Houghton, Mifflin and Company, 1884. (1st edition, 1878.)

STRONG, JOSEPH (V.D.M.). *The Duty of Singing, considered as a necessary and useful Part of Christian Worship.* Illustrated and Inforced in a Sermon, Delivered at a Singing-Lecture, in a Parish in Simsbury, March 18, 1773, On the Occasion of introducing regular Singing into the public Use in the Worship of God there. Published at the Request of the Hearers. New Haven: Printed by Thomas and Samuel Green, 1773.

"Sudbury, Massachusetts, Records of the Town." Manuscript records on file in the office of the town clerk,

SWAN, TIMOTHY. *New England Harmony.* Containing, a variety of Psalm Tunes, in Three and Four Parts, adapted to all Metres: also a number of Set Pieces of Several Verses each, together with a number of Anthems. Northampton: Printed by Andrew Wright, 1801.

SYMMES, THOMAS. *A Discourse Concerning Prejudice in Matter of Religion, Or, an Essay, to shew the Nature, Causes, and Effects of such Prejudices; and also the Means of Preventing or Reviving them.* Boston: Printed by S. Kneeland, for S. Gerrish, sold at his shop in Corn-hill, 1722.

_____. *A Monitor for Delaying Sinners: A Sermon, studiously adopted to the meanest capacities published by the desire of a society of Young Men to whom it was preached Lord's Day Evening Dec. 7, 1718.* With a Preface by Increase Mather, D.D. Reprinted in Memoirs of the Rev. Mr. Symmes (Newburyport: Printed by Wm. B. Allen & Co., No. 13 Cornhill, 1816).

_____. *Reasonableness of Regular Singing, or, Singing by Note; in an Essay, to Revive the True and Ancient Mode of Singing Psalm-Tunes, according to the Pattern in our New-England Psalm Books, the Knowledge and Practice of which is greatly decay'd in most Congregations. Writ by a Minister of the Gospel.* Perused by Several Ministers in the Town and Country and published with the Approbation of all who have Read it. Boston in N.E.: Printed by B. Green, for Samuel Gerrish, and Sold at his shop near the Brick Meeting-House in Corn-hill, 1720.

_____. *Utili Dulci, or a Joco-Serious Dialogue concerning Regular Singing:* Calculated for a Particular Town, (where it was publickly had, on Friday Oct. 12, 1722.) but may serve some other places same Climate. Boston: Printed by B. Green, for Samuel Gerrish, near the Brick Meeting House in Cornhill, 1723.

SYMMES, WILLIAM. *A Discourse, delivered at an Occasional Lecture in Andover, on Tuesday, April 6, 1779, appointed to promote and encourage the religious art of Psalmody.* By William Symmes, A.M., Pastor of the First Church in Andover. Danvers, near Boston: Printed and Sold by E. Russel, at his Printing-Office, next to the Bell Tavern. 1779.

TANS'UR, WILLIAM. *The American Harmony, or Royal Melody Complete.* In Two Volumes. Vol. 1. Containing, I. A New and Correct Introduction to the Grounds of Music, Rudemental, Practical and Technical. II. A New and Complete Body of Church Music, adapted to the most select Portions of the Book of Psalms, of either Version; with many Fuging Chorus's, and Gloria Patri's to the whole. III. A New and Select Number of Hymns, Anthems, and Canons, suited to several Occasions; and many of them never before printed. Set by the greatest Masters in the World. The Whole are composed in Two, Three, Four and Five Musical Parts, according to the nicest Rules; consisting of Solos, Fuges and Chorus's correctly set in Score for Voices or Organ; fitted for all Teachers, Learners, and Musical Societies. Eighth Edition. By William Tans'ur, Senior, Musico Theorico. Printed and Sold by Daniel Bayley, at his House, next Door to St. Paul's Church, Newbury-Port, 1773. (Note: Vol. 1 is bound with A. Williams' *Universal Psalmodist* which forms vol. 2 of the complete *American Harmony.*)

_____. *The Melody of the Heart: or, the Psalmist's Pocket-Companion.* In Two Parts. Containing: I. The New Version of the Psalms of David New Tun'd, with Musick more proper to the Sense of the Words than any Extant. With an Alphabetical Table of all the Tunes, and what Psalms are proper to each Tune: and a Table of Psalms suited to the Feasts and Fasts of the Church, &c. with Gloria Patri's proper to the Measure of every Psalm in the Book. To which is added, Compendious Instructions on the Grounds of Musick, &c. II. A New and Select Number of Divine Hymns, and Easy Anthems; On several Occasions, &c. The Whole is Composed in Two, Three, and Four Musical Parts, according to the most Authentick Rules (and Set in Score) for either Voice or Organ, &c. The Third Edition, Corrected by the Author according to his Original Manuscript: With large Additions. By William Tans'ur, Who Teacheth the same, Author of the Harmony of Sion. London: Printed by Robert Brown, for James Hodges, 1751. (Note: This edition has been bound together with Tans'ur's *Royal Melody* to form one volume.)

_____. *The Royal Melody Compleat: or the New Harmony of Sion.* In three Books. Containing: I. A New and Correct Introduction to the Grounds of Musick, Rudimental, Practical and Technical. II. A New and Compleat Body of Church-Music, adapted to the most select Portions of the Book of Psalms, or either Versions; with many Fuging Chorus's, and Gloria Patri's to the Whole. III. A New, and Select Number of Services, Chants, Hymns, Anthems, and Canons, suited to several Occasions; and many of them never before printed; Set by the greatest Masters in the World. The Whole are Composed in Two, Three, Four, Five, Six, Seven, and Eight Musical Parts, according to the nicest Rules: consisting of Solo's, Fuges, and Chorus's, correctly set in Score for Voices, or Organ: and fitted for all Teachers, Learners, and Musical Societies, &c. with a Preface on Church Musick, shewing the Beauty and Excellency thereof. The Second Edition. By William Tans'ur, Senior, Musico Theorico. London: Printed by R. Brown for S. Crowder, 1760. (Note: This edition has been bound together with Tans'ur's *Melody of the Heart* to form one volume.)

THACHER, PETER; DANFORTH, JOHN; and DANFORTH, SAMUEL. *An Essay: Cases of Conscience concerning the Singing of Psalms.* Boston: Printed by S. Kneeland for S. Gerrish, and Sold at his Shop in Cornhill, 1723.

TILESTON, JOHN. "Diary," quoted by D. C. Colesworthy, *John Tileston's School.* Boston: Antiquarian Bookstore, 1887.

TUFTS, JOHN. *An Introduction to the Singing of Psalm-Tunes.* Boston: 1726, Fifth edition. Facsimile reprint for Musical Americana (Harry Dichter) by Albert Saifer, Publisher, Philadelphia, 1954.

The Village Harmony, or Youth's Assistant to Sacred Musick. Containing a concise Introduction to the Grounds of Musick with such a collection of the most approved Psalm Tunes, Anthems and other Pieces as are most suitable for Divine Worship. Designed Principally for Use of Schools and Singing Societies. 5th edition. Exeter, N.H.: 1800.

The Village Harmony, or Youth's Assistant to Sacred Musick, containing a concise introduction to the Grounds of Musick, with such a Collection of the most approved Psalm Tunes, Anthems, and other pieces, as are most suitable for Divine Worship. Designed principally for the use of Schools and Singing Societies. 9th edition. Exeter, N.H.: 1808.

The Village Harmony: or Youth's Assistant to Sacred Musick. Consisting of Psalm Tunes and Occasional Pieces, selected from the works of the most eminent composers. To which is prefixed a concise Introduction to Psalmody. 13th edition. Newburyport: Published by E. Little & Co., 1816.

WALTER, THOMAS. *The Grounds and Rules of Musick Explained: Or, An Introduction to the Art of Singing by Note.* Fitted to the Meanest Capacities. By Thomas Walter, M.A. Recommended by Several Ministers. Boston: Printed by J. Franklin for S. Gerrish, near the Brick Church in Cornhill, 1721.

_____. *The Grounds and Rules of Musick Explained: Or, an Introduction to the Art of Singing by Note.* Fitted to the Meanest Capacities. By Thomas Walter, M.A. Recommended by several Ministers. The Second Edition. Boston: Printed by B. Green, for S. Gerrish, near the Brick Meeting House in Cornhill, 1723.

_____. "A Subscription Paper for Thomas Walter's Grounds and Rules of Musick Explained dated Boston, November 12, 1720." In the possession of the John Carter Brown Library, Providence.

_____. *The Sweet Psalmist of Israel, a Sermon preach'd at the Lecture held in Boston, by the SOCIETY for promoting REGULAR & GOOD SINGING, and for reforming the Depravations and Debasements our PSALMODY labours under, in order to introduce the proper and true OLD WAY of SINGING.* Now published at the desire of several ministers that heard it, and at the request of the Society aforesaid. Boston: Printed by J. Franklin, for S. Gerrish, near the Brick Meetinghouse in Cornhill, 1722.

WEBSTER, NOAH. "Diary," quoted in full by E. E. F. Ford, *Notes on the Life of Noah Webster.* Vol. 1. New York: Privately printed, 1912.

WELD, EZRA, V.D.M. *A Sermon, preached at a Singing Lecture in Braintree, May, 21st, MDCCLXXXVIII and now printed at the desire of the Singing Society, in the Second Parish.* Printed at Springfield, Massachusetts, by Ezra Weld.

WEST, ELISHA. *The Musical Concert.* Containing, the Rudiments of Music, and a great variety of Psalm Tunes, together with a number of Anthems, suitable for Churches and Singing Societies, many of which were never before published. The Second Edition. By Elisha West, Philo Musico. Printed, typographically, at Northampton by Andrew Wright for the Compiler, 1807.

Weston, Town of: Records of the First Precinct, 1746–1754 and the Town, 1754–1803. Vol. 1. Boston: Alfred Mudge and Son, 1893.

Weston, Town of: Records of the Town Clerk, 1804–1826. Vol. 2. Boston: Alfred Mudge & Son, 1894.

WHALEY, . . . IAM P. "(Singing) Book," A manuscript tune book with music from both the Tufts and Billings period written by different hands. In the possession of Mr. Irving Lowens, Hyattsville, Maryland.

WHITE, D. A. "Reminiscences of College Life, 1793–97." Manuscript written by D. A. White, Harvard A.B. 1797, in the year 1837. Harvard University Archives HU 797.94.

WHITE, DANIEL APPLETON. . . . *Early Records of the First Church in Salem.* Salem: n.p., 1861.

The Whole Booke of Psalmes faithfully Translated into English Metre. Whereunto Is prefixed a discourse declaring not only the lawfullness but also the necessity of the heavenly Ordinance of singing Scripture Psalms in the Churches of God. Cambridge: Imprinted by Stephen Daye, 1640. A facsimile reprint of the first edition of 1640 entitled, *The Bay Psalm Book* (Chicago: University of Chicago Press, 1956).

WIGHTMAN, VALENTINE. *A Letter to the Elders and Brethren of the Baptized Churches in Rhode-Island, Narragansett, Providence, and Swansy, and Branches Dependent in Places Adjacent.* n.p.: 1725. A copy with a torn title page in the possession of the Massachusetts Historical Society.

WILLARD, SAMUEL. *The Expediency and Proper Application of Sacred Music, a Discourse, preached at Heath, Feb. 21, 1816 as a Musical Lecture.* Deerfield: Printed at R. Dickinson's office, *Graves and Wells, Printers,* 1816.

_____. *The Use and Design of Sacred Music, a Discourse preached Mar. 19, 1811 as a Musical Lecture in Greenfield.* Greenfield: Printed by Ansel Phelps, 1811.

WILLIAMS, A. *The American Harmony, or Universal Psalmodist.* Vol. II. Containing, a Choice and Valuable Collection of Psalm and Hymn Tunes; Canons and Anthems; with Words Adapted to each Tune. The Whole Composed in a New and Easy Taste, for Two, Three and Four Voices; in the most familiar Keys and Cliffs:—Calculated to Promote and Improve this most Excellent Part of Social Worship; and render it both Useful and Delightful; in Quires, as well as in Congregations in the Country. (By A. Williams, Teacher of Psalmody in London.) To which is added a Variety of Favourite Hymn Tunes and Anthems; Collected from the Latest and Most Celebrated Authors; Carefully set in Score, and neatly Engraved. Printed and Sold by Daniel Bayley at his House, next Door to St. Paul's Church, Newbury-Port, 1773. (Note: Vol. 2 is bound with William Tans'ur's *Royal Melody Complete* which forms vol. 1 of the complete *American Harmony.*)

WILLIAMS, THOMAS. *A Discourse at a Public Meeting of the Singers at the North Parish in Wrentham.* 17th May, 1817. Dedham: Abel D. Alleyne, Printer, 1817.

WINSLOW, EDWARD. *Hypocrisie Unmasked, a True Relation of the Proceedings of the Governor and Company of the Massachusetts Bay against Samuel Gorton of Rhode Island.* London: Printed by Rich. Cotes for John Bellamy at the Three Golden Lions in Cornhill, neare the Royall Exchange, 1646. Reprinted from the original edition with an introduction by Howard Millar Chapin. Providence: The Club for Colonial Reprints, 1916.

WOODBRIDGE, TIMOTHY. *The Duty of GOD'S Professing People, in Glorifying their Heavenly Father; Opened and Applyed, in a Sermon Preached at a Singing Lecture in Hartford, East Society, June the 28th, 1727.* By the Reverend Mr. Timothy Woodbridge, Pastor of a Church in said Town. New London: Printed and Sold by T. Green, 1727.

WOODS, LEONARD. *A Discourse on Sacred Music, delivered before the Essex Musical Association at their Annual Meeting, Boxford, Sept. 10, 1804.* Salem: Printed by Joshua Cushing, 1804.

WORCESTER, SAMUEL. *An Address on Sacred Music, delivered before the Middlesex Musical Society and the Handel Society of Dartmouth College at a Joint Meeting held at Concord, N.H., Sept. 19, 1810.* Boston: Printed by Manning and Loring, 1811.

II. SECONDARY SOURCES.

ADAMS, C. FREDERICK, JR. "Notices of the Walter Family." *New England Historical and Genealogical Register,* VIII, 209–214. Boston: Samuel G. Drake, Publisher, 1854.

ALDRICH, GEORGE. *Walpole, 1749–1879.* Claremont: Printed by the Claremont Manufacturing Co., 1880.

ALLEN, MYRON O. *History of Wenham, 1639–1860.* Boston: Bazin and Chandler, 1860.

ALLEN, N. H. "Old Time Music and Musicians," *Connecticut Quarterly* 1, no. 3 (July, Aug., Sept. 1895), pp. 274–279, and no. 4 (Oct., Nov., Dec. 1895), pp. 368–373; 3, no. 1 (Jan., Feb., March 1897), pp. 68–76.

ATKINS, GAIUS GLENN, and FAGLEY, FREDERICK L. *The History of American Congregationalism.* Boston and Chicago: The Pilgrim Press, 1942.

BALDWIN, SIMEON E. *Life and Letters of Simeon Baldwin.* New Haven: The Tuttle, Morehouse & Taylor Co., 1919.

BALTZELL, W. J. "Old Time Community Music," *Music Teachers' National Association: Proceedings for 1922, Series 17;* pp. 67–75. Hartford: Published by the Association, 1923.

BARRY, JOHN S. *Historical Sketch of the Town of Hanover, Massachusetts.* Boston: Published for the Author by Samuel G. Drake, 1853.

BARRY, WILLIAM. *History of Framingham.* Boston: James Monroe & Co., 1847.

BENEDICT, WILLIAM A., and TRACY, HIRAM A. *History of the Town of Sutton, Massachusetts, 1704–1876.* Worcester: Sanford & Co., 1878.

BENSON, LOUIS F. *The English Hymn.* London: Hodder & Stoughton, 1915.

BIRGE, EDWARD BAILEY. *The History of Public School Music in the United States.* Philadelphia, Oliver Ditson Co., 1937.

BLAKE, FRANCIS EVERETT. *History of the Town of Princeton, 1759–1915.* Vol. 1. Princeton: Published by the Town, 1915.

BLAKE, HENRY T. *Chronicles of New Haven Green, 1632–1862.* New Haven: The Tuttle, Morehouse and Taylor Press, 1898.

BLAKE, MORTIMER. *A History of the Town of Franklin.* Franklin, Mass.: Published by the Committee of the Town, 1879.

BLAKE, S. LEROY. *The Later History of the First Church of Christ, New London, Connecticut.* New London: Press of the Day Publishing Co., 1900.

BLOOD, HENRY AMES. *History of Temple, New Hampshire.* Boston: Printed by Geo. C. Rand and Avery, 1860.

History of Bolton, 1738–1938. Bolton, Mass.: Privately published, 1938.

BOLTON, ETHEL STANFORD. *Shirley Uplands and Intervales.* Boston: George Emery Littlefield, 1914.

BOURNE, EDWARD E. *History of Wells and Kennebunk.* Portland: B. Thurston and Company, 1875.

BOUTON, NATHANIEL. *History of Concord, New Hampshire, 1725–1853.* Concord: Published by Benning W. Sanborn, 1856.

BOWEN, CLARENCE WINTHROP. *History of Woodstock, Connecticut.* Norwood, Mass.: Privately printed, 1926.

BRIDENBAUGH, CARL. "The New England Town: A Way of Life," *Proceedings of the American Antiquarian Society for April, 1946, vol. 56,* pp. 19–48. Worcester: Published by the Society, 1947.

BRIGGS, L. VERNON. *History and Records of the First Congregational Church, Hanover, Mass., 1727–1865.* Boston: Wallace Spooner, Printer, 1895.

BRITTON, ALLEN P. "The Musical Idiom in Early American Tune Books," an abstract of a paper read in St. Louis on April 14, 1950 at a meeting of the Midwestern Chapter. *Journal of the American Musicological Society 3,* no. 3 (Fall 1950), p. 286.

_____. "Theoretical Introductions in American Tune Books to 1800." Unpublished doctoral dissertation, University of Michigan, 1949. University Microfilms, No. 1505.

BRITTON, ALLEN P., and LOWENS, IRVING. "Unlocated Titles in Early Sacred American Music." *Music Library Association Notes,* XI (December 1953), 33–48.

BROOKS, HENRY M. *Olden Time Music, a Compilation from Newspapers and Books.* Boston: Ticknor and Co., 1888.

BURNHAM, COLLINS G. "Olden Time Music in the Connecticut Valley," *New England Magazine,* New Series, 24, no. 1 (March 1901), pp. 12–27.

BUTLER, FRANCIS GOULD. *A History of Farmington, Franklin County, Maine, 1776–1885.* Farmington: Press of Knowlton, McLeary and Co., 1885.

CAMP, DAVID N. *History of New Britain, 1640–1889.* New Britain: William B. Thomson & Co., 1889.

CHAMBERLAIN, MELLEN. *A Documentary History of Chelsea, 1624–1824.* Vol. 2. Boston: Printed for the Massachusetts Historical Society, 1908.

CHANDLER, SETH. *History of the Town of Shirley.* Shirley: Published by the Author, 1883.

CHAPIN, ALONZO B. *Glastonbury for Two Hundred Years.* Hartford: Press of Case, Tiffany and Co., 1853.

CHASE, BENJAMIN. *History of Old Chester (Auburn, N.H.).* Auburn: Published by the Author, 1869.

CHASE, GEORGE WINGATE. *History of Haverhill, 1640–1860.* Haverhill: Published by the Author, 1861.

CHASE, GILBERT. *America's Music.* New York: McGraw-Hill Book Co., Inc., 1955.

CHENEY, SIMEON PEASE. *The American Singing Book.* Boston: Published by White, Smith and Co., 1879.

CLARKE, GEORGE KUHN. *History of Needham, Mass., 1711–1911.* Cambridge: Privately printed at the University Press, 1912.

COFFIN, CHARLES CARLETON. *History of Boscawen and Webster, 1733–1878.* Concord: Printed by the Republican Press Assoc., 1878.

COLBURN, SILAS R. *History of Dracut. Massachusetts.* Lowell: Press of Courier-Citizen Co., 1922.

COTHREN, WILLIAM. *History of Ancient Woodbury, Connecticut 1659–1854.* Waterbury: Published by Bronson Brothers, 1854.

COVEY, CYCLONE. "Letter to the Editor." *William and Mary Quarterly 9,* no. 1 (Jan., 1952), pp. 129–133.

_____. "Puritanism and Music in Colonial America," *William and Mary Quarterly 8,* no. 3 (July, 1951), pp. 378–388.

CRAWFORD, MARY CAROLINE. *Social Life in Old New England.* Boston: Little, Brown, and Company, 1914.

CROWELL, ROBERT. *History of the Town of Essex, 1634–1868.* Essex, Mass.: Published by the Town, 1868.

CURRIER, JOHN J. *History of Newbury, Massachusetts, 1635–1902.* Boston: Damrell and Upham, 1902.

_____. *History of Newburyport, Mass., 1764–1905.* Newburyport: Published by the Author, 1906.

CURRIER, MISS LIZZIE B. "Music of Other Days in Methuen." *Methuen Historical Society Publication* No. 1. Methuen: Published by the Society, 1896.

CURTI, MERLE. *The Growth of American Thought.* 2nd edition. New York: Harper & Brothers, 1951.

CURWEN, JOHN S. *Studies in Worship Music.* 2nd ser. London: J. Curwen & Sons, 1885.

_____. *Studies in Worship Music.* 1st ser. 2nd edition. London: J. Curwen & Sons, 1888.

CUTTER, BENJAMIN, and CUTTER, WILLIAM R. *History of the Town of Arlington, Massachusetts, formerly the Town of West Cambridge, 1635–1879.* Boston: David Clapp and Son, 1880.

CUTTER, DANIEL B. *History of the Town of Jaffrey, New Hampshire, 1749–1880.* Concord: Printed by the Republican Press Association, 1881.

DANA, HENRY SWAN. *History of Woodbridge, Vermont.* Boston: Houghton, Mifflin and Company, 1889.

DANIEL, RALPH. "The Anthem in New England Before 1800." Unpublished doctoral dissertation, Harvard University, Cambridge, 1955.

DAVIDSON, PHILIP. *Propaganda and the American Revolution, 1763–1783.* Chapel Hill: University of North Carolina Press, 1941.

DAVIS, CHARLES HENRY. *History of Wallingford, Connecticut.* Meriden: Published by the Author, 1870.

DAVISON, ARCHIBALD T. *Choral Conducting.* Cambridge: Harvard University Press, 1940. Sixth printing, 1950.

DAY, REV. GARDINER M. *The Biography of a Church.* Cambridge: Riverside Press, 1951.

DEFOREST, H. P., and BATES, E. C. *History of Westborough, Massachusetts.* Westborough: Published by the Town, 1891.

DINEEN, WILLIAM. *Music at the Meeting House, 1775–1958.* Providence: Privately printed for the First Baptist Church in America, 1958.

DONOVAN, THE REV. D., and WOODWARD, JACOB A. *History of the Town of Lyndeborough, New Hampshire, 1735–1905.* Lyndeborough: Published by the Town, 1906.

DOW, GEORGE FRANCIS. *History of Topsfield, Massachusetts.* Topsfield: Published by the Topsfield Historical Society, 1940.

History of Dublin, New Hampshire. Boston: John Wilson & Son, 1855.

DWIGHT, JOHN S. "Billings' Psalmody," *Dwight's Journal of Music 3,* no. 1 (April 9, 1853), p. 2.

EARLE, ALICE MORSE. *Home Life in Colonial Days.* New York: Charles Scribner's Sons, 1891.

_____. *The Sabbath in Puritan New England.* New York: Charles Scribner's Sons, 1891.

EDWARDS, GEORGE THORNTON. *Music and Musicians of Maine*. Portland: The Southworth Press, 1928.

ELLINWOOD, LEONARD. *The History of American Church Music*. New York: Morehouse-Gorham Co., 1953.

ELLIS, ARTHUR B. *History of the First Church in Boston, 1630–1880*. Boston: Hall and Whiting, 1881.

ELSON, LOUIS O. *The History of American Music*. New York: Macmillan Co., 1905.

_____. *The National Music of America*. Boston: Page Co., 1899.

EVANS, CHARLES. *American Bibliography: A Chronological Dictionary of All Books, Pamphlets, and Periodical Publications Printed in the United States of America*. Chicago: Blakely Press, 1903–1955.

FELT, JOSEPH B. *Annals of Salem*. 2 vols. 2nd edition. Salem: Published by W. & S. B. Ives, 1845.

_____. *History of Ipswich, Essex and Hamilton*. Cambridge: Printed by Charles Folsom, 1834.

FISHER, WILLIAM ARMS. *The Music That Washington Knew*. Boston: Oliver Ditson Co., 1931.

_____. *Notes on Music in Old Boston*. Boston: Oliver Ditson Co., 1918.

_____. *Ye Olde New England Psalm-Tunes, 1620–1820*. Boston: Oliver Ditson Co., 1930.

FLEXNER, BEATRICE HUDSON. "The Music of the Puritans," *American Heritage 8*, no. 1 (December, 1956), pp. 65–67 and 117–119.

FOOTE, HENRY WILDER. *Three Centuries of American Hymnody*. Cambridge: Harvard University Press, 1940.

GAGE, THOMAS. *History of Rowley*. Boston: F. Andrews, 1840.

GARRETT, ALLEN M. "Performance Practices in the Music of William Billings," an abstract of a paper read in Chapel Hill, N.C., on May 26, 1952, at a meeting of the Southeastern Chapter. *Journal of the American Musicological Society 5*, no. 2 (Summer 1952), p. 147.

GAY, JULIUS. "Church Music, an historical address delivered at the Village Library Company of Farmington, Connecticut, May 6, 1891." *Farmington Papers*, pp. 23–42. Farmington: Privately printed, 1929.

GOLDBERG, ISAAC. "The First American Musician," *American Mercury 14*, no. 53 (May 1928), pp. 67–75.

GOLDMAN, RICHARD FRANKO, and SMITH, ROGER. *Landmarks of Early American Music, 1760–1800*. New York: Published by G. Schirmer, Inc., 1943.

GOULD, AUGUSTUS A., and KIDDER, FREDERIC. *History of New Ipswich*. Boston: Gould and Lincoln, 1852.

GOULD, NATHANIEL D. *Church Music in America*. Boston: A. N. Johnson, publisher, 1853.

GRIFFIN, S. G. *A History of the Town of Keene, 1732–1874*. Keene: Sentinel Printing Co., 1904.

HARASZTI, ZOLTAN. *The Enigma of the Bay Psalm Book*. Chicago: University of Chicago Press, 1956.

HAYNES, GEORGE H. *Historical Sketch, First Congregational Church, Sturbridge, Massachusetts*. Worcester: Davis Press, 1910.

HIBBARD, A. G. *History of the Town of Goshen, Connecticut*. Hartford: Press of the Case, Lockwood and Brainard Company, 1897.

HODGMAN, EDWIN R. *History of the Town of Westford, 1659–1883*. Lowell: Morning Mail Company, Printers, 1883.

HOLMES, PAULINE. *A Tercentenary History of the Boston Public Latin School, 1635–1925*. Cambridge: Harvard University Press, 1935.

HOOD, GEORGE. *A History of Music in New England*. Boston: Wilkins, Carter Co., 1846.

HOUGHTON, WILLIAM. *History of the Town of Berlin, Worcester County, Massachusetts, 1784–1895*. Worcester: F. S. Blanchard & Co., 1895.

HOWARD, JOHN TASKER. *Our American Music*. Third edition. New York: Thomas Y. Crowell Co., 1946.

HOWES, FREDERIC G. *History of the Town of Ashfield, 1712–1910*. Ashfield: Published by the Town, 1910.

HUBBARD, W. L., ed. *History of American Music* (Vol. 8 of *The American History and Encyclopedia of Music*). New York: Irving Squire, 1910.

HUDSON, ALFRED SERENO. *Annals of Sudbury, Wayland and Maynard*. Ayer, Mass.: Published by the Author, 1891.

_____. *The History of Concord, Massachusetts*. Vol. 1. Concord: The Erudite Press, 1904.

_____. *The History of Sudbury, Massachusetts, 1638–1889*. Sudbury: Published by the Town, 1889.

HUMPHREY, ZEPHINE. *The Story of Dorset (Vt.)*. Rutland: Tuttle Co., 1924.

HUNTINGTON, REV. E. B. *History of Stamford, Conn., 1641–1868*. Stamford: Published by the Author, 1868.

HUNTOON, DANIEL T. V. *History of the Town of Canton*. Cambridge: John Wilson and Son, 1893.

HYDE, CHARLES G. *Historical Celebration of the Town of Brimfield*. Springfield: Published by Vote of the Town, 1879.

Hymns, Ancient and Modern. "Historical Edition" with an Introduction by the Rev. W. H. Frere. London: Wilham Clowes and Sons, 1909.

"Incidents in the First Seventeen Years of the Life of Robert Rhythm," *Musical Gazette 1*, no. 15 (August 17, 1846), pp. 113–115. Boston: Published by A. N. Johnson and J. Johnson, Jr.

JACKSON, GEORGE PULLEN. "Buckwheat Notes," *Musical Quarterly 19*, no. 4 (October, 1933), pp. 393–400.

_____. *White Spirituals in the Southern Uplands*. Chapel Hill: The University of North Carolina Press, 1933.

JEWETT, AMOS EVERETT, and JEWETT, EMILY MABEL ADAMS. *Rowley, Massachusetts, Mr. Ezechi Rogers Plantation, 1639–1850*. Rowley: Published by the Jewett Family in America, 1946.

JOHNSON, H. EARLE. "Early New England Periodicals Devoted to Music." *Musical Quarterly 26*, no. 2 (April, 1940), pp. 153–161.

_____. *Musical Interludes in Boston, 1795–1830*. New York: Columbia University Press, 1943.

JONES, EZEKIEL, ESQ. (nom de plume). "Opposition Psalmody." *Musical Gazette 3*, no. 6 (April 10, 1848), pp. 41 f.

JONES, MATT B. "Bibliographical Notes on Thomas Walter's *Grounds and Rules of Musick Explained*," reprinted from the *Proceedings of the American Antiquarian Society* for October, 1932. Worcester: Published by the Society, 1933.

JONES, MATT B. "Some Bibliographical Notes on Cotton Mather's *The Accomplished Singer*," Reprinted from the *Publications of the Colonial Society of Massachusetts 28*. Boston, 1933.

JUDD, SYLVESTER. *History of Hadley*. Northampton: Printed by Metcalf & Co., 1863.

KENT, JOSIAH COLMAN. *Northborough History.* Newton, Mass.: Garden City Press, 1921.

KIMBALL, FISKE. *Mr. Samuel McIntire, Carver, The Architect of Salem.* Portland, Maine: Southworth-Anthoensen Press for the Essex Institute, Salem, Mass., 1940.

"JACOB KIMBALL," *Historical Collections of the Topsfield Historical Society,* XII, 96. Topsfield: Published by the Society, 1907.

KOUWENHOVEN, JOHN A. "Some Unfamiliar Aspects of Singing in New England," *New England Quarterly* 6, no. 3 (Sept., 1933), pp. 567–588.

LEE, DR. WILLIAM. "Instruction in Psalmody in Boston Before 1750," *New England Historical and Genealogical Register* 42, pp. 197–198. Boston: Published at the Society's House, 1888.

LIGHTWOOD, JAMES T. *Hymn-Tunes and their Story.* London: Charles E. Kelly, 1906.

LINCOLN, WILLIAM. *History of Worcester to 1836.* Worcester: Moses D. Phillips and Company, 1837.

LINDSTROM, CARL E. "William Billings and his Times," *Musical Quarterly* 25, no. 4 (October, 1939), pp. 479–497.

LORD, JOHN KING. *A History of Dartmouth College, 1815–1909.* Concord: The Rumford Press, 1913.

LOWENS, IRVING. "The Bay Psalm Book in 17th-Century New England," *Journal of the American Musicological Society* 8, no. 1 (Spring 1955), pp. 22–29.

_____. "Daniel Read's World: the Letters of an Early American Composer," *Music Library Association Notes,* 2nd ser. 9, no. 2 (March, 1952), pp. 233–248.

_____. "John Tufts *Introduction to the Singing of Psalm-Tunes (1721–1744):* The First American Music Textbook," *Journal of Research in Music Education* 2, no. 2 (Fall, 1954), pp. 89–102.

_____. "John Wyeth's Repository of Sacred Music, Part Second: A Northern Precursor of Southern Folk Hymnody," *Journal of the American Musicological Society* 5, no. 2 (Summer, 1952), pp. 114–131.

_____. "The Origins of the American Fuging Tune," *Journal of the American Musicological Society* 6, no. 1 (Spring, 1953), pp. 43–52.

Lowens, Irving, and Britton, Allen P. "Daniel Bailey's *The American Harmony,* a Bibliographical Study," reprinted from the *Papers of the Bibliographical Society of America* 49 (Fourth Quarter, 1955), pp. 340–354.

_____. "*The Easy Instructor (1798–1831):* A History and Bibliography of the First Shape Note Tune Book," *Journal of Research in Music Education* 1, no. 1 (Spring, 1953). pp. 30–55.

LYFORD, JAMES O., ed. *History of Concord, New Hampshire.* Concord: Published by the City, 1903.

MacDOUGALL, HAMILTON C. *Early New England Psalmody.* Brattleboro: Stephen Daye Press, 1940.

MANGLER, JOYCE ELLEN. "Andrew Law, Class of 1775: the Contributions of a Musical Reformer," *Books at Brown* 18, no. 2 (January, 1957), pp. 61–78.

_____. "Andrew Law, Musical Reformer." Unpublished Master's thesis, Dept. of Music, Brown University, 1956.

_____. "Early Music in Rhode Island Churches—Music in the First Congregational Church, Providence, 1770–1850," *Rhode Island History* 17, no. 1 (January, 1958), pp. 1–9.

_____. "The First 'Dissenting' Church Organ." *Choral and Organ Guide* 9, no. 10 (January, 1957), pp. 12 f.

MANN, REV. ASA. "History of Psalms and Hymns and Music of the First Church of Randolph," *Proceedings of the One Hundred and Fiftieth Anniversary of the Organization of the First Congregational Church, Randolph, Massachusetts.* Boston: Beacon Press, 1881.

MANSFIELD, ORLANDO A. "Bedford's Great Abuse of Musick," *Musical Quarterly* 16, no. 4 (October, 1930), pp. 547–562.

MARVIN, THE REV. ABIJAH P. *History of The Town of Winchendon.* Winchendon: Published by the Author, 1868.

MAURER, MAURER. "The 'Professor of Musick' in Colonial America," *Musical Quarterly* 36, no. 4 (October, 1950). pp. 511–524.

McKENZIE, DUNCAN. *Training the Boy's Changing Voice.* New Brunswick, N.J.: Rutgers University Press, 1956.

METCALF, FRANK J. *America Psalmody, or Titles of Books, Containing Tunes Printed in America from 1721 to 1820.* New York: Charles F. Heartman, 1917.

_____. *American Writers and Compilers of Sacred Music.* New York: The Abingdon Press, 1925.

_____. "The Easy Instructor," *Musical Quarterly* 23, no. 1 (January, 1937), pp. 89–97.

MILLER, JOHN C. *Samuel Adams, Pioneer in Propaganda.* Boston: Little, Brown and Co., 1936.

MOOAR, GEORGE. *Historical Manual of the South Church in Andover.* Andover: Printed by Warren F. Draper, 1859.

MORIN, RAYMOND. "William Billings, Pioneer in American Music," *New England Quarterly,* March, 1941, pp. 25–33.

MORISON, SAMUEL ELIOT. *Harvard College in the Seventeenth Century.* 2 vols. Cambridge: Harvard University Press, 1936.

_____. *Three Centuries of Harvard, 1636–1936.* Cambridge: Harvard University Press, 1942.

MORSE, JAMES KING. *Jedediah Morse, a Champion of New England Orthodoxy.* New York: Columbia University Press, 1939.

NEWTON, WILLIAM MONROE. *History of Barnard, Vermont, 1761–1927.* Vol. 1. Burlington: Published by the Vermont Historical Society, 1928.

NOON, ALFRED. *History of Ludlow.* Springfield: Springfield Printing and Binding Company, 1912.

NORTON, ARTHUR O. "Harvard Text-books and Reference Books of the Seventeenth Century." *Transactions, 1930–1933, Publications of the Colonial Society of Massachusetts,* XXVIII (April, 1933), 361–438. Boston: Published by the Society, 1935.

NOURSE, HENRY S. *History of the Town of Harvard.* Harvard: Printed for Warren Hapgood, 1894.

NOYES, HARRIETTE ELIZA. *A Memorial History of Hampstead, New Hampshire.* Vol. 2. Boston: George B. Reed, 1908.

ORCUTT, REV. SAMUEL. *History of Torrington.* Albany: J. Munsell, Printer, 1878.

PAIGE, LUCIUS R. *History of Hardwick.* Boston: Houghton Mifflin and Co., 1883.

PARKER, EDWIN POND. *History of the Second Church of Christ in Hartford, 1670–1892.* Hartford: Belknap and Warfield, 1892.

PARSONS, HERBERT COLLINS. *A Puritan Outpost, a History of the Town and People of Northfield, Mass.* New York: Macmillan Co., 1937.

PATRICK, MILLAR. *Four Centuries of Scottish Psalmody.* London: Oxford University Press, 1949.

PERKINS, CHARLES C., & DWIGHT, JOHN S. *History of the Handel & Haydn Society*. Vol. 1. Boston: A. Mudge & Son, Printers, 1883–1893.

PERLEY, SIDNEY. *History of Boxford*. Boxford: Published by the Author, 1880.

PHALEN, HAROLD R. *History of the Town of Acton*. Cambridge: Middlesex Printing, Inc., 1954.

PICHIERRI, LOUIS. "Music in New Hampshire, 1623–1800." Unpublished doctoral dissertation, Syracuse University, 1956.

PIERCE, EDWIN HALL. "The Rise and Fall of the 'Fugue-tune' in America," *Musical Quarterly* 16, no. 2 (April, 1930), pp. 214–228.

Playford's "Brief Introduction to the Skill of Musick," an Account with Bibliographical Notes of an Unique Collection comprising all the editions from 1654 to 1730 in the possession of Messrs. Ellis, Bookseller. London: Messrs. Ellis, 1926.

POLADIAN, SIRVART. "Rev. John Tufts and Three-Part Psalmody in America," an abstract of a paper read in New York on Feb. 17, 1951, at a meeting of the Greater New York Chapter. *Journal of the American Musicological Society* 4, no. 2 (Fall, 1951), pp. 276–277.

POPE, CHARLES HENRY. *The Cheney Genealogy*. Boston: Published by Charles H. Pope, 1897.

POTTER, ROCKWELL HARMON. *Hartford's First Church*. Hartford: Published by the First Church of Christ, 1932.

PRATT, WALDO SELDEN. *The Music of the Pilgrims*. Boston: Oliver Ditson Company, 1921.

_____ , ed. *Grove's Dictionary of Music and Musicians, American-Supplement*. New York: Macmillan Co., 1920.

Proceedings in Observance of the One Hundred and Fiftieth Anniversary of the Organization of the First Church in Lincoln. Cambridge: University Press, 1899.

PUTNAM, ALFRED P. (D.D.). "Danvers People and their Homes," *Historical Collections of the Danvers Historical Society* 7, pp. 72–74. Danvers: Published by the Society, 1919.

Readings in New Canaan History. New Canaan: Published by the New Canaan Historical Society, 1949.

RICH, ARTHUR LOWNDES. *Lowell Mason, "The Father of Singing Among the Children."* Chapel Hill: University of North Carolina Press, 1946.

RITTER, FREDERIC LOUIS. *Music in America*. New York: C. Scribner's Sons, 1883.

ROURKE, CONSTANCE. *The Roots of American Culture, and Other Essays*. New York: Harcourt, Brace and Co., 1942.

ROWE, WILLIAM H. *Ancient North Yarmouth and Yarmouth, Maine, 1636–1936*. Yarmouth: Printed by the Southworth-Anthoensen Press, 1936.

RUSSELL, THE REV. CHARLES FRANK. *"The First Parish and Church in Weston, A Summary of their Records,"* An Account of the Celebration by the First Parish of Weston, Massachusetts of its Two Hundredth Anniversary. Weston: Printed for the Parish, 1900.

SAVELLE, MAX, ed. *Seeds of Liberty, the Genesis of the American Mind*. See Chapter IX, "Of Music and of America Singing," by Cyclone Covey, pp. 490–552. New York: Alfred A. Knopf, 1948.

SCANLON, MARY BROWNING. "Thomas Hastings," *Musical Quarterly* 32, no. 2 (April, 1946), pp. 265–277.

SCHOLES, PERCY A. *The Puritans and Music in England and New England*. London: Oxford University Press, 1934.

SEARS, REV. E. H. "History of the Oxford Singing School," *Dwight's Journal of Music* 18, no. 15 (January 12, 1861), pp. 331–332, and no. 16 (January 19, 1861), pp. 340–341.

SEEGER, CHARLES. "Contrapuntal Style in the Three-voice Shape-note Hymns," *Musical Quarterly* 26, no. 4 (October, 1940), pp. 483–493.

SEYBOLT, ROBERT FRANCIS. *The Private Schools of Colonial Boston*. Cambridge: Harvard University Press, 1935.

SHIPTON, CLIFFORD K. "Letter to the Editor," *William and Mary Quarterly* 9, no. 1 (Jan., 1952), pp. 128–129.

_____. "Letter to the Editor." *William and Mary Quarterly* 9, no. 2 (April, 1952), p. 288.

_____. *Sibley's Harvard Graduates*. Vols. 6–9. Cambridge: Harvard University Press, 1933–1956.

SHOEMAKER, ERVIN C. *Noah Webster, Pioneer of Learning*. New York: Columbia University Press, 1936.

"The Singing-School Master." *The Message Bird*, No. 37 (Second Year), Feb. 1, 1851.

SMALL, WALTER HERBERT. *Early New England Schools*. Boston: Ginn and Co., Publishers, 1914.

SMITH, FRANK. *A History of Dedham, Massachusetts*. Dedham: Transcript Press, Inc., 1936.

SMITH, FRANK. *History of Dover, Massachusetts*. Dover: Published by the Town, 1897.

SONNECK, OSCAR G. *Bibliography of Early Secular American Music*. Washington, D.C.: Printed for the Author by H. L. McQueen, 1905.

_____. *Early Concert Life in America*. Leipzig: Breitkopf & Hartel, 1907.

SPAULDING, WALTER R. *Music at Harvard*. New York: Coward-McCann, Inc., 1935.

STANDISH, LEMUEL W., ed. *The Old Stoughton Musical Society*. Stoughton: Published by the Society, 1928.

STEARNE, EZRA S. *History of Ashburnham, 1734–1886*. Ashburnham: Published by the Town, 1887.

History of the Town of Rindge, New Hampshire, 1736–1874. Boston: Press of George H. Ellis, 1875.

STEBBINS, RUFUS. (D.D.). *An Historical Address, delivered at the Centennial Celebration of the incorporation of the Town of Wilbraham, June 15, 1863*. Boston: George C. Rand & Avery, Printers, 1864.

STEVENSON, ROBERT M. *Patterns of Protestant Church Music*. Durham: Duke University Press, 1953.

STILES, HENRY R. *History of Ancient Windsor*. Revised edition, vol. 1. Hartford: Press of the Case, Lockwood and Brainard Company, 1891.

STONE, EDWIN. *History of Beverly, 1630–1842*. Boston: James Munroe and Company, 1843.

STOWE, J. M. *History of the Town of Hubbardston*. Hubbardston: Published by the Town, 1881.

SWEET, WILLIAM WARREN. *The Story of Religion in America*. New York: Harper & Bros., 1939.

SWIFT, ROWLAND. *"The Meeting-Houses of the First Church,"* Commemorative Exercises of the First Church of Christ in Hartford at its Two Hundred and Fiftieth Anniversary, October 11 and 12, 1883. Hartford: Press of the Case, Lockwood and Brainard Co., 1883, pp. 135–163.

TEMPLE, J. H. *History of Framingham, Massachusetts. 1640–1880*. Framingham: Published by the Town, 1887.

_____. *History of the Town of Palmer, Massachusetts, 1716–1889.* Palmer: Published by the Town, 1889.

_____. *History of the Town of Whately, Massachusetts, 1660–1871.* Boston: T. R. Marvin & Son, 1872.

TEMPLE, J. H. and SHELDON, GEORGE. *A History of the Town of Northfield.* Albany: Joel Munsell, 1870.

THOMPSON, FRANCIS M. *History of Greenfield.* Greenfield: Press of T. Morey and Son, 1904.

THWING, WALTER ELIOT. *History of the First Church in Roxbury, Massachusetts, 1630–1904.* Boston: W. A. Butterfield, 1908.

TRUMBULL, JAMES RUSSELL. *History of Northampton.* Vol. 2. Northampton: Press of Gazette Printing Co., 1902.

WALKER, GEORGE LEON. *History of the First Church in Hartford, 1633–1883.* Hartford: Brown and Gross, 1884.

WARFEL, HARRY R. *Noah Webster, Schoolmaster to America.* New York: The Macmillan Co., 1936.

WASHBURN, EMORY. *Historical Sketches of the Town of Leicester, Massachusetts.* Boston: Printed by John Wilson and Son, 1860.

WATERS, WILSON. *History of Chelmsford.* Lowell: Printed for the Town by Courier-Citizen Company, 1917.

WELLS, FREDERICK P. *History of Newbury, Vermont.* St. Johnsbury, Vt.: The Caledonian Co., 1902.

WHITE, ALAIN C. (compiler). *The History of the Town of Litchfield, Connecticut, 1720–1920.* Litchfield: Compiled for the Litchfield Historical Society, 1920.

WHITEHILL, WALTER MUIR. "Letter to the Editor." *William and Mary Quarterly 9,* no. 1 (Jan., 1952), pp. 134–136.

WOODBURY, PETER P., et al. *History of Bedford, New Hampshire.* Boston: Printed by Alfred Mudge, 1851.

WORCESTER, SAMUEL T. *History of the Town of Hollis.* Boston: A. Williams and Company, 1879.

WORTHEN, MRS. AUGUSTA HARVEY. *History of Sutton, New Hampshire.* Part I. Concord: Printed by the Republican Press Association, 1890.

Index